# Kansas Opera Houses

## Actors & Community Events

### 1855-1925

Jane Glotfelty Rhoads

*Kansas Opera Houses, Actors, and Community Events 1855-1925*

Copyright © 2008 by Jane Glotfelty Rhoads, Wichita, Kansas 67214

This publication may not be reproduced, stored in a retrieval system, or transmitted in whole or in part, in any form by any means, electronic, mechanical, photocopying, recording, or otherwise without prior permission of the copyright holder.

Unless otherwise noted, illustrations are from the author's private collection and photographs are by John Rhoads.

International Standard Book Number: 978-0-9822050-4-4

Library of Congress Control Number: 2008910931

Designed by Jim L. Friesen

Printed in the U.S.A by Mennonite Press, Inc., Newton, Kansas

# *Kansas Opera Houses,*
## *Actors, and Community Events 1855 - 1925*

I am pleased to present your library with this complimentary copy of *Kansas Opera Houses, Actors, and Community Events 1855-1925*. I am providing my book to all of the public libraries in the state as a "thank you" for the generous assistance I received as I traveled the state researching the book, and also because I wish to contribute to the recorded history of Kansas communities.

*Kansas Opera Houses* highlights the importance of these public spaces to the cultural and social development of Kansas during the last half of the 19th century and the early part of the 20th century. The book features information on the building of Kansas' opera houses and their physical evolution. *Kansas Opera Houses* also highlights the types of civic and cultural entertainments that occurred in these structures as well as the actors who graced their stages.

As a special feature, *Kansas Opera Houses* contains a detailed listing of 900 opera houses located in more than 400 Kansas communities and the activities that occurred in them. From high school graduations to political rallies, local opera houses were a focal point of civic activities.

Thank you for placing this in your collection. My hope is that *Kansas Opera Houses, Actors, and Community Events 1855-1925* will make a valuable contribution to your community's history. Additional copies of my book may be purchased directly from Watermark Books, 4701 East Douglas, Wichita, Kansas, 67218, 316-682-1181 or on line at www.watermarkbooks.com for $30 plus shipping.

*Jane Glotfelty Rhoads*

*Jane Glotfelty Rhoads* • *1141 N. Emporia, Wichita, KS 67214* • *316-264-6026*
*jane.rhoads@wichita.edu*

# CONTENTS

List of Illustrations ............................................................................................................................vi

Chapter 1   The Curtain Rises: Early Theatre in Kansas ...............................................................1

Chapter 2   "The Finest Opera House West of the Missouri": Origins and ..................................7
            Development of Kansas Opera Houses

Chapter 3   It Happened at the Opera House: Community Uses................................................ 19

Chapter 4   The Stage is Set: Opera House Scenery ................................................................... 26

Chapter 5   From Melodrama to Shakespeare ............................................................................ 35

Chapter 6   Now Appearing: Performing in Kansas ................................................................... 45

Chapter 7   Home Grown Talent: Kansas Performers................................................................ 55

Chapter 8   Life as a Performer .................................................................................................. 63

Chapter 9   Ringing Down the Curtain: Fire and Other Natural Disasters ................................ 69

Chapter 10  Final Curtain and Encore........................................................................................ 75

Kansas Communities: Alphabetical listing of 479 Kansas communities with ............................. 85
            information concerning their opera houses.

Notes........................................................................................................................................ 147

Bibliography............................................................................................................................. 154

# ILLUSTRATIONS

Cowboy entertainment ..................................................................................................................1

Atchison, Topeka and Santa Fe Railroad advertisement ........................................................2

Cowboy variety theatre .................................................................................................................4

Ragsdale Opera House, Newton .................................................................................................6

Nuzum/Kelley Opera House, White Cloud ............................................................................10

Dearborn Hall/Opera House exterior, Barnes ........................................................................11

Dearborn Hall/Opera House interior, Barnes ........................................................................11

Crawford's Grand Opera House exterior, Wichita ................................................................12

Crawford's Grand Opera House interior, Wichita ................................................................12

Bohemian National Hall exterior, Jennings/Oberlin .............................................................13

Bohemian National Hall interior, Jennings/Oberlin .............................................................13

Stafford Opera House Company Stock Certificate ................................................................14

Weide Opera House, Stafford ....................................................................................................14

Bowersock Opera House exterior, Lawrence ..........................................................................15

The Forum interior, Wichita .....................................................................................................15

Opera House/Palace Theatre, Kinsley .....................................................................................16

Band, Colby .................................................................................................................................18

High School Commencement, Gove ........................................................................................20

Children's program, Garnett .....................................................................................................21

Dramatic production, Stafford ..................................................................................................23

Prague Cathedral curtain, Cuba ...............................................................................................26

"Drouthy Kansas" curtain, Lawrence ... 27

Grand Drape curtain, Gypsum ... 28

Advertising curtain, Oketo ... 29

Woodland scene curtain, Iola ... 30

Great Western sales room, Kansas City, Missouri ... 31

Grand Drape curtain, Concordia ... 32

"Heart of Chicago" poster ... 34

"Uncle Tom's Cabin" poster ... 38

Booth and Barrett program ... 41

Blind Boone ... 42

Haverlaff's Minstrels ... 43

Eddie Foy ... 45

Louie Lord advertisement ... 49

Harry and Bess Houdini ... 50

The Three Keatons ... 51

Fred and Ed Stone ... 54

Milburn Stone ... 56

North Brothers Stock Company advertisement ... 58

Musical Reeds advertisement ... 61

Call sheet ... 62

Advertising post card ... 64

Advertising post card ... 66

Elks Theatre/Orpheum Theatre, Parsons ... 68

Twilight Theatre, Greensburg ......................................................................................................................... 72

Twilight Theatre, Greensburg ......................................................................................................................... 73

Brown Grand Theatre, Concordia ................................................................................................................... 74

Rogers' Columbian Theatre, Wamego ............................................................................................................. 76

Opera House, Waterville ................................................................................................................................. 77

Opera House, Wilson ...................................................................................................................................... 78

Grand Opera House, McPherson .................................................................................................................... 80

Opera House/Colonial Theatre, Junction City ................................................................................................ 81

Winship Opera House, Phillipsburg ................................................................................................................ 82

Orpheum Theatre, Wichita ............................................................................................................................. 83

Santa Fe Directory .......................................................................................................................................... 84

# Chapter 1
# THE CURTAIN RISES:
## Early Theatre in Kansas

1874 cowboy enterainment as depicted by Henry Worrall. Courtesy of the Kansas State Historical Society.

Steamboats plied the river, towns sprang up, and into this new territory came actors and actresses eager to perform. Because the Missouri River linked pre-Civil War Kansas settlements such as Leavenworth and Atchison to established cities like St. Joseph, St. Louis, Cincinnati and New Orleans it was only natural that in addition to goods and settlers, actors also arrived by river boat.

Leavenworth, situated on the Missouri River, was the site of the first public space specifically fitted up for theatrical productions. This facility, constructed in 1857, just 16 years after the Kansas Territory was officially opened for settlement, was located on the second floor of a commercial building. Several other opera houses or halls, as they were called in the 1850s and 1860s, were also constructed in Leavenworth prior to the Civil War as were performance spaces in Topeka, Lawrence, Junction City, and Olathe. It is not surprising that the oldest remaining opera house in the state is located in White Cloud, a Missouri River town.

The Curtain Rises | 1

The availability of transportation was the key to the development of theatre in Kansas. While the Missouri River provided actors easy access to some communities, the Civil War hindered access to others. The Civil War was a bloody and brutal time for the nation and also for the newly formed state of Kansas. The war's effect on transportation was to halt all rail construction in the state, and also to halt almost all opera house or theatre construction.[1]

Following the war there was an explosion of rail activity as men, hungry for profits, crisscrossed the state with rail lines. This, in turn, brought a tremendous expansion in population as settlers from the eastern United States and from Europe sought new lands, and cowboys drove herds of Texas cattle to the newly created rail heads.

## Coming of the Rails

The great Kansas journalist William Allen White lamented the advent of the Railway Age saying, "The railroad came and everything was changed. I did not know that the smell of coal smoke, which first greeted my nostrils with the railroad engine, was to be the sign and signal of the decay of a town and indeed of pioneer times, when men made things where they used them — all the things necessary to a rather competent civilization."[2] The majority of Kansas's residents, however, did not share White's views. "The child is born and his name is 'success.' Let the Capital City rejoice," was how Cyrus K. Holliday, the driving force behind the Atchison, Topeka and Santa Fe Railroad exuberantly announced the successful completion of negotiations necessary to begin construction of the line.[3]

Residents of Kansas eagerly awaited the arrival of railroads to their communities. Local newspapers issued daily bulletins on the progress of the laying of the rails until the glorious day arrived. The *Wichita Eagle* reflected this excitement generated by the arrival of the first train. "This is a fact, regular through trains reached our depot yesterday. The bosom of our valley 'heaved and sot' with ecstatic emotion. All is joy, and many, very many, are 'too full for utterance.' We are exhausted, bewildered, and can say no more. It is enough."[4] To facilitate the construction of these rail

Atchison, Topeka and Santa Fe Railroad brochure used to attract settlers to Kansas. Courtesy of the Kansas State Historical Society.

lines the federal government gave significant financial inducements to transcontinental railroads in the form of land grants. In Kansas this amounted to almost one-sixth of the area of the state, and by 1918 railroads in Kansas operated 8,806 miles of track.

The first company to build in the state was the Kansas Pacific known first as the Union Pacific Eastern Division. It entered the state in 1863 and reached Denver in 1870. The second major line was the Atchison, Topeka and Santa Fe. Construction began in 1868 and the Colorado border was reached in 1872. Other important lines included the Chicago, Rock Island and Pacific known as the Rock Island; the Missouri Pacific Railway; and the Missouri, Kansas and Texas commonly known as the Katy. Each of these railroads then laid numerous branch lines.[5]

The James Lord Dramatic Company is a good example of how the expansion of rails in Kansas also brought entertainment to the early settlers. From their home base in Chicago, James and Louie Lord toured the midwest from shortly after the Civil War until James Lord's death in 1885. Taking advantage of new rail lines, the company first appeared in Kansas during the winter of 1869-1870 when they performed in towns located in the northeastern part of the state, Atchison, Leavenworth, Lawrence and Topeka. The next season they expanded their tour to include Junction City and played along the newly laid Santa Fe line between Topeka and Emporia. During the 1872-1873 season the Lords traveled by the Missouri River, Fort Scott and Gulf railroad to Fort Scott and by 1876 the company traveled to Texas on the Katy railroad.[6]

## Cattle Trade and Cow Towns

By March 1867 the Kansas Pacific reached Abilene, thus setting the stage for a lucrative cattle trade. The Civil War had first disrupted and then destroyed the Southern shipping routes used by Texas cattlemen, so by the conclusion of the war Texas had huge herds of longhorn cattle but no way to get them to packing plants in Chicago. Abilene, Kansas appealed to Joseph G. McCoy, an Illinois livestock dealer, because of its close proximity to fields to pasture stock prior to shipment, adequate water, and importantly, there were no farmers to object to the cattle. As a result, cattle were driven up the Chisholm Trail from Texas to Abilene, and on September 5, 1867, the first rail shipment of 20 cars left Abilene for Chicago, and a new era of Kansas history began.

Although short-lived, it was certainly an exciting period in the state's history. As the rails pushed ever westward new shipping points developed. Abilene was a cow town from 1867 to 1871; Ellsworth from 1872 to 1875; Newton in 1872; Wichita from 1872 to 1876; Dodge City from 1875 to1885 and finally, Caldwell from 1880 to 1885.[7] The quarantine laws of 1884 and 1885 officially ended the Texas cattle trade, but even without these restrictions the cow town era was coming to an end. Homesteaders with their fenced farmland cut off access to the trails, and the arrival of railroads in Texas made the long cattle drives unnecessary.[8]

## Cowboy Entertainment

The annual summer influx of cowboys with money to spend invited hard drinking by the cowboys and the arrival of many less than upstanding individuals to relieve the cowboys of their newly acquired wealth. Cow towns' populations of gamblers and prostitutes skyrocketed during the summer months.[9] In addition, actors also arrived to entertain the cowboys with variety shows.

In Abilene the Novelty Theatre provided this type of entertainment. This venue, in operation by 1870, was crowded nightly with 300 to 400 fun-seeking cowboys. The manager was credited with putting on some good quality plays and the theatre's front curtain was regarded as most artistic.[10]

Ellsworth, the city that took the cattle trade away from Abilene, also boasted an early theatre. It was a one-story structure, 20 by 75 feet that seated 150 on pine benches. The stage was at one end of the room while at the other end was the entrance with a bar on one side and gambling tables on the other. An evening's entertainment consisted of a variety show that included songs and comedy sketches. On a typical evening the

Cowboy variety theatres featured a stage at one end and gambling and a bar at the other. Courtesy of the Kansas State Historical Society.

patrons, mostly young men, sat on the pine benches while seven or eight "ladies" together with three or four "gentlemen" looked on from above, seated in what were described as "boxes." Boys with trays circulated through the crowd hawking liquor and cigars while the bartender kept time with the orchestra and jig dancers while mixing and shaking drinks.

The "green room," behind the stage, was another location where herders drank and engaged in conversation with the stage girls. It was, apparently, the height of a herder's ambition to obtain admission to the green room and to drink a bottle of wine with the girls. A visit to the green room could cost a dozen head of steers, but Texas cowboys thought it was worth it.[11]

Dodge City, the best-known cattle town, was served by several variety theatres, but by far the best known was Ben Springer's Theatre Comique. In 1877 Ben Springer and Bat Masterson's brother, Jim, opened The Lady Gay dance hall. The following year Springer added a simple stage, changed the name to the Theatre Comique, and booked vaudeville performers. It was onto this stage that the young Eddie Foy and his partner Jim Thompson appeared in their black face and Irish comedy acts.

Years later Foy's recollection of his Dodge City appearance provided a colorful description of frontier entertainment. He began by noting that no movie could ever do justice to the old western amusement halls.

> The sounds are lacking — the songs and patter from the stage at one end, where the show began at eight o'clock and continued until long after midnight; the click and clatter of poker chips, balls, cards, dice, wheels and other devices at the other end, mingled with a medley of crisp phrases: 'Thirty-five to one!'

'Get your money down, folks!' 'Eight to the one on the colors!' 'Keno!' 'Are you all down, gentlemen? Then up she rises!' and a thousand other bits representing the numerous varieties of games that were being played and which, though mostly spoken in a moderate tone, combined to make a babble of sound.

Just as in Ellsworth, the Dodge City theatre featured boxes for the more intimate activities. Foy described them, "All around the room, up above, a sort of mezzanine, ran a row of private boxes-and they were boxes, indeed. As plain as a packing case--where one might sit and drink and watch the show." At the conclusion of the performances there was dancing which might last until 1 a.m. or daybreak. And what of the women who worked at the entertainment establishments in Dodge City? According to Foy they were not as depicted in modern film. "It was an eye-opener to me to discover that the women who entertained Dodge, no matter in what capacity, didn't as a rule, dress in silks and satins, but in gingham and cheap prints; and that goes for the dance-hall girls when they were on duty too…. Their job was to dance with the men, talk to them, perhaps flirt with them a bit and induce them to buy drinks—no more."[12]

From almost the beginning of statehood entertainment in Kansas thrived thanks to the expansion of railroads. Cattle trade brought trail weary cowboys with money to spend and the desire to be entertained into the state and the variety theatres of the cow towns provided that entertainment. The settlers who poured into the state on the newly laid rails also craved entertainment and this in turn brought actors. The settlers, aware of the importance of meeting and entertainment facilities, in turn constructed halls and theatres, some of which stand today.

A drawing depicts the beautiful interior of Newton's 1884 Ragsdale Opera House.

# Chapter 2
# "THE FINEST OPERA HOUSE WEST OF THE MISSOURI"
## Origins and Development of Kansas Opera Houses

No matter the size, early Kansas residents took enormous pride in their community's opera house or hall. The local news paper invariable bragged that theirs was the "finest west of the Missouri."

Settlers arrived in Kansas knowing what opera houses looked like and as these new residents set about duplicating their previous environments, opera houses were included. It was only natural that as town companies were formed and communities developed residents would desire to appear "civilized" and "cultured," not only for themselves, but also to attract new residents. Across the state opera houses or halls, as they were sometimes called, were constructed by local communities, by civic-minded organizations and ethnic groups, or in the majority of cases, by local businessmen.

## Builders of Kansas Opera Houses

**Town and City Halls**

The first builders of meeting halls in Kansas were the communities themselves. While these early structures were not designed specifically for entertainment, performances did occur in them. Leavenworth's Public Hall was built in 1855, just one year after Kansas was opened for settlement. Another early public space was Fort Scott's 1863 City Hall. At least 61 performance spaces in Kansas bore the name of either City or Town Hall. Because early Kansans did not have the luxury of single-purpose facilities, meeting rooms and performance spaces were often part of a building that housed other community offices such as the sheriff's office, fire department or court house. Eventually, the city hall concept evolved into the construction of large municipal auditoriums such as the 1906 facility in St. John, Salina's 1907 Auditorium, Hutchinson's 1911 Convention Hall, and Wichita's Forum constructed in the same year.

Another name for early public meeting spaces was "Union Hall." This is not surprising given Kansas' tumultuous entrance into the Union. The name designation indicated on which side the residents' sympathies lay. Union Halls were located in such eastern Kansas communities as Topeka, Osage City and Burlingame.[1]

**Grand Army of the Republic**

The Grand Army of the Republic or G.A.R., a patriotic fraternal organization composed of Union veterans of the Civil War, constructed many halls across Kansas. These halls ranged from simple wooden structures to the beautiful three-story opera house in Garnett. Between 1883 and 1889 G.A.R. Halls were constructed in at least sixteen communities.[2]

## Faternal Associations

By the end of the nineteenth century fraternal organizations had became extremely popular and many Kansas communities were enriched because of them. The Independent Order of Odd Fellows or IOOF constructed many meeting facilities that were also used for public meetings and for entertainment purposes. The first of these was the 1878 hall in Leavenworth.[3]

Another fraternal organization that made numerous contributions to entertainment in Kansas was Freemasonry. For instance, the Masons constructed the 1885 Masonic Music Hall in Newton. Other Masonic halls that also served as performance spaces were located in Coolidge, Ellsworth, Great Bend, Peabody, and Canton.[4]

Several other fraternal organizations made similar contributions to their communities' development. These include halls constructed by the Knights of Pythias, the Knights of Columbus, and the K of L.[5] Originated in 1868 as a fraternal organization for actors, the Benevolent and Protective Order of Elks of the USA or Elks Lodges soon encompassed the general population and in 1904 the Elk's Lodge of Parsons constructed a magnificent $65,000 four-story theatre.

Other groups responsible for performance facilities in the state included Modern Woodmen of America. Their first hall used for public entertainment was the 1878 structure in Lawrence. The Ancient Order of United Workmen, the AOUW, the AOWL and the AAOW were also responsible for halls.[6]

Agricultural interests also participated in the construction of halls. A very influential turn-of-the-century group, the Grange, provided at least two Kansas structures used for entertainment purposes. These were located in Olathe and Edgerton. Another group with rural interests was the Anti Horse Thief Society with a hall in Andover.

## United States Military

Several of the state's early theatres were related to the United States Military. The first was constructed in 1870 by soldiers at Fort Riley. During the 1880s performances were given in Fort Riley's auditorium, and still later the Post Gymnasium was used as a performance space. Also functioning in the 1880s was the Soldier's Home Opera House located in Leavenworth.

The advent of World War I and the desire to provide good, wholesome entertainment for our troops resulted in a nationwide theatre construction spree. Forty Liberty Theatres were built during 1917 and 1918. Camp Funston, operated in conjunction with Fort Riley, was the site of Kansas' Liberty Theatre.

## Ethnic Influences

The newly established state of Kansas benefited greatly from the arrival of immigrants directly from Europe, and also from the migration of persons who had previously immigrated to the United States. At the beginning of the Civil War only about one-third of Kansas was occupied, but that changed rapidly.[7] Due to economic and political conditions in Europe and to the availability of free or relatively inexpensive land, the population of Kansas grew by more than a million between the beginning of the Civil War and 1890.[8] By 1890 46,423 Germans had immigrated to Kansas. In addition, the state was home to 18,086 English; 17,096 Swedes; 15,879 Irish; 9,801 Russians; and 3,022 Bohemians.[9]

European immigrants added significantly to the culture of the state and also to the construction of performance spaces. The German Turnverein Society, basically an athletic club, constructed many facilities across the state. These buildings, Turner Halls as they were often called, were community centers and were also used as performance spaces by traveling theatrical troupes.[10] The 1869 Turner Hall in Lawrence and Hanover's 1874 Turner Hall are still standing.

Another nationality responsible for several attractive community halls was the Bohemians who came to Kansas from other parts of the Midwest in search of cheaper land. The Bohemian settlement in Wilson constructed the 1901 Wilson Opera House. This facility, beautifully restored by the community, is in use today. Other halls erected by Bohemian Lodges include the 1906 hall in Jennings; the 1907 hall in Cuba; and Holyrood's, 1910 hall. The Jennings Lodge, still in use for community activities, has been moved to Oberlin, and although the first Cuba Hall was destroyed by fire, the 1930 Cuba Hall serves as a community center.

While agriculture attracted many European immigrants to the state, the coal mining industry of Southeastern Kansas was also responsible for bringing still more residents to the state. Beginning about 1876 immigrants from a variety of European countries arrived in response to the development of major coal fields in Crawford and Cherokee counties, and in 1877 for the lead and zinc mining in Galena.[11]

The 1918 Armistice Celebration in Osage County provided an excellent example of the diverse nature of the southeastern Kansas population. One of the participants recalled the event.

> The band was playing and the people singing 'Over There' and all those familiar war songs, right in the center of the four square. A platform was built and nearly all nations were represented. They went up on the platform and sang their native song. The French were first called upon and a very fine mixed chorus sang 'The Marseillaise.' Next came the Italians, who were also represented by a nice group of mixed voices. They sang 'Con Spirite,' 'Noi Siame Conseritti Siam Uomini Fatti,' and also gave us a good program. The English were also called and sang the very appropriate song, 'God Save the King.' All the crowd sang 'America'...On the same platform the band played dance music and everybody danced, old and young...We came home in the small hours of the morning, call it one more perfect day.[12]

The names of the opera houses in mining communities often reflected the town's major occupation. This can be seen in Frontenac's Miners Opera House and Corona's Miner's Union Hall.

Other nationalities also made their mark on the state. The most distinctive Danish community in Kansas, Denmark, was founded in 1869. The very attractive Denmark Hall, dedicated February 24, 1912, is in use today. The French influence can be seen in the construction of the 1883 Florence Opera House. Well educated, musically talented French immigrants wished to establish culture in their newly founded Kansas town and this opera house was the result.[13]

Lindsborg, the best known Swedish settlement in Kansas, was also a cultural center and the host to traveling theatrical companies. Bethany College's Ling Hall was the location of such productions.

**Private Investors**

While the first halls and opera houses in the state were constructed by the local communities then later by civic, fraternal, and ethnic organizations, the majority of the opera houses and halls in Kansas built during the heyday of opera house construction, the 1880s and 1890s, were built by private citizens. These performance spaces could be as simple as an empty second floor room with a platform at one end, to structures as elaborate as the Crawford Grand Opera Houses located in several major Kansas cities.

Opera houses were never in constant use. Although important events such as school plays and commencement exercises, political rallies, visiting speakers, and traveling theatrical troupes appeared in the opera houses, much of the time these facilities were "dark," a theatrical term for "not in use." For this reason a second floor hall made a great deal of sense. A business man could construct a two- or three-story building, locate businesses in the basement and first floor, rent office space along the street side of the second floor and still have room for a one- or two-story opera house in the remainder of the building. The opera house was a way to make money from unused space.

Profit was not the only driving force behind the construction of opera houses. Many successful businessmen built opera houses as a way to support their communities. The 1897 Mallory Opera House in Paola built by C. H. Mallory and Girard's Painton's Hall built by Thomas Painton were good examples of this. These privately financed opera houses were sometimes named for the person who constructed them, sometimes for the community, and sometimes the name of the opera house changed every time the building changed hands.[14]

Located on the Missouri River, the 1862 Nuzum/Kelley Opera House in White Cloud is the state's oldest remaining opera house.

# The Evolution of Performance Spaces

The earliest performers in Kansas appeared in any public space available, but the state's rapid development was reflected in the performance spaces constructed. While it is impossible to divide these structures into rigid categories, there was certainly a definite progression in terms of the types of spaces that were viewed as halls or opera houses. This evolution in architectural style related to the development, size, and needs of the communities, the availability of funds, and current trends in design.

Generally speaking there were two major types of performances facilities constructed between 1860 and 1925. The majority of the opera houses in Kansas were constructed on the second floor or second and third floors of commercial buildings. Later, owing to the deterioration of these earlier spaces and due to concern about fire safety, ground floor, single use facilities became popular.

**Second Floor Opera Houses**

The earliest opera houses in the state were plain, second floor rooms located above businesses. The box office was nothing more than a window on the side wall. At one end of the hall there was a small stage and because the ceiling above stage was low, scenery that rolled up and down was used. Seating was portable which allowed the space to be used for a variety of purposes including dinners, roller skating, and dances in addition to events taking place on the stage. The opera houses in White Cloud and Hartford are examples of this type of hall.

As time passed opera houses became more elaborate. First the "proscenium arch" or the opening through which the audience viewed the performance became wider and higher, and small, back stage dressing rooms were added. The auditoriums began to include small balconies and fixed seating. Examples of this type of theatre can be found in the 1880's Mound City Opera House; the 1895 Dearborn Hall/Opera House in Barnes; the 1909 Roesler Opera House in Claflin; and the 1901 Opera House in Morrill.

Even more elaborate second floor opera houses featured still larger proscenium arches and wider and deeper stages, larger auditoriums with fixed seating, large balconies and occasionally a second smaller balcony. Finally, the peak of elegance in second-story opera houses occurred during the 1880s in larger communities. True Victorian opulence was exhibited through the use of elaborate proscenium arches and boxes on either side of the

The Dearborn Hall/Opera House in Barnes, constructed in 1895, is a second floor opera house located above commercial space.

stage, elegant seats, intricate painting and decorations on the walls and fronts of the balconies and boxes. The stages were large and scenery was housed above the stage in a space referred to as a "stage house" and "flown" or lowered into place. Some examples of opera houses in this category included the 1881 Crawford Opera House in Topeka; the 1882 Whitely Opera House in Emporia; the Bowersock Opera House in Lawrence; the 1884 Ragsdale Opera House in Newton; and the 1888 Crawford Grand Opera House in Wichita. Unfortunately, none of these theatres is standing.

**Ground Floor Theatres**

The earliest ground-floor theatres were halls with stages. The simplest halls were hastily constructed facilities used to entertain cowboys in the cattle

The interior of Dearborn Hall/Opera House in Barnes features a simple stage.

Larger communities were home to more elaborate opera houses such as Wichita's 1888 Crawford Grand Opera House. Courtesy of the Wichita-Sedgwick County Historical Museum.

towns of Kansas. Not designed for luxury but for rowdy good times, these structures were wooden, ground floor facilities with a small stage and rough lumber benches located at one end, and gambling tables and a bar in the end closest to the street. With the exception of the front roll curtain these early theatres contained little or no scenery. Examples of cow town theatres include the 1870 Novelty Theatre in Abilene; the 1872 Variety Hall in Wichita; Ellsworth's 1873 McClelland and Freeman Opera House; and two 1878 establishments in Dodge City, the Comique and the Varieties.

The elaborately decorated interior of Wichita's Crawford Grand Opera House seated 1,500 in upholstered opera chairs. Courtesy of the Wichita-Sedgwick County Historical Museum.

Smaller communities constructed multi-purpose facilities such as this 1906 Bohemian National Hall originally built in rural Jennings and now located in Oberlin.

Roller rinks, while not as elaborate as most opera houses, were more finished than the earlier cow town theatres. Built between 1885 and 1890, the rinks featured finished walls, a small stage in one end and a large smooth floor with no fixed seating. An example of this was the 1885 McCarthy's Rink in Dodge City. It boasted a 100' x 300' maple wood floor and no pillars.[15] These rinks were also used for stage performances.

The most elaborate halls with stages were the community centers. Built between 1905 and 1922, these featured a large multi-purpose hall with no fixed seating, an attractive interior and a stage with scenery, and sometimes a kitchen facility. Fortunately, a number of community centers remain in use including the 1905 Oketo Community Center; Jennings' 1906 Bohemian Hall, now located in Oberlin; and the 1912 Denmark Hall.[16]

The Jennings/Oberlin Hall is still in use.

At the beginning of the twentieth century as the opera houses of the previous century were showing their age and fire safety became a concern, communities saw the need for attractive public auditoriums or theatres. These theatres with their separate box offices, fixed seating, large stage and dressing rooms answered that need.

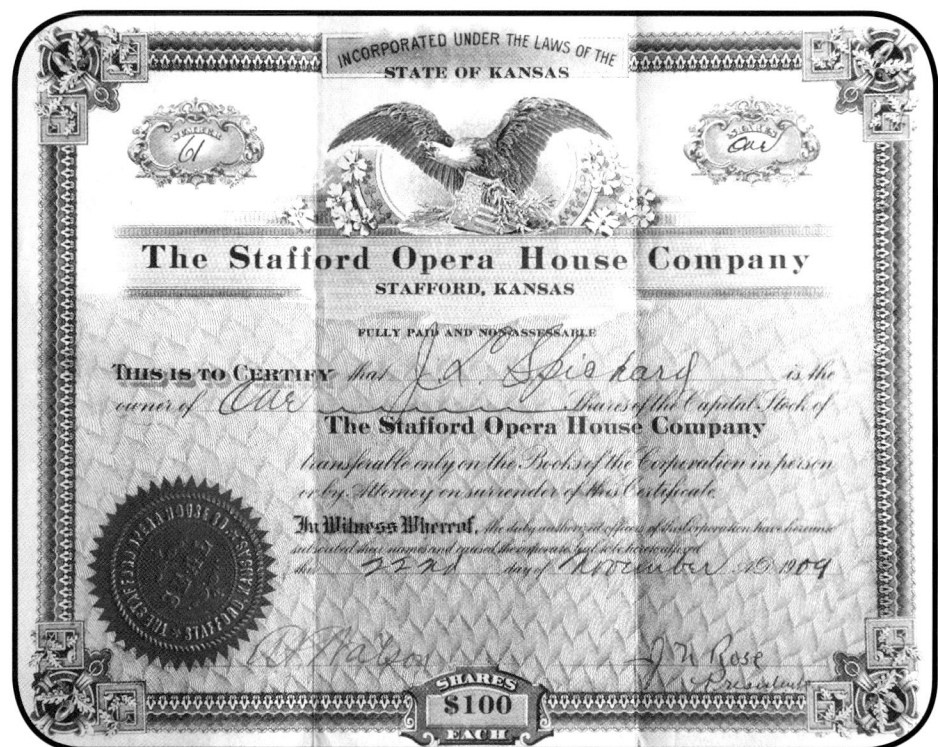

Stock certificates for $100 were issued by the Stafford Opera House Company in 1909. Courtesy of the Stafford County Historical and Genealogical Soceity.

The Weide Opera House in Stafford is an example of a community financed ground floor theatre.

Good examples of this type of ground-floor theatre are the 1901 Strong City Auditorium, the 1903 Waterville Opera House, the 1906 St. John Opera House/Convention Hall, and the 1910 Stafford Weide Opera House.[17]

Even before the turn of the century, larger communities were home to elegant ground-floor theatres. Early examples of this type of architecture included the 1888 Winfield Grand Opera House, the 1888 Arkansas City Fifth Avenue Opera House, the 1889 Junction City Opera House, and McPherson's 1889 Grand Opera

Constructed in 1912, the Bowersock Opera House in Lawrence is an example of an elegant ground floor theatre.

House. Fortunately, the McPherson and Junction City Opera Houses are still standing. Later opera houses in this category that are still in use include the 1907 Brown Grand Theatre in Concordia and Lawrence's 1912 Bowersock Opera House.

These elegant ground-floor theatres contained box offices, large auditoriums with fixed seating, and one or two balconies. Large elevated stages were set off by high proscenium arches. Back stage were fly lofts that housed many sets of elaborate scenery and dressing rooms.[18]

Municipal auditoriums, such as Wichita's Forum built in 1911, were home to everything from livestock shows to operas.

The Finest Opera House West of the Missouri | 15

Ground floor, turn-of-the-century municipal auditoriums, while falling outside the category of "opera house," were the location of community events that included plays by traveling acting companies. An example of this type of public space is Hutchinson's 1911 Convention Hall. Wichita's 1911 Forum, no longer standing, was another example of this type of architecture. These large municipal auditoriums were characterized by a very large flat ground floor with portable seating, a circular balcony that surrounded three sides of the auditorium, and a large, well equipped stage. Everything from circuses to Easter pageants and from operas to livestock shows appeared in these entertainment spaces.

Built near the end of the opera house era were ground-floor theatres that were called "opera houses," but because of the scarcity and expense of traveling acting companies, also showed moving pictures. After the advent of talking pictures and the need for sound equipment that was often located on the stage behind the screen, these late opera houses became almost exclusively movie theatres although some continued to present occasional stage productions. These later theatres contained a box office and an auditorium with fixed seating and a projection booth located in the balcony. There was also a well equipped stage, and in some instances a fly gallery that contained scenery. There were also dressing rooms. A number of these theatres remain and are in use as performance spaces such as the 1910 Electric/Jayhawk Theatre in Atwood and Kinsley's 1917 Opera House/Palace Theatre.[19] Opera houses of this style that were constructed for vaudeville, but soon converted to moving pictures, include Scott City's Opera House/Majestic Theatre and El Dorado's El Dorado Theatre both constructed in 1921, and Wichita's 1922 Orpheum Theatre.

The 1917 Kinsley Opera House/Palace Theatre presented a combination of live entertainment and moving pictures.

Whether constructed by local citizens or towns themselves, and whether elegant or plain, the opera house or hall was a source of community pride and an integral part of the community's life. One Severance native lovingly summarized the importance of that community's local opera house. "The Theatre, a place of entertainment and amusement, was a great part of those early years...The opera house was a tribute to those sturdy hearts who were looking forward to better things in 1880 and built a structure that was a place of wonder in the hearts of those who were once young and gay."[20]

The Colby band, pictured here, was an example of the many community events that occurred at local opera houses. Courtesy of the Kansas Historical Society.

# Chapter 3
# IT HAPPENED AT THE OPERA HOUSE:
## Community Uses

To celebrate their high school graduation the senior class of Garnett decorated the opera house stage with their class motto and with paper streamers in the class colors. In Severance the teachers and school board members were seated on the stage along with the graduating seniors who each delivered an oration that had taken weeks to prepare and to learn. As a Severance native observed, "These events were carried on with much ado and the theatre would be packed. Folks came and sat on the straight hard chairs to listen and admire their young people."[1]

While visiting actors and actresses might bring excitement, amusement, and a hint of glamour to the stages of early Kansas opera houses, by far the most memorable events featured the local citizens themselves. Community functions that ranged from dinners to funerals, from graduation ceremonies to church services all took place at the opera house. The facility provided seating for large numbers or a space large enough to host banquets or to play a basketball game. But, the best remembered community events were the graduation exercises. In a time when advanced education was costly and rare, commencement was a rite of passage and a stamp of accomplishment.

High school graduations weren't the only ones celebrated at the opera house, eighth grade ceremonies also occurred there. A Kiowa resident graphically described the fear he felt as he commenced from eighth grade.

> The school principal was from Ohio and he was full of eastern ideas. The general idea was that we were to prepare what was called an oration, or a reasonable facsimile thereof, and go out on the opera house stage under our own power--no one was allowed to hold us up--then before an audience of relatives and friends, tell them how we proposed to scale the mountain heights and cross the burning sands to victory.
>
> That night the opera house was packed. Everyone was there; even the saloons closed. There were four girls and four boys in the class. We were told to follow the professor single file out on the stage, then execute a left turn, face the audience and nonchalantly and gracefully seat ourselves.
>
> We followed the professor all right. We executed the left turn, gazed out on the sea of faces and then the class of 1891 collapsed. After that it was everybody for himself.
>
> Just before the time for my little offering of oratory, the boy next to me pressed a piece of paper into my clammy hand. As I read it with glazed eyes, I saw it was a farewell message from the professor. It said, 'Stand up straight and don't let your knees wobble.'
>
> How I got to the front of the stage without a pair of crutches I never knew. It seemed to me I was gazing into the eyes of a thousand Eddie Cantors. My mouth was parched; there was a ringing in my ears; I saw spots before my eyes; my knees wobbled; I heard a voice a thousand miles away that I never would have believed was mine.
>
> That night when I got home, I found I was carrying a roll of parchment that said I finished the 8th grade. I thought the 8th grade had about finished me."[2]

Many Kansans received their high school diplomas on the stages of the state's opera houses. Pictured here is the 1906 commencement ceremony of the Gove County High School. Courtesy of the Gove County Historical Society.

Even grade school children appeared on the stages of Kansas opera houses. A proud Courtland audience member observed,

> The Opera House was full and standing room was at a premium Tuesday night to hear the program by the grades of Courtland School. Everyone from the little tots in the primary to the would-be 'Freshies' of the eighth grade took part. The little playlets were simple, yet entertaining, the drills appropriate, and the children cleverly trained, the costuming unique and pretty; all showing painstaking effort on the part of the teachers in designing and training. In all respects the program was a success as all things in which our children are concerned are bound to be.[3]

Opera house use wasn't limited to commencements. Following the destruction of the Sedan Opera House by fire, the local newspaper made an impassioned and successful plea for the construction of a new opera house.

"A large public hall in Sedan is as much a necessity as is the courthouse. The town needs one continually. It is a public benefit and a public need. It is used by the churches, the schools, political parties, commercial clubs and everybody. It is one of the strong features of any town to have a house or hall large enough for public gatherings."[4]

Any community event that required seating for a large number of persons took place at the opera house. This included activities ranging from high interest court cases to funerals of prominent residents. In 1881, these two functions merged in Olathe through the life of one man, Col. Josiah E. Hayes. One week prior to his death, Hayes offered his newly constructed opera house for use as the county court house.

The following week Col. Hayes passed away in Eureka Springs, Arkansas, where he had gone for his health. Hayes' body was returned to Olathe and his funeral was held in his newly completed opera house. The casket was placed at the front of the stage which was heavily draped in mourning. The choir was positioned to the right of the casket. The auditorium was densely packed for the service where the funeral address was given by the governor of the state.[5]

It was not unusual for newly formed religious congregations to meet at their local opera houses until money could be raised to build their own churches, and before these same churches were enlarged to include kitchens and dining rooms, opera houses were the location of church dinners that often required tables, dishes, water and food be carried up steep flights of stairs. In the early days of communities an opera house was occasionally pressed into service to house a school. And, before the advent of high school auditoriums, band concerts, school plays, operettas, home talent productions, and even basketball games took place at the opera house.

Roller skating became quite popular during the opera house era and communities often built their auditoriums with portable seating so that the floors could be used for skating. The noise caused by roller skaters in the second floor Woodston Opera House caused the local paper to observe, "If one can judge from the sound, the girls can strike the floor about as hard as the boys can."[6]

Children's programs were a popular form of entertainment. This children's program occurred at the Garnett Opera House about 1907.

The opera house era followed closely on the heels of the Civil War and community remembrances of veterans and other patriotic celebrations often took place at the opera house. A Lyons' native remembered a Decoration Day celebration.

> Nearly every man who died and was buried in Graceland Cemetery was a veteran (of the Civil War) and on Decoration Day folks came from far and near to honor the nation's dead. They brought flowers for the graves. There were several companies of blue clad men with funny slanted caps on their heads and bayoneted rifles over their shoulders to march in the parade to the cemetery behind an improvised band and followed by hundreds of wagons and other vehicles. After an address and prayer and platoons had fired salutes over the graves, the assembly came back to the square for picnic dinners on the grass. In the afternoon everyone went to Butler's Opera House on the north side of the square for the oration of the day, then hurried home before nightfall."[7]

The Kuhnle Opera House in Miltonvale was also the location of various patriotic celebrations. One Fourth of July the opera house was the site of an afternoon program that consisted of a speech by an out-of-town speaker, then a presentation by the children of the community. The boys and girls, dressed in white with bunting sashes, would drill, moving in march step from one formation to another. Special recognition was also given to the community's old soldiers.[8]

The 1892 Fourth of July celebration in Hutchison featured the production of a military drama, "The Federal Captain" at the opera house. "In the afternoon the play was presented to a large crowd and in the evening it was again produced. The play, like all military dramas, has a thrilling plot and the various characters were well personated."[9]

Politicians of national prominence also appeared on the stages of Kansas opera houses. Mary Ellen Lease and Jerry Simpson, both Populists, spoke at the Goodland Opera House, as did Charles Curtis. And both Susan B. Anthony and General Custer's sister spoke from the stage of the McPherson Opera House.

Stockton Hall in Leavenworth earned a place in Kansas history because on December 3, 1859, Abraham Lincoln spoke there. Two days later a crowd, too large for the auditorium, forced him to speak outside in front of the building. The speech Lincoln delivered that day was reported to have been very similar to the speech he later gave in New York City that won him the presidential nomination. An Eastern reporter who witnessed the Leavenworth occasion observed, "It was the largest mass meeting ever assembled on Kansas soil and the greatest address ever heard there."[10] Less than 100 years later a noted Kansan, Dwight David Eisenhower, declared his candidacy for the Presidency from the stage of Abilene's Plaza Theatre, the renovated Seeley Opera House.

Local politics could get quite heated and the opera house was often the site of spirited debates. When a controversial issue arose in Severance, a meeting was called at the opera house where representatives of both sides expressed their opinions. One resident observed, "The arguments would become heated and it took many a pitcher of water to quench the thirst of a lusty candidate, tussling with words, and making his point."[11]

A Marquette resident recalled yet another way opera houses were associated with politics. He remembered that on election night when he was a young boy a large party would assemble at the opera house and he would run the latest election returns from the telegraph office to the opera house where the returns were posted on a bulletin board.

Traveling speakers often appeared at the opera house. Topics ranging from politics to feminine hygiene were expounded upon. Emporia audiences were treated to such varied lecture topics as ornithology, a display of the supernatural, and an interesting pair of lectures, "Origin of Life - men only" and "Diseases of Woman - women only." In 1903 the Rev. Charles M. Sheldon, a Topeka pastor and author of *In His Steps*, appeared at the McPherson Opera House as did William Allen White in the 1920s.[12]

Opera house seating was often portable so that the chairs could be moved to allow dancing. In 1885, Latham's opera house was opened with a grand ball held on Christmas Eve. This was so successful that several other balls followed in close succession. During the same period the Latham residents who danced the nights away at the Opera House, on Sunday worshiped at the M.E. Sabbath School, also held at the Opera House.[13]

The 1881 Christmas celebration in the fledgling community of Old Kiowa was indeed a memorable one.

Someone brought in a huge cedar tree, set it on the floor and nailed the top to the ceiling. A nice big star was made out of heavy paper and covered with tin foil off tobacco and placed high on the tree with one lone candle. With true Western spirit it was decided that everyone should be remembered with a gift of some kind, and as all buying was done at the one and only store, owned by A.W. Rumsey, he was told to lay in a good stock of bright colored silk handkerchiefs, knives, and plenty of candy.

...as the cowboys and cattlemen rode in their names were written down and pinned to a gift of some kind. As there was nothing to trim the tree with, not even candles, all packages were opened up, the contents draped (in all their splendor) over the tree, and they certainly made a fine showing. A small stage had been erected back of the tree, with a calico curtain across and after lighting a few coal oil lamps and singing several songs, we listened to a short talk fitting the occasion. Then a hush came over the room as we heard sleigh bells ringing (bells that someone had brought from back East) and the curtains parted and there was old Santa riding on a handmade sled--but what a thrill to the few little children there--and maybe to some older ones.

Santa was impersonated by our dear old friend, Mr. Rumsey, and as he had a great sense of humor, he made it very amusing especially in reading the names of the little folks, and we were all eager to hear our own names called.

The Weide Opera House at Stafford was the scene of this dramatic production. Courtesy of the Stafford County Historical and Genealogical Society.

It Happened at the Opera House | 23

...Picture if you can a dimly lighted room, the walls lined with men dressed in all the paraphernalia of their trade, who had sheepishly offered as an excuse for their coming that they 'just wanted to see what the little folks would do when old Santa appeared,' but when their names were called they, too, remembered the wonderful story they had heard their mothers tell, and they wondered how Santa had learned they were coming. But he had been sworn to secrecy, under pain of death, so they could only say, 'Golly, it's nice to be remembered.' There were only eight or nine families and six or eight children in Old Kiowa at that time, but no one, young or old, went out empty handed.

Some of the cowboys had ridden over 50 miles to attend the celebration. And, after the presents were given out, the room was cleared and a dance was held. It was reported that it was customary for cowboys to bring dancing slippers with them. This way they could remove their boots and not tear the ladies' gowns with their spurs.[14]

A long remembered New Years Eve party occurred on the night of December 31, 1885, at the Community Center in Buffalo Park. It was quite cold and one native described the event. "People threw great heaps of hay in the wagons, quilts were thrown over the hay and the children were put into this warm nest while father and mother rode up on the spring seat and thus whole families came to the dance." But, during the party, a major snowstorm began. Before revelers were able to return to their homes three feet of snow had fallen. As a result, the rural partygoers were forced to stay in the Community Center or with town folks for the next two days.[15]

An event of a very different nature occurred on March 3, 1908, when seventeen orphans from the Children's Aid Society appeared on the stage of the Washington Opera House. The children, who arrived in Washington on the B and M Railroad, were fed at the Nims Hotel and then taken across the street to the opera house where 700 people had gathered to see them. There were 70 applicants for the 17 orphans. In order to be considered an applicant had to sign a contract after showing the committee that he or she could support the child and had to have the endorsement of the committee before receiving a child.[16] A similar event was reported during the 1920s at the McPherson Opera House. Ads were placed in the McPherson paper saying that the children were well-disciplined and that families were responsible for their upbringing until they reached the age of 18. One group of orphans included 12 children ranging in age from 10 months to 11 years.[17] From 1886 to 1930, between 5,000 and 6,000 children were placed in Kansas homes.[18]

As movies made their way onto the entertainment scene, the opera house was often the location of the first moving pictures seen by the locals. Kiowa residents caught an early preview of things to come when Edison's kinescope was exhibited in a big tent west of the Commercial Hotel during a big three-day Street Fair and Race Meeting in September 1899. By 1909, ten years later, the owner of Kiowa's opera house showed occasional moving pictures along with the stage shows.[19] In spite of these early showings, the transformation to moving pictures in Kiowa was not complete until the advent of sound in the late 1920s.

Even though they were still in the developmental stage, early motion pictures fascinated audiences. A LeRoy resident vividly recalled the 1922 or 1923 showing of the notorious "Birth of a Nation." Because of the picture's publicity, everyone wanted to see it and came from miles around. The LeRoy Opera House, where the movie was shown, was filled to capacity and some folks were even standing. "The whole event was out of this world. Stirring battle hymns, marches, hoe downs, and sweet melodies were played along with the show to accentuate the changing scenes. It was also in 'color.' The film was tinted in different shades as it was projected to coincide with the tempo and mood of the script."[20]

For years many opera houses struggled to survive, but the declining availability of road shows and the popularity of moving pictures eventually forced even the most grand of opera houses to close. The McPherson Opera House was a good example of this. After giving up the struggle to present live entertainment, the opera house closed and remained vacant for two years during which time it was renovated and converted to a movie theatre. Seating in the top gallery was removed to allow room for a projection booth that contained equipment for both silent and talking films. Much the same thing happened in Delphos where the final owner of the opera house turned that venue into a moving picture theatre and installed a Wurlitzer electric player piano which offered special musical effects.

The Neal family of Lenora bridged both entertainment worlds. Henry Neal purchased the Lenora opera house in 1930, renovated the theatre, and for more than 25 years offered moving pictures, but he also headed an acting company, the Neal Players, who used the theatre for live dramatic productions.

From the excitement surrounding the building of a community's first opera house to the end of the live entertainment era, the opera house played an important role in the life of a community. Countless numbers of Kansans commenced from the stages of the state's opera houses. Patriotic ceremonies, community meetings, local talent productions, and visiting speakers brought entertainment and enlightenment to the residents of the state. The opera house was a source of pride and a symbol of the community's emergence from the unsettled plains of the Kansas frontier to become part of mainstream America.

# Chapter 4
# THE STAGE IS SET:
# Opera House Scenery

The Prague Cathedral stage curtain, located in the Cuba Community Center, reflects the community's ethnic origin.

"Lighted with their kerosene lamp footlights and the tin reflectors, their magnificent scenery and curtains, many stirring scenes were enacted."[1]

W.F. Pride

A train with wings, a ferocious bull, giant stocks of grain, all were scenes on early roll curtains. Mirroring the exuberance of early cowboys and settlers, the scenery in the state's early halls and opera houses celebrated life on the Kansas frontier.

In 1868 the curtain in Topeka's Union Hall heralded the newly arrived rail system. Extending across the top of the curtain was an engine at full speed throwing off a cloud of smoke and a jet of steam followed by five or six winged cars. Below the fast moving train was a painting depicting the streets of Topeka and around the boarder of the curtain were cards advertising the various Topeka businesses. The lower left corner of the curtain carried a depiction of Gov. Burnett, the last chief of the Pottawatomie nation and in the opposite corner was "Kaw Charley" an eccentric half-breed Kaw Indian.[2]

A drawing by Henry Worrall entitled "Drouthy Kansas" was the inspiration for a curtain located in the 1870's Liberty Hall in Lawrence. Courtesy of the Kansas State Historical Society.

While Topeka's first curtain reflected the importance of rail travel, Ellsworth's 1873 front curtain celebrated the cowboy trade. The theatre itself was a low one-story building 20' x 75' with an interior that was unplastered and unpainted except for the proscenium arch and front drop curtain, but what a curtain! It was a testament to the Texas cattle trade. On one side was a festive depiction of a cattle herder dressed like a Spanish don complete with a lace trimmed crimson jacket, plumed Castilian sombrero and gaudy spurs riding an awe-inspiring horse. The other side of the curtain contained a painting of a roped longhorn attempting to escape, and between the two was a huge gold and silver glitter-covered star.[3]

Liberty Hall, an early Lawrence theatre, boasted yet another Kansas theme with its humorous look at agriculture. The 1870 hall's front curtain contained a representation of Henry Worrall's "Drouthy Kansas" cartoon. Designed to show his Eastern friends that Kansas was indeed the "land of plenty," the drawing by Worrall depicted a Kansas farmer climbing a ladder to harvest a gigantic grape, another farmer using a team of horses to bring in a large pumpkin, a man carrying a huge ear of corn and another dragging a bolder sized potato by a rope.[4]

Painted scenery had been a theatre staple for years. During the first half of the 19th century major American theatres employed their own scene painters who produced scenery for specific plays. But, as rail transportation lead to the growth of communities and that, in turn, lead to the erection of opera houses, changes occurred. Traveling theatrical troupes often could not afford to transport their own scenery and relied on the scenery present in the local theatres. This scenery, rather than being painted by in-house artists, was most often purchased from scenic companies. And, rather than being designed for a specific production, was fairly standard in nature and appropriate for most plays.

This 1922 Gypsum Community Center curtain is a good example of a grand drape.

The type of scenery used in Kansas opera houses was known as "wing and drop" scenery. The sides of the stage were masked by what were called "wings" or flats. These were wooden frames covered with canvas and painted to represent an extension of the setting created by the drop curtain. Wings prevented the audience from glimpsing off-stage activities and allowed actors the space needed for stage entrances and exits. These wings were held in place by a system of grooves located in the floor and suspended overhead.

The drops were large pieces of canvas, usually ten- to twelve-feet tall and 20- to 25-feet wide that were painted with a particular scene. The drops were either hoisted up, flown above the stage when not in use, or in theatres without enough height above the stage, rolled up on wooden cylinders using a rope system.

A stock set of scenery consisted of a front drop curtain and four other drops, two interior, and two exterior, known as "front, back, timber and town." The "front," the most often used interior, was an elegant parlor scene. Commencement ceremonies, concerts and many public functions often occurred in front of this drop. The other interior or "back," was a room more rustic in nature that could be used as a kitchen, a jail, or a poor person's bedroom. The two exterior scenes were a woodland scene referred to as the "timber," and a city street scene or "town" completed the set.

In order of appearance from the audience perspective, the first curtain visible was the front drop curtain or grand drape. This was the most carefully executed curtain, often in colors that complimented the color scheme of the interior of the opera house, and usually contained a landscape such as a lake, mountains, or castle. This scene was often surrounded by what appeared to be a large gilt frame, which in turn was decorated with a painted velvet drape. The best example of this type of curtain in Kansas is the grand drape of Concordia's Brown Grand Opera House that features a scene of Napoleon seated on a white horse and backed by his troops. This painting is contained in what appears to be an elaborate gold frame draped with an ornate green velvet curtain. Another good example of this style of front curtain is located in the 1922 Gypsum Community Center. The curtain, a rural landscape surrounded by a picture frame that is in turn surrounded by a beautifully painted rich green drape trimmed in gold, was painted by the Kansas City Scenic Company. And in Kinsley, the 1920 Princess Theatre features a front curtain that portrays a stone wall with a window, through which can be seen an Arabian city.

Communities took great pride in the beauty of their opera houses' scenery. An account of the 1887 opening of the J. C. Merril Opera House in Westphalia reported that,

> The building was filled with the many people who came to see the hall and scenery. There were six different scenes, all very attractive, and could compete with any opera house in the state. The drop curtain had a large picture in the center, representing the Westphalia Driving association, one of our future institutions. Surrounding this were the advertisement of the merchants and businessmen.[5]

A variety of scenes adorned the front curtains in Kansas opera houses. The 1909 Ellis Opera House contained a replica of "The Spirit of 76" painting. A bay with a city in the background graced the front curtain of the Morrill Opera House and the first scene visible to Ness City audiences at the Barnd Opera House was one of a lake in the Alps with an ancient castle in the distance. And, when the Powell Opera House in Belleville opened in 1887 its front curtain contained a view of the Bay of Naples.

Several years after the completion of the outer shell and basement of the Ladies Opera House in Blue Rapids, money was raised to finish the interior of the theatre and the Kansas City Scenic Company was hired to provide the scenery. This theatre's front curtain contained a view of the Blue River. The artist from Kansas City reported that he was so pleased with the scene that he was going to paint it on other curtains throughout the country.[6]

Located behind the grand drapery curtain or taking its place, was the ad curtain. This curtain was similar to the grand drape except that the outdoor scene was reduced in size and was surrounded by advertisements for local

The Oketo advertising curtain shows a rural scene surrounded by ads for various community businesses.

The Stage is Set | 29

businesses. Opera house owners sold the space for these ads to help offset the cost of the curtain. For instance, Clay Center's Bonham Opera House curtain contained a central scene depicting a street in Antwerp, Belgium surrounded by advertisements. The 1916 Ransome Opera House boasted $300 worth of fine scenery from the Kansas City Scenic Company and featured a curtain with a scene from the Arabian Knights, around which appeared the advertisements for the community's various business firms. While most of the ads that appeared on opera house curtains were quite straightforward, stating the name of the company, perhaps a company slogan or motto, and in later years a telephone number, a humorous ad appeared on the curtain of Emporia's Whitley Opera House. The ad, commissioned by the famous Kansas newspaperman, William Allen White read, "Cuss the Gazette, but read it."[7] Although very little painted scenery has survived, the ad curtain is the one most likely to have been preserved because it contains the commercial history of the community.

The street scene, located a few feet behind the ad curtain, was often used as a backdrop for the vaudeville numbers that occurred between acts in the plays. Following the street scene was the curtain that contained the plain interior scene, and the fancy parlor scene followed that. The woodland scene appeared on the final curtain and was often hung at the very back of the stage. This location allowed it to serve as a backdrop for many of the non-dramatic activities that took place on stage.[8]

The size of the community and of the theatre determined the number of sets of scenery that an opera house contained. For instance, the 1885 Price's Opera House in Atchison boasted 20 scenes, and in 1889 Wichita's Crawford Grand Opera House reported fifteen sets of scenery. The 1885 Ragsdale Opera House in Newton featured 32 sets of scenery painted by Sosman and Landis of Chicago. Charles S. King, an employee of the company who supervised the scenery's installation pronounced the scenery, "the finest in the west."[9, 10, 11]

In order to meet the scenery needs of an opera house that was under construction a salesman, bringing with him photographs or painted renderings of scenery options, would meet with the builders of the opera house. Selections were made, the stage measured, and the order sent. The scenic studio would then build the flats, sew the draperies, construct the wings and paint the roll curtains. Two methods were used to paint these large drops. One was to suspend the drop on a frame and the artist painted from a bridge that could be raised or lowered.

This curtain of a woodland scene is now located at the Bowlus Fine Arts Center in Iola.

Pictured here is the sales room of the Great Western Stage Equipment Company, Kansas City Missouri. Courtesy of William McGeehee.

The second method was to spread the canvas on the floor and the artist would paint it in that position. While the wings and set pieces could be easily shipped, the large drops were more difficult to transport. To prevent the paint cracking, the drops were rolled onto cylinders and transported by rail. A representative of the scenic studio would accompany the scenery and see to its installation and do any needed touch up work.

A number of major studios supplied scenery to Kansas opera houses. By far the most often represented was the Kansas City Scenic Company.[12] Other major scenic houses that provided Kansas opera houses with scenery included Sosman and Landis of Chicago, Noxon, Halley and Toomey of St. Louis, and the Twin City Scenic Company of Minneapolis, Minnesota.[13]

The grand drape found in Concordia's Brown Grand Theatre is a beautiful example of the scene painter's art. In 1907, the Twin City Scenic Company painted the original grand drape curtain that hung in the theatre for many years. Then, in June 1967, a tornado passed over the theatre taking off the stage house roof. Subsequent rain badly damaged the curtain. Later, when the town of Concordia was in the process of restoring the theatre, the curtain was returned to the Twin City Scenic studio in hopes that a replica could be painted, but the curtain was too badly damaged to be used as a source. The original curtain contained a reproduction of the painting "Battle at Wagram" found in the Hall of Battles in the Palace of Versailles.

The Grand Drape found in Concordia's Brown Grand Theatre was originally painted in 1907 at the Twin City Scenic Studio and reproduced in 1979 by the same studio.

W. R. Brown, retired owner of the Twin City Scenic Company and another retired painter came out of retirement to paint the new curtain and when it was unveiled to the public on January 7, 1979, their finished product was proclaimed "as beautiful as the original." This curtain has particular significance because it was the last to be painted by that great company. The next year the scenic studio was destroyed by fire.[14]

Less well known scenic studios also produced curtains for Kansas opera houses. These included the Jessie Cox studio in Esterville, Iowa, the Omaha, Nebraska, studios of William Grabach and Jack Ballard and Son, and a Kansas City firm, the Graham and Davis Scenic Artists.[15] Located in Kansas, were the C. W. Sewell Scenic Company of Larned, Monarch Art Studio of Dodge City, and J. S. Jones and Son of Wichita.[16]

In addition to scenic studios, scenery was also painted by itinerate artists and local artists.[17, 18] One Kansas community even benefited from the terrible flu epidemic of 1918. Because theatres nationwide were closed due to the epidemic, Jimmie Shaw, a scene painter for the Castle Square Stock Company in Boston, came to Almena to stay with his father-in-law and while there painted a beautiful curtain for the Lyric Theatre that featured "The Spirit of 76."

It was not uncommon for an opera house to have more than one set of scenery during its life. Scenery wore out with constant use and local audiences became bored with what had once been new and beautiful. In 1892 the ten year old Hutchinson Opera House was renovated. Work included new paint and wall paper on the interior. The "Clipper" a local theatrical paper bragged about the work of the Kansas City Scenic Company,

No part has been overlooked. From the gallery to the stage every inch of surface has been touched and brightened by paper or paint….The old scenery has been disposed of and the seventy-five pieces of new scenery makes the stage equal of that in any opera house in the state.[19]

As the entertainment world changed, so did the need for painted scenery. While it was not unusual for a newly constructed moving picture theatre or community auditorium to contain a front ad curtain, there was less need for the other types of scenery. As orders for painted scenery became fewer, scenic studios turned to producing scenery for fraternal societies. This scenery, beautifully executed and preserved, is almost all that remains of this artistry, once so important to the opera houses of Kansas. Kansas is fortunate that the Scottish Rite Centers in Topeka, Lawrence, Fort Scott, Salina and Wichita all contain scenery painted by Sosman and Landis Studio of Chicago. Wichita's scenery was painted in 1907.

The painted canvas scenery of the late 19th and early 20th centuries was an integral part of opera house history. This scenery, roll or fly, crudely or masterfully painted, added much to the theatres and to the communities' pride as newly founded Kansas towns grew and prospered.

Audiences were entertained by thrilling special effects in plays such as Lincoln J. Carter's "Heart of Chicago."

# Chapter 5
# FROM MELODRAMA TO SHAKESPEARE

A damsel in distress, a villain twirling his mustache, these are images that come to mind when we think about late 19th and early 20th century theatre. "Melodrama" is the type of play associated with that period, but in reality an astonishingly large number of acting companies presented a wide variety of entertainments to Kansans of that period. In fact, it is likely that 19th century Midwesterners were better versed in Shakespeare than are the current residents of the state. And, while scenic effects lacked 21st century technology, train wrecks, tornadoes and mine explosions thrilled turn-of-the-century audiences. Early residents of the state were also delighted by the music and skits of Minstrel Shows, as well as by performances by nationally recognized opera companies. And, patriotic dramas that were staged by the residents themselves celebrated the brave soldiers of the Civil War.

## Types of Companies

**Resident Stock Companies**

The development of theatre in Kansas coincided with the growth of the state. Even before statehood, Leavenworth, located on the Missouri River, was the site of the state's first theatrical activity. Actors reached Leavenworth via the Missouri River from such locations as St. Louis and New Orleans, and by March 1858 there was a permanent theatre in Leavenworth, the Varieties Theatre, which later became the Union Theatre.

During the early days of theatrical activity in the state it was the common practice for a theatre to have a resident company of actors who presented a variety of plays. Because overland transportation was difficult and the river was often blocked by ice during the winter, a resident company was a practical way to provide continuous entertainment. Between 1858 to 1867 Leavenworth had several resident companies.[1] Following the Civil War and the explosion of activity in the railroad industry, the need for resident theatre companies diminished and the era of the traveling theatre company began.

**Traveling Theatrical Companies**

It is impossible to estimate the number of theatrical companies who appeared in Kansas from the late 1860s to the advent of World War I, but the number was considerable. For instance Emporia, located in the middle of the state, being of a fairly substantial size and blessed with a number of rail lines and an impressive opera house, bustled with theatrical activity. Approximately 590 acting companies appeared in Emporia between 1882 and 1913 when the Whitley Opera House was destroyed by fire. Between 1878 and 1925 Concordia, located in north central Kansas and smaller in size than Emporia was visited by 183 companies. While these two communities are relatively close together, 173 miles apart, only 43 companies appeared in both locations.

Garden City, located in western Kansas, was visited by 244 companies between 1886 and 1921. Twenty-four of these companies also appeared in Wichita, a much larger community. Wichita, while not incorporated until 1871, saw the appearance of 605 acting companies between 1872 and 1920. This is not surprising because by 1890 Wichita's was the second largest city in the state and by 1920 it was the largest.

Most companies played in a community only once, but a few appeared year after year. Residents of Emporia were treated to performances by the Andrews Opera Company on five occasions and by Lincoln J. Carter and his spectacle dramas eight times. John Dillion, when appearing in Emporia, presented a different melodrama on eight different occasions between 1882 to 1899, while J. C. Lewis visited the city eight times always offering the same show, "Si Plunkard." Another favorite, the Morey Stock Company's appearances in Emporia spanned a 23-year period. During their eleven visits this company presented 42 different plays. Charles Yale's "Devil's Auction" Company showed 12 times between 1893 and 1908 and Concordia audiences viewed one of their favorite companies, Hilman's Ideal Stock Company, ten times between 1907 and 1924.[2]

Several factors influenced the number of companies that appeared in a community. First, and most important, was whether the town was situated on a railroad line. While an "in-land" community, a city without a rail line, was not totally ignored because an acting company would occasionally rent a wagon and travel from the nearest rail stop, the town's location was crucial. The number of rail lines running through a town was also a consideration, as was the population of the community. Larger communities such as Topeka, Lawrence, Atchison, Leavenworth and Wichita were visited more frequently and by larger and better known companies than were smaller communities. Another factor in attracting good companies was the size of the opera house. Both its seating capacity and stage dimensions were relevant. The greater the seating capacity, the more tickets that could be sold and the larger the potential for profit, while the size of the stage dictated the size of production that could be staged.

**Dramatic Repertoire Companies**

There were several types of traveling theatrical troupes. Early in the period it was common for a company to come to a town, stay a week and present seven different shows in six days then move on to another community. One of the best-documented examples of the dramatic repertoire companies was the James A. Lord Chicago Dramatic Company. This troupe, one of the most popular and enduring in Kansas, made its first tour of Kansas in 1869. The company appeared for six days in Atchison, then in Leavenworth for seven days, followed by Lawrence for six days and finally in Topeka for eleven days. In each community six or seven different plays were presented. During this tour they gave 35 performances in 33 working days.[3]

From time to time Harry Corbet of Emporia, younger brother of Fred Corbet who managed Emporia's Whitley Opera House, joined traveling companies as a piano player. His diary for late May and early June of 1909 gave an indication of the life as part of the Jefferson Stock Company. Because it was summer and too hot to appear in unairconditioned opera houses, the company appeared in outdoor theatres called Air Domes.

| | |
|---|---|
| Tuesday - May 18 | Arrived Arkansas City 7:00 am. - "Kippewas' Secret" - bum biz |
| Wednesday - May 19 | Rehearsed in AM. "Home and Honor" - fair biz |
| Thursday - May 20 | Rehearsal AM "Paid A Debt" - fair biz |
| Friday - May 21 | "Counterfeiters" |
| Saturday - May 22 | Big biz, drew $8.00 |
| Sunday May 23 | Left Ark City at 12:30, arrived Winfield 1:30, laid over till 6:30; Arrived Wellington at 1:30 |
| Monday - May 24 | Rained - no show |
| Tuesday - May 25 | Band Concert |
| Wednesday - May 26 | "Lear" - capacity business |
| Thursday - May 27 | "Home and Honor" - Bum biz |
| Saturday - May 29 | No show |
| Monday - May 31 | "Paid a Debt" - good biz |
| Tuesday - June 1 | "Kippewa's Secret" - Fair biz |
| Wednesday - June 2 | "Father Against Son" - biz poor |

| | |
|---|---|
| Thursday - June 3 | "Paid A Debt" - fair biz |
| Friday - June 4 | "Cheerful Liar" - good biz |
| Saturday - June 5 | "Heart of A Slave" |
| Sunday - June 6 | Left Wellington at 8:50 AM; Changed at McFarland, arrived Manhattan at 3:30. Left Manhattan at 1:30; Arrived at St. Marys at 2:30; presented a play |
| Monday - June 5 | Left St. Marys at 7:21; arrived in Kansas City at 11:00 am; left Kansas City at 6:40 and arrived at Trenton, Missouri at 12:30. |

During the two-week period prior their entrance into Missouri the company presented eight different plays.[4]

**One Show Companies**

"One nighters" were companies that presented only one play, a one night stand, and moved on to a new town after almost every performance. The Trousdale's, an Iowa family with years of theatrical service, appeared in Kansas on several occasions. During the fall of 1910 Merle Trousdale's "Man on the Box" company entered Kansas from Nebraska and then, appearing in a different town every night, proceeded to play in Norton, Holton, Hiawatha, Seneca, Burlingame, Osage City, and Council Grove. Later that month they played Humboldt then Eureka followed by Severy, Neodesha, Independence, Altoona, Sedan, Belle Plaine, Englewood, Ashland, Coldwater, Medicine Lodge, and Kiowa before moving into Oklahoma.[5]

Finally, coming full circle, resident companies again became popular for a brief period of time. During the teens, toward the end of the opera house era, Wichita was the location of several resident companies including the Wolfe Stock Company at the New Auditorium and the North Brothers Stock Company at the Princess Theatre. During the 1915 season the Nestle Players was the resident company at the Home Theatre in Hutchinson.

# Types of Theatrical Productions

**Melodrama**

A wide variety of entertainments delighted rural audiences, but melodrama was the mainstay of frontier theatre. The plays presented at opera houses in Kansas reflected the values of the audience, the values of family, hard work and patriotism. This type of drama has been characterized as "drama to re-affirm what the audience already believed....People saw on the stage, the difficulties, illusions and ambitions of their own time."[6]

Today we view the overly dramatic plots of melodrama with amusement, but these plays pre-dated social security, disability insurance, and unemployment compensation. If several seasons of drought caused crops to fail, Kansans literally lost their farms and were forced to move, often leaving the state and returning to the shelter of relatives' homes. If a fire destroyed a general store and the owner did not carry insurance, that shopkeeper was forced to begin again from scratch. And medicine, even when doctors were available, was far from the sophisticated science we know today. Infant death, farm and workplace injuries, and disease were a tragic part of frontier life. There was, unfortunately, truth to the old children's prayer, "If I die before I wake, I pray the Lord my soul to take." While exaggerated, many of the situations portrayed in melodramas were real. And, temperance plays such as "Ten Nights in a Bar Room" and "The Drunkard," reflected serious social problems.

Just as the hardships presented in melodramas had a basis in reality, the values portrayed by these plays were also the values of the settlers. Early audiences knew the perils and physical demands of frontier life, but they also knew the joys of home and of family life. The settlers of Kansas believed in hard work and honesty, and church activities were an integral part of their social and religious life.

By far the most popular melodrama of the era was "Uncle Tom's Cabin." This stock poster was used by the Neal Stock Company of Lenora.

The selection of plays was rather limited in the mid to late 19th century. Many of the early melodramas were imported from Europe. Some appeared originally in play form while others were adapted from novels. Examples of European dramas were favorites such as "East Lynne," "Lady Audley's Secret," "Faust," "Monte Cristo" and "Fanchon the Cricket." In addition to their availability, another advantage to European dramas was that U.S. copyright laws did not apply, thus acting companies were not required to pay royalties. Plays such as "Hazel Kirke," "The Galley Slave," "Davy Crockett," "Two Orphans," "The Octoroon" and "Ten Nights in a Bar Room" delighted audiences during the 1890s. Later audiences enjoyed such plays as "The Sorrows of Satan," Dixie Land," "Woman Against Woman" and "The Convict's Daughter."

As time passed audiences wanted to see new material. Unfortunately, the "new" plays were often old plots renamed or rewritten, and the pirating of scripts was common. From 1880 to 1922 a company existed whose sole purpose was to pirate plays. A former actor, Alexander Byers, founded the Chicago Manuscript Company in 1880. He hired stenographers to attend plays, take down the dialogue in shorthand and transcribe it. The manuscripts were then sold under new names. This deception was possible because it wasn't until 1909 that a complete script of a play was submitted for copyright. Prior to that only the title was submitted.[7]

**Uncle Tom's Cabin**

Of the many plays presented in Kansas between the Civil War and World War I, "Uncle Tom's Cabin" stood out for its enduring popularity. For example, between 1885 and 1914 the play was performed seventeen times in Newton. This made it the community's most often viewed play, while "East Lynne," the second most often performed play, was presented only nine times. "Uncle Tom's Cabin's" phenomenal popularity relied on far more than just its anti-slavery sentiment. It was a dramatic extravaganza.

"Uncle Tom's Cabin" written by Harriet Beecher Stowe was first published as a novel in 1852, but when asked to turn it into a play, she refused and as a result never received a penny for the dramatic rights to "Uncle Tom's Cabin." Unprotected by copyright, the novel was originally dramatized by George Aiken and his brother Frank. When first produced, the play ended with the death of little Eva, but soon two additional acts were written, featuring the famous ending where the slave Tom, on his deathbed, said, "Don't call me poor fellow.... Heaven has come! I got the victory! The Lord has given it to me! Glory be to his Name!" And George, his master responded, "Poor old Uncle Tom — he's gone!" followed by the very popular transformation scene where Little Eva appeared, as if from heaven, and off stage voices sang, "The poor old slave has gone to rest, we know that he is free; Disturb him not but let him rest way down in Tennessee."[8]

Spectacle played a large part in the play's popularity. When McFadden's Boston Double Uncle Tom's Cabin Company appeared at the Eureka Opera House, the company's publicity proclaimed that it was composed of 25 performers including ten colored Plantation Singers, two imported Irish trick donkeys and six monster bloodhounds. In Norton the arrival of the Uncle Tom's Cabin Company was heralded by a spectacular parade. A brass band lead by a colored man who twirled a baton was followed by flat wagons that carried the various characters in scenes from the play, and concluded with a number of black children, a group of Negro singers with banjoes, and a pack of big bloodhounds.

Ads for "Uncle Tom's Cabin" always billed the production as the "best ever" and bragged about the size of the production. When Stetson's Uncle Tom's Cabin Company appeared in Hutchinson the company was reported to be composed of "fifty men, women and children, all capable actors, actresses, singers and dancers. As a scenic production it is said to be better than any other. Among other worthy of special mention are the Ohio River by moonlight, the beautiful vision scene and the gorgeous transformation scene at the close." And, "A number of prize Shetland ponies, trick mules and Col. Sawyer's splendid pack of genuine Siberian bloodhounds are special features."[9]

On one occasion when the well known Kansas theatrical company headed by Wallace Bruce presented "Uncle Tom's Cabin," Bruce's young daughter, Virginia aged six, played Little Eva. Virginia remembered one particular scene where she (Little Eva) was lying dead on the stage with one of the actors crying over her body.

It made Virginia so sad to see that actor whom she knew crying that she burst into tears too. Through clenched teeth her father whispered, "Be quiet, you're supposed to be dead."[10]

Popular "Uncle Tom's Cabin" companies who appeared in Kansas included McFadden's Mammoth Double Uncle Tom's Cabin Company and the Boston Double Company. While the majority of companies appeared during the latter part of the 19th century, Stetson's Uncle Tom's Cabin Company was active in the state between 1902 and 1923, and Burk's Company played Garden City five times during the same period.

Not all "Uncle Tom's Cabin" companies delighted their audiences. An 1889 review from a Washington, Kansas, paper stated, "Uncle Tom's Cabin Company played here Tuesday night. All the actors were miserable failures except the donkey who seemed to appreciate the execrable acting of the balance and made special efforts to please."[11]

An article in an 1897 *New York Dramatic Mirror* reported a disaster that was supposed to have occurred when one unlucky "Uncle Tom's Cabin" company performed in Kansas. The report, submitted by an actor from a rival company appearing in the same town, was quite critical of the opera house, the audience, and the company that presented the play.

> The theatre was a dingy upstairs affair, long, narrow and abominably dirty. The audience, an unspeakable aggregation, had come in from sagebrush and adobe during the afternoon, and each particular household had brought along its especial dog, or dogs. That evening when the choice crowd had assembled in the 'opera house,' the little aisles presented the formidable appearance of some unhallowed bench show, for each and every dog was disposed at the side of its master. The canine contingent behaved at the onset rather better than the human collection, and the opening scene went fairly well.
>
> There were sixteen players on the program and six on the stage, but the really enthusiastic spectators never suspected a double. And there was one player who didn't double, and he it was who caused the trouble. This artist, be it known, was the amiable mongrel cur who masqueraded as a 'sagacious Siberian bloodhound.' His business, of course, was to trot merrily across the stage in the wake of George Harris and Eliza at the ice episode, and so much he attempted to do. But no sooner had he reached the center than there went up from the house a howl of appalling significance.
>
> The actor dog paused uncertain for an instant, and that instant was his finish. Every canine in the aisles had marked the cowering yellow beast upon the stage as its legitimate prey, and there was a wild, furious stampede for the footlights. At a bound, the attacking army reached the stage, and in another moment the supposed ice scene was obscured by a snarling, snapping canine pyramid. The actors rushed out with staves and brooms, the spectators climbed up with sticks and whips, and in a few minutes the enthusiastic curs had been chased off the stage — all but the mongrel object of assault. A little yellow heap lay motionless in the center of the platform as the curtain was lowered. The 'Tom' people went on to the next stand without their 'Siberian' bloodhound.

**Spectaculars**

In an era that preceded radio, moving pictures, television and computer animation, Midwestern audiences were thrilled by the special effects presented in the plays that appeared at the local opera houses. One of the premier designers of spectaculars was Lincoln J. Carter. The titles of his plays indicated the types of effects Carter devised: "Fast Mail," "Tornado," "Remember the Main" and "While Frisco Burns." The special effects included a train that roared across the stage with whistle blowing and sparks flying, Niagara Falls, a tornado that destroyed a farm, two ships colliding at sea, elaborate fire scenes, automobile races, and battle scenes.

While Lincoln Carter produced a new play each year, another well known company manager, Charles H. Yale, toured the same spectacular play for at least 22 years. "The Devil's Auction's" first appeared in Wichita in 1886 and featured, according to its advertisements, 60 people, including 16 dancers, a dramatic company of 20, 22 sets of scenery and its own calcium lights. The same year an Emporia audience was delighted by the troupe's first appearance in that community.

The Whitley opera house was jammed last night, up-stairs and down, to witness the presentation of the Devil's Auction. The play was put on in the style, each character seeming to be selected especially for his part. The costumes were rich and becoming, and the scenery was gorgeous. The acrobatic feats were unusually good and the hat throwing from the gallery much enjoyed by the boys. The troupe of fairies with their dancing queen was perhaps a little flashy, but taken as a whole the performance gave more than usually good satisfaction and ranks far above the average.... We bespeak for the company a crowded house wherever they go.[12]

**Grand Opera**

The same Midwestern audiences who thrilled to the scenic effects of Lincoln Carter and the "Devil's Auction" were also exposed to a more cultural form of entertainment, grand opera. The first appearance of opera in Kansas occurred in 1869 when Pasquale Brignoli performed at Frazer's Hall in Lawrence and later at the Leavenworth Opera House. "Don Pasquale," the opera presented, was sung in Italian with piano accompaniment. These first operas were presented by concert companies that consisted of one or a few soloists singing to piano accompaniment, but by the 1880s full operas became prevalent.

During the later part of the 19th century and the early part of the 20th century numerous full opera companies appeared in Kansas. Among the most popular were the Emma Abbot Grand English Opera Company, the Andrews Opera Company, the Boston Ideal Opera Company, and the Boston English Opera Company. When "English" was used in the title it referred to the language the opera was sung in rather than the national origin of the company. The operas presented by these companies included such favorites as "Il Trovatore," "Said Pasha," "The Bohemian Girl," "Mascotte," "Rigoletto," "Chimes of Normandy," "Pirates of Penzance," the "Mikado," "Martha" and "Faust."

The interest in grand opera peaked in the 1880s and 1890s but declined in later years. Changes in audience taste and over familiarity with the operas presented took their toll. Also, increased railroad rates made it much more expensive for the large opera companies to travel from city to city.

**Shakespeare**

In addition to grand opera, Kansas's audiences were also exposed to the classic plays of Shakespeare. In 1888 Edmund Booth, the greatest of all 19th century Shakespearean actors appeared in Wichita in "Julius Caesar" and "Othello," and again in 1893 in "Julius Caesar." Lawrence Barrett was also featured in these productions. A young supporting member of the Booth and Barrett Company, Charles B. Hanford, later

Kansas audiences were quite familiar with Shakespeare. This program was from Edwin Booth and Lawrence Barrett's 1888 appearance at Wichita's Crawford Grand Opera House.

brought even more Shakespeare to Kansans. After appearing with Booth and Barrett Charles Hanford went on to appear with Thomas Keene, another great Shakespearean performer who presented such plays as "King Richard III," "Julius Caesar," "Hamlet" and "Othello" to Kansas audiences.

Upon the retirement of Booth and Barrett, Charles Hanford bought their scenic equipment for "Julius Caesar" and began touring with his own company.[13] Hanford and his wife Marie Drofnah (Hanford spelled backwards) appeared in Emporia eight times between 1902 and 1910 in the "Taming of the Shrew," "The Merchant of Venice," "Julius Caesar," "Anthony and Cleopatra," "Othello," "Hamlet" and "Macbeth." The couple's last appearance in Wichita was in 1917. Other actors who brought Shakespeare to Kansas included Sanford Dodge, Louis James, and E. H. Southern and Julia Marlo.

**Black Entertainment in Kansas**

By far the best remembered opera house entertainer in Kansas was the pianist John William Boone, better known as Blind Boone. The *Hutchinson Clipper* described a performance by Blind Boone.

A large audience greeted the Blind Boone Company last Tuesday evening. Blind Boone has visited this city before, but his reception last week was more enthusiastic than ever given him in this city. Boone and Stella May both rendered several plantation songs, which were highly appreciated. His imitations on the piano of the old darky and his fiddle, the fife and drum, music box, etc. were perfect and received hearty encores from the delighted audience."[14]

An enthusiastic Severance, Kansas, audience member described Boone's appearance in that community. "He played the piano wonderfully and one selection 'The Storm,' was a true story of a Cyclone he had experienced when a small boy down in Missouri and it was beautifully given. With him traveled a couple known as the Lang's. Lang carried a big Green Parrot, named Lorita on his arm, to the delight of the school children. The Hall was packed for these performances."[15] To Kansas audiences one of the most remarkable features of Blind Boone's performances was his ability to hear a number played and then to repeat it exactly.

Boone traveled extensively for 39 years, performing ten months a year with six concerts per week for a total of 8,650 concerts. Just like other performers whose careers were affected by the advent of moving pictures and the closing of opera houses, Boone's career declined steadily from 1916 until his death in 1927.[16]

The second major black entertainer who appeared in Kansas was Sissieretta Jones, nationally known as Black Patti. Sissieretta received the name Black Patti when a newspaper compared her to the world-famous Italian soprano, Adelina Patti.[17]

By far the best remembered performer of the opera house era was black pianist John William Boone, better known as Blind Boone, seen here on the right. Pictured with Boone is his agent of many years, John Lang. Courtesy of Dennis Coffey.

42 | Kansas Opera Houses

The Black Patti Troubadours appeared in Kansas numerous times. Commenting on the company's appearance, a Hutchinson newspaper informed its readers that, "Through the remarkable talents of its versatile members, the extraordinary excellence of the stage performance and its phenomenal popularity, it has become one of the most valuable pieces of theatrical property in the country."[18]

The Black Patti Troubadours performed for 20 years, breaking up in 1915. Like Blind Boone and so many other attractions, the company fell victim to changing audience tastes and to new technology.

**Minstrel Shows**

Minstrel Shows were perennial favorites in Kansas. While they began in the South prior to the Civil War, this form of entertainment did not reach Kansas until the railroad expansion of the 1870s. Sanford's Georgia Minstrels, with its 1878 appearance in Concordia, was one of the first companies to perform in the state. By the early 1880s Kansas was visited by the best companies in the United States, Hi Henry's Minstrels, Haverly's Minstrels, Barlow and Wilson's Minstrels, I. W. Baird's Minstrels, and Pringle's Georgia Minstrels. Other well-known troupes that appeared in the state included Kersand's Colored Minstrels, the Belmont Happy Minstrels, the Maharani Minstrels and Lou Docksteadeer's Minstrels.[19]

Minstrel shows grew out of parodies of the Black culture. Early Minstrel companies featured white entertainers in blackface, but as time passed black entertainers also performed in black face.[20] Later the Minstrel format evolved

Minstrel companies were popular with Kansas' audiences. Pictured here are the Haverlaff's Minstrels at Kelley's Opera House in White Cloud. Courtesy of the Kansas State Historical Society.

From Melodrama to Shakespeare | 43

into a vehicle for amateur performances by fraternal and community organizations. Through the mid-20th century these blackface productions were quite popular and could be found as fundraisers in many communities. Wallace Bruce, a Hutchinson entertainer, would be hired by civic organizations to direct their local minstrel shows. Bruce would provide scripts that included music, jokes and stage directions, and direct the productions.

**Military Pageants**

With the Civil War still fresh in the minds and hearts of the nation, plays with a patriotic flavor were popular with Kansas audiences. Often these pageants were presented by the local G.A.R., Grand Army of the Republic, posts with some of the actors actual Civil War veterans. Popular plays included "The Blue and the Gray," "The Spy of Atlanta," "The Spy of Gettysburg" and "Dixie." An 1891 Hutchinson production of "Drummer Boy and Spy" was, according to its review, "a thrilling war drama with special scenery and beautiful tableaux." And, still another production, George T. Ulmer's war drama, "The Volunteer" was described as, "possessing many extremely powerful situations."[21]

Even before statehood, Kansas's settlers were entertained by traveling theatrical troupes. These early troops traveled by wagon and riverboat, and then as rails spread across the state, even more theatrical troupes presented a wide variety of entertainments. Melodramatic plays were always the staple of opera house entertainment, but other types of productions flourished as well. From Shakespeare to military pageants, from grand opera to minstrel shows, a multitude of troupes entertained Kansas's audiences.

# Chapter 6
# NOW APPEARING:
# Famous Performers and Their Kansas Appearances

What was it like performing in Kansas during the early days of the state? The remembrances of several frontier performers answer this question.

**Eddie Foy**

A very colorful chapter in the state's history revolved around the Texas cattle trade and the glory days of the Kansas cow towns. While short lived, this period was certainly colorful and brought not only cowboys to the state, but also performers to entertain the cowboys. Eddie Foy was one such entertainer. Thanks to Foy's recollection of his 1878 appearance in Dodge City, we have a vivid account of entertainment in a Kansas cow town.

Foy described his and his partner Jim Thompson's arrival by rail. "One of the most vivid yet remaining of my first impressions of Dodge City is that of dust; heat, wind and flat prairie too, but above all dust!"

As they approached the town they passed huge piles of bones beside the track. This sight caused Jim Thompson to suggest that perhaps they were killing people in Dodge more rapidly than they could bury them. Later Thompson and Foy learned that these were buffalo bones awaiting shipment to manufactures of fertilizer.

Foy and Thompson opened at Springer's dance hall and saloon on the night of their arrival and felt that they were fairly well received. "I didn't hesitate to josh the town a bit in my original parodies and patter. Had I known the West better then, I might have been more careful, but even as it was I suffered no ill consequences."

Years later a Dodge City historian wrote this account of Foy's first appearance in Dodge.

> Eddie Foy, one of the greatest comedians of our day, made his debut or about his first appearance at Dodge City. He dressed pretty loud and had a kind of Fifth Avenue swaggering strut, and made some distasteful jokes about the cowboys. This led to their capturing Foy by roping, fixing him up in a picturesque way, ducking him in a friendly way in a horse trough, riding him around on horseback and taking other playful familiarities with him, just to show their friendship for him.

As a young performer Eddie Foy, pictured here in "Up and Down Broadway," was a favorite of the Dodge City cowboys.

Foy observed, "My bearing on that occasion must have given the town an exaggerated idea of my courage, for I was presently offered an opportunity to enlist as a hired gunman…an offer which I declined."

The Dodge City historian continued, "Foy took these pranks with such good grace that he captured the cowboys completely. Every night his theatre was crowded with them, and nothing he could say or do offended them; on the contrary, they made a little god of him."[1]

Foy's career took him from Dodge City to the mining camps of Colorado and eventually to all of the major stages of the country.

**Jefferson DeAngelis**

Jefferson DeAngelis, who went on to national recognition, was a teenager appearing in his family's show when the troupe encountered dire circumstances in Kansas. The company, while working its way to California, had traveled through Missouri. Business was good and they made a modest profit. But, at St. Joseph they realized that something was wrong and decided to move on to Atchison, Kansas. What these actors hadn't paid attention to were reports of a grasshopper plague, and what they did not know was that this scourge of the land would continue all the way across Kansas.

After the company's first and only appearance in Atchison, they were so broke they couldn't even afford train tickets to the next town. At that point DeAngelis' father found a farmer whose crops had been eaten by the grasshoppers, and persuaded the farmer to join the company, using his wagon to transport the troupe. First they played the larger Eastern Kansas towns such as Leavenworth, Lawrence, Topeka and Emporia. But, because they were traveling by wagon and could only make short jumps of ten to 20 miles a day, they were also forced to stop at many small communities that had never seen a show.

DeAngelis described the company's preparations to appear in one of these villages.

> We had printed handbills, with date and place of performance left blank. As soon as we reached a town we hustled about and engaged some place for our performance. It might be a courthouse, a school house, the town hall, a hotel or restaurant dining-room, a warehouse, anything that would hold 50 to 100 auditors. Schoolhouses were the commonest, but sometimes the trustees doubted whether they ought to be used for so coarse a function as a professional variety show.
>
> Having found a place, we would scribble its name and the date (it was always 'Tonight' if we got the arrangements completed in time) on our bills and distribute them about the town, shoving them under doors and throwing them into farmers' wagons. If the room we engaged had no stage or rostrum, we must build one. This we usually did by borrowing from some contractor or lumber dealer a few of those four-legged 'horses' used by carpenters and some rough boards, which were lent us the more cheaply on condition that we were not to saw a piece or drive a nail into any of it. With such stuff we constructed stages that were decidedly precarious for dancing and acrobatic work, but which were better, after all, than some others that we contrived by grouping the tables in hotel dining-rooms. That none of us suffered from broken bones or sprains during that tour was a miracle.
>
> In many cases there were not enough chairs available, and we had to make benches, too, from our rough lumber, laying the planks across boxes or blocks of wood. Then we must borrow a piano or a cottage organ if we could; otherwise Gerard with his fiddle was our only music. As for the piano, I had to play that, and I knew nothing but the simplest of chords.
>
> The village and country folk were hungry for entertainment but they had little money to spend on it. Many a night we did only five or ten dollars' worth of business. We discovered that some who had no cash would come to the show if they could pay in farm produce, and as we presently began camping out and preparing our own meals we let it be known that we would accept potatoes, cabbage, turnips, eggs, chickens, butter, grain or any other edible for man or beast at current prices; with the result that our 'box office' frequently resembled a 'grocery store.'
>
> As we worked westward through Kansas, the towns were farther and farther apart, and there were

times when we couldn't reach shelter, but must sleep in the open. The women always slept in one of the wagons, the men usually on the ground around the camp fire. But with performances scarcer and overhead higher, the inevitable finally happened. We contracted debts that we couldn't pay, and sheriffs seized first a trunk full of costumes, and then at another place they took our wagons from us. The debt was only trivial--perhaps ten or twelve dollars — but to us at the moment it might as well have been ten thousand.

The troupe managed to travel by stagecoach until DeAngelis' father convinced another farmer to join the troupe and provide transportation. They progressed on West, always hoping to make money. Often they did not and had to resort to midnight escapes from hotels to avoid paying their bills and pawning possessions, including Gerard's fiddle, to eat. But, eventually the beleaguered company arrived in California where the family lived for many years, always making a living in some form of entertainment.[2]

**Luke Cosgrave**

As a small boy living in Ireland, Luke Cosgrave dreamed of the American West and read countless stories about cowboys and Indians. In 1870, when he was still a child, his family moved to America, living first in Zanesville, Ohio, and later in Kansas City. While in Ohio Cosgrave developed an interest in the theatre and attended performances by such great actors as Effie Esler in "Hazel Kirke," Frank Mayo in "Davy Crockett," Thomas W. Keene in "Richard III" and Edwin Booth in "Hamlet." And, by watching these performers, Cosgrave began to learn how to act.

After the family's move to Kansas City, Luke Cosgrave began to give recitations and to take part in amateur dramatics. It was at this point that the Grace George Dramatic Company appeared in Kansas City putting on "Fanchon, the Cricket." They were in need of an actor and Cosgrave applied. He was hired at the salary of fifteen dollars a week and told that the company would leave town on Sunday and open on Monday in Garnett, Kansas. Cosgrave was elated.

> I left Miss George, went out and walked the streets. Even the air was different. It was being breathed by a new man, a professional actor. There is always a point where the tide begins to turn. I felt this was it. I did not know where I was going in the theater, nor did I need to know. All that mattered was that something had happened to make my boyhood dreams begin to take shape. The actor in my dreams was about to merge with the man.

When the Grace George Company arrived in Garnett, Kansas, Luke Cosgrave discovered what it really meant to be an actor. "Mr. and Mrs. George (or 'Miss' as she was known) were both able to charge themselves and their company with an air of romance blended with authority. It spelled THEATER TONIGHT."

During the day the company went from house to house distributing small program playbills that featured a picture of Miss George wearing a piece of lace on her head. Also, Mrs. George directed the rehearsal of their opening plays while Mr. George took care of advertising. The first night's fare was "Lady Audley" followed by the farce "Bibbs and Bibbs, or the Quiet Family." The next night the company performed "The Hidden Hand or the Romance of Hurricane Hall" and finished with the Irish comedy drama "Kathleen Mavourneen."

Following Garnett, the company played in LeRoy, Kansas, where the Georges employed a unique attention getting technique. About ten o'clock in the morning a carriage arrived at the entrance to the hotel. Red velvet banners proclaiming "Grace George — Theater Tonight" were draped on either side of the horses and carriage. Two of the company's actresses were already in the carriage when Miss George made her grand entrance in a dress of red silk brocade and a wide-brimmed black hat with white plumes. By this time a small crowd had gathered. To give the townspeople even more time to assemble, Miss George, in great distress, announced that her keys were lost, and sent her son back into the hotel to locate them. Eventually he reappeared and the promenade began. The carriage, driven by Mr. George and containing the three actresses, proceeded around the community, and then returned to the hotel where an even larger crowd had gathered.

The LeRoy opera house was located on the second floor of a building that is still standing. At the time of their appearance the theatre, according to Cosgrave, needed a lot of sweeping and the kerosene lamps smoked and often needed tending. To attract attention to the opera house a little cloth sign that read, "Theatre Tonight" was hung over the entrance to guide the country folks who came in for the performance and who also brought their lanterns. The company's appearance in LeRoy was followed by an engagement in Westphalia. By this time Luke Cosgrave was beginning to feel comfortable in his new parts. Cosgrave summarized the rest of the company's Kansas appearances.

>All that autumn we toured the vast open spaces that were the Kansas of 1886. They were perfect days. I met storekeepers, farmers, peace officers; old fellows who knew Wild Bill Hickock at Abilene; pioneer bankers. The weekly newspapers sometimes mentioned us.
>
>This was the West that Ned Buntline told about in "Dashing Charlie" and "Buffalo Bill's Fight With Spotted Tail." The prairie grass, the Indians and buffalo were gone. The great ranges were fenced with barbed wire, and lightning rods glistened on schoolhouse and church. The big crop of corn was being gathered. Railroad cars were on a siding to receive it. The whole town could hear the trains screaming by.
>
>Even the religious people came to the theatre sometimes, just to look at bits of color or get a flash of the great world. And the towns? Mulvane, Burlingame, Cimarron, Fort Scott, Manhattan, Abilene, Howard--we booked them all....In some towns we met a Medicine Show in a tent. A long-haired doctor, dressed in gray homespun frock coat and a wide white hat, sold Kickapoo remedies for a dollar a bottle, while minstrel boys played banjos and sang the latest Negro melodies.
>
>At other places, evangelists in gospel tents told the great old story of the glad tidings of Redemption, sang Psalms and hymns. This was called The Sawdust Trail. One old pioneer in Mulvane remarked, 'These two institutions are all the people of Kansas have to keep their bodies and souls together!'

The Grace George Dramatic Company continued to make its way west playing in such towns as Little River, Solomon City, Dighton, Ness City, Greeley, Tribune, Leoti and Coronado. Today Coronado consists of a grain elevator and one house, but in 1886 it was much larger. It was while playing in this part of the state that Cosgrave had a real western adventure.

Leoti and Coronado were rivals for the county seat. These "county seat wars" as they were called, were often hotly contested battles. A great deal was at stake because gaining the county seat meant that the community would grow and prosper. In order to insure their success, the residents of Coronado went to Leoti and took the county seat safe and records, put them on a wagon and returned to Coronado. That night six horsemen from Leoti went to Coronado to shoot up the town, but the Coronado boys anticipated this and were waiting upstairs in the printing office to ambush the Leoti gunmen. When the Leoti riders rounded the corner, the Coronado men opened fire and dropped four men out of their saddles.

This is where the matter stood when the Grace George troupe arrived. The company's second performance was "Uncle Tom's Cabin" and for that, guns were needed. This was Luke Cosgrave's exposure to the "true west."

>Mr. George asked me to borrow a couple of sure-fire revolvers for the escape scene. Kansas had very strict prohibition, so men usually gathered at the drug store. Because of the Leoti trouble, several gunmen were in town, among them the well-known Pat Shugra from Dodge City.
>
>I asked the druggist if he could borrow a couple of sure-fire guns for me. So he said, 'Will any of you boys lend this young fellow a couple of sure-fire guns for the show?'
>
>'Sure-fire?' they yelled. 'What other kinds are there?' And they laid out on the counter the most variegated assortment of artillery I ever saw. Smith and Westons, Colt single barrels, ivory handles, walnut handles, black and silver barrels. Even Pat put his up.
>
>Pat squinted a little, because one of his eyes was powder-burned. He was short, very broad, rather a good shot. He picked out two showy guns, very kindly extracted the bullets, filled the cartridges with candle grease, and — we had a nice little clatter of harmless gunfire for the escape scene.[3]

**Louie Lord**

Perhaps more than any other, Louie Lord epitomized the frontier performer. Born in 1851, Louisa Simms was a 17-year old Chicago girl who had trained to be a teacher when she married James Lord, a Civil War veteran

18 years her senior. His acting company, the James Lord Company, which soon became known as the Louie Lord Company, performed in Kansas from the late 1860s to the 1880s. An Atchison newspaper article proclaimed, "Louie Lord, with her husband and company were to the small towns of Kansas what Henry Irving and Ellen Terry are to the British theater--the zenith and perfection of dramatic art."[4]

During the early years of their career the Lord's presented an amazing number of plays ranging from Shakespeare's "Othello" to melodramas. Their first tour of the state in 1869-70 featured 15 different plays and the next year 21 different plays were presented. But, this style of production gradually changed. By the 1880s Louie Lord limited her offerings to a few plays that were, according to the company's publicity, written especially for her or by her. This was due in part to stricter enforcement of the copyright laws.[5]

In 1903, a newspaper commentary on Louie Lord's skills as an actress summed up the frontier theatre very well, "Actors of thirty years ago in Kansas were brave beyond conception. They would storm the heights of a Shakespeare play with the same intrepidity with which they skirmished in the fields of simple melodrama. Desdemona, Portia, Topsy, Lady of Lyons, were to Louie Lord such a small tax on her versatility that she passed from one to the other with no effort at all."[6]

From 1869, when she first appeared in the state, until the 1880s, Louie Lord was one of Kansans favorite performers.

## Harry Houdini

Houdini, the most famous magician of the early 20th century, was born Ehrich Weisz in Budapest, Hungary, on March 24, 1874. The son of a rabbi, he, along with his family, immigrated to the United States in 1878. Ehrich Weiss, as he was known after his move to the United States, was the middle son in a family of five boys. The family, quite poor, eventually moved to New York City. There the teenage Ehrich worked in a neckwear-cutting firm, took other odd-jobs, and because he was passionate about sports allegedly ran ten miles a day to train for long distance events.

In 1891 Ehrich teamed up with another youth from the neckwear-cutting firm to form a magic act. They called themselves the Brothers Houdini. The name alluded to the French conjurer Jean Eugene Robert-Houdin, the founder of modern magic. It was about this time that Ehrich anglicized his name to "Harry." In 1893 the Brothers Houdini played the World's Columbian Exposition in Chicago, but the act broke up a year later when Harry married eighteen-year old Wilhelmina Beatrice Rahner, known as Bess, and she became his partner.

Houdini was a short man, five-foot-five or six, and Bess was even more diminutive, at five feet. He appeared in a tux and she in tights and bloomers or in a Little Lord Fauntleroy outfit of black knickerbockers, white shirt

A young Harry and Bess Houdini appeared in Kansas in 1897 with Dr. Hill's California Concert Company. Courtesy of the Library of Congress, LC-U5762-112443.

with a flowing lace collar, and velvet jacket. During these early years of their partnership Houdini perfected the two acts he would be best remember for, the disappearing act "Metamorphosis" and the ability to escape from a variety of handcuffs.[7]

The Houdinis' Kansas performances came about because of the couple's financial misfortunes. In 1897 they had been appearing at a music hall in Milwaukee but were swindled out of their salary by an unscrupulous manager. This was followed by still another financial disaster brought on by Houdini himself. In order to try to recoup their losses Houdini, then 23, entered into a crap game where he lost the couple's last sixty dollars leaving them destitute. But, a new chapter in their professional life was about to begin.

The couple received an offer to join Dr. Hill's traveling medicine show, known as The California Concert Company, at $25 a week plus board and traveling expenses. Since this was a fifteen-week engagement, the offer was very good news. In addition to Dr. Thomas Hill, a very charismatic pitchman, the show boasted Swiss bell ringers, a German dialect comedian, and at some point, a singing, dancing, and acrobatic family, Joe and Myra Keaton. In addition to individual vaudeville acts, the company also presented melodramas.

It was while playing in Garnett, Kansas that Harry first introduced spiritualism into his act.[8] The California Concert Company appeared in Garnett on November 26, 1897. In order to insure a big audience and make enough money for the company to leave town, it was announced that a séance would be held. The success of this performance was reported in the local newspaper. "The California Concert Company sold 1,030 general admission tickets Monday night and this is the largest audience that has ever attended a pay entertainment in the history of the city (Garnett). The special feature for this night was a spiritual séance and this was the cause of such a large attendance."[9]

Later Houdini recalled that his phenomenal performance was possible because in preparation he had visited the Garnett cemetery and also talked with local residents. While in the cemetery Houdini found the grave of Joe Osborne, the six-year old son of Mr. and Mrs. Harry Osborne. At the performance Mrs. Houdini was put into a trance and spoke, "Don't cry, mamma. There'll be another one soon to take my place." And, it was true, Mrs. Osborne was pregnant. Years later Houdini admitted that this was simply a shrewd guess on his part and sent a letter of apology to the couple.[10]

After leaving Garnett the California Concert Company continued to play across Kansas. From Houdini's diary we know that their 1897 Kansas appearances included Pittsburg, Cherokee, Columbus, Galena and finally, Weir City.

After the Houdinis left the medicine show they appeared briefly with a circus and then went on to small time vaudeville. In 1899 Martin Beck, a great vaudeville impresario, saw the couple's act and recognized Houdini's showmanship and talent and sent him a telegram that read, "You can open Omaha March 26th, sixty dollars, will see act probably make you proposition for all next season." Years later Houdini noted, "The wire changed my whole life's journey."[11]

## Buster Keaton

We remember Buster Keaton as the sad faced comic of silent movies, but his career began much earlier. Buster was actually the third generation of his family to enter show business. His mother, Myra Cutler Keaton, was four-feet-eleven inches tall, weighed ninety pounds, and was born into show business. Her father, F. L. Cutler was one of the owners of the Cutler-Bryant 10-cent Show. Myra was a musician who played the base fiddle, the piano and the cornet. She was also, according to her son, the first woman in the United States to play a saxophone. Buster's father, Joe Keaton, was five-foot-eleven, a dancer and comedian, and a great socializer. Among his acquaintances were Will Rogers, Harry Houdini, Fred Stone, George M. Cohan, Al Jolson, McIntyre and Heath,

Joseph Frank Keaton, better known as Buster, was born October 4, 1895, in Piqua. Buster is pictured with his father and mother when they appeared as the Three Keatons. Courtesy of The Museum of Modern Art Film Stills Archive.

Now Appearing | 51

Gus Edwards and again according to Buster, about everyone else who was around and up and doing in the old two-a-day days. Buster considered his father to be the most gifted man in taking a fall that he ever saw.

The medicine show with the Keaton's as performers was making a one-night stand in Piqua, Kansas, when Mrs. Keaton went into labor. She was taken to the home of a Piqua couple where Joseph Frank Keaton was born. Myra and her baby remained in Piqua for two weeks and then rejoined the show.

According to Buster Keaton, it was during the time that the Keatons and Houdinis were playing with the same show that Buster received his name. Young Keaton, then about six months old, tumbled down the stairs of a boarding house where they were staying and landed at the feet of Harry Houdini. Houdini picked up the crying child and said, "My, that was a buster," and from then on that was the child's name.

One night while both families were performing together Bess Houdini was on stage singing when she heard a voice cry, "Hogan's Hotel is afire." Joe Keaton was in the dressing room and didn't hear the alarm, and neither did Myra Keaton who was accompanying Mrs. Houdini on the piano. Bess realized that Buster was back at the hotel asleep so she jumped over the gas footlights, ran up the aisle, down the street and into the smoky hotel, all the time wearing her short bespangled dress. Bess rushed up stairs and grabbed the baby. As she returned to the lobby with Buster, Joe, Myra and Houdini, followed by most of the audience, came charging in the door.

Buster claimed that as a toddler he got into so much trouble back stage, his parents thought they might as well put him into the act. In truth, Buster was five when he joined the act, and that was the making of the Keaton family's vaudeville career. A 1906 theatrical trade paper featured eight-year old Buster on its cover and proclaimed him to be, "the ace in vaudeville's pack of winning cards" and predicted his future success when it concluded, "watch out for Buster."[12] Several years later, in a letter to Harry Houdini, Joe Keaton wrote that his undersized eleven-year-old son, Buster, would grow up to be not much larger than "little Bessie," but was "excruciatingly funny."

From obscurity, the Keatons moved into the headline position in vaudeville. And from vaudeville, Buster went on to silent movies and lasting fame.[13]

**Pearl White**

Names that are recognizable today because of their association with the moving picture industry also appeared on the stages of Kansas.

Pearl White, who became famous in the silent movie series "The Perils of Pauline," received her start in Kansas when she joined a road company that was appearing in the state.

As a child Pearl was much attracted to show business and had even played Little Eva when an "Uncle Tom's Cabin" company came to her small Missouri town. Her family, like many families of that time, was opposed to her becoming an actress, but she eventually won the struggle.

A few months before her 18th birthday Pearl began answering advertisements from traveling companies that appeared in the *New York Clipper*, a theatrical paper. While answering ads didn't pay off, she finally landed a job through an agency in Kansas City and was scheduled to join the troupe on the 4th of March, the day on which she turned 18. In preparation for joining the company Pearl secretly sent her trunk to the train station. Then, at about eleven the night before her birthday, she announced to her family that in an hour she would be 18 and could do whatever she pleased, and therefore, was departing on the 1:30 a.m. train. Pearl reported that her father acted like a sportsman. He said simply, "Well, girl, I have lost. I have tried to change your mind and failed. Therefore, I can but wish you good luck."

Pearl White then boarded the 1:30 a.m. train and joined the Truesdale Stock Company at Galena, Kansas. Unfortunately, she only lasted about eight weeks with the company before she was fired because, in her words, "It seems that I simply didn't make good. This was quite a blow to me, but I was determined not to return home until I had become a success. So I was left in Emporia, Kansas, flat and alone, with precious little money in my possession."

Pearl White went on to become a successful actress with various Midwestern touring companies and then moved to California where, because she had laryngitis and needed money to tide her over until her voice was better, auditioned for a part in a silent movie, and made a name for herself in the "Perils of Pauline" series.[14]

**Boris Karloff**

"Boris Karloff and Miss Margot Beaton are the two greatest leading people I ever saw at any price and I've seen a few of the big ones," was how J. J. Newcomb, manager of Newk's Theatre in Burlington, Kansas, described two young actors who appeared at his theatre with the Harry St. Clair Company.[15] Born William Henry Pratt in London, England, the future actor immigrated to Canada in 1909. After holding many day-laborer jobs and a few brief acting engagements, Boris Karloff as he had become, joined the Harry St. Clair Company in 1912 for two years then rejoined the same company a short time later. Through his association with this company Karloff received valuable acting experience, playing as many as 106 roles in one year. It was during this period of his career that Karloff appeared in Burlington and came to the attention of J. J. Newcomb.

Karloff eventually joined the Billie Bennett road company of "The Virginian" and again played through Kansas in December 1917 on the company's cross country trek to Los Angeles. After a few years of playing in West Coast stock companies Karloff found work in films.[16]

Other fledgling actors who made appearances in the state included Lon Chaney who appeared with a road show in Norton; the young Ginger Rogers who performed with her father and mother in Salina; and Douglas Fairbanks who acted with the Sport North Company sometime before 1916 at a salary of $75 a week.[17]

During the height of the opera house era, Kansas audiences delighted to the performance of literally thousands of actors. Some were young, just beginning their careers, others seasoned professionals, and a few true stars.

Fred Stone, who went on to fame on Broadway and in the movies, was 14 and his brother was 12 the first summer they toured with a circus. Courtesy of the Kansas State Historical Society.

# Chapter 7
# HOME GROWN TALENT: Kansas Performers

Fred Stone, the first Scarecrow in the "Wizard of Oz"; Sidney Toler the most famous Charlie Chan; and Milburn Stone, Doc in "Gunsmoke" were nationally known performers who called Kansas home. While entertainers from all parts of the country appeared in Kansas, the state was certainly not lacking in home grown talent. Sometimes these individuals or companies only appeared a few times, but others brought years of enjoyment to audiences within the state and even the nation.

**Fred Stone**

Two of the best known Kansas entertainers, Fred Stone and Milburn Stone were related. Fred, born in 1873, began his autobiography, "The western frontier and I grew up together. Watching a country grow up is always interesting, but being a part of the West as it came of age was the most exciting experience a boy could have."[1]

Because his father was constantly on the move, never living more than two years in any one place Fred observed that, "...I was in time to take part in the last act of the grandest super-spectacle this continent ever witnessed — the covered-wagon parade into the Wild West."[2] The Stone family moved from Colorado where Fred and his brother Ed were born, to Kansas, living in Garden City, Dodge City, Nickerson, Hutchinson, Burrton, Halstead, Newton, Wellington, North Topeka, and Kansas City.

Fred was nine and living in Wellington, Kansas, when a mountebank, a professional tightrope walker, came to town. Watching this performer gave direction to Fred's life.

> I sat on the edge of a wagon with my legs hanging over the side, right under the rope, and watched so hard I got a crook in the back of my neck. The mountebank was a dazzling figure in a pair of tights covered with spangles. Back and forth he went over the wire, performing his tricks, and then he came down to pass the hat. He had a trapeze bar hanging from the center of the wire and he announced that, if he got enough money, he would do his trapeze act.
>
> The idea of being paid for having fun was new to me. And it was obviously more fun to balance high in the air, clad in spangles, than to work on a farm or in a barbershop.
>
> A bold plan began to take shape in my mind. I was going to be a trapeze performer! Presently the mountebank did some other stunts, none of them very remarkable, but I watched him almost without breathing, following every move he made, studying the way he kept his balance--until the spangles began to fall off his costume. After that, I climbed down from the wagon and walked under the rope, picking up the spangles as they fell. By the time the performance was over, I had a whole glittering handful.
>
> I took them home and raced into the house. 'Mother,' I asked anxiously, thrusting the spangles into mother's hands, 'will you please sew some tights on these?'[3]

Stone's career began that day. He spent the summer practicing until he could do all of the tightrope walkers' tricks, and at age 11 joined the Cole circus for two weeks when it performed in Harper, Kansas. Then Fred and his brother worked out acts together. While young, the boys began touring with small circuses. The first summer their parents let them travel with a circus, Fred was 14 and his brother was 12-years old.

Stone progressed from circus acrobat to the vaudeville stage as one half of the Montgomery and Stone blackface comedian act. The pinnacle of his career occurred when he appeared as the Scarecrow in the first production of "The Wizard of Oz." The show opened in Chicago in 1902 to rave reviews and then moved to New York. Stone went on to appear in numerous Broadway musical comedies and also in motion pictures.

**Milburn Stone**

Another actor Kansans are proud to call their own is Milburn Stone, second cousin of Fred Stone. While Fred performed at the beginning of Kansas' live entertainment era, Milburn's involvement occurred toward the end. Milburn Stone, born on July 5, 1904, in Burrton, began acting in small Kansas towns and ended his career in Hollywood with his well known television role as Doc Holliday in "Gunsmoke," for which he received an Emmy for best supporting actor in 1968.

Upon graduation from high school Stone had been awarded an appointment to the U. S. Naval Academy at Annapolis, but broke his mother's heart by leaving town with the Helen B. Ross Company, a Kansas theatrical troupe. While in Kansas Stone also appeared in the Arthur Names Company, the Harold English Players, and then the Wallace Bruce Players of Hutchinson. Stone also married a young woman from Delphos, Kansas.

Milburn Stone, best known as Doc Holiday of Gunsmoke, acted with several Kansas companies early in his career. Courtesy of the Kansas State Historical Society.

Milburn appeared on Broadway with Fred Stone in the 1934 production of the "Jayhawker"; made his first movie appearance in 1936; and from movies moved into television in "Gunsmoke." The show was an immediate success and ran for 20 years. Stone was 71 when he retired from "Gunsmoke."[4]

**Sidney Toler**

Sidney Toler, the most famous Charlie Chan, was a member of a prominent Wichita family. His father, Hooper G. Toler, brought the family to Kansas in the 1880s, first to Anthony and then in 1886 to Wichita. After a successful business raising and selling award winning horses, Hooper Toler purchased a large, frame auditorium located on the southwest corner of St. Francis and First streets in Wichita, spent $10,000 renovating the structure, and named it the Toler Auditorium. This theatre was the site of many great performances including appearances by Sarah Bernhardt and Paderwski.

Sidney, one of the three Toler sons, was encouraged in his dramatic interests by his mother, Sally. In fact, his first role was in the premier presentation of the play, "Tom Sawyer," adapted for the stage by his mother.[5]

After graduation from high school Sidney Toler enrolled in the University of Kansas, but during his freshman year ran away from school to pursue acting. Early in his career Toler appeared with various theatrical companies before moving to Hollywood in 1929 to seek a career in film. After several years of playing character roles, he was chosen to replace Warner Oland in the role of Charlie Chan, the famous fictional detective. Toler's first Chan movie, "Charlie Chan in Honolulu" premiered in 1939. This was followed by 24 additional Charlie Chan movies. Sidney Toler passed away in 1947 at the age of 59.[6]

**L. M. Crawford**

One man, L. M. Crawford, stands above even the most famous actors for his theatrical contributions to the state. Crawford, a Topeka native, who began his career at the age of 14 by selling peanuts, popcorn, fruit, and cigars in the territorial legislature of Kansas, went on to own an extensive chain of legitimate theatres.

Crawford, born in 1845, entered the entertainment business in the 1870s when he rented Topeka's Old Union Hall. Then, in 1880 Crawford purchased his first theatre, Costa's Opera House that he remodeled and named the Crawford Opera House. Critics objected to the name change but Crawford asserted, "I intend to have my name on everything I have anything to do with."

The remodeled Crawford Opera house opened in the fall of 1880, but was destroyed by fire just ninety days later. Although insured, the settlement was not enough to rebuild, so Crawford borrowed $20,000 and built a new theatre. This theatre, the New Crawford Opera House, opened in 1881 and was quite successful. Crawford later bought Topeka's Grand Opera House and over the years also owned several other theatres in Topeka.[7]

Crawford's theatrical holding included far more than the Topeka theatres. In 1901 Crawford was the General Manager of The Amusement Syndicate Company, a corporation owning and managing theatres in Topeka, Leavenworth, and Wichita, Kansas; Lincoln, Nebraska; St. Joseph, Missouri; Albuquerque, New Mexico; El Paso, Texas; and Phoenix and Prescott, Arizona. The same company also owned and controlled the bill posting business in many of those cities.

In addition to owning theatres, Crawford also controlled bookings in many communities. His son, O. T. Crawford, managed this circuit known as the New Crawford Circuit. This was an arrangement whereby theatrical companies would sign up with a circuit and then appear in theatres operated by the circuit. Crawford's circuit boasted a number of first class performers including Mrs. Fiske, Primrose and Dockstader (Minstrels), Yon Yonson, Sol Smith Russell, Murray and Mack, Alice Neilson Opera Company, and acting companies that presented such favorites as Hoyt's "A Milk White Flag," "Sign of the Cross," "Blue Jeans," "Under the Dome" and "A Prisoner of Zenda." L. M. Crawford also brought such noted artists as Clara Louise Kellogg, Joseph Jefferson, Booth and Barrett, and Emma Abbott to Kansas.[8]

Later in life Crawford moved to Wichita where he lived until his death August 6, 1944, at the age of 99. At that time he owned only three theatres, ones in Wichita, El Paso and St. Joseph.

**Sport North**

Kansas produced a number of theatrical troupes of state and regional importance, but the most significant of these companies was the one founded by Sport North. William Allen White once labeled the Norths, Sport and Genevieve, "the Barrymores of Kansas," and never missed a performance when the company appeared in Emporia.

Born Caelon Chapin in Maple Rapids, Michigan, May 10, 1873, Sport received his nickname in childhood. Later, as young men Sport and his brother Harry were working with a small stock company in Montana doing vaudeville when the manager of the company gambled away the company's receipts and left the entire troupe stranded. At this point the two brothers changed their name to North, probably to make light of their dire financial situation because they had only $31 between them, and along with two friends, formed their own company.

Sport North married his leading lady, Genevieve Russell, and adopted her young son, William Edward Steinal, known as Ted. When he grew up Ted North became a noted showman in his own right. For over 30 years the North brothers and later Ted North presented quality drama to Midwestern audiences. They appeared from Saskatchewan to Texas with, as one theatre historian noted, "a wide reputation for excellent productions."

Throughout this era Genevieve Russell was the company's preeminent leading lady.

In 1916, Sport and Genevieve bought a house in Holton, Kansas, where they had played many engagements. Holton became their home base, but like all working actors, they spent much time on the road performing.

Early in his career Neil Schaffner, another major Midwestern theatrical figure, was a member of the North Company. Years later, Schaffner sang the praises of Sport North. "Working with the North brothers was an experience no actor could forget. Sport North, the star, was truly one of the great actors of the American stage and working with him in 'The Great John Ganton' was one of the supreme privileges of my life; his portrayal of John Ganton was the most incisive and powerful that I ever witnessed."[9]

Sport North passed away in his hotel room in Council Grove, Kansas, on January 10, 1926, following a successful Saturday night performance in "Danger, Go Slow." North was 52 years of age.

Following North's death the company was reorganized under the direction of his adopted son Ted and opened ten days later in Coffeyville as the Ted North Players. This company toured for the next ten years playing opera houses in the winter and tents in the summer. This show business tradition came to an end on September 2, 1939, in Topeka, Kansas, with the final curtain of "Home on the Range."

The closing of the Ted North Players represented the end of not only this company, but symbolically of live repertoire theatre. The June 13, 1940, Bill Bruno's Bulletin carried the following ad that began, "for Sale Cheap, Tent, 65 x 115 feet, with poles and nearly new ten foot wall, $500.00," and concluded "come and look this over in Topeka, or write 'Ted North, 2800 Kentucky Avenue, Topeka, Kansas."[10]

The North Brothers Stock Company, featuring Sport and Genevieve North and later headed by Ted North, were popular Kansas entertainers. Courtesy of the Jackson County Museum.

**Harriet Nelson**

Harriet Nelson, wife of Ozzie and mother of David and Ricky, also had a Kansas tie. At the time of her birth in 1909 her parents, the Hilliards, were members of the Sport North Troupe. To celebrate her birth the company produced Guy Bates Post's play, "The Heir to the Hoorah," and Harriet Hilliard received her show business start at the age of six weeks when she was carried on stage on a pillow.[11]

**Wallace Bruce**

Wallace Bruce, a beloved Kansas showman, was 16 when he got his start in the business in 1914 when he joined a vaudeville company. It was while doing vaudeville that Bruce worked with such greats as the four Marx Brothers and Houdini. Upon his return to his home in Hutchinson, Kansas, Bruce formed a singing group, The Salt City Trio, then a year later joined the Nestell Players when they appeared at the Home Theatre.

Still in his teens Bruce joined Marvin Bybee's company in Larned where he met his future wife, Ruby Clare, who was also part of the company. In true show business fashion Wallace and Ruby were married between the morning rehearsal and the matinee on January 2, 1919.

In August of the same year the young couple took their first show on the road as the Wallace Bruce Players. This company, whose territory included Kansas and Oklahoma, played three days or a week in each town. In 1922 the first of Bruce's daughters, Virginia Bruce Renfro, was born. Virginia recalled that beginning at the age of five, she and her sister would dance between acts of their parents' show. The children were only allowed to travel with the show on weekends during the winter months because they attended school in Hutchinson. Virginia also recalled that a typical company schedule included the City Hall in Lyons on Friday night and on Saturday a matinee in Holyrood and a night performance in Claflin.[12]

Later the couple and their company presented Broadway plays at the Riverside Park theatre in Hutchinson, and in 1934 the company took to the road in a big tent. At that time the Wallace Bruce Players traveled with 25 including the cast, tent men, scenic artists, advance agent, and orchestra. Two actors who went on to Hollywood fame performed with the Wallace Bruce Company, Milburn Stone and Chill Wills, who later became a screen cowboy.

The advent of World War II and the scarcity of male actors caused Bruce to temporarily give up show business. For a number of years Bruce ran movie theatres, first in Dodge City and then in Lyons, and finally in 1958 Wallace and Ruby Bruce returned to the stage, this time playing in school auditoriums, their shows sponsored by local organizations as money making projects. Wallace Bruce passed away November 12, 1968, the day after the company performed in Council Grove.

The closing number for Bruce's show, adapted to fit the city where the performance took place and sung to a variation of "Good Night Ladies," sums up his career and life.

"Good Night--ladies--Good night ladies
Good Night ladies-and all you men folk too.
Merrily we played for you, sang for you,
Danced for you.
We loved every one of you--we hope you love us too.
BECAUSE, you (fill in town's name) people
Are wonderful people
The best in the land, we think you are grand.
There's no people, like you people
We love you so--but now we must go.
We've enjoyed these two hours with you
And we hope that you've liked it too.
But good night people-sleep tight people
You're all right-so GOOD NIGHT."[13]

**Marvin Bybee**

Between 1915 and 1930 Marvin Bybee and his wife Ethel toured a six-state area with their stock company known as the Bybee Show or Bybee's Players. Bybee, a Kingman, Kansas, native, began his show business career at the age of 17 when he worked selling candy, peanuts, soda pop and gum at performances of the Campbell's Circus and later as a billposter and advance man for another circus before abandoning show business to become a barber.

It was in 1906 while barbering that Bybee met and married Ethel Moss and moved to Larned, Kansas. In 1912 Bybee and Earl Freeland organized their first traveling stock company. They paid $70 for equipment that

Home Grown Talent | 59

included a 35′ x 70′ tent and a few seats. With two weeks rehearsal they took their eight-person cast on the road. Salary for the first cast was $18 a week for a single person and $35 a week for a couple. By the time the show closed in 1930 the pay had risen to $35 to $50 for a single actor and $75 to $90 for a team. Following the closing of his road show Marvin Bybee worked as a theatre manager.[14]

**J. A. Wolfe**
Beginning in 1908 and spanning a six-year period, J. A. Wolfe was associated with the Toler Auditorium in Wichita. When Wolfe became manager of the facility in 1908 he expanded the stage to accommodate large productions and changed the name of the theatre to the New Auditorium. Later Wolfe shared the management of the theatre with the Toler sons. It was during this period that Wolfe also managed the Wolfe Stock Company. One member of that company, Jane Morgan, eventually played the role of Mrs. Davis, the landlady, in the "Our Miss Brooks" television series.

**Guy Caufman**
Born in Pennsylvania in 1875, Guy Caufman spent much of his life associated with Kansas. A resident of Holton when he wasn't on the road, Caufman was a busy actor, author and company manager. The letterhead on Caufman's stationary proclaimed, "Plays for Hire, The Plays of the actor-author Guy Caufman, Original…Exclusive…Distinctive…Different Plays that Please."[15]

Caufman and his wife created a small theatre on the second floor of a downtown business in Holton. Guy Caufman passed away in Flint Michigan in 1947 at the age of 72.

**Henry Brunk**
Henry Brunk, born in Missouri, moved to Wichita, Kansas, with his family in 1910. His career really began when he was a small child assisting his older brothers. While the family was living in the West Texas community of Hereford, the seven Brunk brothers saw a presentation by a traveling musician who sold musical instruments. The two older brothers were so impressed that they bought horns and worked diligently to master them. Thus began the family's involvement in show business. The Brunk boys, as they matured, joined various bands and finally, in 1916, opened their first tent show, Brunk's Comedians. At its peak the Brunk's Comedians had 12 shows on the road simultaneously, and beginning in the 1920s Henry Brunk managed his own company.

Henry, his wife Mercedes, and their company usually stayed on the road 35 weeks a year, putting on six different plays each week. The company started out in April in Colorado, circled down to South Texas and returned to Wichita for the winter. The couple eventually retired their tent show in 1960.[16]

**Arthur Names**
Arthur Andrew Names, born in 1891 in rural Kansas, later moved to McCracken, Kansas where he began writing plays while still in his teens. In 1912 he, along with his cousin, Leonard Ryan, leased the opera house in McCracken and presented plays. Then, in 1916 and 1917 the two erected an Air Dome in McCracken and showed motion pictures. Names eventually formed his own acting company, the Art Names Players and hired the young Milburn Stone.

In order to stay in business after the advent of motion pictures closed many theatres to live performances, Names bought a tent and took his acting company on the road. The show continued through the Depression bringing entertainment to impoverished Midwestern audiences. One Kansas native said Names' show was one of the few bright spots during the long, hot summers of the Depression. She also recalled that Names' tent had so many patches it looked like a crazy quilt.[17]

**The Musical Reeds**
The Musical Reeds from Quinter, Kansas, was an example of an entertainment company that existed for

a few years, brought a great deal of enjoyment to their audiences, and then disbanded. The group was composed of Mr. Reed on the trumpet and Mrs. Reed at the piano, and their children Effie on the violin and Harry on the drums. Their ad for a performance at the Grainfield, Kansas Opera House proclaimed them to be, "Distributers of Sunshine, Mirth and Music...WE will Mobilize glee and Gladness in our Big Regiment, and our Instruments of War are the Quibs and music that shoots Good Cheer to your Hearts and Laughter to your Lips."

The Reed family played opera houses, fairs and Chautauquas during the teens and disbanded when the children grew up and left home.[18]

### Helen B. Ross

The Helen B. Ross Players appeared in Kansas, Oklahoma, Nebraska, Colorado and Missouri from 1906 to 1928. A Medicine Lodge resident remembered that in a performance Joe Sims and his wife, Helen B. Ross and their children played many parts.[19]

### Henry Neal

Lenora, Kansas was the home base for the Neal Stock Company. Henry Neal purchased the Lenora Opera House in 1930 and used it to show moving pictures and also to present live performances. The ever-popular "Uncle Tom's Cabin" was part of the Neal Stock Company repertoire.

Quinter was home to the Musical Reeds.
Courtesy of Jaquetta Houser.

### The Lockes

The Lockes headed the week-long celebration in 1904 that opened the Logan, Kansas Opera House. The first play they presented, "The Princess of Patches," was heralded as "especially strong." The local paper went on to remind the readers that on Friday night the company would present their noted play, "A Kansas Sunflower."[20]

The Lockes performed for a number of years, and at some point combined with another company to form the Kerkhoff and Locke Dramatic Company which was organized in Osborne, Kansas.

Kansans were entertained by a wide variety of performers. Many with national reputations visited the state while on cross-country tours. But, the state was also blessed with many native companies that brought endless years of entertainment to the residents of the state.

Home Grown Talent | 61

## CALL

**CRESTON CLARKE**

IN

## The Power that Governs

Management of JULES MURRY

THE LADIES AND GENTLEMEN OF THIS COMPANY WILL PLEASE NOTICE.

Next Stand *Dodge City Kan*
Date *March 3* Nights *one* Matinee —
Leave *Hutchinson* at *8:20* a.M
Via *Same* R. R. *134* Miles
Depot (You are required to be at the Depot 15 minutes before train time) *Same*
Change cars at —
Breakfast at — Dinner at —
Arrive at *Dodge City* at *2* P.M
Hotel Baggage Ready and Down Stairs ___ M
Theatre Baggage Ready after last Performance Always.
Theatre *Opera House*
Orchestra Rehearsal *7 P.M.*
Company Rehearsal
Super Rehearsal

| HOTELS. | Single. | Dble. 1 Bed. | Dble. 2 Beds. | Fires. |
|---|---|---|---|---|
| *Harvey* | $3.00 | | | |
| *Gray. Western* | 1.50 | 1.50 | | |
| *O. Neals E* | .50 | .75 | | |

From Depot I advise you to take Omnibus. Electric Car. Walk.

Remarks *C. F. Zimmerman*
*Company will leave Dodge City 1 AM Rail Road time arrive La Junta 7:15 AM*
*Harry Dornton* Stage Manager.
*Fred P. Wilson* Manager.
Date *March 2* 1908

**J.R. CLANCY SYRACUSE, N.Y.**
ESTABLISHED 1885
THEATRICAL STAGE HARDWARE
STAGE CARPETS, GRASS MATS, ETC.
SEND FOR NEW CATALOGUE

**AGENCIES**
Boston, Mass. 27-29 Eliot Street
Brooklyn, N. Y. 639 Fulton Street / 50 Rockwell Pl.
Chicago, Ill. 71-73 Randolph St.
Cincinnati, Ohio 515 Central Avenue
Columbus, Ohio 247-253 So. Front St.
Denver, Colo. 1520 Arapahoe St.
Kansas City, Mo. 2331-37 Grand Ave.
Los Angeles, Cal. 720 South Broadway
Minneapolis, Minn. 2819-21 Nicollet Ave.
New York, N. Y. 314 W. 42nd Street / 229 Bowery
Philadelphia, Pa. S. E. Cor. Ridge Ave. and Callowhill Street
Pittsburg, Pa. Seventh Ave. & Grant St.
St. Louis, Mo. 822-823 Holland Bldg.
San Francisco, Cal. 902 Eddy Street
Seattle, Wash. 106 Occidental Avenue

Actors traveled from town to town by train. This notice, posted back stage in a Hutchinson theatre, informed the actors of when they were to leave Hutchinson for their next stop, Dodge City. Courtesy of Joyce Cavarozzi.

# Chapter 8
# LIFE AS A PERFORMER

Life on the road held many pleasures and many challenges for the actors and actresses who appeared in Kansas between the Civil War and World War I. The constant need to move from town to town meant that performers spent much of their lives waiting for trains, riding on trains, unpacking their theatre and hotel trunks, performing, packing and then repeating the process the next day or the next week. While prairie actors often faced a financially perilous and sometimes uncomfortable existence, they also enjoyed the same pleasures as their non-acting contemporaries. Couples met and married, children were born, holidays were celebrated, and bereaved families mourned their losses.

Weddings were always a topic of interest in theatrical trade papers. One Kansas opera house manager observed,

> It isn't often that troupers pull any stunts here that I am not wise to, but it happened here last Thursday when Mr. Floyd Eldridge Low, playing "heavies" and Miss Flora May Driesbach, pianist with the Chase-Lister company, slipped quietly up the back alley to the county judge's office and 'got hitched.' It was a mighty neat stunt and they pulled it in fine shape, warning the judge very particularly not to mention it until they left town.

The theatre manager admitted that he should have suspected something because that evening during the performance the groom played the "heavy" character, "like a sixteen year old girl going to a picnic and Miss Driesbach pounded about all the keys off my piano."[1]

On a more somber note, when a trouper passed away, the theatre community mourned his or her passing. The following announcement appeared in a theatrical trade paper. "Minnie Seward has answered her last curtain call. On April 2nd, the Angel of Death lowered the curtain which separates her forever from the footlights of this mundane sphere. She has responded to her last encore. May Peace eternal be her portion."

Even though troupes were constantly on the move, holidays were celebrated. When his company appeared in Pittsburg, Kansas, Harry Sohns, manager of the No. 1 Hillman Ideal Stock Company hosted a Christmas banquet at the Depot Hotel. Table decorations furnished by the women of the company included candles, Christmas greens and place cards. And, following an elaborate banquet, the manager of the company presented sterling silver gifts to each company member.[2] The members of the Garrett Stock Company celebrated a memorable Christmas as they traveled from one Kansas engagement to the next. Manager Edwin Holt described the occasion.

> Talk about Christmas dinners! We surely had our share. First Doctor Hall and his good wife gave us a real one before leaving Harlan (Kansas); then on Sunday at Colby, Kansas, while laying over between trains, Mr. and Mrs. Arrington of the Walter Arrington Stock Company who were playing there, sent a big box down to the depot, filled with turkey, cake, fruit, candy, and everything good; then on our arrival at Collyer, Manager Glass met us at the station with two big cars and whisked us away to his suburban home and then proceeded to fill us up on everything that could be imagined that was good.

The company's celebration continued because they opened in Collyer on Christmas Day to good business.[3]

Just as the personal lives of the performers corresponded to those of their audiences, the actors' fortunes also reflected regional and national conditions. From the grasshopper plagues of the 1870s to the oil field boom

Post Cards were a form of publicity. This card advertised the 1908 appearance of "The Road to Yesterday" at the Bowersock Opera House in Lawrence.

of the teens, performers' lives were affected by the economy of the region. The audiences' ability to pay the price of admission often depended on the state of Kansas's agriculture. Good crops meant money to spend on pleasure; poor crops often spelled economic doom.

Agriculture wasn't the only economic consideration. Local industries also had a bearing on theatrical troupe profits. The opera house manager in Chetopa, in an effort to lure companies to his theatre, included the following description of the community in a theatrical guide. "Railroad division shop employing about 300 men and pay out over $10,000 monthly to railroad employees." And so that the theatrical troupes would know when the residents had the most money, "Pay days 19th and 30th of each month."

Mining employed a number of workers in the southeastern part of the state. Fort Scott was a coal mining community, as was Pittsburg. Galena, another southeastern town, emphasized its lead and zinc mining industry in an 1889 theatrical guide by claiming, "The most prosperous mining district in the West, and a good place for a good troupe."[4]

The Kansas oil boom of the late teens did not go unmentioned by opera house managers or unnoticed by troupe managers. In 1916 the manager of the Augusta opera house, wishing to attract the attention of the best companies reported that, "The new oil fields have more than doubled the population and the conditions were never before more promising than at the present time." And, the next year the manager of the same opera house, Joe Bianoazzi, boasted, "booming oil town, capacity business."[5]

If opera house owners bragged about the economy, so did theatrical troupe managers. Billy Arthur with The Dubinsky Brothers Stock Company reported that the troupe was playing the oil fields of Kansas and Oklahoma and added, "You live managers will do well by booking the opera house at Towanda, Kansas. This is a new oil town, and business is capacity every night. This is a small one, but there's real money here for you live ones." And, in El Dorado, just a few miles from both Towanda and Augusta, E. W. Brice, a company manager reported, "I am now located at the city of Oil and let me tell you folks something: this is some oil town. There are two houses here playing tab shows and vaudeville with change of bills twice a week to mighty big business."[6]

Weather also played a large role in company profits. It is no wonder that theatrical diaries kept by actors and managers, in addition to listing the town's name, the play presented, and the profits for the night, also contained a notation about weather. The rural population was an important component of any audience, so road conditions were very important. This was a time before paved roads, therefore, too much rain or snow made country roads impassable to wagons and later on to cars. The manager of the Eureka opera house, in reporting on the business done by the "This Is the Life" company's January 1916 appearance reported that the company played to poor business in one of the worst storms in years. And the same company encountered not only bad weather, but illness when it played a February 1916 engagement in Sedan. Other factors affecting opera house attendance included local events such as school activities, church socials, county fairs and circuses. But, even more serious were the effects of World War I, and the devastating flu epidemic of 1918.

While the era of traveling theatrical troupes was on the way out, some companies were still performing in the late teens. However, America's entrance into World War I caused these companies several problems. As a result of the War Tax levied on opera houses and theatres several Kansas houses closed including the theatres in Harper and Kiowa. This tax was lifted after a few months, but other war-related issues continued to plague the theatre. Coal to heat theatres was difficult to obtain due to the war. And, train transportation, so vital to acting companies, became a problem because fewer trains were available and costs were higher. As a result, some shows closed, while others played longer at each location, and some companies even began to move by truck.

Another effect of the war was that male actors became scarce. Many answered the call to the colors by enlisting in the services while others were drafted. When Glen Brunk of Brunks Comedians left for Camp Fort Sill on July 1, 1918, his theatrical troupe band escorted him to the station.[7] Issue after issue of theatrical trade papers reported performers who were in the service and where they were stationed. Then, sadly, these same papers also began reporting the deaths of troupers.

Men were not the only performers to serve their country. Women of the theatrical world were active in Red Cross and other volunteer efforts. For instance, the women of Brunk's Comedians No. 1 spent their afternoons at the Red Cross workroom rolling bandages. Opera house managers also assisted in the war effort by making their theatres available for war bond rallies and other patriotic gatherings.

World War I presented the acting profession with many challenges, but the war effort also brought a brief resurgence in theatrical activity through the creation of Liberty Theatres. The United States Army's Liberty Theatres was a project of the War Department's Interim Commission on Training Camp Activities. This Commission, mobilized on April 26, 1917, and demobilized on August 31, 1919, was a civilian agency created to maintain the morale of conscripted soldiers in the U.S. training camps. During its brief tenure the commission constructed 40 theatres that were divided into two circuits, the "blue" where the theatres seated 3,000 and the "red" with theatres that seated 1,000. In Kansas the Liberty Theatre, located at Camp Funston at Fort Riley, opened May 13, 1918, and closed June 2, 1919.

In order to make it possible for the service boys who lacked the funds to attend performances, there was a national campaign to sell "Smilage Books." Civilians purchased these books that were in turn distributed to servicemen. The coupons contained in the books provided free admission to the Liberty Theatre performances.

The advent of Liberty Theatres brought new hope to the beleaguered theatrical community. For a brief period there were a number of new theatres in need of entertainment and many theatrical companies eager to oblige. This project came to an end shortly after the end of World War I.[8]

There was much celebrating when World War I ended on November 11, 1918. While the U.S. involvement in the war had been brief, only nineteen months, it was a brutal conflict and the signing of the Armistice was cause for much rejoicing. A theatrical troupe appearing in Concordia when the war ended participated in the town's parade and described festivities. "Concordia went wild at the news from the front, and we helped celebrate

This "Mutt and Jeff" promotion claimed that the show was, "The biggest success in years and the greatest laughing show on earth."

here. Had a dandy float in the parade Monday night. A big touring car draped in white, with the word 'peace' in white and red from the front to the back of the top of the car with a white dove surmounting it, also American flags. We burned oodles of red fire. It was a gala night."[9]

While the end of the war was celebrated with gusto, the fall of 1918 brought another type of devastation, the influenza epidemic. This worldwide pandemic began with a relatively mild initial assault on March 4, when the first case was reported at Camp Funston. The flu spread rapidly, but seemed to be relatively mild. Then, a few months later, it exploded world wide killing millions.[10] To put the death toll in perspective, 2,500 Kansans died in World War I, while 5,500 died as a result of the flu.[11]

Once again the theatrical community's fate was closely tied to that of the nation. There seemed to be no stopping the flu and the only recourse was to attempt to limit personal contact. As a result, theatres nationwide were closed during the winter of 1918-1919. While necessary, this was devastating to a profession whose only income came from performing in theatres. The manager of the "Boy With A Smile" company lamented, "The influenza closing order, coming just after lean theatrical days of summer unemployment, caught most of the profession in this part of the country with bank rolls flatter than the acting of a hated rival. Salaries stopped when the houses closed so real work was necessary if eating was to be continued as a habit and sleeping indulged in with such incidental converts as beds."[12]

Another company manager echoed this sentiment; "The flue seems to have demoralized the whole theatrical game for this season. Some of the girls were fortunate enough to get jobs in the department stores and offices, while others preferred to take things easy - hoping for an early resumption of vaudeville activities." Eventually trade papers began carrying the inevitable announcements of even more serious consequences of the epidemic, the death of performers. "James O'Leary who has been identified with various Midwest attractions died at Kansas

City last week from flumonia." And another contributor to that same issue summed up the situation by saying, "The flue has certainly spoiled the show business for this winter - nothing like it in the history of the business."[13]

Some actors and actresses sought outside employment while the theatres were closed, but if the company was financially able, it simply stayed where it was and waited for the theatres to reopen. One such troupe was the "Freckles" company stranded in Almena, Kansas. The company's manager pointed out the positive side of the situation, "This makes about four weeks layoff for us, but it can't be helped so we will 'grin and bear it.' At least we are pleasantly situated here as everyone in town is pleasant to us, and are doing all they can to make our stay a pleasant one."

The citizens of Almena cared about the stranded actors as evidence by an article that appeared in an Almena newspaper.

> These times of Spanish Flu are most trying to road theatrical troupes, who are forced to lay off entirely. What with time lost, heavy running expenses, and the tangling of their dates, just now the lot of the actor and actorine is far from either agreeable or profitable. One such company has been 'holed up' in Almena for the past week - the Freckles Co., which has arranged to appear here at the first opportunity permitted by the state health authorities, which will be next Monday night. In the meantime we can imagine that being stuck in a town the size of Almena for a week or two, with no visible occupation, and only such entertainment as may be derived from inspecting the city water works, or admiring the flowering shrubs in the bank window, might perhaps be scarcely an ideal condition.[14]

From the sadness of war and influenza to the ordinary celebrations of life, the lives of turn-of-the-century theatrical troupers were similar to their non-nomadic counterparts in Kansas and across the nation.

Fire was a major destroyer of opera houses. Pictured here is the 1939 fire that destroyed Parson's Elks Theatre/Orpheum Theatre. Courtesy of the Parsons Historical Museum.

# Chapter 9
# RINGING DOWN THE CURTAIN:
# Fire and Other Natural Disasters

The sight of billowing clouds of smoke and the clanging of the fire bell filled frontier town residents with panic. These early Kansans feared not just the destruction of their personal property, they also feared for the future of their emerging communities. Fire was a major threat to early Kansas towns because most had few, if any, resources for fighting fire. Not only did these early communities lack fire departments with carts and hoses, but there was sometimes a limited supply of water. For this reason, when a fire occurred the emphasis was on saving the contents of the buildings, slowing the spread of the fire, and avoiding the loss of life. A fire could mean not just the end of the businesses that were destroyed, but it could also change the town's future. During February 1907, Mound Valley, Kansas, was ravaged by fire not once, but twice. These fires that destroyed much of the downtown business district including a newly erected $12,000 opera house had a major impact on the growth of the community.[1]

Another community severely affected by fire was Glasco, Kansas. Fire broke out in Davidson Auditorium between 1:30 and 2 a.m. on November 28, 1911. The fire spread rapidly and although the community fought valiantly, most of the downtown businesses were destroyed. In addition to the entire population of Glasco turning out to fight the fire, the telephone operator, before she was driven from her office by the fire, notified the rural population who responded as well. Battling the Glasco blaze was hindered by the lack of water and every resident's well was pumped dry, but even after they had no more water to contribute, the resident's continued the fight. One man explained, "Just as soon as a man had done all that was humanly possible to save his own business, or saw the last of his lifetime work go up in smoke. Did anyone sit down or moan over the loss? Not on your life, we were fighting for the very existence in our little city where our businesses have been, our friends and the good Lord knows that there is no worse enemy than fire." The total loss was estimated at $200,000 to $250,000 with only $40,000 covered by insurance.[2]

The loss of the town's opera house was a major disaster. An 1895 account graphically recounted the horrors the night the WaKeeney opera house was destroyed.

> About 4 o'clock Tuesday morning our citizens were aroused from their slumbers by the ominous clanging of the fire bell. As usual they were prompt to respond and soon a large crowd was hurrying to the scene of the conflagration, which even then lighted up the whole city. It was soon apparent that our beautiful opera block, the pride of our city, was doomed and although everything possible was done to stay the flames, they soon spread to every part of the building and in less than two hours nothing remained but the bare and blackened walls.[3]

A similar report from the *Emporia Gazette* recounted that community's valiant efforts to save the Whitley Opera House. This fire, described as one of the most destructive in the history of Emporia, occurred on June 18, 1913. The fire was discovered at 10:25 p.m. when thick clouds of smoke were seen pouring down the baggage stairway. Less than an hour later at 11:10 p.m. the blaze had burned through the roof and by 11:32 p.m. the entire building was burning. While the city firemen responded promptly, they could not stop the advance of the fire because the water pressure was insufficient to lift the water streams high enough. The *Emporia Gazette* of the next day reported that the firemen, "made a splendid fight against the big fire, but accomplished little, except in saving surrounding buildings." While never proved, the fire in the Whitley Opera house was thought to have been caused by the wiring in the first floor store below the opera house.[4]

Opera house fires most often originated in the stage area. This is not surprising because for a number of years stage and auditorium lighting was provided by gas. Pipes of gas and gas burners hung over the stage and open gas flames acted as footlights in the footlight well located along the front of the stage. Another flammable form of lighting for rural Kansas stages was the kerosene lanterns supplied by audience members. These lanterns, needed to find their way home in the dark, were strategically placed on stage to provide illumination for the shows, and if knocked over could easily ignite a fire. Also, as electricity was introduced, defective wiring was responsible for some fires.[5] Auditorium heating could also lead to fires. Nineteenth century opera houses were often cold, drafty, places for both the audiences and the actors. Auditoriums were generally heated by large coal or wood stoves placed at intervals throughout the auditorium, and small kerosene stoves located on either side of the stage provided what little heating there was for the actors. Improper care of these stoves was another cause of fires.

A fire that began when a kerosene filled lamp exploded destroyed the Alton Opera House in Milan, Kansas. On August 11, 1899, as Mr. I. S. Alton was closing up his business he took a hand lamp and went into the opera house to make sure that the windows were secure because it was a stormy night. As Alton opened the dressing room door the lamp exploded, causing severe injuries to his hand and face and filled the room with burning oil. First Mr. Alton extinguished the fire on his body then ran down stairs and sounded the alarm. The men and boys of Milan responded and through their efforts, the rest of the town was saved. Unfortunately, the opera house, its contents, and the businesses below were destroyed.[6]

To alert local citizens to a fire in the opera house, or anywhere in the community, the town's fire bell was rung. But, in Junction City this was difficult because the opera house was located in the City Building, which was also the location of the fire department, the fire bell, and the fire itself. On the night of the Junction City opera house fire few people heard the bell because the bell's rope burned off after only three taps of the bell. The local paper reported, "The department got action on itself quicker than it ever did in its history, but it was to no avail, and at no time did Chief Ziegler think that the building could be saved."[7]

A common time for opera houses fires was between the end of the show and the early morning hours. These fires could usually be attributed to improper care in extinguishing the back stage or house lighting or heating, or to cigarettes left smoldering in back stage dressing rooms. Unfortunately, by the time a fire was discovered, it was often too late to contain it. On January 1, 1915, the Ragsdale Opera House in Newton, Kansas, burned to the ground. At 2:30 a.m. a small fire was noticed in the southwest room off of the stage. According to a local newspaper account,

> The wooden interior of wings, stage, dressing room floors, contraptions and whatnot behind the stage were all ablaze and fed the fire on to the wooden floors and joists of the story above and below. In less than an hour the flames licked up the offices and shops at the west end and swept through the McManus dry good and clothing store at the front of the building and the south wall and belfry were down.[8]

It was tragic when opera houses were destroyed by natural causes, but it was an even more devastating blow to the community when arson was suspected. Such was the case with the Mallory Opera House in Paola. For a number of years the Mallory Opera House was central to the town's cultural and community life. The theatre owner, Lucy Mallory, along with another woman and a doctor lived in the opera house building. Late in the evening of October 27, 1921, fire was discovered in the building and while the residents escaped with their lives, all of their belongings were destroyed. The building could have been saved because the fire began in the basement, but water pressure was not adequate to extinguish the blaze. This was ironic since the structure was less than half a block from the fire station. In less than ninety minutes after the fire was reported, the entire structure was in ruins. Eventually the owners of the battery shop located in the basement of the opera house were accused of setting the fire for the insurance that they carried on their shop.[9]

A burning curtain was responsible for the 1885 stage fire at the Rink in Garden City, Kansas. The I. W. Baird's Mammoth Minstrels and Spectacular Military Show was interrupted when a curtain that was being lowered gave way at the top, fell into the footlight, and was ignited. The initial response of the audience was panic, but disaster was averted. A local newspaper reported, "The audience at once rose and started en-mass for the doors but a few cool-headed ones kept them back and the fire being extinguished that might have resulted in great loss of life ended in a fizzle."[10]

While opera house fires were devastating to communities, fires also had serious consequences for the actors involved. Traveling theatrical troupes, upon their arrival in a town, would send their personal trunks to a hotel or boarding house and their professional trunks and scenery to the theatre. Each actor's professional trunk contained all of the costumes the actor owned. During this period actors were responsible for supplying their own costumes so their loss created great financial hardship for the individual actors, just as loss of scenery did for the company's manager.

Caldwell, Kansas' opera house was remodeled in 1917 and received compliments from companies that appeared there. A company manager reported, "We opened the opera house at Caldwell, Kansas, week of December 3rd to a packed business and played to a good week. The old house has been thoroughly overhauled and put into excellent condition and it is a comfortable, roomy and well equipped house to play."[11] Only two months, later tragedy struck. On February 18, 1918, the newly redecorated opera house was destroyed by fire. The loss to building was reported to be $15,000 while insurance covered only $8,000. The disaster, from the performers' point of view, was equally devastating. An *Opera House Reporter* account detailed the extent of the damage.

> The Giersdorf Concert Company gave one of the best musical concerts ever heard in Caldwell, February 18th, and were to show on the 19th, but a disastrous fire wiped them out. Never was there a time when the building could have burned when the loss was so great. H. A. Colvin, vaudeville and talking picture show had the place leased for five years and had just moved here, stored his wardrobe, films, personal clothing, etc., previous to moving in a house. Everything went up in smoke. Everything being a total loss. Haley also suffered total loss of dogs. Giersdorf Band and Concert Company met with very heavy loss. The opera house caught fire about an hour after the show and burned to the ground. Company lost everything except a few small instruments. His loss estimated as about $5,000.[12]

An opera house with a very short history was located in Winona, Kansas. An announcement in the February 16, 1917, *Opera House Reporter* indicated that a new opera house was being built in Winona, Kansas by J. N. Thouvenell. The new theatre was to be located on the ground floor with a seating capacity of about 400. A few months later J. N. Thouvenell placed the following announcement in the *Opera House Reporter*.

> We wish to advise you of our bad luck since you last heard of our new opera house…Saturday evening a fire originated in our garage just north of the new opera house which completely destroyed our garage, opera house and fixtures and nine cars besides all the other small items. The total loss to me is about $10,000. However, I wish to say that we intend to rebuild. In fact, we have men at work already clearing the rubbish away and will begin in earnest before long.[13]

A second opera house with a very short history was located at Coolidge. The opera house, built by E. H. Peck, burned after just one performance. This occurred on August 25, 1888, during a fierce thunder storm.[14]

Sometimes the opera houses destroyed by fire were rebuilt. The Sedan, Kansas opera house may be unique because it was twice destroyed by fire and twice rebuilt. W. H. Bryan opened the first Sedan opera house in 1885. Five years later this opera house was destroyed by a fire that originated in a stove on the first floor of the building. Tremendous efforts were extended to save the opera house. "The boys worked like heroes in flames and smoke when it was necessary to throw entire buckets of water on them to keep their clothes from catching fire. G. W. Arnold was badly singed, and came near losing his life. Marion Denni's eyes were in bad shape that evening." At that time the only fire fighting method available was by bucket brigade. People made a line from the nearest well to the fire and passed buckets of water hand-to-hand and poured them on the blaze.

The damage to the Sedan Opera House was extensive and as the local newspaper reported, "Our town can ill afford the loss of this building." Five years after the initial blaze, the lot of the former opera house was purchased and work commenced on a new Opera House. The opening was held March 20, 1896. A fire that originated from a gas stove also destroyed this opera house. The fire broke out during the night after a performance and by 2:15 the next morning, the opera house was completely destroyed.

Community sentiment ran high that a new, larger opera house was needed. The local newspaper announced that, "The opera house will be longer, safer, and finer than before. A large public hall in Sedan is as much a necessity as the court house. It is one of the strong features of any town to have a house or hall large enough for public gatherings." Finally, on August 12, 1904, the *Weekly Times Star* proclaimed that the opera house had reopened. And that it was, "One of the handsomest and best new opera houses in Kansas."[15]

While we can't know the exact number of Kansas opera houses destroyed by fire, we know that at least 78 were lost in this manner. But, fires were not the only natural disasters to destroy opera houses. Tornadoes claimed the opera houses in Greensburg, Mulberry, Washington, Wilmore, and Harper.

The Rothwell Opera House in Harper opened June 25, 1884. Constructed by J. S. Rothwell at a cost of $45,000, this elaborate building was 50' x 90' with a stage 25' x 50'. The second floor theatre that seated 700 boasted an orchestra pit, an elaborate cut glass dome, and a balcony. Reported to be one of the finest opera houses in the state, the opera house had large stoves in each corner of the auditorium, gas lighting on stage, and a massive chandelier hanging mid-theatre in the auditorium. The opera house was used for many community and dramatic events until on May 27, 1892, the building was heavily damaged by a tornado. The Harper *Sentinel* reported this tragic event.

> Toward the close of the afternoon the appearance of the heavens indicated another rain, but as we have been having so much this spring it produced no alarm. Between 6 and 7 however, a change took place, causing many an anxious inspection of the clouds. They seemed concentrating in the northwest, where a

Constructed some time prior to 1915, the Miller-Wacker Auditorium in Greensburg was later known as the Twilight Theatre.

Following the devastating tornado of May 4, 2007, this is all that remained of the Twilight Theatre. Courtesy of *The Wichita Eagle*.

heavy black cloud with ominous appearance began forming. The wind was blowing briskly from the southeast but suddenly veered around until almost in an opposite direction. Shortly after this there was almost a dead clam, then the wind sprang up again soon bringing dashes of rain. Hail soon began falling, most of them being of enormous size--larger than a hulled black walnut. The forces of the wind increased, the small trees bending almost to the ground. Buildings began to tremble, and loose boards and boxes were flying through the air in every direction. As these would crash against the dwelling houses and business rooms it would awaken feelings in the inmates that can not be described. Shingles would be torn from the roofs, chimneys were crumbling, and house were crushed by the forces of the wind like egg shells in a mortar.

Amazingly, only four deaths were attributed to the tornado, but, the destruction caused by the tornado became an area-wide tourist attraction, as, "Thousands of people have been here to see the ruins of our city. Last Saturday and Sunday every train was loaded and thousands drove in from neighboring cities and the country." One of the fatalities of the tornado was Harper's Rothwell Opera House. Although the opera house was rebuilt following the storm, it never regained its previous elegance or status in the community.[16]

The Greensburg tornado of 2007 destroyed the entire community including the Twilight motion picture theatre that began life around 1915 as an opera house.

A flood claimed one opera house in Kansas, the Shaw Theatre in Hutchinson. Constructed in 1901 this theatre was badly damaged by a flood when it was only two-years old. Repairs were made, but during the flood of 1929 the stage house of the theatre collapsed and the structure was later razed.

Many risks were associated with life in the emerging communities of the Kansas frontier; not the least was fire. With the majority of the buildings constructed of wood, the use of kerosene and gas for illumination, and the lack of adequate fire protection, it is not surprising that fire claimed a number of early opera houses. However, tornadoes and a flood were also responsible for the destruction of several other early Kansas theatres.

The Brown Grand Theatre of Concordia was constructed in 1907 and has been magnificently restored.

# Chapter 10
# FINAL CURTAIN AND ENCORE

To those who lived during the lush days of the Opera House the building stood as a tribute to the sturdy hearts who were looking forward to better things in 1880 and built a structure that withstood many things and remained a place of wonder in the hearts of those who were young and gay…There will never come again to its stage such performances and fun, that was experienced by those people, but it was something for its day and age.[1]

## Going Dark: Why the Opera Houses Closed

What happened to the opera houses of Kansas? What happened to these structures that were the object of community pride and such important cultural spaces? Fires and tornadoes provided dramatic conclusions to some of them, but more often it was old age and the changing times that took their toll. The vast majority of opera houses in the state simply wore out and were torn down.

In many communities it was the building of a new high school containing an auditorium that marked the end of the opera house's active use. Time and again the conclusion of the opera house era was marked by the phrase, "Let's see, 19__ was the last commencement held in the opera house. After that it just…" Also, communities such as Salina, Hutchinson and Wichita built large municipal auditoriums to house public functions.

For many years the opera house in Little River was the largest meeting room in town, but each new public building that was constructed took more activities away from the opera house. It began in 1902 with the Mason's building, followed two years later by the Odd Fellows. Then in 1905 the Congregational church enlarged, as did the Methodist Church. In 1909 Little River's first movie theatre was built, but the final blow came in 1921 when a large ground floor building that was used as the school gymnasium and auditorium was constructed.[2]

The development of the state also affected the disposition of several opera houses. The Old Kiowa and Old Ulysses opera houses were moved to new locations and used for other purposes when the communities themselves moved. In other instances, towns that contained opera houses no longer exist.[3]

The type of entertainment itself contributed to the downfall of the opera house era. Plays that were fresh, new and exciting in the 1880s and 1890s were tired and shop-worn by the teens. Audience members had seen them all--many times over. As an example, two popular plays that appeared in Emporia were the "Devil's Auction" presented eleven times between 1886 and 1908 and "Uncle Tom's Cabin" presented at least 23 times between 1884 and 1908. And, scenic effects that amazed and dazzled turn-of-the-century audiences were less interesting as technology evolved. The dramatic train wrecks, mine explosions and shipwrecks of melodramas were rendered outmoded by their real life counterparts shown in the fledgling moving pictures. And, lecturers talking about far away places were supplanted by moving pictures showing the same exotic locations.

Audiences were always intrigued by the latest technology in entertainment. As early as 1897 an appreciative Norton audience was entertained by W. W. Sears and his graphophone. In 1909, residents of Kirwin and Logan were delighted by demonstrations of Edison's talking machine: the phonograph. Sponsored by the local Edison Phonograph salesmen, Vernon Delhart, Grand Opera star and one of the early performers on Edison records, traveled the country putting on demonstrations. He would play his recordings and sing along with them. Delhart also made wax cylinder recordings on stage for the audience.

A technology even more significant than the phonograph was making its way into the state. The first experimentation with motion pictures began in the late 1800s, but didn't become a serious contender in the entertainment world until the early 1920s. In 1909 Thomas Alva Edison was credited with the invention of the Kinetoscope, a box with a peep hole that allowed one person to watch a film that lasted five seconds. By the end of that century filmmakers were producing short films, and eventually by the 1920s these early attempts evolved into feature length films. The first moving picture to be shown at the Ragsdale Opera House in Newton occurred on

The extensively restored 1895 Rogers' Columbian Theatre in Wamego features ornamentation from the 1893 Columbian International Exposition.

The Waterville Opera House was constructed in 1903 by the city for $8,000.

February 11, 1898. Edison's Vitascopic Productions presented "The Black Diamond Express," "The Pillow Fight" and "Mother's Morning Task" interspersed with selections from the phonograph.[4] But, it wasn't until December 25, 1913, that the first Edison talking picture was shown at the opera house. A phonograph synchronized with the film achieved this effect. Still, at this point film had not taken the place of live entertainment. For example, moving pictures came to Garden City, July 10, 1907, with the opening of the Lyric Electric Theatre, but it wasn't until March 18, 1921, that the first full-length first-run film was shown in the community.

There was no clear, dividing line between the appearance of motion pictures and the disappearance of theatrical troupes. The two existed side by side for a number of years. Because early moving pictures were so short, one approach was to show a combination of film and vaudeville, or film and tab shows, plays that had been shortened to fit the time constraints of the movies. Another approach was to present either a moving picture or live entertainment depending upon availability. In fact, during the early 1920s, long after most opera houses had closed or converted to movies, the Ted North Players and the Hillman Stock Company were still actively playing theatres in the state.

Profit often dictates change and that was the case with live entertainment. It was far more profitable for the owner of the opera house to show moving pictures than to play road companies. If the owner of a theatre

Built in 1901 with volunteer labor from the Bohemian community, the Wilson Opera House is still used for community events.

showed a moving picture, the only expense the owner incurred was the rent on a film and shipping costs. He could then keep all of the profits. On the other hand, if a road company appeared at the opera house the owner of the theatre only received a percentage of the profits. In addition, ticket prices for plays had to be higher because road companies paid both the salaries of the performers and their transportation costs from city to city.

The physical location of the theatre also seemed to be a factor as the older second floor opera houses tried to compete with the new ground floor movie theatres. Too often the opera house lost. As the manager of the Garden City Opera House lamented, "It seems like folks won't climb stairs to see a movie."[5]

It took very little to create an early silent picture theatre, a room, a screen, a projector and benches. Often these new movie theatres went out of business as quickly as they appeared, but a final blow to live entertainment in opera houses was the advent of talking movies. Not only did the audiences find them more enjoyable, but the need for large speakers and screen often took up stage space needed for live shows.

Two other technical advances may have contributed to the decline of opera houses, automobiles and radios. As cars became a common part of rural America, families could travel greater distances to view entertainment. Rural Americans were no longer limited to the distance a team of horses pulling a buggy or a wagon could reasonably travel or the family could comfortably ride on a cold winter evening. Entertainment did not have to come to the community; the community could drive to the entertainment. And later, as radios gained in affordability and stations became more numerous, entertainment was available in each home.

Finally, the country itself was changing. The world went to war. Technology increased rapidly and exposure to other parts of our own country and to foreign countries expanded personal horizons. Urban and rural areas alike became "up-to-date" and "modern."

Toward the end of his career, Wallace Bruce, a well-known Kansas performer lamented the demise of the opera house in this humorous monologue.

## Let the Actors Come Tew' Town

Mebbe Things er better now than in the old time days;
I know thet lots O' people like these movin' picter plays.
Our Op'ry house has nothing else, 'N' people miss their meals
To see "Tarzan Of The Apes," did in forty seven reels.
Jes' feature Reels O' fightin N' single reels O' soup.
It may suit some; but, as fer me, I miss a Standin' roun'
The deepo and the drug store when the actors come to town.
We've had Marlene Dietrich, and Claudette Colbert tew,
Montgomery, Gable and Raft and all the movie crew.
They've visited us often N' put up a first rate show;
But no one ever seen em' come N' no one seen em' go.
They aint no actor living' thet can make much of a spread
If he travels in a tin box in the baggage coach ahead.
An' while perhaps we'll never git' the stars of great renown
I hope I live ter see a few more Actors come to town.
Oh, give us back the good old times, the grand old days of "Rep";
A leadin' lady full of sobs, a hero full of "pep";
A funny feller full O' jokes yew' may 'a' heerd before;
But everytime he springs em' yew jes' got ter' up an' roar.;
A soubrette cute N' sassy, in a dress jest tew' her knees,
With shiny shapely stockings, N' a style jes' like a breeze;
A Villyun with a mustache, who kin snarl, N', sneer, N', frown
An' I'll be out er-waitin' ter' see em' come to town.
I like to hear em' askin What is this lonesome Tank?
I like to have em' call me Hiram, Hen er' Hank.
I like to hear em' talk Belasco-"Yew know my friend Dave"
An' when they see our Op'ry house, I like to hear em' rave.
I like to see em' sewll aroun' the Hotel afternoons
I like to hear their piano play them thar' city tunes.
An' if they give a street parade, Goah! How I chase it down.
I can do without the movies, let the Actors come tew' town.[6]

## Current Uses

What happened to the opera houses that had instilled pride in the hearts of turn-of-the-century Kansas residents? The vast majority of these structures fell into disrepair and were eventually sold for salvage, but not

McPherson's 1889 Grand Opera House is currently undergoing extensive renovation.

all. In several Kansas towns owners of second-story opera houses simply moved down stairs and installed moving picture theatres on the ground floor.[7] In Phillipsburg and Abilene second-story opera houses were renovated and became large one-story movie theatres. And in Mound Valley the second-story opera house was renovated into a one-story community center and gymnasium. In several instances the opera house portion of the building, the second or third floor, was removed and the rest of the building remains.[8]

What of the opera houses that remain? 200 of the approximately 900 opera houses and halls are standing. The oldest of these is the White Cloud Opera House also known as the Nuzum or the Kelley Opera House, which stands vacant in White Cloud, Kansas. This opera house, on the second floor of a general store, was constructed in 1862. Located on the Missouri River, White Cloud was once an active steam boat port.

Performances may no longer take place in many of the state's remaining opera houses, but the structures are put to good use. Fraternal associations meet or have met in spaces that once housed theatres in several locations.[9] Other opera house spaces have been converted to commercial uses such as a shopping mall, an army surplus store, auto repair shops and furniture stores.[10] The newspaper office in Stafford is housed within the former Weide Opera House as is a funeral home in the Leach Opera House of Wamego. Other uses include a feed store, a liquor store, a factory, plumbing shops and several other types of commercial ventures.[11]

In addition to providing the setting for dramatic productions, an important function of Kansas's opera houses was as community gathering places. Therefore, it is appropriate that a number of these structures are still in use in some type of community function. Several are community owned movie theatres and a few are still privately owned movie theatres, thus providing sorely needed rural entertainment.[12]

Some opera houses that still contain their original stages are now used as community centers.[13] Local celebrations and events, meetings, wedding receptions, flee markets, youth recreation programs, as well as occasional dramatic productions, are some of the activities carried out in these facilities. Other opera houses, although no longer containing their stages, are also used as community gathering places.[14]

Other community uses of structures that were once opera houses include a Chamber of Commerce meeting room, a library, and church owned halls. More unusual uses for former opera houses include a school bus barn, a city's heavy equipment garage, and the Emmett Kelly Museum, which is located on the first floor of the opera house building in Sedan.[15] A few opera houses with stages stand vacant, some badly deteriorated, others needing only to be dusted and to have electricity restored to once again come to life.[16]

There are also several theatres that were constructed for live entertainment and were considered opera houses, but were built just as moving pictures were coming into their own. Because they are newer structures, several of these are still in use as dinner theatres, community centers, movie theatres and for live performances.[17]

# Encore

Actors no longer arrive by rail and shows aren't heralded with street parades, but fortunately a few of the states' beautiful opera houses remain, and a few more are being returned to their former glory. Renovated opera houses include the Brown Grand Theatre in Concordia, the Palace Theatre in Kinsley, the former Bowersock Opera House in Lawrence, Manhattan's Wareham's Opera House, the Columbian Theatre in Wamego, Waterville's Opera House, and the Wilson Opera House. Most of these are community owned theatres that

Rebuilt after the original opera house was destroyed by fire, the 1898 Junction City Opera House/Colonial Theatre is in the process of being renovated.

The 1905 Winship Opera House in Phillipsburg began as a second floor theatre and was later converted to a ground floor movie theatre. This is the longest continuous-use entertainment facility in the state.

are once again bringing live entertainment to their Kansas communities. Opera houses in McPherson, Junction City, Grainfield, Meade and a major vaudeville theatre in Wichita, the Orpheum, are being restored.

Bracketed between the Civil War and World War I was a period when the country was agrarian, when the world was often restricted to ones immediate surroundings. Into this world came traveling theatrical troupes crisscrossing the country on the newly laid rails. And into each community traveling performers brought excitement, entertainment and a hint of a world outside the confines of the community.

Little remains of this once vital part of the Kansas' history. The entertainers who trouped the state are no longer with us and many of the opera houses and community centers where they performed have fallen to the ravages of time, but a precious few opera houses stand as beautiful reminders of the excitement and glamour that was entertainment in Kansas.

Built as a vaudeville theatre, the 1922 Wichita Orpheum Theatre is in use while the process of restoration continues.

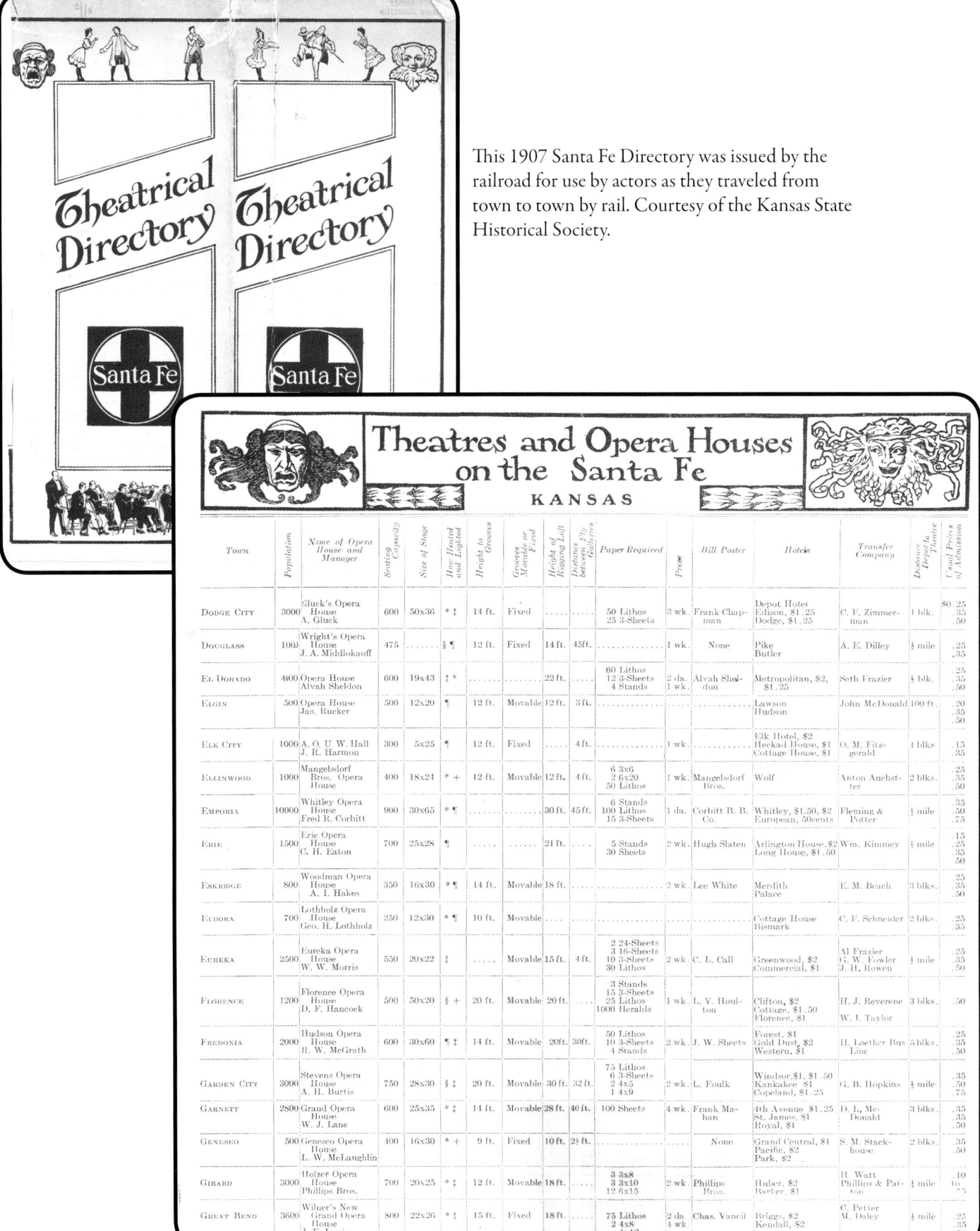

This 1907 Santa Fe Directory was issued by the railroad for use by actors as they traveled from town to town by rail. Courtesy of the Kansas State Historical Society.

A sample of the Santa Fe Directory indicates the relevant information needed by acting companies of the early 20th century. Courtesy of the Kansas State Historical Society.

84 | Kansas Opera Houses

# Alphabetical Listing of Kansas Opera Houses

## Sources of Information

In order to appreciate the information on the individual opera houses in Kansas it is necessary to be aware of the various sources of information used in writing this book, and the contributions made by each. Theatrical guides, local and county histories, the recollections of Kansas residents, and research by the members of the Woman's Kansas Day Clubs and students of theatrical history are at the heart of this book.

## Theatrical Guides

Theatrical guides were the lifeblood of the theatrical community. Published annually, they offered acting companies vital information to use when planning their routes, publicizing their shows, and appearing in the theatres of Kansas. The guides included the town name, population, railroad/s, name of opera house, manager, seating capacity, size of stage, height from stage to rigging loft, number of grooves to hold scenery, depth under the stage, number of trap doors, number of sets of scenery, the name of the stage carpenter, the town bill poster, number and type of posters needed, and the leasing or rental fees for the theatre.

Other information such as the name of the local newspaper, hotels and their rates, and the name of a local doctor and lawyer was sometimes included. All of this was necessary for theatrical troupes as they moved from town to town by rail. Information concerning the stage alerted traveling companies to the size of show the stage could accommodate and the scenery available. Business considerations included the cost of renting the opera house and the auditorium capacity, the potential for profit.

Also important was the arrangement for bill posting, the most common method of advertising. Finally, it was important to know the type of illumination found in the opera house. Lighting ranged from kerosene lanterns sitting on the stage to elaborate gas systems and finally, to electricity. If the opera house contained electricity, the voltage was also noted.

Directories consulted during the course of this research included *Harry Miner's American Dramatic Directory* for the seasons of 1883-1884 and 1884-1885; *Jno. B. Jeffery's Guide and directory to the Opera Houses, Theatres, Public Halls, Bill Posters, etc. of the Cities and Towns of America*, 1879-1889; *Julius Cahn's Official Theatrical Guide* 1910-1911; *Union Pacific Theatrical Diary* 1890-1911; and *Theatres and Opera Houses on the Santa Fe*, 1907.

## Local and County Histories

In addition to theatrical guides, an invaluable source of information concerning the opera houses of Kansas was the centennial histories published by individual communities and counties. These brought the opera houses to life and emphasized their importance to the social and cultural lives of the communities.

## Women's Kansas Day Clubs

Another valuable source of information was two collections compiled by the Woman's Kansas Day Clubs. The first, *Old Opera Houses and Early Places of Amusement*, was compiled in 1952 and the second, *Opera Houses and Entertainment Pre-1950 in 1986*.

## Masters Theses

Several Masters Theses written about opera houses in specific communities included well researched accounts of the construction of the theatres, their physical descriptions, community importance, and the theatrical companies who appeared in them.

## Citizens of Kansas

Finally, an important source of both information and encouragement was the many Kansans who assisted me. Ranging from informal conversations in cafes to research by volunteers in libraries, museums, and city offices, the citizens of Kansas provided vital and personal information, and contributed greatly to this book.

## Notations

The following notations are used to indicate the current disposition of the state's opera houses: NLS - no longer standing; UTD – unable to determinc; Standing – the building still exists, but without a stage; Standing/stage – the structure is standing with its original stage.

# A

| Abilene | 1870s | Novelty Theatre | NLS |
|---|---|---|---|
| | ? | Opera House/Livery Stable | Standing |
| | 1885 | Music Hall | NLS |
| | 1879 | Bonebrake Opera House/ | |
| | 1901 | Seelye Theatre | NLS |
| | 1900 | City Auditorium | NLS |

Abilene, "the first cow town" as it called itself, was the site of tremendous cattle trade activity for a five-year period between 1867 and 1872. Stretching from the Red River country in Texas to Abilene, Kansas, the Chisholm Trail brought cattle, commerce and cowboys to Abilene, and helped to facilitate the early expansion of the city. The first mention of a theatre in Abilene occurred in 1870. That theatre was the Novelty Theatre located on Texas Street between Cedar and Buckeye. An Abilene native remembered the theatre.

> The Novelty Theatre, which stood east of the Pearl Saloon, was usually crowded nightly. Its seating capacity was from 300 to 400 and some very good plays were put on the boards....Such plays were presented as would be creditable to our city today, and often were the better class of people seen before its stage. The drop curtain of that little theatre was by far the most artistic ever before an audience in this city and was painted by the stage manager of the theatre here in Abilene.[1]

This early performance space is no longer standing.

Another early opera house was located in the 400 block of NW 2nd street. Its sign read "Opera House and Livery Stable." This building is now located in Abilene's cow town.

In 1879 J. E. Bonebrake, a hardware merchant who later became president of a bank, built the opera house that was destined to stand the test of time, undergo several renovations, and be in continuous use for over 120 years. The cost of construction of the Bonebrake Opera House was $45,000. This second-floor theatre had a seating capacity of 800, a stage 24' x 48', 11 sets of scenery, and a piano. It was heated by steam and lighted by incandescent lights.

In 1900 Dr. Seelye, well known for his patent medicines, purchased what was known as the Bonebrake Block. Seelye operated the second floor Opera House and located his medicine factory on the first floor where he produced such popular products as Wasatusa and Fro-Zona. Shortly after Seelye purchased the building, he remodeled it. It became a ground-floor theatre with a seating capacity of 800, a balcony, and four boxes located at two levels on both sides of the stage. The stage was large enough, 32' x 65' with a proscenium opening 32' x 21', to accommodate big city productions and there were large dressing rooms. Decorations in the auditorium were in antique ivory, green and gold. The first stage production to appear in the newly renovated theatre was "The Prince of the World," a play that was produced by Hal Reid and featured a real lion.[2] Writing about his early memories of Abilene, Deane W. Malott recalled that, "The theatre's balcony had electric lights all around it, as did the arch that separated the stage from the auditorium, and there was a fire curtain covered with advertisements for local businesses."[3]

During June of 1935 the theatre again underwent extensive renovations including changing the original façade of red brick and many windows to one that featured blond brick with no windows. The renovated theatre, known as the Plaza, continued in business as a movie theatre until 1999 when the roof and one of the side walls collapsed. The remaining structure was later razed.

Other early entertainment venues in Abilene that are no longer standing included a 1885 Music Hall located above the D. G. Smith Drug store, an open air theatre at the corner of Fourth and Spruce operated by Dr. Seelye, and the combined Auditorium, City Hall and Fire Department. This building, opened in 1900, faced Quincy Street between 7th and 8th, and was razed in 1940.

| Ada | 1916 | Opera House | UTD |
|---|---|---|---|

No information is available concerning the Ada Opera House.

| Adams | ? | ? | NLS |
|---|---|---|---|

There is no evidence of an early 20th century performance space remaining in Adams.

| Agra | 1882 | Spangenburg Hall | NLS |
|---|---|---|---|
| | 1894 | Modern Woodmen of America Hall | NLS |
| | 1906 | Opera House | NLS |

Agra was the site of several entertainment spaces. The first of these, a room over a drug store operated by Mr. Spangenburg, was in operation in 1882. This building was later moved to another location when the town moved following the arrival of the railroad in 1889.

Samuel Merrifield and Mr. Glasco who formed a stock company in 1893 or 1894 to erect a two-story building were responsible for the second entertainment space. The Modern Woodmen of America used the upper story for their meeting room and the lower floor housed several businesses.

A variety of types of entertainment occurred in these two structures. There were home talent plays, literary society programs, spelling bees, magic lantern shows, magicians and medicine shows. Revivals staged by the Salvation Army and Free Methodists also occurred in these halls.

In 1906, William Wishman built a large barn-like structure that was called the Opera House. The facility was used for both school entertainments and funerals because it had the largest seating capacity in town. The facility was heated with pot bellied coal stoves that, unfortunately, were inadequate in cold weather. The auditorium had a beautiful maple floor and was used for roller-skating and dances. Silent pictures also made their debut in this theatre. None of these buildings is standing.[4]

| Alanthus | 1916 | | NLS |
|---|---|---|---|

The town of Alanthus no longer exists.

| Alden | 1906 | Alden Township Hall | Standing |
|---|---|---|---|

The Alden Township Hall is still in use today. The second floor probably served as an all-purpose meeting room and community center. It was the location of regular meetings of such groups as the Literary Society, the Masons, the Eastern Star, the Home Demonstration Unity, the 4-H Club, and various civic groups. In addition, theatrical groups performed there. The high school class of 1910 produced the "Merchant of Venice" in the hall and when motion pictures became popular, the Township Hall served as a movie theatre presenting a film each Saturday.

Another type of entertainment to appear at the hall was the medicine show, the last one appearing in the 1930s or early 1940s. The medicine show featured variety acts and a great deal of advertising for their product, a patent medicine designed to cure all ills. Between sales pitches music was provided by a three- or four-piece band and songs and comic routines were also presented. During the breaks the barker would extol the virtues of their products and of the company and would move through the audience selling candy, popcorn and patent medicine.[5]

| Allen | ? | Allen Opera House | NLS |
|---|---|---|---|

The Opera House in Allen was located on the second floor of the town's first hardware store. This structure was destroyed by fire.[6]

| Alma | 1907 | Falk's Opera House | NLS |
|---|---|---|---|

Falk's Opera House, built some time before 1907, is no longer standing. It was a large frame building that contained a first floor theatre.

| Almena | 1916 | Opera House/Lyric Theatre | Standing |
|---|---|---|---|

Morgan P. Smith built the Almena Opera House or Lyric Theater in 1916 at a cost of $6,000. From the beginning, Almena received good reports from managers of theatrical troupes that appeared there. One manager was especially grateful for the town's support during the flu epidemic of 1918. "At least we are pleasantly situated here as everyone in town is pleasant to us, and are doing all they can to make our stay a pleasant one."

The theatre was in use until 1928 when a new, more modern brick building, known as the Rabourn Theater, was constructed. The Opera House has been renovated, the stage removed, and is currently used as the Almena City Hall and Library.

| Altamont | 1889 | City Hall | NLS |
|---|---|---|---|

An 1889 theatrical guide listed the City Hall of Altamont as a having a performance space. This hall, managed by J. C. Murphy, with a seating capacity of 500 is no longer standing.

**Alton**  1889  Rosegrant Hall  UTD

Rosegrant Hall, listed in an 1889 theatrical directory, was reported to have a seating capacity of 300. The manager of the hall was William Rosegrant. There is no current information on Rosegrant Hall, but a one-story frame building identified as Hardman Hall is located on the main street of Alton.

**Altoona**  1900  Opera House/Milton Theatre  NLS

Built prior to 1900, the Milton Theatre or Opera House, as it was commonly called, was in use until the 1930s. Graduation ceremonies and high school plays took place at the opera house. The auditorium, along with several offices, was located on the second floor of the Opera Block. Martin Furniture Company was on the first floor. The opera house in Altoona is no longer standing.[7]

**Americus**  1913  City Hall  Standing/Stage

In 1905, the women of Americus formed the Auditorium Club. The group circulated a petition in 1912 and obtained enough signatures to bring the proposition to build an auditorium to a vote. Their proposition was, "Shall the city of Americus, Lyon County, Kansas, issue bonds to the sum of $6,000 for the erection of a city hall and to purchase a site for the same." The proposition passed by a close vote, 60 to 53. This is particularly significant because in 1912 the very women who proposed the building of a city hall could not vote.

The city hall, built in 1913 by James Phelan, was quite popular for several years, but as time went by it was used less and less and finally stood idle for many years. In 1975, the building was sold for commercial purposes.[8] Although the structure was altered with the office and rest room located at the front of the building under what used to be the balcony and large doors on either side of the auditorium; the stage remains.

**Andale**  ?  Anti Horse Thief Society Hall  NLS
  ?  Kneppels Hall  NLS

The AHTA Hall, Anti Horse Thief Society Hall, was located on the east side of Main Street above Nick Hermes Hardware. Another hall, Kneppel's Hall, was located on the west side of Main Street.[9] Neither hall is standing.

**Anthony**  ?  Union Hall  UTD
  1887  Opera House/Grand Opera House  NLS

The first recorded performance space in Anthony was the Union Hall. While its construction date is unknown, in 1889 the facility was managed by Gaines and Olmstead and had a seating capacity of 350. Nothing is known concerning the fate of this structure.

Constructed in 1887, the opening of the Grand Opera House on December 18th was an event of tremendous significance to the community. The house, including the private boxes, was filled to capacity. "The rich colors of stage fittings, the highly decorated woodwork, the draperies of the private boxes, and the flood of light from the glittering gas fixtures added every necessary effect to the gala scene." Not to be out done by the beauty of the facility, the opening play, "Caprice," starred 22-year-old Minnie Maddern, an actress of national importance.

A joint stock company consisting of prominent residents of Anthony owned the building that housed the Grand Opera House. It was located on the southwest corner of Anthony and Main, had a frontage of 75 feet, by a depth of 100 feet, and was nearly three stories in height with a basement under the entire building. Stores were housed on the first floor of the building. The opera house, located on the second floor of the building, had a seating capacity of 900, with a stage 25' x 63', one trap door in the center of the stage, and four sets of grooves. The theatre also contained four large dressing rooms. By 1907 the facility boasted furnaces and 110-volt electricity. Admission was 25, 50, and 75 cents and $1.

For a number of years the theatre was an important part of the community. Civic and school functions were held there. Many outstanding dramatic performances occurred there including such plays as "Ten Nights in a Bar Room" and "Uncle Tom's Cabin." In 1915 the United States Marine band gave a concert, as did the Kansas City Little Symphony Orchestra. Unfortunately, the decline of the Grand Opera House mirrored that of opera houses across the country. As the cost of travel rose and movies and radio gained in popularity, it became more and more difficult to attract quality road shows.

On January 1, 1928, a member of the *Republican-Bulletin* staff was walking down Main Street when he noticed smoke issuing from under the roof of the opera house building, and immediately turned in an alarm. The blaze was difficult to handle because of its location and the wind and smoke, but after two hours it was under control. While the building was not totally destroyed, a great deal of damage occurred. The opera house was seldom used after the fire and in 1933 the owner sold the building to the city. It was razed and a new municipal auditorium erected.[10]

**Appomattox**  ?  Opera House/Gillispie's Opera House  NLS

The town of Appomattox, located in Grant County, no longer exists. However, in the town's early days dancing at what was known as the Opera House, a large hall located over Mr. Gillispie's store, was a popular form of entertainment.[11]

**Arcadia**  1885  Grant's Hall  UTD
  1889  Arcadia Opera House/
  1896  Richard's Opera House  NLS
  ?  Possibility of another opera house  UTD
  ?  Eagle Theatre/Movie Theatre/
     Opera House  Standing

Arcadia was the home of one hall and two or possibly three opera houses. The first reference to a performance space in Arcadia occurred in 1885, Grant's Hall. Then, an 1889 theatrical guide listed the Arcadia Opera House managed by A. W. Richards. The guide indicated that this facility contained 650 chairs and benches, had a stage 14' x 32' with five sets of scenery, two dressing rooms and no piano. The license to perform was $1.25.

Beginning in 1896 and extending to 1910, the Richard's Opera House, under the management of A. W. Richards, appeared in theatrical guides. The Scenic Artist was L. R. Clare from Kansas City. Seating was 400, the stage dimensions were 12' x 31' with an 18' x 12' proscenium opening. This opera house was listed as a ground-floor theatre. However, a resident of Arcadia reported that the opera house had been located above a blacksmith's shop and was no longer standing. Another resident of Arcadia reported that a one-story brick building still standing downtown, had been a movie theatre, but also presented live entertainment.

**Argentine**  1912  Nokes Opera House  NLS

This theatre will be discussed in the section on Kansas City opera houses.

**Argonia**  1885  Hall  NLS

In 1885 Argonia, the first town in the United States to elect a woman mayor, had a hall with a seating capacity of 300. While this hall no longer remains, there is a record of the town's first Christmas celebration.

Argonia celebrated her first Christmas, December 25, 1883, by giving a program accompanied by a tree and a light house. The town was new and small, but very enthusiastic. The location of the amateur entertainment was held in the new building owned by Mr. And Mrs. John Goss .... Mr. L. A. Salter was chosen chairman of the program; Mr. Hickok, of the committee on tree decoration and presents; F. E. Mummy had charge of the music, with Mrs. Baughman at the organ, Joe Arnold an auctioneer, and the owner of the only fur coat in town was chosen to act as Santa Claus.[12]

**Arkansas City**  1884  Highland Hall/Highland Opera House  NLS
  1888  Fifth Avenue Opera House  NLS

Arkansas City, or Ark City as it is known to Kansans, was the home of two opera houses, neither of which is standing. The first opera house, the Highland Opera House, was located at 110 - 114 South Summit, the current location of the Buford Theatre. In 1885, H. P. Farrar managed the Highland Opera House which had a seating capacity of 700 and boasted 15 scenes. This theatre is no longer standing.[13]

The lavish Fifth Avenue Opera House was opened on October 17, 1888, by the famous actress Lillie Langtry performing her signature role in "As In A Looking

Glass." The theatre was located at 225 East Fifth Avenue, the current site of the Arkansas City Recreation Center. This ground-floor theatre was quite grand with a large stage 40' x 64', a proscenium opening 36' x 36' and seating for 1,400. The stage was elevated nine feet above the auditorium floor with three traps in the stage floor. By 1910 the theatre was owned and managed by W. R. Ranney and the name was changed to Ranney's Fifth Avenue Theatre.

Writing in 1918, Will Locke, a manager of a theatrical company who performed there, painted a vivid picture of the theatre and what it had been. His physical description of the theatre reflected on its beauty.

The old Fifth Avenue Theatre, once one of the largest and finest theatres in the country, still retains its architectural beauty of sweeping curves and graceful lines. Although it has recently been "touched up" a bit, many of the fine old decorations remain. The domed ceiling is a splendid piece of art. Designed in the days when they believed in room, strong walls and bold colors, this old house can give points to many modern houses and come out winner.

Locke went on to reminisce about those who had played the opera house.

"In its palmy days this old stage saw many of the world's greatest stars. Covering the walls around the stage and dressing rooms there may still be seen patches of many old lithographs of old-time plays: 'Shore Acres,' 'Devil's Auction,' 'For Her Sake,' and many others that once 'packed 'em' in here."

But it wasn't merely the remembrance of the plays that impressed itself on manager Locke. He was moved by his discovery of old publicity photographs.

Stacked away in a remote corner of a room off the lobby I found a great collection of old portraits of famous men and women of the stage who had played here…But what interested me most of all was an old photo frame fastened to the wall back in one corner of the stage. I climbed up a stepladder and wiped away the dust-laden cobwebs that almost obscured some of the ancient pictures, and there I found many familiar faces that seemed to be looking out through the windows of the past.

Performers whose pictures he found included Clarence Bennett as a young man; one as he appeared in "Royal Slave" and as John the Baptist in "Holy City." There was also a photo of W. B. Patton in "The Minister's Son"; Eugene Moore, Mitchel Ingraham, Guy Caufman, Harry Billings, J. C. Lewis in "Si Plunkard," Sam J. Burton in "Si Perkins" and one of "Baby Irene Spooner."

The performers had given these photos to the back stage "boys." Manager Locke concluded, "In the halcyon days of old, this picture gallery was the pride of the 'boys' who ran the stage; the actors took pleasure in giving them--the 'boys' found joy in caring for them. But now all is changed. Gone are many of the actors; vanished are the 'boys.'"

The fate of this majestic theatre was the same as that of many others in the state. After the decline of traveling theatrical troupes, the auditorium was used less and less, and finally served as a Masonic lodge. Exactly 40 years after being constructed at a cost of approximately $100,000, the Fifth Avenue Opera House was sold for $2,750 at a sheriff's sale and was later razed after a fire ruined the interior of the building.[14]

| Arlington | 1880 | Pickens and Campbell's Opera House | NLS |
| | 1889 | Town Hall | NLS |

In 1889 there was one performance space in Arlington, the Town Hall, with a seating capacity of 500. This might have been a building constructed in 1880 by Pickens and Campbell and known at that time as the Pickens and Campbell's Opera House. This building, located north of Main and known to later residents as the "picture show building" was dismantled in 1932.[15]

| Arma | 1914 | Pearl Theatre | Standing |

Arma, a mining community, is located near Mulberry and Pittsburg. Constructed in 1914 and managed by Joe Giard, the Pearl Theatre was "up-to-date in every way" and seated 600. George Bubb, manager of the Ikey and Abey Company describe the company's 1918 appearance in Arma in glowing terms as, "…a new show spot on the Kansas map … Our business the record of the house — it being $230.00. Every mine is worked for miles around with advance stuff and all gone over again with the tonight stuff."[16]

The structure now stands vacant.

| Army City | 1918 | ? | NLS |

Army City, constructed during World War I and located close to Fort Riley, no longer exists. The theatre burned on August 4, 1920.[17]

| Ashland | 1887 | Berry Hall/Stephens Opera House | Standing |
| | 1889 | Cooper Hall | Standing |

Ashland is the home of a standing opera house in very good condition. The stage has been removed, but the original stairway and box office remain. The opera house auditorium is currently used as a recreation center for teenagers. The front advertising curtain from the opera house used to hang in the Ashland Museum, but has been taken down due to water damage. However, the curtain from the Liberty school is still in the museum.

Both Berry Hall and Cooper Hall each had seating for 1,000. These halls were located on the second floor of adjoining buildings. The November 3, 1887, *Clipper* stated that Ashland was "…the busiest city in the state for her population." Among the buildings under construction were three buildings being built by King, Berry and Cooper. "All of these buildings are similar in appearance and size, being 25' x 100' feet and two stories high.[18] Berry Hall became the Ashland Opera House and then the Stephens Opera House. The stage was 18' x 35'. Heating was by stoves and illumination was by gas. Admission to the opera house was 25, 50, and 75 cents and $1. Cooper Hall, located next door, became the Masonic Hall and is now an apartment.

| Assaria | 1916 | ? | NLS |

Mentioned in a 1916 theatrical trade paper, the performance space in Assaria no longer exists.

| Atchison | 1866 | Atchison Theatre/Price's Hall/ Price's Opera House | NLS |
| | 1867 | Turner Hall | NLS |
| | 1870 | Corinthian Hall | NLS |
| | 1882 | New Opera House/Price's Opera House/New Atchison Theatre/ Atchison Theatre | NLS |

Atchison, located on the Missouri River, is one of the oldest cities in the state. Because of its age and easy access, it has a long theatrical history. Unfortunately, none of the town's early theatres remains. The Atchison Theatre, located in Price's Building on the northeast corner of Fourth and Main Streets, served as a performance facility as early as 1866. An early advertisement for this theatre gave the price of admission as 75 cents for the parquet and 50 cents for the gallery with productions beginning at 8 o'clock. Frank Frayne, an actor who went on to international fame, appeared there in several productions during the 1866 season.

Built in 1867 by the Turnverein Society, the Turner Hall located on the southeast corner of Kansas Avenue and Sixth Street, was an important part of the German community. It was used for recreation, dramatic productions, lectures and the education of the German members of the community. This structure is no longer standing.

Judge C. G. Voster of Topeka, C. J. Drury and Dr. J. M. Linley of Atchison erected the Corinthian Hall in 1870. The hall occupied the second floor of a building on the west side of Fourth Street between Kansas Avenue and Commercial Street. This facility with its seating capacity of 700 and a stage 23' x 50' contained five sets of scenery and a curtain. The hall rented for $25 a night or $125 a week. The license was $5. The Corinthian Hall appeared in theatrical guides between 1870 and 1885.

The Lord Dramatic Company, featuring the extremely popular actress Louie Lord, opened the theatre with their production of "Dora." Louie Lord's versatility as an actress was apparent because she also appeared in ten other roles during the company's two-week stay in Atchison. Other performers of note who appeared in the Corinthian Hall included Frank Daniels, Mary Anderson, Joseph Jefferson in his signature role in "Rip Van Winkle" and Clare Louis Kellogg. Following the construction of the Atchison Theatre in 1882, the Corinthian Hall fell into disuse and finally in 1960 the Urban Renewal Program razed it.

Erected in 1882 by L. M. Crawford, who eventually owned or managed a chain of 40 theatres, the Atchison Theatre was located on the southeast corner of Fourth and Kansas Avenue. It was a grand, first floor theatre with a stage 35' x 55', a proscenium opening 32′ x 34′ and a seating capacity of 1,100. There were 20 scenes and a piano. The cost of renting the facility was $65 per night with a $5 license fee. Fay Templeton, a noted star of her day, was one of the many performers to appear at the theatre. In 1888 Crawford sold the theatre to John M. Price and the name was changed to Price's Opera House. Price then operated the theatre until 1893 when he sold it to John Seaton. At this point the name was once again changed and the theatre became the New Atchison Theatre. The theatre closed in 1912 and is no longer standing.

During the early 20th century outdoor theatres or Air Domes became popular. It was too hot and stuffy in theatres to attract audiences, so these outdoor theatres were constructed. A manager of one of the companies that appeared at Atchison's Air Dome in the summer of 1916 reported on business that summer.

> The continued drought and hot weather is making it uncomfortable for actors playing Air Dome circuits, but Air Dome managers are reaping good profits. The hot nights are too much for regular movie fans and this business is now going to the Air Domes. It is also unnecessary for Air Dome managers to give out rain checks, as there hasn't been any rain in six weeks. H. M. Ernst, manager of the 'dome' here, reports an unusually good business this season.[19]

| Athol | 1916 | Athol Opera House | NLS |

The 1916 and 1917 the manager of the Athol Opera House was C. H. Niedermeyer. This theatre with a seating capacity of 500 is no longer standing.

| Atlanta | 1889 | Hall | NLS |
| | 1889 | School House | NLS |
| | 1920 | City Hall | Standing/Stage |

An 1889 theatrical guide listed two performance spaces in Atlanta, a hall with a seating capacity of about 200 and the School House with a seating capacity of 250. The performance space in the schoolhouse was listed as having a "good stage." Neither building is standing.

Constructed in 1920, the Atlanta City Hall contains an almost complete set of painted scenery. Like other auditoriums of that period the hall, a large auditorium with a stage at one end, is used for community functions. In recent years the hall has been significantly renovated.

| Attica | 1889 | Attica Opera House | NLS |

In 1889 the Attica Opera House, owned by C. E. Denton, was a second-story theatre that had a seating capacity of 400 and a stage 16′ x 16′ with four scenes. This facility is no longer standing.

A long-time resident of Attica fondly recalled the old second-story theatre. As a child he attended movies there. The movie came from a little hole way in the back of the room. He, along with all of the children, sat right down in front. The children always stomped their feet and clapped their hands to get the show started. He particularly remembered laughing very hard at Charlie Chaplin, a comic who walked a plank, and then that night he couldn't sleep because he kept dreaming that he, too, was walking a beam. The resident also recalled a dance held at the Opera House. During the evening two "really big guys," boys from the country got into a fight. They were fighting so hard they rolled all the way down the stairs and ended up on the floor at the bottom, still locked together.

| Atwood | ? | Cochran Brothers Skating Rink | NLS |
| | 1905 | Shirley Opera House | Standing |
| | 1910 | Electric/Jayhawk Theatre | Standing/Stage |

The western Kansas town of Atwood is the home of two standing opera houses, the Shirley Opera House and the Jayhawk Theatre, formerly known as the Electric Theatre.

The first reference to a performance space in Atwood was to the roller-skating rink owned by the Cochran brothers. When a traveling show came to town, it played on a stage at one side of the rink. Also, in 1906 the Halloween Grand Masquerade Ball was held at the rink. Prizes were given for the best costumes. The rink is no longer standing.

W. R. Shirley, a prominent Atwood resident, built the Shirley Opera House in 1905. The opera house was located on the second floor of a commercial building. A standing-room-only crowd attended the opening of the theatre and was entertained by a band concert. Wrestling matches were also held there. There was also a report that when a Negro group appeared in Atwood they had to cook back stage, and when the show started one could smell their cooking out front in the audience.[20]

A 1917 advertisement that appeared in a theatrical trade paper indicated that the Shirley Opera House was under new management and had recently been remodeled with seating for 350 and electric lights. Although the opera house portion of the building is vacant and the stage has been removed, the first floor has been renovated.

The Jayhawk Theatre, originally called the Electric Theatre was built by Andrew Madsen who operated a general store in the building before selling it. The new owner, Edward Egelston, remodeled the building into a theatre. This was what was known as a "combination house," showing both movies and theatrical troupes. A description of the Electric Theatre that appeared in a 1918 trade paper indicated that the Electric Theatre was a ground-floor theatre that seated 450. The theatre was illuminated by electric lights and contained a piano and two dressing rooms. Egelston, the manager, also managed the Electric Theatre at St. Francis. The Jayhawk Theatre is in use as a community owned movie theatre and also used for dramatic productions. Although the theatre contains a stage, it is not original.

| Augusta | 1885 | Good Templar's Hall | UTD |
| | 1880 | Kuster's Opera House/ | |
| | 1889 | Hindman's Opera House/ | |
| | 1907 | Sander's Opera House | NLS |

The March 11, 1880 *Gazette* proudly proclaimed that, "We thought Augusta had been booming for the past two months, forty buildings have been erected in that time. But the boom actually has just commenced." The article proceeded to describe the current building frenzy that included a public hall fitted up for theatrical purposes. The hall was constructed over two of the buildings, Reynolds drug and grocery store and A. Kuster's confectionery and ice cream parlor. The theatre had a seating capacity of 500 with an 18′ x 21′ stage. The facility was heated by stoves and illuminated by gas. In 1916, electric lights were installed and other improvements were made.

This public hall became known as the Opera House. The *Augusta Journal* reported, "The stage, scenery, properties, etc., are all modern and up to date. To this fact the amusement-loving public may attribute the many first-class attractions appearing at the Opera House last season. It is not a hall but a modern and fully equipped theatre with a seating capacity of five hundred." The opera house was also known as Kuster's Opera House, Hindman's Opera House and Sander's Opera House depending on who owned the ground floor business located beneath the opera house. This facility was the scene of many amateur and professional dramas, as well as vaudeville acts and community functions such as high school commencements. The building was torn down in 1938 and the land used for the new post office.[21]

Augusta's history as an oil town was reflected in the ads for acts placed in trade papers. In a 1916 trade paper the manager of the Augusta opera house reported that, "…the new oil fields have more than doubled the population and the conditions were never before more promising than the present time." The next year there was a different opera house manager, but he advertised the town in the same way. "Would like to hear from Good Shows of all kinds. Booming oil town, capacity business."[22]

No Information is available on the Good Templar's Hall mentioned in an 1885 theatrical guide.

| Axtell | 1889 | Barnes' Hall | UTD |
| | 1893 | Axtell Opera House/ | |
| | | Citizens Opera House | NLS |

The first mention of a performance space in Axtell occurred in an 1889 theatrical guide. Barnes' Hall had a seating capacity of 500. No information is available concerning the disposition of this structure.

Constructed in 1893, the Axtell Opera House located at 103 5th Street is no longer standing. This second floor performance space contained seating on two levels that totaled 500. The stage was 21′ x 21′.

The following account described a birthday celebration by the Hillman No. 1 acting company during their 1917 appearance in Axtell.

> At Axtell, Kansas, we celebrated again, the occasion this time being the birthday of our charming little ingénue, Cora Sohns. Again that fluid that made Milwaukee famous, and has made lots of folks drunk, sparkled on the

table, set in dry Kansas like an oasis in the Sahara desert, only the desert in this instance should be pronounced with the accent on the last syllable. There sure was lots of it, but the ladies of the company had warmed their way into the good graces of the landlord's wife with the result that they took possession of the rear end of that hostelry and turned it into a factory of home cooking; second result being a satisfied bunch of well-fed humans after the party and all hoping to be on hand when charming Cora celebrates again. She received many gifts among which was $100 in gold from friend hubby.[23]

# B

**Baker**      1885    Lillreal's Hall      NLS

The only reference to Lillreal's Hall was found in an 1885 theatrical guide. That structure is no longer standing.

**Baldwin**      1857    Old Castle Hall      Standing

Old Castle Hall, the first building at Baker College in Baldwin, is standing and in use as a museum.

**Barnes**      1895    Dearborn Hall/Opera House      Standing/Stage
            1907    New Hall      NLS

Built in 1895, Dearborn Hall/Opera House with its original stage, is standing and in excellent condition. The building was constructed by Augustus Hiram Dearborn who used stone and lime found on his farm. The first floor of the building was a mercantile.

The opera house is a very good example of a late 19th century, second floor theatre. Such features as the box office window, the wainscoting, the trap door in the stage and the grooves for scenery above the stage remain. In addition, the room contains both knob and tube wiring and gas fixtures. There is also an original seating chart for the auditorium.

The New Hall, a tin structure, was built around 1907. It was used for skating and the second floor was used for plays. An outside stair led to the auditorium. New Hall is no longer standing. During the summer Barnes residents were entertained by a well known Kansas theatrical troupe, the North Brothers who performed at the Barnes Carnival.[1]

**Bartlette**      1920    Town Hall      Standing/Stage

While the outside stone walls of the Bartlette Town Hall are standing and the stage is in tact, the roof has leaked and the floor is rotten. This theatre was the site of productions by touring acting companies including the Neil Schafner Players.

**Baxter (Springs)**    1889    City Hall      Standing

The building housing the Baxter Springs Opera House was constructed in 1872 for use as the county courthouse. However, it was never used for that purpose because Columbus became the county seat. In 1905, an extension was built on to the front of the building and the structure then became the town's library. Remnants of the opera house, located on the second floor of the building, are still visible although a remodeling that occurred in 1988 has significantly changed the appearance of the room. During its days of use, the opera house was the location of community events including home talent plays and high school graduations.[2]

**Beattie**      1889    G.A.R. Hall      NLS
            1889    O'Neil's Hall/Opera House      NLS
            1917    ?      UTD

The 1889 Opera House or O'Neil's Hall that seated 500 is no longer standing. In 1889 Beattie also had a G.A.R. Hall seating 300. An 1895 theatrical guide listed only the G.A.R. Hall with a seating capacity of 450 and a stage 40' x 30'.

A 1917 reference to a ground-floor theatre in Beattie indicated that it was a, "Dandy house on ground floor, good dressing rooms, furnace heat and about sixteen foot height on stage." This facility could have been the O'Neil's Opera House, the G.A.R. Hall or they could have been the same. The Beattie Opera House was destroyed by fire in 1938.

**Belle Plaine**      1885    Opera Hall      UTD
            ?    Opera House      Standing

An 1885 theatrical guide listed an Opera Hall in Belle Plaine. It is not known if this is the brick structure that contained the opera house and fire station shown in a 1914 picture. The interior of the opera house featured a front advertising curtain that contained a picture of water, cliffs and a boat. The room was lighted by gas. This opera house is standing. The stage has been removed and the space divided into shops to form a mall.

**Belleville**      1882 or 1887    Powell's Opera House/Armstrong
            and Co. Theatre/Opera House      NLS
            1916    Rex Theatre      UTD

Powell's Opera House, constructed in either 1882 or 1887, was destroyed by fire in 1934. According to one account, the grand opening of the theatre occurred on December 22, 1887, with the nationally known actress Minnie Maddern Fiske appearing in "Caprice." The opera house was a second-story facility with a stage of 32' x 45' and a seating capacity of 700. The theatre was furnished with the finest of opera chairs, stage settings, and scenery. The front drop curtain contained a scene which represented a view of the Bay of Naples. There was also a fine Mason and Hamlin piano located in the auditorium. The seats could be removed and the space used for dances.

Over the years a number of traveling theatrical companies appeared at the opera house. These include: Docksetters Minstrels; "The Count of Monte Cristo" featuring the father of Eugene O'Neal; Robert Downing in "Ingomar"; Sanford Dodge and Louise Marshall in Shakespearean plays; and stock companies such as Kirkhoff and Locke and Hillman performing such old faithful as "East Lynn" and "Uncle Tom's Cabin." One Belleville resident remembered being taken to "Uncle Tom's Cabin" as a young child and how embarrassed his mother was when, upon learning of Liza's fate, the child cried out "Rats."

Medicine and Indian shows also appeared at the opera house. One such company raked in a great deal of money selling electric belts that were purported to be a cure for every ill. Another type of performance to take place at the opera house was magic acts. Professor Price was a magician who entertained and thoroughly frightened the large audience with his hypnotism and mesmerism. Local residents were shocked to see one of the church elders become so hypnotized that he actually sat down at a card table and not only played cards, but played successfully. The opera house was also used for concerts, recitals, and home talent shows.

One of the worst fires in the history of Belleville broke out in the Opera House on February 14, 1934. The structure containing the opera house and several businesses was totally destroyed. Damage was estimated at between $60,000 and $75,000.[3]

No information is available on the Rex Theatre mentioned in a 1916 theatrical guide. This could have been the opera house re-named or another performance space.

**Belmont**      1887    Turner Hall      NLS

The Turner Hall listed in an 1887 theatrical guide is no longer standing.

**Beloit**      1883    Opera House/Cooper's Opera House/
            Williams Theatre/Williams OH      NLS
            1914    Grand Theatre      NLS

The earliest reference to the Cooper Opera House appeared in an 1883 theatrical guide. The theatre, known simply as the Opera House, had a stage 25' x 42' with four sets of scenery and a seating capacity of 500. It was a first floor theatre. An 1889 listing of the facility gave its name as Cooper's Opera House with J. F. Cooper as manager. In 1910, Ira F. Williams was the manager and the name had been changed to the Williams Theatre. This structure is no longer standing.

In 1914, the Grand Theatre was constructed in Beloit. The *Beloit Gazette* reported that the building was 48' x 142' and "would be one of the neatest and most attractive play houses in this part of the state." It was going to be made as nearly fire proof as possible. The stone structure was to have an arched brick front and a lobby that extended across the front of the building. The *Gazette* also reported that the seating capacity would be 750 with the possibility of expanding by constructing a gallery that would add another 250 seats. When the building was completed and furnished it would represent an investment of about $15,000. The scenery for the theatre was painted in Downs. This structure was razed in 1964.

**Belpre        1912    Opera House                    NLS**

The Belpre Opera House, a brick building with a second-story performance space, was built to serve as a community auditorium as well as for entertainment events. It was also, on March 14, 1912, the site of one of the more notorious events in the community's history. When there was no event scheduled, the opera house served as a meeting place for the local men who played cards and visited. On the evening of March 14th the local men had gathered to witness a wrestling match. During the evening an argument occurred between some of the spectators. It is not known exactly what happened, but a fight ensued. There was a shooting and a stray bullet hit the editor of the local paper. He fell down the stairs to the ground level and was taken to a nearby restaurant where he died. Conflicting stories and a surprise witness made the trial one of great interest and brought notoriety to the community. The Belpre Opera House is no longer standing.[4]

**Bennington     ?       Bennington Opera House         NLS**
               **1909    Bennington Opera House         NLS**

Bennington was the location of two opera houses, neither of which is standing. The first Opera House was located where a house now stands. Robert Quinn built the second Opera House in 1909. This one-story wooden structure was used for touring companies' performances, commencement exercises and as a community center before the brick school with an auditorium was built.[5]

**Bern           1892    Turnverein Hall/Opera House    NLS**

Constructed in 1892 by the Turnverein Society, their hall, also known as the Bern Opera House, was razed in 1972. This structure contained painted scenery. Curved-back wooden chairs were used for seating on the main floor of the hall.

During the depression, years after the era of traveling acting companies, the hall continued to serve as source of entertainment for the community. Every Saturday night there would be a movie at the hall. One of the audience members remembered, "They were silents, and the reels broke, and they were sort of second rate …. Oh, it was tragic if by Friday afternoon you heard that the reels for the picture show hadn't come in on the old Rock Island motor."[6]

**Beverly        1892    Beverly Hall                   NLS**
               **1910    Beverly Opera House            Standing/Stage**

Beverly Hall was located on the second floor of the Fritts Building, a large brick building at the main intersection, on the northeast corner of the block. The building also housed the post office and Fritts Hardware. This structure is no longer standing.

The 1910 Beverly Opera House is a one-story brick structure that stands with its original stage and serves as a community center. A kitchen is located in the rear section of the building. The inside set of doors and box office are original, but the stage portion of the theatre has been altered. The ceiling has been lowered and the stage made smaller to accommodate rest rooms on either side of the stage. However, backstage is totally original with one dressing room and stacks of folding chairs from the auditorium. On stage you can still see the location of the footlight trough. To the right of the stage is a stairway that leads to a very small basement area. None of the original scenery remains.

Home talent plays were popular in the late 19th and early 20th centuries and it was not uncommon for residents of one town to stage their production in a neighboring town. In 1892 some young folks from Brookville put on a play, "The Factory Girl." The play was so successful that it was decided to stage the production in Beverly on April 1st. That day it rained and snowed, but this didn't deter the young actors. They secured rigs from the livery stable and started for Beverly about 10 a.m. Every time they came to a mud puddle the actors got out and walked for fear of getting the rigs stuck in the mud. The tired group finally arrived in Beverly about 5 p.m., thus making the trip of 18 miles in about seven hours.[7]

**Bird City      ?       Opera House                    NLS**
               **1917    Opera House                    NLS**

The first Bird City Opera House was located on the second floor of a hardware store. This building and its contents were destroyed by fire.[8] The second theatre, the Bird City Opera House was built in 1917. An ad appearing in a 1917 theatrical trade paper described the theatre as a ground-floor theatre that seated 400. At the time of its construction it contained electric lights, a No. 4 B. Powers' picture machine, a new piano and furniture, and a stage 20' x 30' with all new scenery. This theatre was also destroyed by fire.

**Bison          1912    Opera House                    NLS**

The Bison Opera House, built by Oscar Bieber in 1912, was torn down in 1950. During its tenure the building was the site of many important civic and cultural events. The second floor of the building was used for the opera house with various businesses located on the first floor. The first event of importance to be held at the Opera House was the presentation of the cantata, "Queen Esther" on April 10, 1912. This same cantata was repeated a month later with the proceeds donated to the rebuilding of the Baptist Church that had been destroyed by the April 20, 1912, tornado. Over the years various uses for both the first and second floors of the building included part-time church, movie theatre, auto garage, some high school classes, doctor and dentist offices, furniture store, bowling alley, roller rink, shoe repair shop, mechanic shop, and gas station.[9]

**Blue Mound     1889    Jenning's Opera House          NLS**

The Opera House in Blue Mound was located on the second floor of a brick building that housed the Bank of Blue Mound. The exact construction date is unknown, but by 1889 the facility was known as the Jenning's Opera House and managed by B. E. Jennings. The structure is no longer standing.[10]

**Blue Rapids    1885    Opera Hall                     NLS**
               **1894    Ladies' Opera House/**
                       **City Opera House               NLS**

Blue Rapids was the location of at least two performance spaces, neither of which is standing. In 1871 Judge W. H. Goodwin of Nashville, Tennessee, erected a building to use as his law office. The second floor was finished as a hall.[11] This is likely the Opera Hall seating 500 that was listed in 1885 and 1889 theatrical guides.

The fascinating story of the second performance space, a large ground floor opera house, began in January 1892, when John McPherson solicited stock for the new opera hall that was going to be "the finest in Marshall County" with a seating capacity of 650 and a stage 24' x 48'. It was proposed that the stock for the opera house, priced at $10 a share, would "draw a fair dividend" for the investors. This, unfortunately, did not prove to be the case.

Two years later an article in the local paper indicated that the building was still unfinished and that negotiations were underway to secure a loan to complete the basement portion of the building. The basement of the building was first opened to the public in February 1895 with an entertainment and a supper. The main room of the basement was described as having a seating capacity as large as the main room of the Turner Hall in Marysville.

During the summer of 1895 the opera house committee struggled to raise the money to complete the auditorium of the building. It was reported that the auditorium could be plastered and floored for $230 and to achieve this it was decided to hold an entertainment.

A standard set of scenery was then purchased for $155. This included a drop curtain, a center door fancy parlor scene, a rustic kitchen scene, landscape wood scene, perspective street scene and the tormentor wings and borders to match. The beauty of the Blue Rapids drop curtain was evidenced by the fact that the Kansas City Scenic Company artist who painted the scene reported that he liked it so well in the future he was going to use it on other opera house curtains. The scene was the view of the water-power and river. A photograph of the scene, taken from the top of the Duncan mill, was used for the drop curtain.

Two years later, the financially-troubled opera house was forced to sell the opera house chairs, lamps and stoves at a constable's sale to satisfy a claim by the Kansas City Scenic Company amounting to about $100. Even more serious financial trouble arose in the February 1897. The Blue Rapids Opera House was in danger of being closed due to foreclosure of the mortgage. In order to complete the building $2,000 had been borrowed from a Missouri loan company. After several months of negotiations and thwarted attempts to hold the foreclosure sale, it was announced that the sale of the opera house by the Kansas City loan company had been called off because of arrangements made by the ladies to pay up the indebtedness. The women of Blue Rapids had raised $1,250 as the first payment and the loan company arranged to loan them the $1,000 balance.

A judge from Manhattan came to hear the motion for an order instructing the Receiver of the Blue Rapids Opera House Company to deed the opera house to the ladies association. There being no objection raised by any stockholder of the old company, the Judge issued the order. From then on the opera house was known as the Ladies' Opera House. The purpose of the new company was to "finish and furnish" the Blue Rapids Opera House and then to deed the property to the city of Blue Rapids. The charter provided that the opera house, after becoming the property of the city, should be open free of charge for G.A.R. memorial exercises, the city school commencements, the Ladies' Library association and for election purposes.

For almost a century the Ladies Opera House of Blue Rapids was used for entertainment and community activities. Finally, in 1985, it was decided that due to the deterioration of the building, it should be razed.[12]

**Bluff City      1889   AOW Hall                                  NLS**

An 1889 theatrical guide indicated that Bluff City "was a good town for small troops." The performance space was the AOW Hall. This structure is no longer standing.

**Bonner Springs   1905   Eagle Opera House              NLS**

The exact date of construction is not known, but in 1905 the Eagle Opera House was the site of an eighth grade graduation. This structure was destroyed by fire some time prior to 1910.

**Brainerd        1889   McLain Hall                             NLS**

In 1889 Brainerd had a public hall, McLain Hall. This structure did not contain a stage, but was used for meetings. The hall is no longer standing.

**Bronson         1885   Holeman's Hall                          NLS**

Holeman's Hall, seating 500, is no longer standing.

**Brookville      1892   Brookville Opera House         Standing/Stage**

The Brookville Opera House, standing with a stage, is an excellent example of a small, second floor opera house. Remnants of scenery hang from the ceiling of the stage and there is a rolled up curtain on the stage. The entrance to the theatre is through the back of the auditorium. The ticket booth is located at the rear of the auditorium, immediately inside the door and under the balcony. The interior of the theatre has wainscoting and hanging light fixtures. The opera house is located on the second floor in one-half of the space over a vacant building. The other half of the second floor was used as a meeting room and where dinners were held.

**Brownell        1920   ?                                        NLS**

In 1920, the performance space in Brownell was owned by Mr. Buxton. This structure is no longer standing.

**Bucklin         1901   Opera House                             NLS**
**                1909   Opera House/Majestic Theatre            NLS**

Bucklin's first opera house was located above the Fisher and Haynes store. Constructed in 1901, this building was eventually used as a Senior Center, and finally razed in 1988. The second opera house in Bucklin was erected in 1909 by C. E. Smith and J. Houston. This Opera House or Majestic Theatre was built at a cost of $10,300 and was said to be the best and most complete on the Rock Island west of Hutchinson. The building was 44' x 120' with a seating capacity of 1,000. The structure featured a large stage with elaborate scenery. It is no longer standing.[13]

**Buffalo         1884   Opera Block                             NLS**

The Buffalo Opera Block, constructed in 1884, was destroyed by fire in 1908.

**Buffalo Park    1885   Hall                                    NLS**

The Hall in Buffalo Park was the scene of entertainment furnished by traveling troupes and supplemented by home talent productions. A dance that would be remembered for years occurred there on the evening of December 31, 1885. It was the custom for whole families to come to dances. The only way for rural families to reach the Hall was by wagon. The parents would throw great heaps of hay into their wagon, place quilts over the hay and nestle their children down into this, and then they would ride on the spring seat of the wagon. During this particular dance, a New Years Eve celebration, it began to snow and before the revelers could return home, snow laid three-feet deep on the ground. Because of this the participants had to remain in the hall or stay with townspeople for two days.[14]

**Bunker Hill     1917   ?                                       UTD**

A 1917 theatrical guide referred to a performance that occurred in Bunker Hill. No mention was made as to the location of the performance.

**Burden          1886   Lyceum and Library Building            NLS**

The Burden Lyceum, constructed in 1886, contained seating for 300 and a stage 20' x 20'. Heating was by stoves and illumination by gas. The building was located on the southeast corner of Main and 6th. Events such as commencement exercises, home talent plays, recitals, benefits, winter lecture courses, and all traveling entertainments were held there. The building was also used by the G.A.R.. When they were young and still active, a long line of veterans of the Civil War would march from their headquarters to the building on Decoration Day to pay tribute to their fallen comrades.[15] This structure is no longer standing.

**Burdett         1917   ?                                       NLS**

The only reference to Burdett occurred in a 1917 theatrical guide. Mention was made that a troupe performed in Burdett, but not where the performance took place. Therefore, it is not known whether Burdett had an opera house. If there ever was an opera house in Burdette, it is no longer standing.

**Burlingame      1883   Union Hall                              NLS**
**                1889   Schaeffer's Hall                        UTD**
**                1904   Shepard's Opera House                   Standing**
**                1917   Panama Theatre                          NLS**

The first reference to an opera house in Burlingame appeared in an 1883 theatrical guide. This second-story facility, known as Union Hall, had a seating capacity of 500, a stage 30' x 50', and five sets of scenery. The building was razed in 1980s. By 1889 there was also another performance space, Schaffer's Hall. No subsequent references to Schaeffer's Hall were found.

Another opera house was reported in a 1904 theatrical guide. The Shepard's Opera House, managed by H. D. Shepard, seated 500, had a 30' x 30' stage, and was heated by stoves and illuminated by electricity. Local residents disagree on the location of Shepard's Opera House. An elderly gentleman indicated that the Shepard's Opera House had been located on the ground floor of the Shepard Hotel. But, he added, the second-story opera house that had been located down the street was much nicer. The Shepard Hotel is standing vacant, but no evidence remains of a theatre. Another Burlingame resident indicated that a brick building that is standing had once housed the Shepard's Opera House.

Finally, a 1917 theatrical trade paper indicated that another performance space existed in Burlingame, the Panama Theatre. This theatre is no longer standing.

**Burlington      1880   Opera House/Jarboe's Opera House/**
**                       Midland Theatre/**
**                       New Wolfe Opera House                   NLS**
**                1885   Hamilton's Opera House                  NLS**
**                1916   Newk's Theatre                          UTD**

Several opera houses were located in Burlington. The Jarboe Block, located on the northeast corner of Third and Miami, constructed in 1880, was the sight of the first one. Over the years this second-story theatre was known by a variety of names, Jarboe Hall, Jarboe Opera House, Midland Opera House, Wolfe Opera House and finally, the New Wolfe Opera House. The first listing for this space appeared in an 1883 theatrical guide. At that time it had a seating capacity of 400, a stage 22' x 18' and a full set of scenery. A renovation must have occurred because in 1896 another theatrical guide gave the seating capacity of the Midland Theatre as 700 with a stage 28' x 45' and a proscenium opening of 20' x 18'. Illumination was provided by electricity. Admission was 25 and 50 cents.

An 1885 theatrical guide listed a second performance space in Burlington, Hamilton's Opera House. This structure was a first floor theatre seating 1,200. The stage was 33' x 48' and contained seven sets of scenery. In 1900, a mass meeting was held at the Hamilton Opera House to help raise a million bushels of corn for the starving in India. The building later served a variety of functions including a roller skating rink, the Burlington Athletic Association gym, the location of many dances, and lastly, for many years a livery stable. This structure was eventually destroyed by fire.

In 1917, J. J. Newcomer managed Newk's Theatre of Burlington. The location of this theatre, or whether it was one of the previously mentioned theatres renamed, is not known. However, because J. J. Newcomb was a steady contributor to the *Opera House Reporter*, a great deal is known about theatre business in Burlington. In 1916 and 1917, Newk's Theatre played such acts as "Henpecked Henry," "This is the Life," "Sis Perkins," "The Missouri Girl," The Scranton Marionettes," and the Giersdorf Concert Band Company. One of the most interesting entries appeared in the October 13, 1916, *Opera House Reporter*. J. J. Newcomb reported that he had played the Harry St. Clair Company during the Fair week to very good business. But what is of special note was his report that, "Boris Karloff and Miss Margot Beaton are the two greatest leading people I ever saw at any price and I've seen a few of the big ones."

| Burns | 1907 | Burns Opera House | NLS |

The Burns Opera House was located over the Burns State Bank. In 1907, the opera house seated 400 with a stage 18′ x 16′. The auditorium was heated by stoves and illuminated by electricity. This structure is no longer standing.

| Burr Oak | 1885 | Opera Hall | NLS |
| | 1899 | Opera House | NLS |

The first reference to the Opera Hall in Burr Oak occurred in an 1885 theatrical directory. The hall, managed by Mann and Gilbert, had a seating capacity of 400. An 1889 guide listed the stage as "fair" but the scenery as "good." The structure is no longer standing.

In 1882 a frame, two-story school was built. This structure was moved northeast across the street in 1899 to make way for its successor. The original school was then remodeled and the lower floor served as an opera house. This structure, known to local residents as the "Octopus," was eventually dismantled.[16]

| Burrton | 1885 | Burrton Opera House/ | |
| | | Howard Opera House | NLS |

The Burrton Opera House or Howard Opera House is no longer standing. This second floor facility had a seating capacity of 400 and a stage 18′ x 47′. In 1907, the room was heated by stoves and illuminated by lamps.

The first attraction to appear at the opera house was the sacred cantata, "Esther." Over the years troupes such as the Grace George Dramatic Company, the Georgia Troubadours, and the Monara Minstrels appeared there along with such standard plays as "Uncle Tom's Cabin" and "East Lynn." Graduation exercises were also held at the opera house.[17]

# C

| Caldwell | 1881 | Opera House | Standing |
| | 1885 | Opera House | NLS |

Caldwell was home to two opera houses, the older of which is still standing. The building has been purchased and is being renovated. The original auditorium was on the second floor, but the stage no longer remains.

The second Caldwell Opera House was a large theatre that was constructed about 1885 and was destroyed by fire in 1918. This opera house seated 800 with a stage 24′ x 30′. While little has been written about the construction of the second Caldwell Opera House, the destruction of the building was well documented through reports by theatrical managers.

Writing in December 1917, Will H. Locke, the manager of a theatrical troupe, set the stage for what was to come. "We opened the opera house at Caldwell, Kan., the week of December 3rd to a packed business and played to a good week. The old house has been thoroughly overhauled and put into excellent condition and it is a comfortable, roomy and well-equipped house to play."

A month later another manager filed a similar report. "Friday at Caldwell, Kans., at the opera house which is now under the hustling management of W. M. Scribner, one of the towns best known business men. The old house has been done over in many ways and many dollars spent to make the house up-to-date in every way and it is now a credit to the town of Caldwell."

Unfortunately, the next month disaster struck in the form of fire. The following report appeared in a theatrical trade paper.

Giersdorf Concert Company gave one of the best musical concerts ever heard in Caldwell, February 18th and was to show on the 19th, but a disastrous fire wiped them out. Never was there a time when the building could have burned when the loss was so great. H. A. Colvin, vaudeville and talking picture show had the place leased for five years and had just moved here, stored all his wardrobe, films, personal clothing, etc., previous to moving in a house. Everything went up in smoke. Haley also suffered total loss of his dogs. Giersdorf Band and Concert Company met with very heavy loss. The opera house caught fire about an hour after the show and burned to the ground. Company lost everything except a few small instruments. His loss estimated as about $5,000…This company has been traveling for about eight years and this is their first serious misfortune. They did not carry any insurance.

While a great loss for the city of Caldwell, the fire was also a financial disaster for the companies who lost everything. But, because their livings depended on their acts, they immediately began rebuilding. The Giersdorf Concert Company appeared in Caldwell at the opening of the 800-seat Air Dome April 3, 1918. H. A. Colvin, the vaudeville performer who lost all of his costumes and motion picture machine in the opera house fire, built this facility. The opening was held on a very cold night, but the people of Caldwell turned out to support the companies.[1]

| Camp Funston | 1918 | Liberty Theatre | NLS |

During World War I a number of entertainment facilities were built on army bases. The 1918 Liberty Theatre at Camp Funston was one of these. Neither the theatre nor the camp remains.

| Caney | 1907 | Caney Opera House/ | |
| | | Truskett Opera House | Standing |
| | ? | Opera House/movie theatre | NLS |

The Caney Opera House or Truskett Opera House, built in 1907, had a seating capacity of 1,000 and a stage 38′ x 50′. Illumination was provided by gas. This theatre was destroyed by fire in 1910. The Caney Elks club then acquired the opera house facilities and rebuilt it for club use. The Elk's Hall was used to organize Caney's Company D in 1917 during World War I.

The façade of the Caney movie theatre is standing. However, the rest of the building has been razed. It is reported that this facility originally served as an opera house.

| Canton | 1889 | G.A.R. Hall | UTD |
| | 1889 | Opera House | UTD |
| | 1905 | Canton Opera House/ | |
| | | Auditorium | Standing |

An 1889 theatrical guide listed two early performance spaces in Canton, the 500-seat G.A.R. Hall, and the 600-seat Opera House. No information is available on the disposition of either building. It is assumed that they are no longer standing.

The Canton Opera House, a two-story brick building, located on the northwest corner of Main and Allen Streets, was built between 1905 and 1907. The Masonic, Star Lodge and Auditorium Association were partners in the building with each part owners of the land on which it was built.

The main floor of the auditorium was used for a number of local activities including high school commencements, class plays, dances and fundraisers such as local minstrel shows. Traveling theatrical troupes like the Wallace Bruce Players came regularly. At one time Milburn Stone appeared with this Hutchinson-based company.

The Masonic and Star Lodges held their meetings on the second floor of the building from the time of its construction until it was partially destroyed by fire in 1967.[2]

| Carbondale | 1889 | Sutherland Hall | UTD |
| | 1913 | Carbondale Opera House | Standing |

No information is available on the 1889 Sutherland Hall in Carbondale. In all probability, it is no longer standing. However, the 1913 Opera House is currently used as the public library. This brick building housed a first floor theatre. In later years it was used for movies, to stage local productions, and as a skating rink. The stage was removed a number of years ago. The former box office window is now the book return for the library.

| Cawker City | 1885 | Grand Army Hall | UTD |
| | 1887 | New Opera House/ | |
| | | Cawker City Opera House | NLS |

Cawker City was the location of two performance spaces, at least for a short period of time. An 1885 listing in a theatrical guide indicated that the Grand Army Hall seated 300 with a stage 22' x 25' that contained seven sets of scenery. The last listing for this facility was in an 1889 guide. The final disposition of this structure in unknown, but it is unlikely to be standing.

In 1878 A. Parker erected the First National Bank building. The opera house, located on the second floor of this building, was opened to the public September 1887. This structure was known at various times as the Cawker City Opera House, the New Opera House and the Grand Army Hall. The main entrance to the opera house was located at the southwest corner of the building with the ticket office at the foot of the stairs. The stage was 18' x 50' and four dressing rooms were located at the north end of the building. The front curtain contained a picture of an historical battlefield scene. Seating was 500.

In addition to the traveling companies and home talent performances, the opera house was used for G.A.R. meetings, Memorial Day programs, school graduations and town meetings.[3] This facility was destroyed by fire on October 24, 1924. At that time it was used for picture shows and a hardware store occupied the ground floor where the bank had once been located. A Cawker City resident described the fire as "really something" because the heat caused the ammunition and paint housed in the hardware store to explode.

| Cedar | 1917 | | NLS |

The only reference to a performance space in Cedar was found in a 1917 theatrical trade paper. This structure is no longer standing.

| Cedar Bluffs | 1916 | Woodman Hall | NLS |

The two-story building that housed the Woodman Hall is no longer standing.[4]

| Cedar Vale | ? | Kennison Opera House | NLS |
| | 1904 | Polson Opera House | NLS |
| | ? | Mystic Theatre | NLS |

Cedar Vale was the home of three opera houses. None remains. The first opera house was the Kennison Opera House. Nothing further is known about this structure. The second, and much better known facility, was the Polson Opera House. It was located on the second floor of a building constructed by T. M. Polson in 1904. The Polson Block was 50' x 110' and housed the opera house on the second floor and the Cedar Vale National Bank and a general merchandise store on the first floor. The opera house had seating for 600 and a stage 24' x 30'. Illumination was provided by gas. In 1907, the admission was 35 and 50 cents. After it was no longer used as an opera house, doctors' offices and apartments occupied some of the second floor. This structure was razed in 1990.

Bill Leonard operated the Mystic Theatre. The Leonards moved to Cedar Vale in the fall of 1907 and purchased the drug store. They later added show business to their activities. First Mr. Leonard took over management of the opera house and then operated the Mystic Theatre. He also edited "The Mystic Murmur," a weekly paper that informed people about local events and show business.[5] The Cedar Vale museum houses two side flats containing ads that are reported to be from the Mystic Theatre.

| Centralia | 1885 | City Hall | UTD |
| | 1887 | G.A.R. Hall | NLS |
| | 1889 | Opera Hall | UTD |
| | 1917 | Opera House | NLS |

Early theatrical guides list three performance spaces in Centralia that might all be the same facility. These are the 1885 City Hall, the 1889 Opera Hall with seating for 200 to 250. Finally, an 1887 city atlas listed a G.A.R. Hall located one lot from the corner on the Northeast corner of Commerce and 5th. This structure is no longer standing, and no information is available on the City Hall or Opera Hall.

A reference in a 1917 theatrical trade paper described the Centralia Opera House as being a ground-floor theatre with a fair stage, dressing rooms and well heated with stoves. This structure is no longer standing.

| Centropolis | 1916 | ? | NLS |

The only reference to Centropolis concerns the 1916 appearance of an acting company. There was no indication as to where their performance took place.

| Chanute | 1880 | Williams Hall/ | |
| | | Williams Opera House | Standing |
| | 1904 | Hetrick Theatre | NLS |
| | 1884 | Roof Garden Theatre | Standing |

George Williams, the first blacksmith in Chanute, built the Williams Opera House in 1880. This facility was first called Williams Hall and then Williams Opera House. It had a seating capacity of 500 and a stage 14' x 50'. It also had "a fair amount of scenery." The performance space must have been renovated because in 1896 another theatrical guide listed the Williams Opera House as having seating for 800 and a stage 25' x 50' with a proscenium opening 26' x 14'. This was a second floor theatre. The scenic artist was R. L. Close of Kansas City. Another renovation must have taken place because by 1904 the Williams Theatre had a seating capacity of 920, a stage 30' x 48' with a proscenium 27' x 18'. This was a second floor theatre, but the dimensions would indicate that the stage house had been heightened to facilitate a fly space for scenery. This structure, while having the stage removed and being radically altered, is standing. For many years it was a furniture store, but it is currently vacant.

The Hetrick Theatre, completed in early 1904, was opened with Sousa's "El Capitan." On this special occasion the theatre was filled to capacity and Mr. Hetrick and his wife sat in a private box. The monogram "F. H." was painted on the highest point of the ceiling and also appeared on the plush stage curtain. The Hetrick Theatre was a second and third-story theatre with a seating capacity of 1,100 and a stage 50' x 60' with a proscenium opening was 37' x 36'. Gas and electricity provided illumination. The theatre burned in 1925.

The *Kansas City Times*, reporting on the destruction of the Hetrick Theatre, commented on the irony of Hetrick's life.

> The Hetrick Theatre was built by Fred Hetrick, a poor farmer who made his fortune from oil and gas leases. Not knowing what to do with his newly acquired wealth, Hetrick decided to build a theatre. In order to do this he pledged all of his property holdings except his house to build the $60,000 theatre. Eventually the price of oil slumped and his rentals declined and Hetrick could not meet his payments and creditors foreclosed. Eventually, Hetrick became a bill poster for the very theatre he built.

Chanute was the location of one other turn-of-the-century theatre. The Roof Garden Theatre, 112 E. Main Street is standing, although very little remains of the original structure. Apparently this was a theatre on the roof of the second floor, which has now been removed. Osa Johnson is reported to have sung there in the 1940s. The construction date was some time before 1884.[6]

| Chapman | 1917 | Opera House | Standing |
| | | (Opera House portion removed) | |

The original Chapman Opera House was on the second floor of a variety store. In the 1920s Arnold, a State Representative, took the second story off the building and turned the first floor into a movie theatre. This structure, with the movie theatre stage, is standing and is currently in use as a recreation center.[7]

| Chase | 1887 | Chase Opera Hall | NLS |

In 1887, six years after the founding of Chase, the Chase Opera House Company was formed. The June 21, 1887, *Chase Record* reported, "The Opera House Company have organized and all the stock subscribed to give us one of the best halls of the kind in this vicinity. Work to commence immediately." A month later the July 28, 1887, *Lyons Republican* reported that, "the building will be under way as soon as the brick can be burned."

The 1887 brick structure could be the same that was later identified as the Chase Opera House. A 1914 picture indicates that the Chase Opera House was located above the Chase Hardware and Implement Company. The opera house was also used for a variety of functions including picture show, dances, and roller-skating. The room was heated by two coal-burning stoves, one at each side. The stage was fairly good sized with several painted drops.

This description vividly described the enjoyment attached to attending events at the opera house.

> It was exciting to climb those steep, inside stairs with my family and wait eagerly for my father to buy the tickets so we could pass through the wide double doors where the ticket-taker stood. Then we would rush to the front to try for seats beside friends. Those seats were wooden folding chairs set up in rows across the auditorium and divided into three sections by aisles. Sometimes these seats became very uncomfortable before a program ended. However, during a school play or a thrilling western movie, the seats could become as hard and bumpy as rocks and we children wouldn't have made a peep about them.[8]

After the new high school was constructed in 1923 the opera house was seldom used. It is no longer standing.

| Cheney | 1889 | Joslyn Hall | NLS |
|---|---|---|---|
| | 1898 | Joslyn Hall | Standing |
| | 1911 | City Hall | NLS |

In 1889 Dr. Joslyn, a druggist, moved Joslyn Hall from the community of Marshal to Cheney. This frame building is no longer standing. Then, in 1898 Dr. Joslyn and Mr. Collins built a large, two-story stone building that housed Dr. Joslyn's drug store in one half of the bottom floor. Upstairs above the drug store was a lodge hall. Upstairs above the other half was the Hall that was used for entertainment. Later, the hall and lodge were combined. There were also doctors' offices across the front of the second floor. This building is standing, but if there ever was a stage, it has been removed.

The City Hall, built in 1911, was the site of graduations, home talent shows and minstrel shows. This facility with a stage and painted scenery is no longer standing.

| Cherokee | 1885 | Walker's Hall | NLS |
|---|---|---|---|

In 1885, Cherokee was home to Walker's Hall with a seating capacity of 250. This structure is no longer standing.

| Cherryvale | 1880 | Opera House/Carson's Opera House | NLS |
|---|---|---|---|
| | 1885 | Powell's Opera House/ Cherryvale Opera House | Standing |

The Cherryvale Opera House Company, organized in 1880, constructed a one-story frame hall that was used as an opera house, town hall and school. In addition, both the Baptist Society and the First Presbyterian Church met in the Opera Hall until they constructed their own buildings. An 1885 theatrical guide reported that O. F. Carson managed the Cherryvale Opera House. Seating was 400 with a 16' x 30' stage and a proscenium opening of 22'. There was very little scenery. This may have been the Opera House Block that was destroyed by fire in 1901.

The 1885 theatrical guide listed a second opera house in Cherryvale, Powell's Opera House managed by J. M. Powell. This theatre had a seating capacity of 900 a stage 23' x 55' with eight scenes. An 1889 theatrical guide listed only one opera house in Cherryvale, Carson's Opera House. This theatre had a seating capacity of 1,000, a proscenium opening 22' and a stage 23' x 55'. There were eight scenes. It would appear that this was the same facility as Powell's Opera House. This was a ground-floor theatre illuminated by electricity.

A former Cherryvale resident described the Opera House at Neosho and Main as "truly remarkable in its likeness to famous old-world opera houses." The balcony was circular and terminated in a private box at each side. The stage contained a colorful drop curtain and there was an orchestra pit. This structure is standing; however the interior has been gutted.[9]

| Chetopa | 1883 | Chetopa Opera House | NLS |
|---|---|---|---|

Constructed in 1883, the Chetopa Opera House was a first floor theatre. The auditorium seated 500 and the stage was 38' x 21' with a proscenium opening 19' x 12 1/2'. There were six sets of scenery with an elegant drop curtain, and three dressing rooms. In 1889 the facility was lighted with Edison incandescent electric lights and heated by furnaces. This structure was razed in 1939.

| Cimarron | 1907 | Luther's Opera House/ Dorean Opera House | Standing |
|---|---|---|---|

A 1907 theatrical guide listed the opera house at Cimarron as Luther's Opera House while a history of Cimarron refers to the same building as the Dorean Opera House. It was a second-story theatre with a stage house. This brick structure, minus the stage and stage house, is still standing. The opera house contained seating for 225 and a stage 14' x 18'. Heating was by stoves and illumination by lamps. Two large framed murals now hang on the walls of the lodge hall that occupies the former opera house space. It is probable that these were made from the opera house scenery.

In 1917 an appreciative company manager, George Lucas, reported that "The Lucas Show (NO. 1) is playing their third week in Kansas and doing nicely. Cimarron, Kan., is a crackerjack show town for the right kind of a show. Upstairs house; nice, clean place and Mr. Bean, the manager, a prince of a fellow. Shows don't want to miss this one--the Dorean Opera House."[10]

| Claflin | 1909 | Roesler Opera House | Standing/Stage |
|---|---|---|---|

The Roesler Opera House, built in 1909, is an excellent example of a second floor theatre. Every aspect of the theatre is preserved including the original stage.

The opera house is located above the local bank, now owned by the First Kansas Bank at Hosington. Bill Brannon, the previous owner of the bank, grew up in Claflin and had many memories of the opera house. Brannon said that the auditorium had been a dance hall in the 1930s and used for motion pictures from 1939 to 1943. It was during World War II that the scenery was taken out. Alterations to the original appearance of the hall include disconnecting the electricity, the removal of the chandeliers and the chairs that were on wooden strips. During the depression a Merchant Appreciation ticket and 10 cents would get you in if you were a child. Adults had to pay a quarter.

Remembering his childhood experiences at the opera house, Mr. Brannon recalled how proud he was to see his father's name on the roll curtain. Performers he remembered included Wallace Bruce with his Toby wig and suspenders. Other performers remembered by Brannon included The Georgia Troubadours and Frank North. Brannon's favorite performer was Anna May Wilborn from Chicago. She was a black clarinetist who was "as beautiful as Lena Horn" and traveled with her own band. At that time Kansas was fairly segregated, but the Claflin hotel made an exception for her and fed her band in the dining room, so she made Claflin her stop on the way to Denver.[11]

| Clay Center | 1885 | Gollober's Opera House | NLS |
|---|---|---|---|
| | 1886 | Bonham's Opera House | NLS |

Located at the corner of Fifth and Court, the first opera house in Clay Center, Gollober's Opera House, was in existence in 1885. The entrance was an outside stairway on the west side of the building. This was a second floor facility with seating for 500. The stage was 20' x 47' and contained four scenes and a piano. Graduations, plays, and political speeches were held in the opera house. This structure was eventually razed by Mr. Gollober who then constructed another building about twice the size of the original one. However, the new building did not contain a theatre.

The second opera house in Clay Center, Bonham's Opera House located next to the Bonham Hotel, opened in 1886. The opening of this opera house was a grand event. "Women trailed down the aisle in beautiful gowns, each one wearing an opera bonnet. One woman had on a gold satin dress with lace all over it." The Bonham Opera House was quite splendid with box seats on the ground floor and also on the level of the first of the two balconies. The stage was hung with two curtains, one an asbestos curtain and the other the outer or decorative curtain that contained a large central scene depicting a street in Antwerp, Belgium. Around the border of the curtain squares were marked off for advertising. Each square cost $2.50.

The Bonham Opera House was a first floor theatre with seating for 750 and a stage 35' x 66' with a proscenium opening 36' x 33'. The theatre was used as an opera house until 1920 when it was remodeled and used as a first floor movie theatre. This theatre was razed in 1954.

Numerous companies appeared at the Bonham Opera House during its 35-year life. The Andrews Opera Company presented "Carmen." "Polly of the Circus" was presented by a cast of 50 actors and featured live horses on the stage. Other favorites included "Uncle Tom's Cabin" and the Lou Docksteaders Minstrels. On the walls of the dressing rooms were autographs by such famous actors and actresses as Minnie Maddern Fiske, Joseph Jefferson, Mrs. Potter Palmer and Edna May, a star of musical comedies.[12]

| Clearwater | 1897 | IOOF Hall and Opera House | NLS |

An early photograph shows a two-story frame building with "1897," "IOOF" and "Opera House" on the front of the building. In 1913, the second-story opera house was known as the Star Theatre. The manager, Bill Schweisberger, showed motion pictures and directed a number of plays. The theatre closed in 1929 when talking pictures came in. The theatre is no longer standing.[13]

| Clifton | 1879 | Hanan's Hall and Opera House/ | |
| | | G.A.R. Hall | NLS |
| | 1885 | Elson's Hall | UTD |
| | 1889 | Miller's Hall | UTD |
| | 1910 | MWA Hall | Standing |

Hanan's Hall, also known as the G.A.R. Hall, was in use from 1879 until 1925 when it was razed. The G.A.R. hall was located on the second floor with the Clifton Theater occupying the ground floor. Nothing is known about either the 1885 Elson's Hall or the 1889 Miller's Hall. It is possible that they are the same structure. The 1910 MWA Hall or Mighty Woodmen of America Hall is standing.[14]

| Climax | 1916 | Opera House | UTD |

A 1916 issue of the *Opera House Reporter* carried the following ad, "Up-To-Date Opera House. Want good shows on per cent, good country to draw from, clean house, stage 12' x 15', scenery, gaslights, 2 dress rooms, Good piano. Good show town for the size." It is not known whether this structure is standing.[15]

| Clyde | 1885 | McDonald's Opera Hall | UTD |
| | 1889 | Clyde Opera House | UTD |
| | 1895 | Derse and Longtin's Opera House | Standing |
| | 1910 | Beachtel Opera House | Standing |
| | 1916 | Wonderland | UTD |

Over the years Clyde was the home of several opera houses. Listed in an 1885 theatrical guide, the McDonald's Opera Hall had a seating capacity of 250 with a stage 16' x 20', four scenes and a drop curtain. A. S. Bender managed this theatre. In 1889 the Clyde Opera House was listed with similar stage dimensions, 19' x 15', but with seating for 400. Illumination was from gasoline lamps. The managers were Derse and Longtin. In 1895 The Derse and Longtin's Opera House was either a new structure or greatly expanded because its stage dimensions were 40' x 16' with seating for 500. The building that contained this theatre is standing but the second floor theatre no longer exists.

The best remembered opera house in Clyde was the Beachtel Opera House constructed in 1910. It was also a second floor facility. The room that contained the theatre is empty, but you can see where both the stage and balcony were located. The curtain from this opera house is reported to be in a museum in Grand Island, Nebraska. The Beachtel Opera House, constructed and operated by J. D. Beachtel, had seating for 600 and a stage 30' x 40'. There were six dressing rooms and two large coal-burning stoves provided heat. The main entrance to the theatre was on the east, with the box office at ground level. Businesses were located on the first floor of the building.

During its hay-day from 1904 to about 1930, the opera house was a community gathering place used for school plays, graduation and baccalaureate exercises, home talent plays, lecture courses, minstrel shows and winter Chautauqua courses. Companies who performed there include Frank and Sport North Players with Ted North and the Chick Boyes Company. These companies usually played a week in Clyde because it was known as a good show town. Following the demise of the road, the theatre was operated as a motion picture house until a new movie theatre was built. The theatre portion of the building was dismantled in 1940.[16]

| Coffeyville | 1871 | Perkins Opera House | Standing |
| | 1883 | Wells Hall/Wells Brothers | |
| | | Opera House | NLS |
| | 1901 | Auditorium Theatre | Standing |
| | 1906 | The Jefferson | NLS |

The first reported opera house in Coffeyville was the 1871 Perkins' Opera House built and managed by Luther Perkins. The seating capacity of this second floor theatre was 400 with a stage that featured a proscenium 18' x 14'. Illumination was provided by gas. This structure is standing, but without its stage. The first floor is the location of the Chamber of Commerce.

Another early opera house in Coffeyville first appeared in an 1883 theatrical guide. Wells Hall or Wells Brothers Opera House had a seating capacity of 600 and a stage 30' x 50' with a "fair amount of scenery." This theatre, located above the Wells Brothers General Merchandise store on Walnut Street between 8th and 9th is no longer standing.

J. B. Tackett opened a third performance space in Coffeyville in 1901. It was located at Seventh and Maple. This ground-floor theatre, the Auditorium Theatre, was managed by Tackett with Neal Turner as scenic artist. The theatre had a seating capacity of 800 and a stage 40' x 80'. Illumination was provided by electricity. John Tackett and his brother brought such great artists as Madame Schumann-Heink to Coffeyville. This theatre, with the upper floor or floors removed, is standing and in use as a commercial property.

In addition to the Auditorium, at various times John Tackett also operated two Air Domes and a vaudeville house located on Union Street. One of his ventures known as Tackett's "Barn" was the site of many dances. One Coffeyville resident reminisced, "The cotillions were quite lovely. I remember Will Rogers and his brother, Clem, often attended." The Barn, a crude building in downtown Coffeyville, is no longer standing.

The Jefferson Theatre was housed in a four-story brick building on the corner of Ninth and Maple. Built in 1906 at a cost of $60,000, the Jefferson was a large theatre with a stage 40' x 70' that seated 1,200. The theatre was gutted by fire in 1924.[17]

| Colby | ? | Bean's Hall | NLS |
| | 1887 | Armory | NLS |
| | 1908 | New Opera House | NLS |

The first social event in Colby was a dance held in the partially completed store building of M. Donelan. This occurred on June 10, 1885. Another space where early entertainments were held was the second floor of the original courthouse. This was the location of meetings and other community events. A third early space was Bean's Hall. Unfortunately, no information exists on this space.

An important entertainment venue in Colby was the Armory. Its inauguration was Memorial Day, May 30, 1887, although its formal opening wasn't until June 23, 1887. Emma G. Hatcher, America's only colored emotional actress, presented the opening performance. The Armory was used for a variety of types of entertainment ranging from home talent plays to traveling troupes. Court was also held in this building when the case being tried was of enough local interest to attract a large crowd. The Armory and the original courthouse are no longer standing.

Interest in an opera house to replace the old Armory began in 1902, but it wasn't until January 2, 1908, that the new Colby Opera House opened. This two-story brick structure located at 265 W. Fourth Street proved unprofitable even though traveling road shows and Chautauquas were held there. In 1920 it was sold and turned into a movie theatre, but this venture also failed. In 1924, the Baptist Church of Colby purchased the building. Finally, in 1947, the former opera house was made into temporary armory quarters. These quarters were used until the new Armory was opened. The structure was razed in 1959 and the brick used to build a house at 215 E. Walnut.[18]

| Coldwater | 1886 | Rich's Opera House | NLS |
| | 1909 | Harbaugh Opera House/ | |
| | | Pike Theatre | Standing |

In 1886 H. H. Rich built a large hall or opera house. This structure, constructed primarily for roller-skating, had a seating capacity of 1,000. It was also used for dances, band concerts and other forms of entertainment. Mr. Rich razed the structure in 1896 because it was not profitable.

A second opera house opened June 17, 1909, when J. E. Harbaugh erected a building that housed the Home Mercantile Company, bank and opera house, later known as the Pike Theatre. When it opened, the Harbaugh Opera House was advertised as being the largest dancing floor in Western Kansas. There was a stage at the south end where plays and other forms of entertainment took place. The Peoples Bank now owns this structure. The opera house portion of the building is vacant and the stage has been removed.[19]

| Collyer | 1890s | Zeman Hall | Standing |
|---|---|---|---|
| | 1893 | G.A.R. Hall | NLS |
| | 1916 | Opera House | UTD |

There are three references to performance spaces in Collyer. One credits Zeman's Hall with being the first performance space. Prior to that entertainments were held in private homes or the schoolhouse. The hall was commodious and was the site of school plays, traveling troupes and public dances. This hall is still standing but not in use. There is also a reference to an 1893 Grand Army of the Republic Hall. No further information is available concerning this space or the next one. The third performance space, an opera house that was new in 1916.

On November 20, 1916, the *Opera House Reporter* announced that, "a new opera house has been opened at Collyer, Kan., with S.F. Glass as manager." Manager Glass received noting but praise from the acting companies who appeared at his opera house.

The Musical Reeds, a Kansas company, reported, "Mr. Glass, the manager of the opera house, met us at the train with a pleasant greeting and stayed on the job and provided for us with everything we ask for to make us comfortable during our short stay. We want to say to companies coming this way, do not pass up Collyer, because it is a small town, for Manager Glass will get you the business and make your stay as pleasant as is possible. It is sure a pleasure to meet managers of this kind."[20]

| Colony | 1917 | Opera House | NLS |
|---|---|---|---|

The Opera House in Colony, referred to in a 1917 theatrical guide, is no longer standing.

| Columbus | 1883 | Harland Brothers Opera House/ Columbus Opera House | NLS |
|---|---|---|---|
| | 1905 | McGhies New Theatre/Liberty Theatre | Standing |

Harland Brothers' Opera House, first listed in an 1885 theatrical guide, was a large second floor theatre with seating for 900 and a stage 63' x 21' with nine scenes and a piano. By 1896 the name of the theatre had been changed to the Columbus Opera House. The last reference to this structure was in a 1904 guide. The theatre was later destroyed by fire.

W. E. McGhie constructed a new opera house, a ground floor facility, in 1904. An article in the June 29, 1905, "Modern Light" reported that, "W. E. McGhie certainly deserves credit for the class of amusements he furnished Columbus theatre goers in the past season. Of course the handsome new opera house aided in the class of plays he could secure ... This year he is on the Crawford circuit and he will unquestionably give Columbus theatre goers the finest opera season ever presented to a people in a town of our size." At some point the theatre was renovated and turned into a motion picture house. The renovations included Tiffany glass trim on the windows, the door to the phone booth, the doors on the restrooms, the window of the "cry room" and the box office. In 1973, the box office was purchased and removed and is now in storage at Lincoln Center. The stage has been removed and the structure now houses a commercial business.

| Colwich | 1886 | Opera House (Opera House portion removed) | Standing |
|---|---|---|---|

The State Bank of Colwich, located on the northwest corner of Wichita and Colorado Avenue, was organized in 1886. The second story of the structure was called the Opera House. This facility was used for a variety of activities including church services, literary entertainment, dances, roller-skating, club meetings, reading circles and bean suppers. The second floor of the bank structure was removed in 1948. The first floor is still standing.[21]

| Concordia | 1878 | Grand Opera House/ LaRocque's Opera House | Standing |
|---|---|---|---|
| | 1907 | Brown Grand Theatre | Standing/Stage |

Concordia has excellent examples of both a second floor and a ground-floor theatre. LaRocque's Opera House and the Brown Grand Theatre are in good condition and contain many original features.

The LaRocque's Opera House, located on the second and third floors of a downtown business, was built by brothers Fred and Joseph LaRocque in 1878 and was in use for the next 30 years. When constructed, the hall had no balcony, stage, dressing rooms or scenery. Although traveling theatrical troupes carried their own scenery and costumes, the facilities did limit what could be staged there. To remedy this problem, in 1884 the LaRocques remodeled and finished the hall. The roof was raised 12 feet to make room for the gallery. The stairway, formerly in the center of the hall was moved to the east and outside the building. The box office was located in the hallway before entering the seating area. The stage was constructed in the north end of the hall and dressing rooms were probably located behind the stage. Eleven sets of scenery were ordered from Kansas City and the hall was provided with 700 chairs. In 1888 the seats at the back of the auditorium were placed on a raised platform to improve visibility.

The list of acting companies that performed in LaRocque Hall form a catalogue of late nineteenth century dramas. Such stars as Nellie Boyd in "Fanchon, the Cricket"; the Kendall Combination and Comic Opera Company's "H.M.S. Pinafore"; and Louie Lord's "Forget Me Not," "A Celebrated Case" and "Hazel Kirk" appeared at the LaRocque. Numerous "Uncle Tom's Cabin" troupes appeared there over the years and vaudeville and minstrel shows and the occasional medicine show were also popular.

Following a performance on the evening of November 28, 1895, a fire gutted the dressing rooms and stage end of the opera house. Although the opera house was insured, it was a year before the hall was completely renovated. Even though further improvements were made in the hall, there was growing concern about the building and the need for a new, larger facility.

In January 1904, the "Kansan" editor wrote, "The great Chicago fire brings to mind the opera house is a fire trap of the worst sort. Today if we do not do something, we will have a catastrophe that will prove this true." Since the LaRocque Hall had only one stairway, fire safety was one of the determining factors in the decision to build a new opera house. Following the opening of this theatre, LaRocque Hall was fitted with a new hardwood floor and the space converted to a skating rink known as the Convention Hall Rink. This early performance space is standing. The curved balcony added during the 1884 renovation still exists, but the stage is a modern addition.

Due to increasing concerns about the inadequacy of the LaRocque Hall, in 1905 Colonel N. B. Brown announced plans to build a fully outfitted opera house. His son, Earl V. D. Brown, supervised construction. W. T. Short of Concordia was the construction supervisor with Carl Boller from Kansas City as the theatre architect. This three-story stone and brick building, when completed, was 60-feet high and 100-feet long and cost $40,000. The front entrances led into a tiled lobby that contained the owner's private office and ticket office. Seating capacity of the theatre was about 1,000 with eight box seats, 400 seats on the orchestra floor, 200 seats in the balcony and 300 chairs in the gallery. The interior color scheme was green, gold and white. The stage is 57' x 34' with six dressing rooms, a restroom, scene gallery and scene shop. The opening was held September 17, 1907, and to celebrate the occasion, Earl V. D. Brown had ordered a magnificent drop curtain as a gift to his father.

Under the direction of the Browns, father and son, the theatre prospered, but by 1911 both Browns were deceased and the management of the theatre fell to the two widows. They gave the theatre to the city, but in 1915 the city of Concordia returned the theatre to one of the widows and her husband Ray Green, the editor of the *Blade Empire*. The Greens ran the theatre for the next ten years. In 1925, it was sold to the Concordia Amusement Company and began its life as a motion picture house.

This theatre, the Brown Grand, is magnificently restored and the best example of an early 20$^{th}$ century, ground-floor theatre in the state. The restoration of the theatre by the town of Concordia took place from 1974 to 1980 at a cost of $500,000. The interior is white with gold trim, and green velvet is used for drapes and seat upholstery. There are two balconies, but the most striking feature of the theatre is the painted grand drape curtain.[22]

| Conway Springs | 1885 | McKibbin's Hall | UTD |
|---|---|---|---|

The only reference to a performance space in Conway Springs was found in an 1885 theatrical guide. McKibbin's Hall was listed as related to the Odd Fellows and managed by them. The hall had a seating capacity of 300. It is unlikely that this structure is standing.

| Coolidge | 1887 | Masonic Hall | Standing |
|---|---|---|---|
| | 1888 | Coolidge Opera House | NLS |
| | 1889 | Potter Opera House | UTD |

During the boom years of Coolidge, a Masonic Hall and a $75,000 opera house were constructed. The opera house, built by E. H. Peck in June or July of 1888, burned after one performance. That performance, August 25, 1888, was provided by a New York Company. The cause of the fire was not determined, but lightening was suspected. One Coolidge resident remembered, "I know one thing though, it was sure raining to beat the dickens the night it burned. It was in the fall and I had been herding cows north of town on Spring Creek. It started raining so hard that I stayed the night with a man named Crane. His home was located two or three miles north of town and although we couldn't see the blaze, the entire sky to the south was lit up."

The Masonic Hall, constructed at about the same time as the opera house, is still standing. It may also have served as an opera house. Potter Opera House with G. T. Potter, Blacksmith, proprietor was also listed in a theatrical guide. Its current disposition is not known.[23]

**Cooperstown**    1916    ?    NLS

Cooperstown, no longer on the map, was mentioned in a 1916 theatrical guide as the location of a performance. It is not known whether Cooperstown contained an opera house.

**Corona**    ?    Miner's Union Hall/Opera House    NLS

The performance space in Corona, a mining camp in northern Cherokee County, was located above the merchandise store. The structure that housed the Miner's Union Hall and Opera House was destroyed by fire in the mid 1930s.

**Coronado**    1887    ?    NLS

Coronado, now just a house and an elevator, was once a rough and tumble frontier town. It was into this setting that the Grace George Dramatic Company made their 1887 appearance. In his autobiography, Luke Cosgrave recounted the company's performance.

We had to borrow seats from the hotel, and chairs from the furniture store for reserved seats. The numbering was somewhat mixed up as a result. A gentleman and his lady came back and said someone had their seats. Would Tom Kaylor--the door tender--kindly get the couple out?

Tom went down and told the people they were in the wrong seats. The lady said, 'Who wants our seats?' She peered back and saw who it was.

'Humm,' she commented. 'Well, I guess we just won't give them up.'

Tom went back to the office.

'What about it?' demanded the lady.

'I can't get them out,' replied Tom.

'Oh, yes, you can,' said the gentleman as he drew his gun.

Tom was scared. 'No, don't do anything like that. You'll break up the show!'

He kept pleading with the man. Finally the fellow cooled off a little, and the couple took two vacant seats. The play was 'The Hidden Hand,' and in one scene there was a lighted candle on the stage. In the middle of the act, the same gentleman said, 'I can snuff that candle. I can even put the candle out without knocking it over!' He had that gun out again.

Someone else in the audience yelled, 'Don't do it, Doc! That's not a wall. It's just canvass. The poor people are behind there dressing. You might kill them!' But he kept up the threatening at intervals all through the show, which at least intensified the interest of the audience in our humble efforts![24]

**Cottonwood Falls**    1907    Music Hall    Standing

The Cottonwood Falls Music Hall was located on the second floor of what is now the Exchange National Bank. If this facility ever had a stage, it is no longer there. Another performance space in Cottonwood Falls was the 1916 outdoor lyceum or Air Dome. This was an open air space used in the summer. It had a center aisle with seats on either side and a stage at the east end.

| Council Grove | 1883 | Opera House | UTD |
|---|---|---|---|
| | 1889 | Etta Opera House | NLS |
| | 1916 | Stella Opera House/ Ritz Theatre | Standing/Stage |

The first recorded theatrical activities in Council Grove occurred in 1880 prior to the construction of the first opera house. An amateur opera company composed of home talent, produced the opera "Fatanitza" and reproduced the opera at Emporia, where the company was highly complimented. Another pre-opera house production, "East Lynne" was staged on a platform in the courthouse and played to crowded houses.

Theatrical guides provide references to three Council Grove opera houses. The first was an 1883 listing for an Opera House owned by Henston and Sims. No further information is available on this space.

In 1889 the Etta Opera House was operated by H. W. Gildemeister. He built this theatre so his daughter, Etta, a talented musician, would have a place to perform. She was a singer who graduated from the University of Kansas about 1900 and later went to Chicago where she taught music. This second-floor facility that seated 800 is no longer standing.

The third opera house, the Stella Opera House, was built in 1916. This facility is standing with its original stage, although the interior has been completely remodeled. Built by T. W. Whiting, the theatre is named "Stella" for his daughter to whom he presented the deed.[25]

**Courtland**    1905    Courtland Opera House    NLS

Constructed in 1905, with funds gained from the sale of stock, the Courtland Opera House was a frame building that contained a ground-floor theatre. A ticket booth and a stairway that led to a small balcony were located in the vestibule. The theatre had seating for 500 with a stage 21' x 24'. The editor of the local paper boasted that, "The new Opera House was seated as comfortable as the Grand or Willis Wood Theater in Kansas City." One Courtland resident described the roll curtain and stage scenery as being, "out of this world. Beautiful trees graced part of the back scenery and the other set made you feel right at home in the inside room which was always the same regardless of the stage families' social standing."

While the theatre and scenery received raves, the heating system left a great deal to be desired. There were two huge heating stoves at either end of the hall that distracted from the dramatic action. As one theatregoer remembered, "Just as sure as a particular high point was about to occur on the stage, the janitor would decide to fill the stove with a whole bucket full of coal."

The Courtland Opera House was quite popular and when traveling troupes appeared, the house was always full. A particularly popular attraction was Blind Boone, a Negro pianist. He came to Courtland once a year, and as one resident remembered, "played his heart out for the music lovers. He always stopped at the corner hotel and they enjoyed having him."[26]

**Coyville**    1899    ?    NLS

The Trousdale family performed in Coyville in 1899. There is no information on where their performance took place. No buildings of a sufficient age remain in Coyville.

**Crope**    1916    ?    NLS

This 1916 reference is to the appearance of a dramatic troupe in Crope, not to a specific performance facility in the town. Crope no longer exists.

| Cuba | 1885 | Boyer's Hall | UTD |
|---|---|---|---|
| | 1908 | Cuba Opera House/Bohemian Hall | NLS |

Cuba was the location of two performance spaces, neither of which is still standing. There is an 1885 reference to Boyer's Hall. This structure had a seating capacity of 250. S. B. Boyer was the proprietor. The last reference to Boyer's Hall occurred in an 1889 theatrical guide. The second facility, the Cuba Opera House/Bohemian Hall, was constructed in 1907-08 by three Bohemian fraternities, Z.C.B.J., C.S.P.S., and J.C.D., at a cost of about $6,500. This structure was destroyed by fire, February of 1928. The lodges immediately reconstructed the hall that was then used for meetings, basketball games, plays and movies, as well as dances. This new structure was erected on the foundation of the burned building. The new hall's original name was the "Ceska Narodni Sin" or the Bohemian National Hall. Today this new hall contains much of its original scenery, with the most impressive piece being a large drop featuring the Cathedral in Prague, Czechoslovakia. As membership in the lodges diminished, the hall was turned over to the city of Cuba to be used as an auditorium.[27]

**Cullison**  1889  City Hall  NLS
 1910  Toews Hall  NLS

An 1889 theatrical guide listed Cullison as having a City Hall, proprietors Jenkins and Sutler. Nothing else is known about this structure. The second structure, Toews Hall was located over Toews Hardware store. A long-time resident of Cullison remembered that in "about 1905 - 12, there was an auditorium over Toews store, where the Woodmen and Odd Fellows met. There were sometimes traveling acts, such as someone hitting a punching bag, a lady in tights, dancing, or music. They sang songs like 'I Wonder Who's Kissing Her Now' and others."[28]

**Culvar**  1916  ?  NLS

There are references to acting companies who performed in Culvar in 1916 and 1917, however, nothing is known about a performance space.

**Cunningham**  1918  ?  UTD

According to a theatrical guide, a performance occurred in Cunningham in 1918. There is no information on where the performance took place.

# D

**Damar/Demar**  1916  ?  NLS

A 1916 reference in a theatrical trade paper to a performance taking place in Damar did not indicate the location of the performance. It is not known whether there was an opera house in Damar.

**Delphos**  1885  Delphos Opera House  NLS

The opera house and grandstand were built in 1885 by public subscriptions. The theatre, a spacious, high-ceilinged frame building, was erected in four months at a cost of $2,600. Scenery cost $285 and chairs, 250 of them, cost $8 per dozen.

A variety of events occurred at the Delphos Opera House that ranged from the Delphos Band concerts to a Silver Wedding party, a Masquerade Party and a G.A.R. Ball. The facility was also the site of school commencement exercises and on rainy days, the Memorial Day program was held there. Home talent shows and traveling troupes also appeared at the opera house and one member of a traveling troupe latter married a Delphos girl, Nellie Morrison. The actor she married was Milburn Stone.

The final owner of the Opera House used it as a motion picture theatre and installed a Wurlitzer electric player with attached synchronized orchestra effects. This furnished a "big band" sound of sorts to accompany the moving pictures. In 1936 when the opera house was torn down, lumber from the building was used to erect a new Bohemian Hall ten miles west of Delphos.[1]

**Denmark**  1912  Denmark Hall  Standing/Stage

The Denmark Hall, standing with its original stage, was dedicated February 24, 1912. The public hall had a seating capacity of 400 to 500 and was lighted by acetylene gas and heated by a furnace. The residents of Denmark were justifiably proud of the building.

Prior to its opening there was a controversy concerning the naming of a facility. Was it to be an "opera house" or a "hall"? One resident expressed the opinion that the structure was much better than the Bryant Opera House in Lincoln. He felt the Denmark facility should be compared to the Willis Wood Theatre in Kansas City and called an opera house. Eventually, however, the supporters of calling the building simply, Denmark Hall prevailed.

This opera house/hall was used for practically everything: plays, operettas, recitals, funerals and Memorial Day services, and occasional large church services and banquets. Today the structure is used as a church hall. The interior is in excellent condition. A kitchen facility has been added.[2]

**Dexter**  1908  ?  UTD

The reference to Dexter is from a 1908 appearance by the Trousdale acting company. Current residents of the community though that there might have been an opera house in Dexter, but specific information was not available.

**Dighton**  1887  Wolf Hall  UTD
 1889  Wishards Opera House  UTD
 1908  Opera House  Standing

The first reference to an opera house in Dighton was to an 1887 Wolf Hall. The Chicago Comedy Company's presentation of "Rip van Winkle" was the first play ever presented in that facility. The next reference to a performance space was to the 1889 Wishards Opera House. It is unlikely that either of these facilities is standing.

In 1907, the Opera House Company planned the construction of a two-story brick building to be located on the west and south sides of the First National Bank building. This structure, completed in February 1908, was a second-story opera house with a seating capacity of 400. Milburn Stone performed there and Jersey Joe Walcot fought there.

After serving as an opera house for traveling actors, the theatre was used for moving pictures. Although in later years the stage was removed and the room was used as a lodge hall, the stairwell and original box office remain. The stairwell is particularly interesting because it is papered with movie posters.[3]

**Dodge City**  1878  Comique Theatre  NLS
 1878  The Variety Theatre/
 1878  Hoover Hall  NLS
 1879  Kelly's Opera House/
 1898  Gluck's Opera House  NLS
 1884  McCarthy's Rink/Opera House  NLS
 1915  Chalk Beeson Theatre  Standing

Dodge City, with its rich history as a frontier cow town, has been home to a number of theatres. The first recorded theatrical activity in Dodge City took place in 1878 in the Comique Theatre. This theatre was located on the south side of the railroad tracks on the southeast corner of Trail Street and Second Avenue. The name was borrowed from a famous theatre in New York City. Local citizens, however, referred to the Comique as the Commie-cue. It was here that Eddie Foy and his partner, Jim Thompson, appeared on their first trip west. The Comique had a stage at one end, a bar at the other and gambling tables in-between. A row of boxes where patrons could sit and drink and view the productions circled the room.

The competition for the Comique was provided by The Variety Theatre built the summer of 1878. The "Varieties" as it was known, had the distinction of being one of the first houses of entertainment in Dodge City to present the Can-Can. As exciting as this was, the Varieties was not successful and closed before the end of the summer. During the same summer, Ben Springer rented the structure and renovated it with a stage and scenery. While Springer's other establishment, the Comique catered to the cattlemen trade, this new venue known as Hoover Hall sought a more refined clientele. This structure is no longer standing.

In 1879 a large two-story frame building, 30 by 80 feet, was constructed at the corner of First and Front Street by James "Dog" Kelley. The first floor housed a restaurant, saloon and barbershop. The opera house and meeting hall were located on the second floor. This structure, known as Kelley's Opera House and the Opera House saloon.

In November 1885, a fire that apparently began with an oil lamp, consumed the heart of the business district including the opera house. Jim Kelley rebuilt his Opera House at a cost of $20,000. In an 1891 ad for the opera house it was reported to be a "house in fine condition, lighted with electricity." Later, during depressed economic times, Kelley sold the structure to Adolphus Gluck, a jeweler, for $3,800. Gluck operated the opera house from 1898 until it burned in 1912. This structure was rebuilt and is still standing as commercial space and apartments.

Another entertainment facility was built in 1884 by Dr. T. L. McCarty, The McCarty Skating Rink and Opera House contained a 100' x 300' maple wood floor with no pillars to obstruct the skating. The first stage performance to appear in the new structure was the Alice Wilson Opera Company's presentation of Gilbert and Sullivan's "H.M.S. Pinafore." This skating rink/theatre is no longer standing.

Music was a very important source of entertainment on the frontier. In 1878 a fund-raising drive was conducted to secure money to purchase instruments for the Dodge City Silver Cornet Band. In 1880 the organization changed its name to the Dodge City Cowboy Band. Chalk Beeson was the driving force behind this band. Between 1884 and 1888 it performed at stockmen's conventions in Denver, Kansas City, St. Louis and even went on tour and was eventually invited to Washington, D. C. to participate in the inaugural festivities for Benjamin Harrison in March of 1889. The cowboy band disbanded in 1890.

In 1915, Merritt and Otie Beeson constructed the Chalk Beeson Theatre at a cost of $40,000, as a memorial to their father. The theatre, which opened December 15, 1915, had a seating capacity of 900 with a stage 21' x 30'. There were four dressing rooms with hot and cold water and showers, boiler room and toilet rooms, orchestra pit, and two storerooms for stage properties. Curtains and murals preserved the atmosphere of pioneer days. The first play presented there was "The Only Girls" and featured a Dodge City girl, Elsie Baird, and despite a raging snowstorm, the theatre opened to a capacity audience.

The advent of motion pictures made it difficult for theatre to survive. It was then converted to motion pictures but was never very successful. Following its use as a movie theatre it was remodeled and boxing matches were held there. In 1935, the building was remodeled in a Spanish motif and divided into retail spaces and the upper part was used as a ballroom. During World War II the building housed an USO facility and after that war it was a snooker room. The building is still standing.[4]

**Dorrance     1916   Reiffs Hall/Opera House          Standing/Stage**

Reiff's Hall, located above Reiff's Store in a large stone building, was constructed some time prior to 1916. This second floor theatre with its original stage and box office, tin ceiling and lighting fixtures is standing. The building containing the theatre is being restored as the Dorrance museum.[5]

**Douglas      1884   Wright's Opera House             NLS**
**             1900   Wright's New Opera House/**
**                    Wright's Opera House             NLS**

In 1884 Levi E. Wright built the original opera house in Douglas. In September of 1900 a fire destroyed this opera house and much of the block in which it was located. Mr. Wright's half-brother, C. M Ranger, then reconstructed the opera house. The new hall was credited with being the finest opera house in Butler County at the time of its construction. Finally, on November 3, 1963, this building was also destroyed by fire.[6]

**Downs        1888   Wolfert's Opera House            Standing**

John Wolfert constructed the opera house in Downs in 1888. The large brick structure had shops on the first floor and the opera house on the second. The hall was used very little after 1912 except for home talent shows, school plays and graduation exercises. Following its use as a theatre, the stage was removed and the space converted to apartments. The structure remains standing.

An interesting announcement appeared in the *Downs Times*, May 17, 1894, "A special policeman has been appointed to do duty at the opera house at all public gatherings. Those who have been annoying the speakers and audience by their rude behavior will be ejected and dealt with according to law." Popular entertainments to appear in Downs were "Uncle Tom's Cabin" and ventriloquists.[7]

**Dresden      1900   IOOF Hall                        NLS**

During the latter part of the nineteenth century, private homes and the schoolhouse in Dresden were used for meeting places and for entertainment. Around 1900 the Odd Fellows bought a hall and the upper story was used by several orders, including the KKK, school and church people. This structure is no longer standing.

# E

**Edgerton     1904   Grange Hall/Community Hall       Standing**
**             1917   Electric Theatre                 UTD**

The Edgerton Grange Hall, constructed in 1904, is standing, but the stage has been removed. In 1917, there was a mention of the Electric Theatre in Edgerton. This might be the Grange Hall, re-named.

**Edmond       1916   Edmond Opera House               NLS**

The John G. Rae company opened the Edmond Opera House, located on the north side of Main Street behind the Stickney Store, on November 23, 1916. The Edmond Opera House was a ground-floor theatre seating 250 with a good piano, electric lights and comfortable opera chairs. The scenery was from the Jessie Cox company in Esterville, Iowa. Unfortunately, this theatre is no longer standing.

Other acts appearing at the Edmond Opera House during its first year included the Garrett Stock Company, Ida Weston Rae, and McCann's "Western Girl." In later years the Neal Show Troupe from Lenora appeared there. During the week the structure was used for roller-skating and sometimes for dances. The building was torn down in the 1920s.[8]

**Edna         1912   Opera House                      NLS**

The Edna Opera House, constructed in 1912, was a tin and wood frame building. For 30 years it was the location of many activities. The building was razed in 1943.[9]

**Effingham    1885   City Hall                        NLS**
**             1895   Woodman Hall                     NLS**

Neither the 1885 City Hall nor the Woodman Hall remains standing. The building housing the Woodman Hall was built by that organization in 1895. The hall was also used as an opera house and rented to groups for dances, dinners, and skating parties.[10]

**El Dorado    1882   Ellet's New Opera House          Standing**
**             1918   Belmont Theatre                  UTD**
**             1921   El Dorado Theatre                Standing/Stage**

Built in 1884, Ellet's Opera House is still standing. The second floor opera house is vacant, without a stage, and is located in a building now occupied by an insurance company. The theatre was named for its builder, an important El Dorado Civil War hero, Alfred W. Ellet. Ellet and his son, Edward, along with Nathan Frank Frazier organized what later became known as the Farmers and Merchants Bank. The Ellets were also responsible for the Florence, El Dorado and Walnut Valley Railroad, later a part of the Santa Fe system, that was built though El Dorado in 1883.

Ellet's Opera House seated 600, had a 19' x 43' stage, was heated by stoves and illuminated by electricity. It was 22' to the rigging loft. In 1913, the theatre was advertised as being thoroughly renovated and was named the Lyric Theatre. The renovation included new curtains, new electric lights, and a fine carpet in the aisles, lobby and stairways. Beautiful panels adorned the walls and the lobby was paneled in green and burlap. The renovated theatre was intended to show moving pictures and to offer high-class vaudeville. The *Walnut Valley Times* of January 9, 1913, advertised, "The Cottie Trio — A high class vaudeville — will open the theatre. Three reels of first run pictures will be shown."

El Dorado was an oil boom town and this was good news for theatrical company managers because it meant that the population had money to spend. E. W. Brice, a former theatrical company manager who settled in El Dorado reported that, "the city of Oil and let me tell you folks something: this is some oil town. There are two houses here playing tab shows and vaudeville with change of bills twice a week to mighty big business."

A 1916 theatrical trade paper announced that the Munson Brothers of El Dorado were going to build a ground-floor theatre housed in a three-story structure 120' x 50'. Whether the theatre lived up to its initial plans is not known, but the 1918 *El Dorado City Directory* listed the Belmont Theatre located at 124 W. Central managed by Elmer Munson. The building is no longer standing or has been altered to the point that it is not recognizable. The Belmont Theatre appeared in the 1923 and 1929 directories with its name changed to the Palace Theatre, but was not listed in the 1935 directory.

The El Dorado Theatre, constructed adjacent to the El Dorado Hotel, opened in 1921. Originally serving as a vaudeville theatre, this facility was converted to a moving picture theatre and remained in business until 1969. In recent years it has housed a variety of functions. The theatre is standing and contains its original stage.[11]

**Elgin        1907   Elgin Opera House                NLS**

The Elgin Opera House, reported in the 1907 theatrical directory, is no longer standing. The opera house had seating for 500, a stage 12' x 20', and was lighted by gas. This theatre was probably a second floor performance space.

| Elk | 1910 | Woodmen Hall | NLS |

Constructed in 1910, the Woodmen Hall was destroyed by fire in 1923. Nothing remains of the community.

| Elk City | 1889 | Noland's Rink/Opera House | NLS |
| | 1907 | AOWL Hall | NLS |
| | 1910 | Star Theatre/Opera House | NLS |

In 1889 Noland's Rink with a seating capacity of 600 was located In Elk City. This rink was used as an opera house during the summer season. This structure is no longer standing. The 1907 AOWL Hall, with a seating capacity of 300, a stage 5' x 25' and gas lighting, is also no longer standing. The final reference to a performance space in Elk City was a 1910 report that the, "Star theatre, a movie house, was made over to be an opera house as well…" This theatre is no longer standing.[12]

| Elk Falls | 1871 | Hall | NLS |
| | 1889 | Hull's Hall | NLS |

The first public entertainment space in Elk Falls, a two-story frame building, was built by F. Bloodgood in 1871. This structure is no longer standing. In 1889 Elk Falls had one performance space, Hull's Hall. This structure, that might have been the same as the 1871 Hall, is no longer standing.[13]

| Elkhart | 1916 | ? | UTD |
| | 1918 | Doric Theatre | Standing |

A reference to Elkhart is contained in a 1916 theatrical trade paper account of a troupe's appearance in Elkhart. There was no reference to the specific location of the performance. In 1918, the Doric Theatre was built as a combination vaudeville house and movie theatre. When talking moving pictures became popular the theatre was renovated and no longer used for live performances. It has since been gutted.[14]

| Ellinwood | 1874 | Maniker Hall | Standing |
| | 1886 | Rotzel Opera House | Standing |
| | 1888 | Rohlfing Opera House | Standing |
| | 1889 | G.A.R. Hall | UTD |
| | 1889 | Kimpler's Hall | UTD |
| | 1891 | Mangelsdorf Brothers Opera House | NLS |

Ellinwood was the location of a number of performance spaces, some with stages, some that probably never had stages. The 1874 Maniker Hall was built by German settlers. This space, used primarily for dances, does not have a stage. The building is standing, but not in use. The 1886 Rotzel Opera House is standing without a stage. It was an IOOF Hall. The 1888 Rohlfing Opera House is also standing without a stage. Its last use was as apartments. These two structures were both second floor performance spaces located above businesses. No information is available on the 1889 G.A.R. Hall or the 1889 Kimpler's Hall. It is doubtful that either of these buildings is standing.

Ellinwood's major opera house, the Mangelsdorf Brothers Opera House, opened in 1891. The Mangelsdorf brothers had a long history as merchandisers in Ellinwood. They purchased their first store in 1877 and then built two, two-story brick buildings, one that contained the opera house. The entire structure was known as the Opera House Block. The Mangelsdorf Brothers Opera House was destroyed by fire.[15]

| Ellis | 1889 | G.A.R. Hall | NLS |
| | 1889 | Opera House | NLS |
| | 1909 | Ellis Opera House | Standing |
| | | (Opera House portion removed) | |

Ellis was the home of three performance spaces. The 1889 G.A.R. Hall and the 1889 Opera House are no longer standing. The first floor of the 1909 Ellis Theatre is standing, but the second and third floors that contained the opera house were removed in the 1937.

The Grand Army Hall, built by Civil War veterans and located on Jefferson Street, was a popular spot to hold dances. This ground floor hall with seating for 550 contained a 20' x 40' stage. In 1889 a second performance space in Ellis, the Opera House, was listed in a theatrical guide. This structure that seated 400 with a stage 16' x 48' was located in a two-story frame building decorated with a cornice-trimmed gable. The facility was destroyed by fire some time between 1904 and 1909.

Constructed in 1909 at a cost of $33,000, the Ellis Opera House opened on April 11, 1909, with the Barrie Stock Company's presentation of "St. Elmo." This second and third floor opera house was quite lavish. The ceiling, which is now the ceiling of the remaining one-story building, was made of tin with a theatrical mask design.

The opera house stage curtain was the replica of the famous paining, "The Spirit of '76" with a drummer, fife player and flag bearer. Entrance to the theatre was gained by going up a wide staircase at the back of the building. Midway up the stairs was a landing where the tickets were sold. The lobby was located on the second floor with a stairway leading to the third floor balcony. Seating on the first floor of the theatre was on wooden chairs that could be removed and stacked against the walls if space was needed to hold a dance. The theatre seated 700 with a stage 30' x 40' feet.

Over the course of the years, numerous companies performed in the Ellis Opera House. Some of these included the North Brothers, the Wallace Bruce Players, Blind Boone and even the Ziegfield Follies.[16]

| Ellsworth | 1873 | Ellsworth Theatre/McClellan and Freeman Opera House | NLS |
| | 1889 | Masonic Temple Opera House | Standing |
| | 1889 | Jackson's Opera House | UTD |
| | 1904 | Ellsworth Opera House | NLS |

Ellsworth was the home of three, or possibly four, opera houses, however, the first entertainment in Ellsworth occurred not at an opera house, but at the Drovers' Cottage. Late in February of 1873, the Sixth Cavalry soldiers from Fort Harker came to Ellsworth and put on a play at the Drovers' Cottage. Later the same year, a theatre was built that provided entertainment for the Texas cowboys. It was a one-story frame structure operated by McClellan, Freeman and Company. Talent came from St. Joseph, Kansas City and St. Louis. The entertainment included plays, dancing and singing. The McClellan and Freeman Opera House was a low one-story building 75 by 20 feet. The room was unplastered and unpainted except for the proscenium arch and the drop curtain. The stage was at the opposite end of the building from the entrance and plain pine benches offered seating for 150. At the right of the entrance was a bar and at the left was a monte gambling table. To the left of the stage was the box where the gaily decorated and dashing "ladies" were seated. This early theatre is no longer standing.

The next reference to theatres in Ellsworth came from an 1889 theatrical guide. This publication listed two theatres, the Masonic Temple Opera House and Jackson's Opera House. The Masonic Temple Opera House had a seating capacity somewhere between 300 and 600. The stage was approximately 18' x 30'. This opera house may still be standing. The current Masonic Hall is located on the second floor of what was originally the Williams Block. A long time Ellsworth resident reported that at this time the Masonic Hall does not contain a stage, but at one time it did.

The second theatre listed in the 1889 theatrical guide was the Jackson Opera House with a seating capacity of 600 and a stage 13' x 38'. Nothing further is known concerning this theatre. A fourth theatre in Ellsworth was the Ellsworth Opera House. The Ellsworth Opera House was a first floor theatre with a seating capacity of 400 and a stage 20' x 30'. Illumination was provided by electricity. This theatre is also no longer standing.[17]

| Emporia | 1871 | Bancroft Hall/Jay's Opera House | NLS |
| | 1878 | Eskridge Hall | UTD |
| | 1882 | Whitley Opera House | NLS |

Emporia was the home to several performance spaces, none of which remains standing. The first reported performance space was Bancroft Hall. The actress Louie Lord opened this third floor facility in 1871. This was the same space that in 1879 was known as Jay's Opera House. Located at 503 Commercial, the opera house seated 600 and contained a stage 18' x 24' with four scenes and a curtain. Jay's Opera House was not large enough to attract many traveling companies and was used mostly for Home Talent productions and lodge entertainments. In 1878 there was a reference in a theatrical guide to Eskridge Hall with a seating capacity of 250. Nothing else is known about this facility.

For years Emporia was known as "the Athens of Kansas," a phrase attributed to William Allen White. The Whitley Opera House, built by a stock company headed by H. C. Whitley, was certainly one of the major reasons for this distinction. The opera house opened January 30, 1882, with a national touring company production of "Fanchon or Cricket on the Hearth." In addition to its other amenities, the Whitley Opera House was lighted with gas, and was probably the first public building in Emporia to use that type of illumination. This illumination was provided by a 24-light chandelier that hung from the dome and by 12 double bracket lights hanging above and below the balcony area, all with cut glass globes. Electricity was added in 1910.

The Whitley Opera House stage was 36' x 60'. The house could accommodate an audience of 1000 giving it, according to Emporia accounts, the largest seating capacity of any theatre in the state at that time. The theatre was heated with hot air, which allowed the fumes from the gas lights to be carried away. Originally, the opera house seats were placed on the level and not attached to the auditorium floor, but after a month the chairs were placed on successive rises in order to improve the sight lines.

There were two entrances to the opera house, one on Sixth Avenue used by the actors and one on Merchant Street used by the audience. This entrance had double doors that led to a stairway to the second floor where the entrance to the auditorium was located. A circular-shaped ticket booth was located in the southeast corner of the lobby and the northeast corner contained a stairway that led to the balcony on the third level. Wainscoting lined the stairways, entrance area and back and sides of the auditorium.

The scene curtain was green with advertisements for local businesses. At the bottom a large advertisement read, "Cuss the *Gazette*, but read it." This slogan also appeared in the Whitley programs because William Allen White, editor of the *Gazette*, was fond of it.

After 17 years of service, the Whitley Opera House was renovated in 1897. The *Emporia Daily Republic* described the lavish additions.

> The walls have been frescoed a beautiful pink that is restful to the eye and a harmonizing background to all decorations. The balcony front is painted a delicate green with the panels pink; the boxes are in corresponding colors.
>
> But it is the curtain and scenery that have been given the artist's touch. The old style rolling curtain has been done away with and a sliding one put in. It represents a large picture of a rolling lake shore set in a heavy gilt frame, around and above which is a rich red plush, artistically draped with gold cord.

Over the years literally hundreds of performances took place at the Whitley including "Oliver Twist," "Camille," "Pygmalion," "Romeo and Juliet," "East Lynne," "Henry VII," "Hamlet," "Uncle Tom's Cabin," "The Mikado," "The White Slave," "A Wonderful Woman" and "A Member of Congress." Famous performers who appeared there included Joseph Jefferson and the Shakespearean actors Charles Hanford and Marie Drofnah.

The theatre was also used for other important functions. Public receptions such as the one for Mr. DeBelle, Danish minister to the United States, were held there. The Order of Railway Conductors met at the opera house and bands including Sousa's and the Royal Canadian Band appeared there. In 1889 the first annual commencement exercise of the Lyon County Schools was held at the Whitley Opera House. In addition to commencements, the stage was used for local productions such as the Elk minstrel shows.

Described as "one of the most destructive fires in the history of Emporia," the Whitley Opera House was destroyed on Wednesday, June 18, 1913. The loss totaled $40,000. It is a sad irony that as a result of this fire the City Commissioners of Emporia decide that a paid fire department had become a necessity for the safeguarding of Emporia.[18]

**Englewood**     1910     ?     NLS

The opera house in Englewood was razed a number of years ago.

**Enterprise**     1870s     Enterprise Opera House/
                           Buhrer's Opera House     NLS
                  ?         Koch's Theatorium     UTD

The Enterprise opera house, constructed in the 1870s, was known as Buhrer's Opera House. The auditorium seated 300 with a stage 20' x 40' feet. This was a second floor theatre located in a brick structure built by J. F. Buhrer. A hardware store was located on the main floor. The structure was razed in 1994 because portions of it had collapsed the previous winter. In addition to the opera house, mention has been made to Koch's "Theatorium" where stock companies presented plays and musicals, and to an Air Dome, an outdoor movie theatre that was operated for several summers by Roy Williams. No further information is available concerning the Theatorium and it is assumed to be no longer standing.[19]

**Erie**     1908     Erie Opera House     NLS

The Erie Opera House, constructed in 1908, was an excellent example of a fairly elaborate second and third floor theatre. The auditorium seated 700 and featured a horseshoe balcony. Molded plaster ornamentation surrounded the proscenium arch. The stage, 25' x 28', contained one trap door. A small heater was located back stage to provide some warmth in the winter. The box office was located at the top of the stairs next to the doors leading into the auditorium.[20]

**Esbon**     1908     Opera House     NLS

The Esbon Opera House, constructed in either 1905 or 1908, is no longer standing. The Methodist congregation held services there until the completion of their church in 1909.

**Eskridge**     1907     Woodmen Opera House     Standing

In 1907, the Woodman Hall in Eskridge also functioned as the opera house. The two-story stone building contained a second floor theatre with a stage 16' x 30' and seating for 350. Heat was provided by stoves and illumination by gas. Entrance to the facility was by an outside stairway. The building remains standing, but there is no stage.

**Eudora**     1907     Lothholz Opera House     Standing/Stage

In existence in 1907, the Lothholz Opera House was located at the corner of 7th and Main above the Kaw Valley State Bank. The building is standing and the opera house portion contains its original stage. The space is currently in use as an apartment. In its opera house days the community uses included Lyceums and Chautauquas, school programs, and graduations. School and public dances were held in this facility until the 1950s, and silent movies were also shown there prior to the construction of a motion picture theatre.[21]

**Eureka**     1883     Eureka Opera House     Standing
              ?        ?     UTD

Eureka is the home to one, and possibly two, standing opera houses. Neither has a stage. The first opera house, constructed in 1883, was a second floor facility that has been converted to apartments. The second opera house, if it is standing, is in use as a grocery store. The 1883 second floor Eureka Opera House had a seating capacity of 600 with a stage 20' x 42' and a piano.[22]

**Everest**     1885     Clevenger's Hall/Clevenger's
                          Opera House/City Hall     UTD
              1916     ?     UTD

There are references to two performance facilities in Everest. It is doubtful that either of these remains. It is likely that Clevenger's Hall, Clevenger's Opera House and City Hall all with a seating capacity of 200, were the same facility. A 1916 reference may or may not be the same facility. It is not known if any of these is standing.

# F

**Fairview**     1916     City Hall     NLS

The Fairview City Hall, an attractive one-story wooden structure, is no longer standing.

**Fall River**     1885     Wade's Opera House     UTD
                1889     Grand Opera House     NLS
                ?         Connell's Hall     UTD
                ?         Brown's Hall     UTD

There are references to several performance spaces in Fall River, but very little is known about their current disposition. In an 1885 theatrical guide mention was made to Wade's Opera House with a seating of 500 managed by J. S. Wade. It is assumed that this structure is no longer standing. The Grand Opera House, first listed in an 1889 theatrical guide seated 1,000 in chairs, had a stage 30' x 50' with ten scenes and a piano, and is no longer standing.

A local history reported, "Plays were presented at the Opera House, in the Brown Building and Connell's Hall.... Traveling entertainers provided most of the talent. The most famous was Blind Boone, the noted pianist."[1] There is a possibility that one of the previously mentioned buildings is standing. A Fall River resident indicated that a one-story stone building on Main Street had once been an opera house.

| Florence | 1884 | Florence Opera House | Standing |
|---|---|---|---|

The Florence Opera House, constructed in 1883 at a cost of between $14,000 and $15,000, opened January 24, 1884. This three-story stone structure contained a first floor dry goods store. Offices were located at the front of the second floor. The remainder of the second and third floors contained the opera house. The Louie Lord Dramatic Company opened the theatre with the play, "The Linwood Case." The structure was destroyed by fire and rebuilt twice, once in 1891, and again in 1894. The building was closed to show presentations in 1917. After that it was used for motion pictures. This impressive stone building with the word "OPERA" chiseled on the cornice is still standing. The stage has been removed.

During its use as an opera house, the facility seated 650. The stage was 50' x 25' with five scenes and a piano. Heat was provided by steam and lamps supplied the illumination.

"Uncle Tom's Cabin" was one the best remember plays of the period, but one performance in Florence was especially noteworthy. During the presentation a donkey kicked over the footlights and oil ran over the floor and back of the stage. This oil then ignited and the resulting fire spread rapidly. It was extinguished but not before one of the men trying to put out the flames under the stage almost landed in the dry goods store below when the floor gave way. Following this experience, a barrel of water, buckets and blankets were kept handy back stage in case of another fire.[2]

| Fort Riley | 1870 | Theatre | NLS |
|---|---|---|---|
| | 1880s | Auditorium | NLS |
| | 1910 | Post Gymnasium | NLS |

An early Kansas theatre was located at Fort Riley. The March 19, 1870, *Union* reported on the accomplishments of a group of soldiers, "After much labor and unceasing energy, success has crowned their efforts in the erection of a fine spacious theatrical hall, a credit to any town or city east of us of 30 times the population."

The frame structure was 135' long and 68' wide. The stage was 60' x 65' and the auditorium seated 800. The cost of the building and scenery was $6,000. The performers were reported to include Mrs. Tannehill and Miss Alice Raymond, both from the Boston Theatre, and 12 members of the theatre association. The opening night production was "The Gentleman from Ireland." Barry's band from the city provided the music. Both the theatre and its performers were greatly appreciated by the community surrounding Fort Riley.

This theatre was in existence for about a year until the school of instruction for Light Artillery was discontinued and the Batteries distributed to their respective headquarters. On March 11, 1871, the following notice appeared in the *Union*, "The Fort Riley Theatre, with scenery and furniture, will be sold at auction by Booth and Kennedy, on Wednesday the 15th. Those wishing to make a safe investment should not lose this opportunity."

The next attempt to bring drama to Fort Riley occurred in November 1871 when a company of fourteen enlisted men of the Sixth Cavalry was organized as the "Sixth Cavalry Dramatic Association." The theatre opened with the "Golden Framer" in January 1872. This theatre, located in one of the old gun sheds formerly used by the artillery, lasted for two months. After the 1880s, performances by amateur groups and minstrel troupes were given in the mess hall and the auditorium, which later was used as the library.[3] In the early part of the 20th century performances took place in the Post Gymnasium. The stage was 30' x 60' and the auditorium seated 1,000. This structure, along with the 1880's auditorium, is no longer standing.

| Fort Scott | 1863 | City Hall | NLS |
|---|---|---|---|
| | 1865 | McDonald Hall | Standing |
| | 1875 | Davidson's Opera House/Patterson's Opera House/Davidson's Theatre | Standing |
| | 1900 | Convention Hall | NLS |

Fort Scott had a long history of theatrical entertainment. The second floor of City Hall, built in 1863, was used as a court house and when the court was not in session, for a variety of other purposes including political meetings, religious services, convention caucuses and amateur dramatic club performances. Local actors produced shows that ranged from "Black-eyed Susan" to "Hamlet." This structure is no longer standing.

McDonald Hall, a stone building constructed in 1865, is standing, but the stage has been removed and the second floor has been converted to apartments. In 1869 McDonald Hall was fitted with new chairs, three chandeliers and eight side lamps, and as a local paper reported, "It is now one of the best halls in the state." The first time this structure was referred to as being used as a theatre was after the arrival of the railroad in 1869. *The Monitor* of January 16, 1870, reported that the National Theatre Company had arrived the night before and that the theatre company would open Monday night at McDonald's Hall

There may have been public objection to the moral character of the theatre because the management offered a Saturday afternoon Family Matinee for women and children. Assurance was given that they, the theatre company, would "confine themselves strictly within the limits of legitimate drama, and no need stay away…on that point." One objection seemed to be its location. A bar was located at or near the entrance to the hall and the patrons of the show had to "run the gauntlet" of patrons of the bar. In addition, were the odors of tobacco smoke, alcoholic liquor and the "assemblage of obnoxious characters" who gathered at the bar.

In 1870 the newspaper reported on the state of entertainment in Fort Scott.

> Fort Scott just now has a varied and liberal variety in the amusement line. The 'Opera House' presents its peculiar attractions nightly: the Wizard Oil men hold forth daily and nightly at the street corners — and their performances are by no means the least pleasing of the catalogue; the Stereopticon is setting the children wild with delight at McDonalds Hall; Orton's Circus pitched their pavilion here on Friday; the Nationals will revisit us next week, and we shall have the fascinating and eloquent Olive Logan with her 'Girls' on the 25th.

Thanks to the convenience of the railroad and the enthusiasm of Captain George J. Clark, Freight Agent of the Gulf Railroad, Opera House Excursions were organized. The first occurred in November of 1870. The excursion train left Fort Scott on Wednesday at 1:30 p.m. arrived in Kansas City in time for supper, then a theatre performance at the Coats Opera House. The return train left Kansas City at 11:30 p.m., which meant arrival in Fort Scott about daylight Thursday. The cost was $2.50 for a round trip railroad ticket, Kansas City transportation, supper and theatre ticket. During the 1871-1872 season, four excursions were arranged.

Captain Clark not only organized theatrical excursions to Kansas City, he also organized the locals into an amateur theatrical group. This troupe was first known as the "Egotistical Dramatic Club" which was shortened to the "Egotisticals." The group was formed in 1873. During the 1873-1874 season performances were at McDonald Hall. There "Kansas in '56," an original drama by T. F. Robley, was produced. *The Monitor* described this play, "…as a true picture of Kansas life during the most exciting and dramatic period of her history — the time of border forays, when were waged upon Kansas soil the first bloody conflicts of the slaveholder's rebellion."

The major opera house of Fort Scott, Davidson's Opera House, formally opened January 1, 1875. The opera house was converted to apartments a number of years ago, but the building remains standing. When constructed, the theatre occupied the second and third floors of the building. The seating capacity was 700 and the stage was 25' x 30'. There were sixteen scenes on flats and a furnace provided heat. The floor was level and when not in use as a theatre its chairs were moved and the space was used for other activities. The opening night play was "The Fireman," performed by a local cast. In 1886 the theatre owners, the Chenaults, remodeled the opera house. At that time the stage was enlarged to 36' x 50', the floor of the auditorium was elevated three feet in the rear, and seating was increased to 900. A final remodeling occurred in 1902.

From 1892 until 1912 the theatre was managed by Harry Ernich who visited New York City at least once a year to book acting companies. In addition to plays and concerts, the opera house was used for a variety of other activities including speeches, high school entertainments and the Elk's Minstrels. Typical of the fate of other opera houses, the advent of movies was the major cause for closing the opera house. It ended operation in 1915, exactly 40 years after its gala opening.

On May 5, 1900, Fort Scott's Convention Hall was opened. This large three-story frame building contained a stage 18' x 56'. The auditorium had two galleries, one of which extended around three sides of the structure, the other across the back of the hall. Seating in the galleries was on benches, while patrons on the main floor sat on folding chairs. The seating capacity was 3,000. The Convention Hall is no longer standing.[4]

| Fowler | 1916 | Opera House | NLS |

The opera house in Fowler was a second floor theatre located above the Fowler State Bank. This structure was razed in 1973 and replaced by a new one-story bank.

| Frankfort | 1869 | ? | NLS |
| | 1870 | Brady and Davis Hall | UTD |
| | 1870 | Sentinel Hall | UTD |
| | 1873 | Newell Hall | UTD |
| | 1889 | Opera House | Standing |
| | 1894 | Anderson Hall | UTD |
| | 1900 | Weiss Opera House | Standing |
| | 1917 | Royal Theatre | Standing |

Frankfort was the home to a number of halls and performance spaces. The first hall was located over the Sullivan House, a hotel. This structure was in existence in 1869. About 1870 the Brady and Davis Hall was built. Another hall, Sentinel Hall, was also built in 1870. This hall was the site of numerous dances and social functions, and the 1888 and 1889 high school graduation exercises were held there. Newell's Hall, the first actual theatre in Frankfort, was built in 1873. Finally, Olaf Anderson built a hall in 1894. It is likely that these halls were all large rooms over commercial building. It is not known whether any of these structures remain.

The Frankfort Opera House, built in 1889 by C. C. Mason, is a stone building that is standing vacant without its stage. The downstairs rooms of this structure were used for mercantile purposes and the second floor for the opera house. There was a large stage built across the south end of the auditorium. The Sterling Comedy Company opened the theatre on November 28, 1889. A grand ball was held after the opening performance. After the Weiss Opera House was built, the Frankfort Opera House was converted to a Lodge Hall.

The Weis Opera House, built in 1900 by Charles Weis, was reported to have been one of the finest in that part of the state. This structure is standing vacant, without a stage. Over the years the Weiss Opera House was an important public structure providing the community with a location for entertainment and meetings. Events included school plays, commencement exercises, Home Talent Plays, Blind Boone's piano performances, and plays such as "Rip Van Winkle," "East Linn," "Dr. Jekyll and Mr. Hyde" and "Way Down East."

Community events held at the opera house included political rallies, Booster meetings, Liberty Loan Drives, Memorial Day programs and band concerts. The auditorium of the opera house had a fine polished floor that was used for dances. Also, prior to churches having dining rooms, church suppers were served in the Opera House. In order to facilitate this, a kitchen was set up in the west end of the hall. This necessitated carrying oil stoves, dishes, tables, food and water up to the second floor room. "Nero and the Burning of Rome" was the first major moving picture shown at the Weiss Opera House. This occurred in 1903. The opera house continued in use for a number of years as a moving picture theatre.

The final theatre in Frankfort where live performances occurred was the Royal Theatre. In 1917, Mr. and Mrs. Hardman purchased a stone building and renovated it for use as a motion picture theatre, but touring theatrical companies also performed there. This building is standing vacant, without a stage.[5]

| Fredonia | 1885 | G.A.R. Hall | UTD |
| | 1889 | Willett's Opera House | Standing |
| | 1889 | Blume's Hall | UTD |
| | 1889 | Hudson's Opera House | NLS |

Several halls were located in Fredonia prior to the construction of Hudson's Opera House in 1889. The first of these was the G.A.R. Hall with a seating capacity of 200 listed in 1885 and 1889 theatrical guides. The second public space was Willett's Opera House with a seating capacity of 1,500, and finally, Blume's Hall, seating capacity of 750. None of these facilities appears in any guide published after 1889. Nothing is known about the disposition of the G.A.R. Hall or Blume's Hall, but it is assumed that they are no longer standing. Willett's Opera House, a second floor facility above Hollis Hardware is standing vacant.

Hudson's Opera House, opened in 1889, had a seating capacity of 600 with 400 parquet chairs. The stage was 30' x 60' with a proscenium opening 24' high. Natural gas and electricity provided heating and illumination. Such favorites as "East Lynn," "St. Elmo" and "Ten Nights in a Bar Room" were seen in the Hudson Opera House. The class of 1914 was the last class to graduate from the stage of the opera house. This structure was razed in 1990 following its partial collapse.

Another location for entertainment was a lot at the Northwest corner of the square where the Dubinsky Brothers would to bring their 10 and 20 cent tent show in the summer.[6]

| Freeport | 1889 | Odd-Fellow's Hall | NLS |

An 1889 theatrical guide contained a reference to an Odd Fellow's Hall that seated 500. This structure is no longer standing.

| Frontenac | 1918 | Miners Opera House | NLS |

The name of the opera house in Frontenac, located close to Pittsburg, was a reflection of the chief occupation of the region, coal mining. The Miner's Opera House was located above the Miner's Hall. This structure was destroyed by fire a number of years ago.

| Fulton | 1889 | Dail's Hall/Fulton Rink Hall | NLS |

The only reference to a performance space in Fulton was found in an 1889 theatrical guide. Dail's Hall with a seating capacity is no longer standing.

# G

| Galena | 1883 | Galena Opera House | UTD |
| | 1900 | Sapp's New Theatre | NLS |

An entry in an 1889 theatrical guide credited Galena with being "the most prosperous mining district in the West, and a good place for a good troupe." The Galena Opera House, first mentioned in an 1883 theatrical guide, had a seating capacity of 500 chairs, a stage 20' x 26', "fine scenery" and a piano. It is not known what became of this structure.

Edward E. Sapp, an attorney and ex-probate judge built a second opera house, much larger than the first. He erected the Opera House Block in 1900 to house his law offices and the opera house. This opera house, a second floor facility, with a seating capacity of 900, and a stage 47' by 36' was destroyed by fire in 1931.

The most interesting pieces of information about a performance in Galena concerned the magician, Harry Houdini. Like most performers, Houdini kept a record of his performances. An early diary entry contained a reference to his appearance in Galena in January of 1898. From the entry we know that spiritualism was part of the performance because of a notation, "Spiritualism $86." The entry continued, "Bus. Fine Played to about $700 on 8 shows. 75/25." The latter was a reference to the profit split between the performers and management.[7]

| Garden City | 1886 | Stevens Opera House | NLS |

The Stevens Opera House, constructed by John A. Stevens in 1886 was an outstanding example of theatre architecture. Stevens did not enter into the venture for profit, but rather as a community project. The building was three stories high with a 50-foot freeze. The theatre was located on the second and third floors. Two businesses occupied the ground floor. A six-foot wide stairway, located between the two stores, led to the opera house ticket booth. From there entrances on either side of the ticket booth led to the auditorium. The entrance on the right of the ticket booth led to another flight of stairs and the gallery on the third floor, while the entrance on the left opened into the auditorium's main floor.

At the time of its opening in 1886 a local newspaper described the interior of the opera house indicating that its "walls are profusely frescoed and ornamental with fine sculptured work." The proscenium arch was framed with four private boxes. The red drapes on the boxes matched the upholstery on the chairs and the act curtain. The main floor seated 370 while the circular gallery seated 120 with bench seating. Illumination was provided by gas. Gas lights lined the gallery, box seats and both side walls of the auditorium. There was also a large gas chandelier suspended from the auditorium ceiling. The building was heated with steam and as was necessary due to the gas lights, ventilated by windows located high up on both sides of the auditorium.

The Stevens Opera House boasted a stage 50' x 50' with a 22-foot proscenium opening. The act curtain was a red velvet-like material. There was also a traditional drop curtain that advertised local merchants. Like the auditorium, the stage was lighted by gas that provided footlights and overhead illumination. The seating capacity was 800. Scenery for the opera house, purchased from the L. P. Culberson Company of Kansas City, cost approximately $800.

Bad weather caused a unique, impromptu performance to occur in Garden City. A late winter storm in March of 1912 stranded a train in Garden City. The train was carrying the Three Twins Company so the manager of the opera house persuaded the manager of the Three Twins Company to put on a play at the opera house. The snow storm had everyone stranded so the Garden City residents wanted something to do and the actors needed some way to make up for their missed performance in Dodge City, so a great time was had by all. Tickets were sold to everyone on the stranded train and the manager of the telephone company had his operators call every home in town. Within a few hours a show was presented to a packed house.

The builder, Stevens, was forced to sell the opera house in 1893. It passed through several hands and 1929 was converted to a commercial property. It is no longer standing.[8]

**Garfield** ? ? NLS

Nothing is known about the opera house in Garfield except that it no longer exists.

**Garland** 1916 Grand NLS

The one reference to a performance space in Garland was found in a 1916 theatrical trade paper. The manager of the Grand theatre reported playing the Ida Weston Rae Company at 50 cents to $444. There were 10 people in the company and they traveled with special scenery. The Grand is no longer standing.

**Garnett** 1871 Stouch and Vreeland Hall/
　　　　　　　　Stouch's Hall/ Stouch Opera House/
　　　　　　　　Garnett Opera House/Wagstaff's
　　　　　　　　Opera House NLS
　　　　　1884 New Opera House/Grand Army
　　　　　　　　Opera House/Grand Opera House NLS

The first reference to the Stouch and Vreeland Hall in Garnett occurred in the January 5, 1871, *Garnett Plaindealer*. "The new hall, just completed by our enterprising citizens Messrs. Stouch and Vreeland, was dedicated on last Friday night by the proprietors. A large and elegant party of ladies and gentlemen assembled therein to 'trip the light fantastic toe.' It was the grand occasion of the season. The guests, in addition to the dancing, were entertained by a troupe of minstrels, composed of a number of our own citizens."

The hall, lighted by chandeliers, was 60' long by 25' wide with a stage 20' x 14' with dressing rooms on either side and seated 400. In 1881 the stage was extended to the width of the hall and new chairs and dressing rooms were added.

In 1884 William Wagstaff and Dr. Pilkington purchased the hall with Wagstaff acting as manager, and the name changed to the Garnett Opera House or Wagstaff Hall. In 1892 the Wagstaff Hall was reported to be out of show business with Company G purchasing the scenery and other paraphernalia and placing it in the armory. This hall is no longer standing.

Veterans of the Civil War built the Grand Army Hall, later known as the Opera House, in 1884. This beautiful facility stood on the north side of the Garnett Square near the east end of the block. It was a large second-story theatre above commercial spaces. The stage was located on the west side of the large room and a balcony was built across the east side. The audience area had removable seats. A small stairway on the west side of the building lead to the stage area and a wider stairway on the east side led from the sidewalk to the hall.

The local paper carried the following announcement of the theatre's opening.

The Haymakers, an operatic cantata, was presented in the new Opera House last night (October 29th). This performance opened our beautiful structure to the public. The Opera House is lighted with gas from 150-light gas machine. The ventilation of the house is perfect. From the ten-foot ventilator in the ceiling there hangs a twelve-light chandelier. The auditorium is 51 by 70 feet and 25 feet from the floor to the ceiling. The windows on the north and south are eighteen feet high and are set with colored glass. The stage is 26-feet wide and extends across the entire west end of the building. It is open from the floor to the roof. On the west end also are five dressing rooms, the property room and gas room. There are two magnificent drop curtains with scenery to match. The painting of the scenery was done by the L. R. Close Company of Kansas City, and the painting of the auditorium was done by Claire E. Lincoln of this city.

On November 26, 1897, The Great Houdini, while appearing with Dr. Hill's traveling medicine show or the California Concert Company, on their tour of southeastern Kansas, appeared in Garnett at the Opera House. This was early in Houdini's career, and although in later life he fought against spiritualism, when he appeared in Garnett, Houdini gave an emotion filled séance. He later wrote a letter of apology to the bereaved father to whom he had given a supposed message from his recently buried son. It was also in Garnett where Mrs. Houdini, Bess, recalled taking one-year old Buster Keaton to the courthouse park in the afternoons while his parents, also with the company, were rehearsing.

In 1898 the Grand Opera House was overhauled. The gas lights were removed and electricity installed. Prior to this the opera house had its own gas plant. In 1910, a substantial porch was built on the front of the opera house and a fire escape. While never a financial success, the opera house was the location of community events for 40 years. Some of the activities taking place there included high school and grade school graduating exercises, home talent shows and traveling shows, high school dramatic and vocal productions, dances and basketball games.

High school graduations were always very special events. A Garnett resident described one such event, "The senior class decorated the high stage with paper streamers of the class colors and the motto. Each graduate was given a subject, and was required to write an oration and deliver it for the Commencement program." After the ceremony tea or punch was served in a room in the Opera House that was filled with well-wishers.

On February 15, 1924, a fire destroyed this longstanding community resource.[9]

**Gaylord** 1885 City Hall/Meadows' Rink NLS
　　　　　1889 Cowgill's Hall NLS
　　　　　1916 Gaylord Theatre/Opera House UTD

The earliest reference to a performance space in Gaylord occurred in an 1885 theatrical guide. City Hall, also known as Meadows' Rink, had a seating capacity of 400 and a stage 25' x 60'. The next reference to a public hall occurred in an 1889 guide. This was to Cowgill's Hall with a seating capacity of 200. Neither structure is standing.

Although the exact construction date of the Gaylord Theatre or Opera House is not known, there is a record of activities that occurred there because the Gaylord Theatre manager was a regular correspondent to the *Opera House Reporter*, a theatrical trade paper. From the manager's reports, 1916 was a good year for the theatre, but in January of 1917 the following announcement appeared in the *Opera House Reporter*, "Manager Geo. P. Leary of Gaylord, Kan., announces that he will close his opera house for the balance of the season on account of poor business." The final correspondence from manager Leary appeared in the May 24, 1918, *Opera House Reporter*, "The opera house at Gaylord, Kansas, has been turned into a dance hall; the stage has been removed." It is not known what happened to this structure, but it is unlikely that it is still standing.[10]

**Geneseo** 1907 Geneseo Opera House NLS
　　　　　? Geneseo Opera House Standing

The first Geneseo Opera House listed in a 1907 theatrical guide is no longer standing. This structure, located on the northeast corner of Main, contained a stage 16' x 30' with seating for 400 and was heated with stoves and illuminated by lamps. The second Geneseo Opera House is standing vacant without a stage. It is located above the post office.

Kansas Communities | 105

| Girard | 1879 | Painton's Hall/ Painton's OH |
| | | Holtzer Opera House/Swart Hall  Standing |

The first minstrel show to appear in Girard was Foster's Ethiopian Serenades in January 1870. This was a small company that included home talent and was well received. The following year the Girard Dramatic Corps staged a program to raise funds to be used for the children of the Episcopal Sunday School. In 1872 the Union Dramatic Troupe advertised a program of dramas and farces to be held at the Presbyterian Church, but the board of trustees of the church decided against it, and the appearance was canceled.

The first public hall, and the location of many early entertainments, was on the second floor of a brick building on the east side of the square constructed by Thomas Painton in 1879. In 1883 Painton constructed a second building next to the first with a broad stairway between them for entrance to the hall. Other changes were made to improve the convenience of the hall making it 47' x 80'. From 1883 to 1889, theatrical guides listed Painton's Hall and then Painton's Opera House as having a seating capacity of 300. The stage was 16' x 20' with four scenes.

Painton's Hall was the location of many and varied entertainment events. Shortly after its opening in 1880, the Old Settlers supper and dance was held there. And, in 1881, a band of Kaw Indians gave an exhibition. An elaborate event occurred in June of 1886. This was a "Kermis" or church fair, held to raise money for the construction of the new stone Episcopal Church. Also in 1886 the Andrews Opera Company presented the "Mikado" and two years later they returned to perform "Mascott."

The "H. M. S. Pinafore" was presented in 1888 by Girard residents who later took their entire home talent troupe to Weir City for a performance. Then, following the mine explosion at Frontenac, they presented the same program as a benefit for the Frontenac suffers. The Southern Kansas Railway ran a free train to bring people from Pittsburg to attend the performance. The effort was a great success as more than $100 was raised for the sufferers from Frontenac. The hall continued to be the location of interesting productions. In 1892 Susan B. Anthony spoke there, as did Eugene V. Debs in 1900.

The original building housing Painton Hall is standing. What was once the hall is located above a café. The space's last tenant was a bowling alley that is no longer in use. A fire destroyed the second floor of the newer structure.

Like many communities of pre-air-conditioned Kansas, Girard was the location of an Air Dome, an outdoor entertainment facility erected on the northeast corner of the square. Performances were given nightly, except for Sundays. This Air Dome was in operation until at least 1916.[11]

| Glasco | 1898 | Opera House/Davidson Auditorium | NLS |

In 1898, L. F. Davidson purchased the building known as the Glasco State Bank building, a large stone structure 52' x 80' and two stories high. The front rooms on the second story were offices, the rear was an opera house.

On Tuesday, November 28, 1911, some time between 1:30 and 2 a.m., a fire began in the Davidson Auditorium and spread quickly. This fire destroyed almost all of the business section of Glasco. Before they were driven from their office the telephone operators spread the alarm to rural people. Rural citizens hurried to town to assist with fighting the fire, but battling the blaze was hindered by the lack of a city water system.

The *Glasco Sun* of December 1, 1911, reported that, "Every residence well was pumped dry….Just as soon as a man had done all that was humanly possible to save his own business, or saw the last of his lifetime work go up in smoke. Did anyone sit down or moan over the loss? Not on your life, we were fighting for the very existence in our little city where our businesses have been, our friends and the good Lord knows that there is no worse enemy than fire."

The total loss was estimated at $200,000 to $250,000 with $40,000 covered by insurance. The fire hastened the decision to bring electricity and city water supply to Glasco and six months later Glasco businesses and many residences had electricity and city water.

Many residents suspected that an arsonist was at work when it was learned that the Jamestown business section was almost wiped out on the same morning by a devastating fire. This suspicion was compounded by the report of a fire in Courtland. These three communities are located within 20 miles of each other.[12]

| Glen Elder | 1889 | McPhegley's Hall | UTD |
| | 1906 | Opera House/Plaza Theatre | UTD |

The first listing for a performance space in Glen Elder appeared in an 1889 theatrical guide. McPhegley's Hall seated 200 to 300 but contained no scenery. Nothing further is known about this structure.

William Davis and James Taylor built the first opera house in Glen Elder in 1906. It was a frame building 40' x 100' covered with galvanized steel. The inside was covered with attractively painted tin. The stage was in the north end of the building and a balcony was built over the entrance hallway.

As with other communities, the opera house was used for a variety of events. A popular stock company, the Hillman show troupe would play in Glen Elder for three or four nights in a row. Some of their offerings would be comedies, others melodramas. Another company that came to Glen Elder about once a year and drew good crowds was the Mahara Minstrels. In the winter Lyceum courses were held in the opera house. Usually eight or twelve persons would sign up. These courses consisted of musical numbers, lecturers, magicians, contortionists and playlets. Entertainers who appeared in Glen Elder would travel by train and stay at the local hotels. The owner of the dray line reported that he would haul as many as 30 trunks or pieces of baggage to the opera house for a show troupe.

In 1931, the Glen Elder Opera House was remodeled using a Spanish theme and renamed the Plaza Theatre. It was then used for the presentation of talking pictures. One source reported that the building is standing but had been gutted by fire. Another resident of Glen Elder remembered performing high school plays on the stage of the movie theatre "up the street," but the exact location of the theatre was not specified.[13]

| Goddard | 1889 | Barrick's Hall | UTD |
| | 1889 | Lyman's Opera House | NLS |

Two performance spaces in Goddard were listed in an 1889 theatrical guide. No information is available on the first listing, Barrick's Hall. However, Lyman's Opera House played an important role in the life of Goddard for a number of years. Al Lyman built the community hall/opera house that was in operation by 1889. The hall seated 600. Later it became the I.O.O.F. Lodge with the city hall on the first floor and the lodge on the second. The city hall was used for numerous community activities including a traveling Chautauqua Lyceum series, high school plays and the occasional Saturday night movie. This structure was razed in 1935.[14]

| Goff | 1916 | ? | Standing/Stage |

Goff is the sight of a one-story brick hall with a raised platform. This structure is likely to be the one mentioned in a 1916 trade paper as the location of a performance. The hall contains portable seating, a box office and a small stage. It is no longer in use.

| Goodland | ? | Thorsen's Hall | UTD |
| | 1888 | Goodland Opera House/Walker OH/ | |
| | | Crystal Movie Theatre | NLS |
| | 1906 | Grand Old Opera House/ | |
| | | Hodgkinson's OH | Standing |
| | | (Opera House portion removed) | |

The first reference to a performance space in Goodland was to Thorsen's Hall. Nothing is known about the location of this space or to its current disposition. Fortunately, a great deal more is known about subsequent performance spaces. W. P. K. Hedrick built the first opera house in Sherman County in Goodland in 1888. This facility was located on West 10th Street between Sherman and Center Avenues. The Goodland Opera House or Walker Opera House, as it was later called, was of frame construction 46' x 100' with a stage 26' by 46'. It was the largest of its kind in that part of the state. The drop curtain contained a center picture of a landscape and was surrounded by advertisements. The theatre boasted a hard wood floor suitable for dancing and roller skating. The only drawback to the theatre was the lack of heating in the winter. One resident remembered that two stoves provided the only heat in the opera house so that no matter how interesting the entertainment on stage, it wasn't easy to forget how cold ones feet were.

Until the construction of a second opera house, this theatre was the center of the town's activities. L. D. Lewelling spoke there in 1891 when he was running for governor on the Populist ticket, as did Mary Ellen Lease and Jerry Simpson, two other proponents of the party. Charles Curtis also spoke there. From 1909 to 1914 the Goodland Opera House was known as the Crystal Movie Theatre. After the movie theatre relocated, the building was often empty and was finally destroyed by fire.

The second opera house in Goodland was built in 1906 and occupied the top two stories of a building located on the corner of 10th and Main. This building is standing, although the third floor has been removed. The Grand Opera House, as it was known, was operated by F. B. Hodgkinson. In addition to a large stage, the theatre featured dressing rooms, a "U" shaped balcony, box and parquet seats, and a ticket office. The theatre opened on December 10, 1906, with "Nature's Nobleman" presented by the Kerkhoff-Hillman Company.

The Grand Opera House was the site of some memorable performances. One of these occurred on Christmas Day, 1917 when a band concert was held for the soldiers leaving for World War I. Also, Milburn Stone who went on to fame as Doc on the television series "Gunsmoke," appeared at the opera house.[15]

| Gove | 1894 | Comedy Hall | UTD |
| | 1916 | Odd Fellows Opera House | UTD |

In 1894 the Presbyterian Church of Gove was discontinued and for many years the building was used as a town hall until 1916 when the Methodists purchased it for use as a church. While in city-use the structure was known as the Comedy Hall. It is unlikely that this building is standing.

In 1916, the Odd Fellows constructed an opera house. S. A. Mitchell who was also County Clerk managed the house. The following humorous item appeared in a 1917 issue of a theatrical trade paper:

> This is an inland county seat, fourteen miles from the railroad. Found it a good one. The Odd Fellows have recently completed a new home, and the first floor is used for theatrical purposes. S. A. Mitchell is the manager....Mr. Mitchell is also County Clerk and can be found at the Court House, where he will sell you a marriage license for two dollars or a dog license for three dollars. It costs a dollar more to be a dog in Kansas than it does to be a married man.[16]

| Grainfield | 1887 | Grainfield Opera House | Standing/Stage |

An opera house that is not only standing with a stage, but also currently being renovated, is located in Grainfield. The Grainfield Opera House, best known for its elaborate galvanized iron façade manufactured by the Mesker Brothers of St. Louis, was built in 1887. The first high school classes were held in this building on the north side of the first floor. Also, at one time a private school with 100 students met on the second floor of the opera house.

Access to the auditorium is from exterior stairs. These could become quite dangerous when they were icy or wet and actually resulted in a death. Following this misadventure, the stairs were covered. The large second-story auditorium is decorated with wainscoting and a circle of electric lights in the ceiling.

Performers who appeared at the opera house included the Musical Reeds, Dr. Charles M. Sheldon, and Blind Boone. One Grainfield resident observed, "Being on the 'kerosene circuit', it was used by all the early-day show troupes."[17]

| Great Bend | 1889 | Great Bend Opera House | NLS |
| | 1896 | New Grand Opera House/Williams Grand Opera House | Standing |

On May 10, 1877, an item that related to entertainment in Great Bend appeared in the local paper.

> The famous Gen. Tom Thumb, the smallest man in existence, and known all over the world, and who is now making a tour of the new West, arrived here Wednesday and gave two entertainments. Tom was never before in such a beautiful country and had never seen so pleasing a landscape as he found in our Barton County. True to his American instinct the cheap land fever seized him and a choice tract of government land he must have in the great Arkansas Valley. So Tom - the veritable Tom Thumb - took a claim in Barton County and goeth on his way.

Another item of interest concerning a veteran performer appeared in the January 12, 1917, *Opera House Reporter*.

> Charles Andress, a retired circus man and theatrical magnate who owns a 1,000 acres of valuable wheat land near Great Bend, has made arrangement with the city whereby he purchases fifty acres of land, adjoining the corporation limits, that he will convert into a city park and amusement grounds, including quarters for the Barton County Fair Association. The park, with the concessions and other buildings that Mr. Andress will erect, will represent a gift of thirty or forty thousand dollars.

There are references to two performance spaces in Great Bend. The first, the Great Bend Opera House, seated 500 in opera and wooden chairs. Its 30' x 30' stage contained five sets of scenery. This facility might be the opera house that was located on the second floor of the Masonic Hall on the northeast corner of Broadway and Main. This structure is no longer standing.

The New Grand Opera House, located at 2103 Forest, was constructed in 1896. The opera house was located on the third floor of the building. Although this building is standing, the stage was removed a number of years ago. The new Grand Opera House seated 800 with a stage 26' x 34' and in 1901 was illuminated by electricity. Stones from the demolished Fort Zarah were reportedly used in the construction of the building.[18]

| Greeley | 1885 | Truefit's Hall | NLS |
| | 1905 | Gerhold Opera House | Standing/Stage |

The earliest performance space in Greeley was Truefit's Hall, listed in both 1885 and 1889 theatrical guides. This hall that seated 150 was located in a room above a store that is no longer standing.

A second performance space, Gerhold's Opera House, was located above Henry Gerhold Dry Goods and Grocery Store. Construction began on March 30, 1905. The facility was 30' x 85' with 200 new seats. On August 25, 1905, a grand ball was held to celebrate the opening of the opera house. Sometime around 1910 Laura Belle Gerhold, who attended the Emporia School of Music, gave a recital in her father's opera house. This facility was in use as late as 1948. The structure housing the grocery store and opera house is standing vacant. The raised platform that was used as a stage is still located on the second floor.

| Green | 1918 | Green Opera House | NLS |

The Green Opera House, located on the southeast corner of First and Martin, was constructed in 1918. The structure was later razed. A report by the Locke Players in a 1918 theatrical trade paper indicated that Green was, "a good little town with a live manager, G. H. Byarlay - a regular prince, and well liked in his town."

| Greenleaf | 1889 | Greenleaf Opera House | NLS |

In 1889 the Greenleaf Opera House, known locally as "The Pink," seated 500 and was the location of many community activities. It was a good-sized wooden structure with a stage. School plays, as well as traveling shows, were presented there. In addition, it was used for dances, skating, and basketball games until the school auditorium was built in 1932. The Pink was torn down some time in the 1930s.[19]

| Greensburg | 1890s | Opera House | NLS |
| | 1910s | Miller-Wacker Auditorium/ Twilight Theatre | NLS |

C. W. Myers built the Greensburg Opera House, located in the Myers Block at the corner of Florida and Main, some time in the early 1890s. The opera house occupied the second story of the building. On March 21, 1892, the county leased the room to the rear of the bank on the 1st floor, and several rooms on the second floor, and the opera house served as a county courtroom when needed. Rent was $30 monthly. After several years very few road shows came to Greensburg, but the opera house continued to serve a vital function as a community center. Such events as dances, home talent plays, graduations, revivals and political meetings were held there. Among the performers to appear at the opera house were Blind Boone, Mary Ellen Lease and "Sockless" Jerry Simpson. This facility was destroyed by fire March 17, 1913.[20]

In 1915, Charlie Spainhour leased the Miller-Wacker Auditorium, and showed motion pictures when the auditorium was not used for stage shows. This theatre, later known as the Twilight Theatre, was owned by the city of Greensburg and was operated as a movie theatre. The interior of the theatre was renovated in the 1930s. Improvements included reducing the projection of the stage into the auditorium, the elimination of the balcony and the installation of new proscenium arch. The theatre was destroyed by the devastating tornado of 2007.

| | | | |
|---|---|---|---|
| Grenola | 1885 | New Opera House | NLS |

The Grenola Opera House or New Opera House, as it was known in 1885, is no longer standing. This structure seated 400 with a stage 29' x 16'. There were five scenes and a piano. The opera house was the site of Lyceum courses and many home talent plays.

| | | | |
|---|---|---|---|
| Gridley | 1917 | ? | NLS |

The opera house at Gridley is no longer standing.

| | | | |
|---|---|---|---|
| Grinnell | 1917 | Theatre | Standing |

An item in a 1917 theatrical trade paper concerning the theatre in Grinnell indicated that, "The house is small but comfortable and the manager, Mr. James O. Evans, is going to enlarge at once, building on a stage at the rear, and will then have a nice little house large enough to accommodate the people." This structure is standing, but in ruins.

| | | | |
|---|---|---|---|
| Gypsum City | 1888 | Opera House | NLS |
| | 1925 | City Auditorium | Standing/Stage |

In 1886 the Town Company of Gypsum, in conjunction with Thomas J. Kingman, began building a 100' x 50', two-story structure located on the northeast corner of Maple and Sixth streets. The first floor of the building contained stores and the City Hall was located on the south side of the second floor. In January of 1888 a movement began to form a stock company to put a stage and scenery in the City Hall and to renovate it so that first class touring companies could come to the town. This was accomplished and on February 29, 1888, the Opera House opened with the comedy "Uncle Josh."

The Opera House was used for many community functions including wrestling matches, moving picture shows, school plays, dances, orations and traveling theatre groups. In 1914, the Opera House was renovated to accommodate basketball practice and was in constant use. Then, in August of 1917 the Opera House was remodeled for use as a lodge hall by the Modern Woodman of America. This structure was destroyed by fire in 1934.[21]

The Gypsum City Auditorium, constructed in 1925, still contains the original front roll curtain. This beautiful and rare example of theatre art depicts a rural scene and was painted by the Kansas City Scenic Company.

# H

| | | | |
|---|---|---|---|
| Haddam | 1885 | Swan Opera House | NLS |
| | 1912 | City Hall/Opera House | Standing |

John Swan who homesteaded near Cuba, Kansas in 1879 and later moved to Haddam where he was engaged in the livery business, put up one of the first store buildings, was instrumental in getting the railroad through Haddam and built the Swan Opera House. Although the opera house's exact date of construction is not known, an article that appeared in an 1885 *Haddam Items* indicated that a scenic artist from Kansas City had contracted with John Swan to paint scenery and a drop curtain. The article concluded by saying, "Mr. Swan does not hesitate to do anything that will benefit and be a credit to our town and in this enterprise he will spare no pains to fix up the Opera Hall that it will compare favorably with any town of this size in the State." John Swan died two years later in 1887.

The Swan Opera House, located on the second floor of a two-story building, was destroyed by fire on December 29, 1909. The fire probably started due to a defective flue in W. V. Chappell's grocery store located below the opera house. In addition to the grocery store and the opera house, the fire destroyed many other buildings on the block.

Several years later, in 1912, a new City Hall/Opera House was built. While the stage has been removed and the balcony closed off, the structure is in use as the Haddam City Building and is the location of many community events and also houses the library.[1]

| | | | |
|---|---|---|---|
| Halstead | 1877 | Opera House | NLS |
| | 1879 | City Hall | NLS |
| | 1907 | Auditorium | UTD |

Standing in 1877, the Opera House in Halstead was located above the Lehman Brothers dry goods store. Road shows appeared there frequently, as did home talent productions. In addition, both the Presbyterian and Methodist Churches held services there before their church buildings were constructed. This structure no longer exists.

The 1879 City Hall, a one-story frame building in use for almost 100 years, was located where the current City Hall stands. In addition to its function as the city hall, it was used for entertainments and graduation exercises.

A 1907 theatrical guide referred to an Auditorium managed by J. Sloan. The seating was 500 with a stage 12' x 26'. Furnaces and gas furnished the heating and illumination. This could have been the 1877 Opera House, re-named.[2]

| | | | |
|---|---|---|---|
| Hamilton | 1899 | ? | UTD |
| | 1916 | ? | UTD |

There are two references to performances that occurred in Hamilton. The first reference was to an 1899 appearance by the Trousdale family. The second was a reference in a 1916 theatrical trade paper. In neither instance was the name of the performance space mentioned. Only one two-story building remains in Hamilton, the Senior Citizens Center. It is not known if this structure was ever an opera house, but the second floor does not contain a stage.[3]

| | | | |
|---|---|---|---|
| Hanover | 1874 | Turner Hall/Opera Hall/ German Hall | Standing |
| | 1916 | Gem Theatre/Electric Theatre | NLS |

The Turner Hall built by the Turnverein Society of Hanover in 1874 is standing. Over the years it has been doubled in size and the stage has been removed. This hall, now used for storage, is a brick structure. Contemporary theatrical guides list the original hall as having seating for between 250 to 400 with a stage 20' x 24'. Plays, medicine shows, dances, church bazaars, and basketball games were held there.

In 1916, the Gem Theatre was another performance space in Hanover. In 1917, the name was changed to the Electric Theatre. It is no longer standing.

| | | | |
|---|---|---|---|
| Harlan | 1916 | Elite | NLS |

The Elite Theatre of Harlan was opened in October of 1916 by the John G. Rae Repertoire Company. This theatre, managed by C. W. "Doc" Hall, the local doctor and druggist, is no longer standing

| | | | |
|---|---|---|---|
| Harper | 1884 | Rothwell Opera House | NLS |

Opened with a grand ball on the evening of June 25, 1884, Rothwell's Opera House was a magnificent structure. Unfortunately, its grandeur was short lived because just a few years later, in 1892, the structure was severely damaged by a tornado. Although rebuilt, it never returned to its former status. Finally, after being empty for a number of years, the building was demolished.

J. S. Rothwell built the opera house at a cost of $45,000. It was a 50' x 90' structure with businesses on the first floor and an opera house on the second and partial third floor. A wide stairway led from the street to the second floor. Offices occupied the front of the second floor. Behind these was the opera house portion of the building. The main floor and balcony of the auditorium were furnished with first class opera chairs. Contemporary theatrical guides listed seating between 450 and 900. The stage was 40' x 50' with fifteen sets of scenery and a piano. The stage was reported to be "the largest in Kansas and was built with the intention of allowing plenty of room to accommodate companies playing spectaculars, or any other dramas requiring it, with better arrangements than either the Gillis or Coates opera houses in Kansas City." The front roll curtain held advertising messages and behind that was a plush double curtain used to open and close acts. Gas lighting was used on stage and in a massive gas chandelier hung in mid-theatre. There was also a solarium glass dome that provided interior natural light during the day. Large heating stoves stood in each of theatre's four corners. Surmounting the front façade was a flag that read "Rothwell's Opera House."

The first troupe to perform at the opera house was the Hyere Colored Musical Comedy Company and the first home talent play to be presented was "A Wronged Wife" presented in August 1884. The advertisement claimed that "Particular pains have been taken to prepare and present this drama in a strictly first class manner." Blind Boone performed there and "Sockless" Jerry Simpson spoke there. Other activities at the opera house included dances, high school graduations and traveling stock companies.

On Friday night, May 27, 1892, a tornado brought terrible destruction to the city of Harper. While the persons killed by this tornado all lived in the country, the commercial section of the city, including the opera house, was nearly destroyed by the fierce storm.[4]

**Harris**      1918    ?                         NLS

The reference to a performance space in Harris is from a 1918 theatrical trade paper. No further information is available concerning this facility. It is no longer standing.

**Hartford**     1885    Opera House Block/Opera House/
                           Maxson's Opera House       Standing/Stage

The opera house in Hartford, located above a hardware store, is an excellent example of a plain, second floor hall with a stage at one end. The opera house seats are still arranged around the room. These portable opera chairs were placed in front of the stage for productions and moved to the side for roller-skating or dances.

The opera house in Hartford was first listed in an 1885 theatrical guide, Maxsay and Lanpher, managers. In 1889 the opera house's name was given as Maxson's Opera Hall with a seating capacity of 400. Although the names were misspelled in the 1885 theatrical guide, information about the owners of the opera house can be found in Hartford's history. The 1884 incorporation petition for Hartford contained the signature of S. Emory Lamphear, and an 1896 report on Hartford mentions a doctor by the name of G. D. Maxson.

Another reference to the performance space in Hartford reported that in 1895 two large brick buildings on the west side of the street, including the Maxson's Opera House and the IOOF hall burned. If this is true, then both buildings were either rebuilt or repaired because they are still standing.

While information on the opera house in Hartford is scarce, recollections of the performances that occurred in Hartford are more numerous. One of the most often performed plays was "Uncle Tom's Cabin." A popular performer who came to Hartford was Blind Boone who could play by ear any selection he had ever heard. He would call for a volunteer from the audience to play a selection and then he would play the same selection, just the way it had been played.

Medicine shows were another popular type of entertainment. During the winter months they would be presented in the opera house, but more often, they occurred out of doors. One performance of this type was particularly memorable. A man selling patent medicines came to town and asked for the fastest horses in town. He was taken to the livery stable where he hired a driver and team. He then opened his suitcase and from it took the regalia of an Indian chief, donned it and was driven around town. This made quite a sight. He then stopped the team, stood in the buggy and proceeded to tell the assembled crowd why they should buy bottled Kickapoo Indian Herb Remedy. "It is good for your rheumatism, good for your bowels and good for your wife and children," he shouted. The cost was $1 per bottle. After 15 minutes of sales pitch, the "Indian" began selling his remedy. When all the bottles were sold, he told his driver to take him to Emporia as quickly as possible, and they exited the town, horses' manes and tails and his feathered headdress flying.[5]

**Hays**          1877    Opera House/
                           Eastman's Opera House       Standing
             1901    Grand Army Hall                UTD

Hays was the home of an early opera house and a hall. While it is unlikely that the hall remains, the opera house is standing, its stage removed years ago.

Pioneer merchant Henry Krueger built what is now referred to as the opera house building in 1877. The opera house, located on the second floor, was the site of home talent plays and traveling troupes who made Hays their last stop between Abilene and Denver. Louie Lord, a well-known Midwestern actress of the 1870s, appeared there in such favorites as "East Lynne" and "Ten Nights in a Barroom." The opera house was also home to traveling minstrel shows, church sociables and dances.

Entries in theatrical guides give various dimensions for this theatre. Seating is reported to be from 300 to 500 and the dimension of the stage from 10' x 20' and 20' x 30'. The opera house billed itself as "the best ventilated hall in the country." The Hays museum contains several sets of wooden theatre seats that reportedly came from the opera house. These seats were decorated with patterns of holes drilled into the seats and backs of the chairs. A wire hat holder was located on the under side of each seat. The town band practiced once a week in a room located on the third floor of the opera house building. In later years, the third floor of the building was the home of the Essex Club, the premier social organization in Hays.

The Grand Army Hall first appeared in a theatrical guide in 1901. This was a ground floor facility with a stage 20' x 26'. No further information is available on this structure.[6]

**Hazelton**     ?       Hazelton Opera House            NLS

The Hazelton Opera House was located on the second floor above the Betty General Store. This structure is no longer standing.

**Healy**          ?       IOOF Hall                        NLS

The Healy IOOF Hall was located above the Farmers Store. This second floor hall contained a stage and curtains. During the 1920s movies where shown there. Milburn Stone also appeared there. The structure is no longer standing.

**Herington**    1888    Herington Opera House            NLS

Built in 1888 by M. D. Herington and J. W. Creech, the Herington Opera House was a grand structure. The first floor of the building contained retail stores while the opera house was located on the second floor. Seating was 850 on folding opera chairs. The 21' x 30' stage contained fifteen sets of scenery and a piano. In addition, there were seven dressing rooms. The building was heated with steam and illumination was provided by electricity. The opening show was "The Buckeye."

Following the advent of movies, the opera house was converted into the Broadway Hotel. Later it was used for various businesses and on February 19, 1969, the structure was destroyed by fire.[7]

**Herndon**     1888    Opera House                        NLS

The Herndon Opera House was a joint venture with the Burlington and Missouri Railroad. Constructed in 1888, the opera house was the center of the town's social activities. These included town meetings, political rallies, musicals, stage plays, school programs by both the public and parochial schools, and graduation exercises. Other activities such as wedding dances, public dances and roller-skating took place there. It was also the site of the showing of the town's first movie, scenes from the 1906 San Francisco earthquake.

Following the construction of the 1936 City Auditorium, the opera house was converted into a bowling alley then razed in 1940.[8]

**Hewins**       1916    Hewins Opera House              NLS

The Hewins Opera House seated 200 with a stage 12' x 20'. In 1916 the manager of the opera house, C. A. Polson, described Hewins as a, "Dandy little show town." This opera house is no longer standing.[9]

**Hiatville**     1885    Wallace and Potter's Hall           NLS

Wallace and Potter's Hall of Hiatville seated 150. A reference to this structure appeared only once, in an 1885 theatrical guide. The hall is no longer standing.

**Hiawatha**    1881    Hiawatha Opera House           NLS
                   1889    G.A.R. Hall/Armory Hall          NLS
                   1916    Royal Theatre/                    UTD
                   1917    Victoria Theatre                  UTD

1880 was known as a "boom year" in Hiawatha and one of the buildings erected during that period was the Opera House. It was a 75' x 80' structure. Three stores were located on the ground floor with the opera house located on the second floor. It seated 300 and the stage contained four sets of neatly painted flats. Dressing rooms were located on either side of the stage. The entrance to the opera house was by a broad, straight stairway.

An interesting story about one of the companies that performed in Hiawatha concerned the London Gaiety Girls. The company's 1891 appearance in Hiawatha resulted from the company drinking too much the night before they were scheduled to perform at Falls City, Nebraska. Unfortunately, the majority of the actors were too full of whiskey to take their parts on the stage and the Falls City manager refused to pay them. After leaving Falls City the actors got as far as Hiawatha before

Kansas Communities | 109

they ran out of money. They performed in Hiawatha, earned enough to be on their way, and left.

At 4:30 a.m. on May 22, 1896, a fire was discovered at the Opera House. The fire was extinguished before doing much damage to the structure, but the stage, scenery and dressing rooms were destroyed. By this point the theatre was not making money and other performance spaces in the city had been built, so the theatre was not rebuilt. Apartments replaced the opera house on the second floor of the building. Over the years the building continued to deteriorate until 1985 when it was razed.

In addition to the Hiawatha Opera House, an 1889 theatrical guide listed another performance space, the Armory Hall or G.A.R. Hall. The Armory Hall, which is no longer standing, was a ground floor performance space that seated 1,000. The dimensions of the stage were approximately 18' x 22'. In 1910, the theatre boasted new electric lights and four new fire exists.

A third facility in Hiawatha was the Royal Theatre managed by C. Wagensvelt in 1916. Wagensvelt was also listed as manager of the Victoria Theatre in 1917. These two were probably the same structure. This theatre showed both live performances and moving pictures. The disposition of this structure is not known.[10]

| Highland | 1858 | Irwin Hall | Standing |
| --- | --- | --- | --- |
| | 1893 | Woodmen Hall | NLS |

Highland had two facilities that were used for entertainment. The first was Irwin Hall, the second was the Woodmen Hall. The Presbytery of Highland, Kansas Territory founded an Academy at Highland as a mission to the Indians. The Academy building, built in 1858, was called Irwin Hall and was used for church services and for entertainments. This structure is still standing but does not contain a stage. The Woodmen Hall was constructed in 1893 by the Woodmen Lodge and destroyed by fire in 1914.[11]

| Hill City | ? | Mollete Opera House | NLS |
| --- | --- | --- | --- |
| | 1886 | Hill City Opera House | NLS |

Local newspaper accounts of Hill City list two opera houses, neither of which is standing. The Mollete Opera House was located on Main across the street from a livery stable. Its seating capacity was 800. The second performance space was the Hill City Opera House located on the second floor of the Boston Store. The store was on the corner of the present McFarland Street and Pomeroy Avenue. J. P. Pomeroy, a Boston merchant, built the 60' x 100' structure in 1886. A bakery and storage occupied the basement. The first floor contained the Boston Cash Store with its five departments, and the second floor housed a doctor's office, a dentist's office, and the opera house. The Hill City Opera House had seating for 400 and a 14' x 16' stage. In 1919 the opera house space was remodeled into apartments, and on May 15, 1922, the Boston Department Store was completely destroyed by fire.

According to the *Opera House Reporter*, a theatrical trade paper, the 1916 and 1917 season was a busy one. Performers who appeared at the Hill City Opera House included Dr. G. W. White and his medicine show, John G. Rae's Company in "The Tenth Commandment" and the Ida Weston Rae Company. The most popular company to appear in Hill City that season was the North Brothers Stock Company with Sport North and Genevieve Russell. The next year was not so successful. The final notice from Hill City to appear in the *Opera House Reporter* stated simply, "The Opera House at Hill City, Kansas is closed and there is no possibility of it being opened again this season."[12]

| Hillsboro | 1904 | Auditorium | NLS |
| --- | --- | --- | --- |

The only reference to a performance space in Hillsboro was from a 1907 theatrical guide. The information indicated that J. D. Hirschler was the manager of an auditorium located in the elementary school. This facility that seated 250 with a stage 20' x 24', heated by steam and illuminated by gas, is no longer standing.[13]

| Hoisington | ? | Opera House | Standing |
| --- | --- | --- | --- |
| | 1916 | Princess Theatre | UTD |

The opera house in Hoisington, a second-story performance space, was located in a building that is standing. The stage has been removed, but the rest of the auditorium remains in tact. It is likely the 1916 listing for the Princess Theatre was also located in the same space. One elderly Hoisington resident remembered attending moving pictures at that location.

Entertainment in Hoisington included one night shows and weekly stands at the opera house. Shows performed at the opera house include "Dora Thorne," "Camille," and "Sappho." A favorite was "Uncle Tom's Cabin." In the summer months it was performed in a tent. Other favorites included "The Face on the Barroom Floor" and hypnotism shows. Blind Boone, a well-known mid-western pianist, also appeared at the Hosington Opera House.[14]

| Hollenberg | 1889 | G.A.R. Hall | NLS |
| --- | --- | --- | --- |
| | ? | Hall above Hyland store | NLS |

The only definite reference to a performance space in Hollenberg, the G.A.R. Hall, occurred in an 1889 theatrical guide. This Grand Army of the Republic Hall is no longer standing. Another source mentioned a hall above the Hyland store in Hollenberg. It is not known whether this space had a stage or whether dramatic performances took place there. The structure is no longer standing.[15]

| Holton | 1889 | Wilson's Opera House | UTD |
| --- | --- | --- | --- |
| | 1890 | G.A.R. Hall | UTD |
| | 1901 | Harmon Opera House/ King's Opera House | NLS |
| | ? | Hinnen Opera House | Standing |
| | 1910 | Perkins Theatre/Arcadia | Standing |
| | ? | Caufman Little Theatre | Standing/Stage |

Thanks to the efforts of dedicated volunteers at the Holton Historical Society, a great deal of information is available concerning entertainment in Holton. Holton's greatest claim to fame in the theatrical area is that it was the home of Sport North, a major Kansas performer. North, his wife Genevieve Russell, and his company, later led by his stepson Ted North, were known regionally for the quality of their entertainment. Another performer from Holton was Guy Kaufman. He first managed his father's company, the Sam Caufman Players, and then for many years operated the company himself.

The first theatrical events in Holton took place in the courtroom of the old Jackson county court house. Louie Lord appeared there in "East Lynn." Then in the 1880s an old skating rink was converted into an opera house and there were week-long appearances by Carrie Anderson and her company. Neither of these structures is standing. Other performers who appeared in Holton included Corse Peyton and John L. Sullivan and his vaudeville company.

Theatrical guides listed several opera houses in Holton. Only one is known to be standing. The first is an 1889 listing for Wilson's Opera House. The facility seated 600 with a stage 18' x 36'. The location of this opera house is unknown. The second facility, the G.A.R. Hall, seated 500 and contained a stage 14' x 18'. The exact location of this space is also unknown. In 1901, there was a listing for the Harmon Opera House. The theatre seated 600 and contained a stage 23' x 14'. This facility, reported to be a ground-floor theatre, is no longer standing. In 1904, a second floor facility with a stage 23' x 13' was known as King's Opera House. This may have been located over what is now a one-story structure that is standing. A facility that is still standing with a stage is a second floor theatre used by Guy Kaufman. Although the structure was not originally a theatre, the stage that was added is still there.

Finally, the community's longest lasting opera house, the Perkins' Theatre, is still standing and in use as a liquor store. The stage has been removed. Formally opened on November 27, 1907, the Perkins was a beautiful theatre. Mr. Stephen Perkins built it at a cost of $12,000 and the enthusiastic support of the town of Holton. One night Perkins told the Commercial Club that if the people of Holton would buy $2,700 worth of tickets for the opening performance, he would build the theatre. The house was practically sold out in half a day.

The building itself was 44' x 92'. The 26' x 44' stage had a proscenium opening of 20' x 26'. The auditorium seated 685, and the theatre contained 425 lights. Scenery and curtain was painted by the Kansas City Scenic Company. The opening performance at the Perkins was "The District Leader," a comedy drama with music.[16]

| Holyrood | 1902 | Ohlemeir's Opera House | UTD |
| --- | --- | --- | --- |
| | 1910 | Bohemian Hall/Theatre | NLS |

On Friday, April 4, 1902, the Cain Comedy Company opened the Holyrood Opera House with a presentation of "Among the Breakers." Admission was children 20 cents, adults 35 cents. It is doubtful that this structure is standing.

In 1910, the C.S.P.S. Hall was completed. The Cesko Slovansky Podporujici Spolek (Czechoslovakian Insurance Fraternity or Organization) constructed this hall, known as the Bohemian Hall. Labor was donated and the rock was quarried from land on local farms. The two-story structure contained the sanction rooms above and a room on the first floor for dances, dramatic productions and other festivities. This structure is no longer standing.[17]

A final theatre, or the C.S.P.S. Hall re-name, appeared in an April 8, 1926, reference to the Wallace Bruce Show Co. appearing April 15, 16, 17 at the Legion Theatre. No information is available on the disposition of this structure.

| Home City | 1892 | Turner Hall | NLS |
|---|---|---|---|
| | 1911 | Opera House/Turner Hall | NLS |

In 1892 Carl Lemmer and Dan Bruensback built a store and hall. The hall was used by the Turner Society and as a community gathering place before being destroyed by fire in 1905.[18]

A photograph in the University of Kansas photo collection shows a large two-story structure. The picture's caption indicated that the building was the Home City Opera House. A Home City resident reported that the Turner Hall was destroyed by fire in 1941. It is likely that the Opera House and the second Turner Hall were the same building.

| Hope | 1886 | Walsh's Hall | Standing |
|---|---|---|---|

Walsh Hall, opened in 1886 with a seating capacity of 200, is standing and in use as a hall by the Catholic Church of Hope. The stage and balcony have been removed and the ceiling lowered, but the original box office door and swinging doors into the hall remain. A kitchen has been added.

| Horton | 1887 | Kemper's Hall/ | |
|---|---|---|---|
| | | Kemper's Opera House | Standing |
| | 1896 | High Street Theatre | NLS |

In 1887, one year after the founding of Horton, W. H. Kemper constructed the city's first opera house. The building that contained Kemper's Opera House, with a seating capacity of 800, is standing. The second floor room contains a stage, but it is not known if this is the original stage or one added later when the room was used for dances.

The High Street Opera House, located south of City Hall, stood on the northeast corner of 1st Avenue East and 7th Street. Built in the 1896, the theatre was the major attraction of Horton's society, and was the location of stage plays and concerts. This second floor theatre boasted a seating capacity of 600 with a stage 35' x 60' with a proscenium opening 28' x 14'. The first manager of the High Street Opera House was W. H. Kemper, the builder of Horton's first opera house.

After the construction of the Liberty Theatre in the 1920s, the use of the High Street Theatre dwindled. For many years it served as the location of the I.O.O.F. and Rebecca Lodges. Finally, a very strong wind caused the north wall of the building to collapse. The structure was then razed.[19]

| Howard | 1883 | Crooks Hall | NLS |
|---|---|---|---|
| | 1887 | Howard Opera House | NLS |
| | 1919 | Robert's Theatre | NLS |

Howard's school building provided the first public meeting place. The next public gathering place was the second story of a structure built in 1883 by Wm. Crooks. Crooks Hall was the location of a variety of activities in 1884 that included a Masquerade Ball and the Howard Dramatic Club's presentation of "Odds With the Enemy." Other performers included the Paragon Minstrels and the Donavan Tennesseers' concert. S. C. Hanna purchased the building in 1888 and installed a stage in the west end of the second story. This space contained a good maple floor for roller-skating. After the space was no longer used for entertainment, Judge A. T. Ayers located his law office there.

The next opera house came into being in 1887 when McKey and Eby doubled the street frontage of their building on the west side of Wabash in the north business block. The upper story became the Howard Opera House. The theatre seated 600 and contained a 20' x 50' stage. Stoves provided the heating and illumination was furnished by gas. A resident of Howard described the opera house lighting as, "a rather brilliant affair."

The Howard Opera House was the location of both professional productions and community activities. In 1887 the Library Association held a "Grand March Ball" and General Prentiss delivered his famous lecture on "Shiloh." In 1889 local talent presented "Maids of Honor," and in 1891 the X.Y.Z. Club of the Presbyterian Church presented an operetta, "Twin Sisters." Other performances that took place there included "Uncle Tom's Cabin" companies and the pianist, Blind Boone, who appeared nearly every year. It was also the location of a memorial service on the death of President McKinley. This opera house went out of existence when the Smith and Goodwin store was damaged by fire on March 27, 1908.

Another location for entertainment was the Air Dome. This structure, an open-air pavilion with outside walls, was constructed after the turn of the century. It was used for roller-skating and picture shows. Later the structure was enclosed and converted to a bowling alley.

The Robert's Theater was built in 1919. The building, originally a two-story horse and hay barn, was converted into a one-story theatre. Stage shows, including an appearance by the Dubinsky Brothers, as well as picture shows, appeared in this facility. It is no longer standing.[20]

| Hoxie | 1916 | Beer's Hall | NLS |
|---|---|---|---|

The first public gatherings in Hoxie were held in the Court House, a structure moved to Hoxie from Kenneth in 1890. Literaries, debates, home talent plays and the occasional traveling show appeared there.

Located above Beer's Dry Goods Store, Beer's Hall was in existence in 1916. It was here that Kansas's political figures made their appearances. Mary Ellen Lease spoke there, as did Carrie Chapman Catt who fought for women's suffrage. Sockless Jerry Simpson and Charles Curtis also spoke in the Hall. Well-known theatrical troupes who performed in the Hall included the Morey Stock Company, the Lucas Show, Ida Weston Rae, the Neal Stock Company, the Ted North Show and Hillman's Stock Company. Such popular plays such as "Ten Nights in a Bar Room" and "East Lynn" were presented by these companies. The building that contained the Hall is no longer standing.[21]

| Hoyt | 1889 | AOUW Hall | NLS |
|---|---|---|---|

Reported to be "large and convenient" by a theatrical guide, the Hoyt A.O.U.W. Hall is no longer standing.

| Hugoton | 1917 | ? | UTD |
|---|---|---|---|
| | 1925 | Gem Theatre | Standing |

A 1917 reference in a theatrical trade paper indicated that there was a performance space in Hugoton. Unfortunately, no information exists as to where the space was located.

An early theatre in Hugoton was the Gem Theatre. In 1925, Russell and Ada Harris purchased this theatre from Charles Nolan. The building is still standing, has no stage, and is vacant. The Harris family showed silent movies in the Gem Theatre. The facility was also used as a skating rink and for performances by traveling theatre troupes. The Hazel Hurd performers appeared there. After performances the seats were often removed and the room used for dances. In 1930, the Harris' built and opened the Harris Theatre that featured the first talking pictures in Hugoton.

The Stevens County Gas and Historical Museum located in Hugoton contains two roll curtains. The one with telephone numbers is from the high school that opened in 1923. It was painted by L. D. Weidesaul from Liberal, Kansas.[22]

| Humboldt | 1869 | Germania Hall | NLS |
|---|---|---|---|
| | 1905 | Opera House/Municipal Theatre | NLS |

Germania Hall, constructed in 1869 by the German population of Humboldt served as the location of local celebrations, entertainments, a school classroom overflow, and even a skating rink. In 1889 this facility had a seating capacity of 300. The structure is no longer standing.

In 1904, construction began on an opera house located at Ninth and Osage Streets. The theatre had a seating capacity of 700, 500 in the orchestra and 200 in the balcony. The stage was 35' x 48'. Illumination was provided by gas.

The opera house was financed by several citizens of Humboldt, but because the theatre attracted few road shows, it was never in a very secure financial position and changed hands several times before it was sold to the city in 1922. In the late

1920s the opera house was used as a movie theatre and finally as a restaurant before it was razed.[23]

| Hunnewell | 1907 | Dance Hall | NLS |

The building that contained the second-story dance hall in Hunnewell is no longer standing.

| Hutchinson | 1882 | Hutchinson Opera House | NLS |
| | 1897 | Riverside Park Auditorium | NLS |
| | 1901 | Shaw Theatre/Home Theatre | NLS |
| | 1911 | Convention Hall | Standing/Stage |
| | ? | Rose Theatre | NLS |

Hutchinson has a long and impressive theatrical history. The first recorded dramatic production, "The Lady of Lyons" presented by Darling's Dramatic Troupe, was staged March 13, 1873, at the first Court House. This was only ten days after Hutchinson officially became the Reno County seat. The Court House where the production took place was a small one-story building. The second Reno County Court House, completed in July 1873 was the location of the first opera seen in Hutchinson, "The Bohemian Girl," presented by the Richings-Barnard Company on July 18, 1877. Neither of these courthouses is standing.

The first opera house in Hutchinson was constructed on the southwest corner of Avenue B and Main during the latter part of 1882, at a cost of $18,000. This was a two-story structure 50' x 100'. The theatre, located on the second floor, had a seating capacity of 800 with a stage 25' x 40'. This theatre, which boasted thirteen sets of scenery and a piano, is no longer standing.

An 1897 performance space was the Riverside Park Auditorium. In 1901, this structure was moved to the Reno County Fair grounds and became the Variety Arts Building. This structure is no longer standing.

Hutchinson's grand opera house, the Shaw Theatre and later known as the Home Theatre, was constructed in 1901 at a cost of $80,000. This large, well-equipped ground floor performance space boasted that it was the, "finest and most commodious theatre in Kansas and was considered twenty years ahead of its time." The theatre also featured "wide aisles and commodious retiring rooms." Constructed of stone at the corner of B and Main, the structure was fireproof. The seating capacity was 1,200 with two balconies. The stage was 40' x 60' and heat was steam and gas, and electricity provided illumination. In 1903 the two-year-old theatre was badly damaged by a flood, and then the flood of 1929 caused the curtain loft of the theatre to collapse. The structure was later razed.

W. A. Loe was the man most responsible for the early success of theatre in Hutchinson. Loe came to Hutchinson in 1885 and opened a printing establishment in the first opera house. He continued in this business for seventeen years and during that time founded a weekly newspaper, *The Clipper*. *The Clipper* combined theatre, sports, bicycling, and local news. In 1902 Loe leased the opera house, and then became manager of the new opera house, the Home Theatre, in 1904.

During the late teens residential stock companies were popular at the Home Theatre. During the spring of 1916 the Nestell Players played to packed houses in such plays as "Paid in Full," "The Third Degree," "The Traveling Salesman," "On the Rio Grande," "Such a Little Queen," and "On the Stroke of Ten." This company was so popular that close to the end of the season the Knights of Pythias lodge in Hutchinson gave the members of the company a party.

Riverside Park opened its summer season on May 13, 1916, beginning with the "Isle of Smiles." In September it was reported that the Riverside Park was still going "full blast, giving four acts of vaudeville shows to from 1,000 to 5,000 every day and as high as 7,000 on Sunday evenings for two shows."

The fall of 1917 the Ted Dailey Stock Company was the resident stock company at the Home Theatre. After twenty-one straight weeks they closed their season with a special production. On their last night the entire company made up in front of the audience and the scenery was shifted with the front drop raised in full view of the audience. It was reported that, "This was a treat to a number of the show fans and went big."

Built in 1911 at a cost of $125,000, Convention Hall, 101 South Walnut, is the only one of Hutchinson's early theatres that remains standing. President Taft laid the cornerstone for this facility. In 1954, the Convention Hall was remodeled. All city offices were housed there until 1958.

Finally, the Rose Theatre, Joan J. Sloan, Proprietor, was a vaudeville house located at 117 S. Main. That theatre is no longer standing.[24]

# I

| Independence | 1878 | Opera House | UTD |
| | 1883 | Payne's Opera House | NLS |
| | 1901 | Band Auditorium | NLS |
| | 1910 | Beldorf Theatre | NLS |

The first recorded theatre in Independence was listed in an 1878 theatrical guide. This structure had a seating capacity of 600. There was no scenery and tickets were sold at McCullagh's Book Store. The last listing for this theatre was 1889. No further information is available.

C. E. and Hugh Payne built Payne's Opera House in 1883 at a cost of $18,000. It was located on the northwest corner of Penn and Myrtle Streets. This second floor facility contained a stage 24' x 24' with nine scenes. In 1893 the theatre was described as, "one of the finest play houses in any Kansas city of 5,500 inhabitants. It is furnished throughout with modern opera chairs, and has a comfortable seating capacity of 750, and is heated and lighted with natural gas." The Andrews Opera Company often played there. This opera house was also used for home talent plays. Some time after 1904 the structure was remodeled into a commercial building, and in 1920 was razed.

Like many Kansas towns, the community band was an important part of the city's cultural life. Independence's first band was organized in 1892, and in 1904 the Band Auditorium, designed by F. N. Bender, was constructed. This structure was located between Eighth and Washington. The Auditorium contained a 24' x 46' stage and had a seating capacity of 3,400. Illumination was provided by gas. This structure was razed in the 1950s.

In 1906 the Independence Theatre Company was formed. Its purpose was to construct the Beldorf Theatre, "one of the finest opera houses in the state." The theatre, built in 1907, was located on the southeast corner of Penn and Chestnut Streets. Publicity for the theatre indicated that, "The magnificent four-story structure was of ample size for a city of 20,000 people." And that, "The interior is of the latest model...and the ventilation and acoustics properties are good. The finishing and decorations are in the latest style and all harmonize, making it a credit to the owners as well as to the city. Independence now has as fine a play house as Topeka or Wichita and is able to accommodate any of the large troupes coming west." After the opening night, the *Tribune*, September 18, 1907, reported, "The attendance was all that could be desired and never before in our city was seen such a display of fine elegantly dressed ladies and gentlemen."

This ground-floor theatre contained a stage 40' x 63' and the auditorium seated 450 in the orchestra; 325 in the balcony; and 400 in the gallery. In 1915, Victor L. Wagner purchased the Beldorf Theatre. He operated it until his death in 1918. At that time his son, William H. Wagner assumed the management duties and operated the theatre continuously, except for a ten-year period, until it closed in 1956. The theatre was razed in 1965. William H. Wagner also owned an Air Dome located directly south of the Beldorf Theatre. The Air Dome was used in the summer months. In case of bad weather, the cast, scenery, and audience were moved into the Beldorf.[1]

| Iola | 1881 | New Opera House/ | |
| | | Iola Opera House | Standing |
| | 1904 | Grand Theatre | NLS |

The New Opera House or Iola Opera House opened October 10, 1881. This second floor opera house had a seating capacity of 350 and a stage 20' by 40' that contained five scenes. The last theatrical guide reference to this theatre occurred in 1889. According to the first Iola City Directory, this Opera House is standing. The stage has been removed and the first floor is currently used for a business. The front of the building reads, "1887" and below that, "A O U W."

The Grand Opera House, located at 110 W. Jackson, opened with the musical "King Dodo" on January 8, 1904. The three-story structure was a first floor theatre with a seating capacity of 1,233. The stage was 35' x 62'. The illumination was gas and electricity and heat was provided by steam. This theatre was destroyed by fire on December 20, 1924.

Iola also boasted a summer Air Dome Theatre that was located on North Washington. Traveling shows appeared there during the warm weather months.[2]

| Ionia | ? | Pound Hall | NLS |
|---|---|---|---|
| | ? | ? | NLS |
| | 1918 | Bertna Theatre | NLS |

In the early 1900s two halls were used for entertainment in Ionia. The first hall was located over the Pound building and other was located on the second floor of a large building that was one block north of the hotel. Because Ionia was what was known as an "inland city," stock companies would hire teams to haul their equipment, consisting mostly of assorted trunks and musical instruments, to Ionia from Otego or wherever they came to on the train. Neither of these halls remains.

Prior to World War I, Mrs. Bert Dusenbery, who owned what was known as the Dugger building, had it rebuilt and converted to a theatre. She named it the Bertna Theater after her daughter, Bertna. At the time of its competition it was one of the nicest, well-equipped theatres in the state, and boasted two high quality projectors. The structure was later owned by the community and used for activities. The structure is no longer standing.[3]

| Isabel | ? | IOOF Hall/Larabee Opera House | NLS |
|---|---|---|---|

Isabel's opera house was located on the second floor of the Odd Fellows building constructed prior to 1900. The Stewart and Larabee Hardware store was located on the ground floor and the Larabee Opera House on the second floor. Various dramatic troupes performed in this facility including the Art Names Stock Company with Milburn Stone. This structure is no longer standing.[4]

# J

| Jamestown | 1911 | French Opera House | NLS |
|---|---|---|---|

The French Opera House of Jamestown, located on the second floor of a large two-story building, was constructed some time prior to 1911. This structure was one of only five commercial buildings left standing following Jamestown's devastating fire of 1911. This fire destroyed 30 buildings in Jamestown and occurred at about the same time as fires in Courtland and Glasco. After its use as a theatre, the French Opera House was converted to apartments and later razed.[5]

| Jeneseo | 1916 | ? | NLS |
|---|---|---|---|

A 1916 theatrical trade paper referred to an acting troupe's appearance in Jeneseo. No mention was made of the name of the performance space. Jeneseo does not appear on current Kansas maps. This reference could also be a misspelling of Geneseo, Kansas.

| Jennings | 1905 | Opera House | Standing |
|---|---|---|---|
| | 1906 | Bohemian Hall | Standing/Stage |
| | | (located in Oberlin) | |

The Jennings Opera House, constructed in 1905, was used for stage shows, stock companies, and dances. The popular Sport North Company appeared there. This theatre is standing and currently in use as a lodge hall.

The local economy figured heavily into the success of acting companies, a fact illustrated by a mention in a 1916 theatrical trade paper. The entry reported that the "Devilish Bunch" troupe appeared in Jennings to only fair business. The manager of the company attributed this to poor crops.

The second performance space in Jennings, the Bohemian Hall, constructed in 1906-1907, was used for dances and the Bohemian Lodge. First located in rural Jennings, the Bohemian Hall was moved to Oberlin where it is currently in use as a community hall and is being restored. The hall has its original stage and roll scenery.[6]

| Jerome | 1916 | ? | NLS |
|---|---|---|---|

In 1916, an acting company appeared in Jerome. It is not known whether Jerome was the location of an opera house.

| Jetmore | 1889 | Miller's Hall | NLS |
|---|---|---|---|
| | 1917 | Dreamland | Standing |
| | 1927 | Majestic | Standing |

In 1889 Professor Miller managed Miller's Hall with a seating capacity of 200. This hall was operated in conjunction with Miller's Academy, an establishment where music was taught. The structure is no longer standing.

The 1917 Dreamland and the 1927 Majestic were combination houses offering both moving pictures and vaudeville. The Majestic opened on February 11, 1927, with "Million Dollar Handicap" and two acts of vaudeville. The buildings that housed both the Dreamland and Majestic are standing, but not as theatres. The stages have been removed.

| Jewel City | 1885 | Emerson Fisher Hall/ | |
|---|---|---|---|
| (Jewel) | | Fisher's Opera House | NLS |
| | ? | J.R. Morris Theatre, Skating Rink | UTD |

The first reference to a Jewel City opera house appeared in an 1885 theatrical guide. The Emerson Fisher Hall was listed as having seating for 600 with "good stage and scenery." By 1889 the name had been changed to Fisher's Opera House. The seating capacity was 700. This structure is no longer standing.

A picture of a large barn-like structure, reported to be located in Jewel, featured painted pictures and lettering on the front of the building. According to the advertising, this building housed the "J. R. MORRIS THEATRE AND SKATING RINK, VETERINARY INFIRMARY, LIVERY FEED AND STABLE." Three pictures also adorned the front of the barn. One showed an interior scene of the opera house. The remaining two pictures related to the other functions of the building. The disposition of this facility is not known.

| Junction City | 1860 | Taylor Hall | UTD |
|---|---|---|---|
| | 1868 | Brown's Hall | UTD |
| | 1876 | Centennial Hall | NLS |
| | 1878 | Streetor's Hall | UTD |
| | 1878 | Turner's Hall | UTD |
| | 1882 | Junction City Opera House/ | |
| | | Blakely Opera House | NLS |
| | 1898 | Junction City Opera House/ | |
| | | Colonial Theatre | Standing/Stage |
| | 1917 | Columbia Theatre | NLS |

Junction City, located in Eastern Kansas, has a long and significant theatre history. Early halls included the 1860 Taylor Hall and the 1868 Brown's Hall. In 1870 soldiers from Fort Riley's dramatic company sometimes gave performances in Brown's Hall. No information exists on the disposition of either of these structures, but it is assumed that they are no longer standing.

On February 10, 1876, the Ladies Reading Club resolved to build a Centennial Hall. This hall was constructed on the southeast corner of Fifth and Adams and, for a number of years, was used for entertainment and for civic events. The hall was purchased by the Universalist Church and was later razed. No information is available concerning the Streetor's Hall or Turner's Hall, both in use in 1878.

The major theatre of Junction City, the 1882 Junction City Opera House, has a long history. In May of 1880 a contingent of Junction City residents visited Abilene to view a performance of "Seven Oaks" at Bonebrakes Opera House and fell in love with the structure. They returned to Junction City determined to build a comparable opera house in their city. Bonds were issued and construction began with a competition day set for April 1881. That date was not met. In fact, on August 6, 1881, a major setback occurred when a large portion of the building fell to the ground. The theatre was eventually opened on January 5, 1882, with the local drama club's presentation of "Miralda" and officially opened five days later by the Clayton Star Concert Company.

The Junction City Opera House was a red brick structure with a tall tower that held a four-faced clock. The front of the building housed the fire department, police department and jail on the first floor, and the city council room was located on the second floor. The interior of the opera house had a seating capacity of 1,000 and was lighted by a gas chandelier. The stage was 20' x 62'. The front curtain was flown up into the fly gallery instead of being raised by the old roller type of system. The front curtain and scenery was by Noxon, Halley, and Toomey of St. Louis, Missouri.

On January 1, 1890, the opera house, which had been known as the City Hall building was given a more formal name, the Blakely Opera House. It was named for William Blakely who served in the legislature, held county offices and was mayor of the city when the opera house was built. The opera house was also remodeled in 1890. At that time the seats were raised to an angle to improve visibility and electric lights were installed. Unfortunately, on the evening of January 14,

1898, the Blakely Opera House burned to the ground. The cause of the fire was never determined.

The local paper reported that,
> Only a few people heard the three taps of the fire bell, but the word that the opera house is on fire ran fast along the street, and as with one bound everybody in the town was at the scene to see the flames burst from the roof. The fire had spread so rapidly through the scenery and along the dry roof that the entire building seemed to be ablaze when the first stream of water was thrown. Only three taps of the fire bell had been sounded when the rope was burned off.... The department got action on itself quicker than it ever did in its history, but it was to no avail, and at no time did Chief Ziegler think the building could be saved.

The city council acted quickly to rebuild. The back half of the building, constructed of native stone, housed the opera house. This theatre seated 820 and contained six private boxes. The walls were decorated in different shades of terra cotta and gold. The large stage had a proscenium opening 25' wide x 30' high. There was a fly gallery and a light board was installed to handle the electric lights. William Grabach of Omaha, Nebraska painted the scenery and front curtain. There were dressing rooms on either side of the stage and a chorus dressing room downstairs beneath the stage. The new opera house was formally opened on October 13, 1898, with Hoyt's "A Milk White Flag."

After an illustrious history, use of the opera house began to diminish. On April 14, 1915, the theatre began running moving pictures in addition to road shows. Later the theatre converted to all movies and still later was renamed the Colonial. The theatre, with its stage, is standing and is in the process of being renovated.

A 1917 article in a theatrical trade paper indicated that the Knights of Columbus were building a new theatre, the Columbia Theatre. This structure, designed by the Boller Brothers of Kansas City, is no longer standing.[7]

# K

**Kanapolis   1887   Opera House                         NLS**

The town of Kanapolis came into being through the efforts of the Kanapolis Land Company. Beginning May 12, 1886, 4,000 lots were offered for sale ranging in price from $300 to $1,000. The company reserved a square of four blocks as the future site for the state capitol. The developers' reasoning was that the state capitol should be located in the geographic center of the state. The venture was successful in one sense; a number of businesses were constructed in Kanapolis including an opera house. The only problem was that the state legislature of Kansas refused to relocate the capitol from Topeka to Kanapolis.

The Opera House, which is no longer standing, was located in the Phillips Block at the corner of Kansas Avenue and A Street. According to a contemporary newspaper article written to advertise the community, the structure was "One of the finest buildings in the west." The lower story of the three-story building contained a bank and three stores. The second floor housed the opera hall with double entrances and four office rooms. Offices and sleeping rooms occupied the third floor. The exterior of the building featured galvanized iron made to represent stone work on the front and north sides, with cornice and window caps of a very elaborate design and finish. The news paper article concluded, "Correspondence solicited. Write for plats and maps."[8]

**Kansas City   1890   Dunning's Opera House           NLS**
             **1901   5th Street Opera House           NLS**
             **1906   People's Theatre                 NLS**
             **1907   Carnival Park                    NLS**
             **1891   Noke's Opera House               NLS**

Kansas City was the location of several theatres, none of which remains standing. In operation in 1890, Dunning's Opera House, located at the southeast corner of State and 4th, had a seating capacity of 500 and a stage 30' x 40'. A 1901 theatrical guide referred to a second opera house, the Fifth Street Opera House managed by Robert Dunning with a seating capacity of 600 with a stage 36' x 28' located at 1109 N. 5th. Still later a 1906 reference listed the People's Theatre in Kansas City, Kansas. No information is available concerning this facility.

Noke's Opera House was located on the south side of Silver Avenue just west of 21st Street in Argentine, now a part of Kansas City. This theatre was the social gathering place for Argentine. In 1891 the first high school commencement was held there. Built between 21st and 22nd Streets, the opera house later owned by the Independent Order of Odd Fellows, is no longer standing.

Kansas City was also home to several public halls that are no longer standing. Union Hall was located at 520 Southwest Boulevard. Built in 1899, the second floor was used as a public hall. The McGeorge Block, built in 1889 by William McGeorge and located at 1207 Kansas City Avenue, included McGeorge's Hall. Eagle's Hall, 1174 Kansas City Avenue, was built in 1890. And, the Electric Theatre was located at 1205 Kansas City Avenue.

An interesting era in the history of entertainment in Kansas City centered around Carnival Park. Located in an area bounded by 14th Street, 16th Street and Armstrong and Barnett Avenues, this facility existed from 1907 to 1912. An early advertisement boasted that it, "would be equal in area to the White City in Chicago and that it would be larger than an amusement park in St. Louis, Indianapolis or any other large city west of New York," and that all the attractions found in Coney Island would be featured. Two hundred thousand lights were used to outline the exteriors of buildings.

In addition to the traditional rides, the park contained such features as Hale's Tours of the World, which gave the park visitor the sense of traveling to various places. Visitors were seated in what appeared to be a train compartment. After everyone was seated by a Pullman Porter there was a cry of "All Aboard," and to all appearances the car began to move. A screen on which a moving picture was thrown was located at the front end of the car. To make the illusion even more real, the car would tilt to simulate going around curves. The wheels under the car moved and it felt as if the train was speeding along a railroad track. Sound effects included the train whistle and bell. The pictures were changed every week.

The Wigwam, Carnival Park's restaurant, was a huge dining hall with a stage at one end. Band and orchestra concerts were held there in addition to vaudeville performances. Due to its financial failure, the Carnival Park was dismantled in 1912.[9]

**Kelley   1916   ?                                    NLS**

A 1916 reference in a theatrical guide reported that an acting troupe performed in Kelley. No information is available concerning the theatre or hall where this company appeared. No theatre is standing.

**Kensington   1905   Opera House                      Standing**
                     **(Opera house portion removed)**

The Kensington Opera House, along with the bank and drug store located across the street, were all constructed in 1905. The first floor of the opera house building is standing, but the opera house itself was removed following a fire.

There was also a movie and vaudeville house in Kensington, but its date of construction is not known. This structure is no longer standing. In addition to the movie theatre, a man with a carbon arc projector would go from town to town showing movies. He would put a sheet up on the side of one of the downtown buildings and use it as a screen.

**Kincaid   1908   Kincaid Municipal Theatre          Standing/Stage**

Constructed in 1908, the Kincaid Municipal Theatre is standing with its stage. Many of the building's original features remain, but the ceiling of the auditorium has been lowered. Mr. Irwin built this ground-floor theatre. Scenery for the theatre was painted by a traveling scenery painter. The structure is currently used as a community center.[10]

**Kingman   1883   Tull's Hall/New Opera House        Standing**
           **1887   Grand Opera House /**
                  **Garfield Opera House              NLS**

The first opera house in Kingman was constructed in 1883 or 1884 and was located in what was then known as the Opera House Block. This structure is reported to be standing but nothing of the opera house remains. This second floor theatre had a seating capacity of 800 with a stage 20' x 30' and six sets of scenery.

The Grand Opera House or the Garfield Opera House opened November 10, 1887. The structure was very important to the residents of Kingman as a symbol of the city's growth and prosperity. The three-story building, located at the corner of A and Cedar streets, was constructed of bricks produced by the Kingman brickyard.

The Grand Opera House had a seating capacity of 1,200 with two private boxes on each side of the large 40' x 75' stage. When the theatre opened illumination was provided by oil and gas, with heating supplied by stoves. By 1891 the theatre was lighted by electricity.

Prof. S. Tschudi, a nationally known scenic artist, painted scenery for the opera house. The *Kingman Journal* reported that, "There are over 1,160 sq. yards of scenery now prepared and ready for use." and the Kingman Courier contributed, "...the scenic displays are brilliant with the rarest evidences of artistic genius and aesthetic conception. When the full power of the electric light was turned on, the dazzle and glitter which art and skill combined to produce evoked universal admiration."

The Grand Opera House and the Baltimore Hotel, both located on West Avenue A, burned in the spring of 1910. Part of the hotel was salvaged, but the opera house was destroyed.[11]

**Kinsley**  1888  Flohr Opera House  NLS
 1917  Palace Theatre  Standing/Stage

The Flohr family owned and operated the opera house in Kinsley. The exact date of construction is unknown, but the facility was in use in 1888. The Flohr Opera House was located in a two-story building that faced west on Colony Avenue. A stairway divided the bottom floor into two rooms. The auditorium occupied the entire second floor and was the location of a variety of activities ranging from theatre to basketball games to dancing and finally, roller-skating.

The opera house hosted numerous traveling stock companies that presented such plays as "The Prisoner of Zenda," "Hamlet," "Paid in Full," "Said Pasha" and "A Ragged Hero." In 1913, the owner of the Opera House closed it because the building was found to be structurally unsound. By January the building had been repaired and strengthened according to the recommendations of experts. Following this, however, the building was not used as heavily, but some shows appeared there including the Bybee Stock Company from Larned. This second floor theatre was destroyed by fire and years later the first floor was also engulfed in flames.

Kinsley had a long tradition of exceptional interest and participation in drama. In 1912 Charles R. Edwards, the son of R. E. Edwards who founded the Kinsley Bank, produced a home talent play at the Opera House. In November of that year Mr. Edwards, along with his sister Mrs. Jouett Shouse and 50 school students, acted in two plays. These productions were given as a benefit with profits going to the school's playground and athletic fund. Following this Mr. Edwards and Miss Lucille DeTar, daughter of a local physician, directed numerous productions in Kinsley.

The activity that really put Kinsley on the map from a dramatic point of view was when the Friday Night Club staged Shakespeare's "Midsummer Night's Dream" as a benefit for the Kinsley Public Library. Mr. Gilmor Brown, a young Shakespearean star was engaged to manage the production. Charles R. Edwards and Jouett Shouse were named as business managers. Gilmor Brown eventually went to Pasadena and in 1917 founded the Pasadena Playhouse and School of Acting.

"Midsummer Night's Dream" was staged on the banks of Coon Creek. Lighting was provided by footlights screened by leaves, and lights strung through the trees. There were no lights on stage. Also trees were reset to form the wings for the stage which had a frontage of 150 feet. Seating to accommodate 800 was provided.

The play, with a cast of 100, involved most of the community in one way or another and gained a great deal of attention. The *Kansas City Star* even sent a reporter to cover the production, as did other Kansas newspapers. To encourage attendance, blocks of tickets were sold to surrounding communities. The three performances of "Midsummer Night's Dream" were enjoyed by a total of 1,800 people.

Two years later, in 1914, Charles Edwards constructed a new amphitheatre, the Meadowbrook, along the Coon Creek close to the location of the previous production. Edwards intended this to be the permanent home of the Arkansas Valley Dramatic Festival. The stage was on the north side of the creek with seating space on a high bank across the creek to the south. The amphitheatre accommodated 700 people. The stage, bordered on either side by groves of trees, extended down a flat, gentle slope. Colored lights were hung in the trees and hundreds of paper flowers were used. It was later reported that the cost of building Meadowbrook was close to $1,000. This time the cast included over 200 members and "As You Like It" was produced. Charles Edwards was the festival master and Gilmore Brown the director. Once again, the production was well received by persons from surrounding communities. One group of people from Great Bend left there at 4:45 in the afternoon, stopped to picnic along the way, attended the play, and reached their homes about 3 a.m. The Great Bend paper even labeled Kinsley as a "sort of a miniature Oberammergau."

The third annual Arkansas Valley Dramatic Festival was held in August of 1916. This time "Twelfth Night" was chosen and the cast numbered 300. Charles Edwards and Lucile DeTar were the directors and an orchestra from Hutchinson furnished the music.

The Arkansas Valley Dramatic Festival wasn't the only dramatic activity in Kinsley. In 1913, Charles Edwards formed the Kinsley Drama Club and in 1916 Lucile DeTar formed the Santa Fe Entertainers. This group provided entertainment including music, readings and dancing in the reading rooms along the Santa Fe. The cast members included Miss DeTar and three other young women from Kinsley.

Charles Edwards formed another local stock company in 1917, the Community Players. They presented one-act plays in the Community Theatre every two weeks for eight weeks. As a culmination of the season the group presented their regularly scheduled play and repeated "The Maker of Dreams" which had been an audience favorite. The company donated 25% of their earnings to the American Red Cross to help in the war effort. Following the final production, the company went on tour with their plays.

The Palace Theatre, built in 1917, is a ground-floor theatre with a seating capacity of over 500 including the main floor and balcony. Sometimes stock companies appeared there and it was always available for local artists. School plays were staged at the Palace until the Kinsley High School auditorium was constructed in 1940. The Palace Theatre, which boasts its original and very attractive front curtain, is owned by a non-profit corporation and is being renovated.[12]

**Old Kiowa**  ?  Hegwer's Hall  NLS
 1881  Convention Hall  NLS

Founded in 1874 as a trading post for the Indians and buffalo hunters, Old Kiowa was located about four miles northwest of the present Kiowa. There are references to two halls where dances were held, Hegwer's Hall and Convention Hall, constructed in 1881. Old Kiowa no longer exists.[13]

**Kiowa**  1886  New Opera House/Campbell's Hall  NLS
 1886  Smith and Finnegan Opera House  NLS
 1905  Opera House  Standing

The Kiowa Town Company was organized August 2, 1884. Through its vigorous efforts New Kiowa was a thriving frontier town of 1,000 within its first year. The first train came to Kiowa over its new track on August 6, 1885, and the first cattle were shipped from Kiowa on August 9, 1885. W. E. Campbell, a founding member of the Town Company built the first brick store building and opera house.

Campbell's Hall, with a seating capacity of 300, was located on the second floor of the Campbell building. The grand opening of this building was held on June 29, 1886, with the Signora Linda Brambilla Concert Company. Campbell was the first manager, but later H. D. "Doug" Records, a prominent Kiowa businessman, managed the hall until it was destroyed by fire in 1904. The fire began when a lamp exploded as a janitor lifted it to the stage as he prepared for a dance. The structure was rebuilt, but without an opera house.

Following the destruction of the Campbell Opera House by fire, its manager, H. D. Records, built and managed a new ground floor Opera House located a block south of Main Street on the northwest corner of Seventh and Miller. The seating capacity was 400 with a stage 16' x 36'. Stoves and lamps provided the heat and illumination. This facility, opened in October of 1905 by the National Stock Company, had a long and varied existence. It is currently standing as an apartment building.[14]

**Kirwin**  1885  Opera Hall/Kirwin Opera House  NLS
 1916  New Opera House  UTD

Kirwin was the location of two opera houses. It is unlikely that either is standing. The first opera hall or Kirwin Opera House was built in the early 1880s and made a significant contribution to the cultural and entertainment life of the community. In 1879 Prof. Smiley formed the Kirwin Cornet Band and a few years later the band formed a corporation and built the Kirwin Opera House at a cost of $5,000. While the exact date of construction is not known, the facility was in operation in 1885. The ground-floor theatre was 125' x 50' with a stage 25' x 50' located at the west end that contained eight sets of scenery. The scenery for the stage and the equipment, including the stage curtains, cost $500. There was seating for 1,000 on folding opera chairs that could be moved for dances or dinners. A balcony was located over the entrance at the east end of the building. Kerosene lamps and pot-bellied stoves were used for lighting and heat. Although it was a frame structure, the interior of the opera house was reported to be quite elaborate.

The Opera House, because of its quality, gained a reputation among traveling shows. Such performers as Cab Calloway, Blind Boone the pianist, and Lawrence Welk and his orchestra appeared at the opera house. An interesting attraction was Vernon Delhart who was a singer on the First Edison phonograph records. He would play his recordings and sing along with them. William Jennings Bryan, a well-known national figure, gave several lectures in Kirwin while appearing on the Chautauqua circuit. The Georgia Colored Strollers, a group that consisted of ten Negro singers, also appeared in Kirwin, as did the popular Kansas acting troupe, the North Brothers. This company would come to Kirwin, perform a different show each evening and then move on to a neighboring town. Blackface minstrel troupes also appeared in Kirwin. Like in so many other opera houses, names of performers covered the dressing room and backstage walls.

Throughout the years the opera house was used for a variety of activities including dances and roller skating. Finally, in 1964 the structure was razed. Of interest is the fact that during the dismantling of the opera house, two bullets were found lodged in the walls.[15]

Although no other information is available, an ad in a 1916 *Opera House Reporter* indicated that in addition to the older opera house there was also a second, newer opera house in Kirwin. The ad read, "F. A. Reeves, manager New Opera House, brick, elevated floor, seats 300, piano, well heated, two dressing rooms, elec. lights up to date. Best dealing a show Co. ever got. Good clean shows only. Try me."
It can be assumed that this theatre is also no longer standing.

# L

**LaCrosse**   ?   Opera House   NLS
          1910   LaCrosse Opera House   NLS

Neither the first nor the second LaCrosse Opera House is standing. The first opera house, owned by J. E. Andrews, was directly south of the Windsor Hotel. On April 18, 1909, the worst fire in the history of LaCrosse destroyed a square block of business, including the opera house. The theatre's piano was saved by rolling it out into the street. The night of the fire the Elliott Brothers were showing motion pictures in the opera house. Fortunately, they were able to save their machine and all but one role of film.

In 1910 the LaCrosse Opera House, located on the northeast corner of Eighth and Elm Streets, was constructed at a cost of $12,500. It was built and owned by a local stock company. The auditorium, that contained a balcony, seated 1,000. The front curtain of scenery at the Opera House featured an Italian Garden. The first performance, held on April 25, 1910, was "St. Elmo." After many years of use, first as an opera house, then as a movie theatre, the structure was razed in 1981.[1]

**LaCygne**   1883   LaCygne Opera Hall   NLS
              1916   K.P. Opera House   UTD

The first reference to an opera house in LaCygne was found in an 1883 theatrical guide. The Opera House or Opera Hall seated 600 and the 21' x 43' stage contained nine scenes. Tickets were sold at the Opera House Drug Store. This structure is no longer standing. In 1916 and 1917, a theatrical trade paper carried reports by Stewart and Young, the managers of the K.P. Opera House in LaCygne. It is not known whether this is the same opera house renamed or a different one.

**LaHarpe**   1910   Peet's Theatre   NLS

There are two references to performance spaces in LaHarpe. A picture identifies a large, ground floor frame building that is no longer standing as the LaHarpe Opera House. A 1910 theatrical guide listed Peet's Theatre managed by R. Peet. This theatre with a seating capacity of 700, a stage 30' x 45', and illumination by gas is no longer standing. It is likely that the Opera House and Peet's Theatre were the same structure.

**Lake City**   1892   Lake's Hall   NLS

Constructed sometime prior to 1892, Lake's Hall was located on the second floor above Ruben Lake's double show room. In 1892 the hall was the site of an old fashioned Irish Dance held on St. Patrick's Day and a Masque or ball. This structure is no longer standing.

**Lakin**   1884   Town Hall   NLS
           1907   Opera House   Standing

The Town Hall in Lakin was formally opened with a ball January of 1884. A description of this important occasion appeared in *The Lakin Herald*, February 1, 1884.

> "The hall was brilliantly lighted, and most tastefully decorated with flags and bunting. At intervals around the walls were arranged the Coat of Arms of the different states of the union, and on the stage in rear of the musicians was a statue of the Goddess of Liberty surrounded by a unique display of flags, relieved by wreaths and bouquets of rare and fragrant flowers. The superb orchestra led by Prof. Geo. Hinkel, played appropriate selections for dancing, which was kept up until a late hour, as if led by enchantment. ...and nothing occurred to mar the splendor and gayety of the occasion."

It is assumed that this structure is no longer standing.

In 1907, Mr. E. S. Snow built a two-story cement block building for his business. The Opera House was located on the second floor. The building is standing but the opera house portion of the structure is vacant and the stage has been removed.[2]

**Lane**   1885   Hall   NLS

1885 and 1889 theatrical guides mentioned a Hall with a seating capacity of 300 in Lane. This structure is no longer standing.

**Langdon**   1917   ?   Standing

The theatre in Langdon, built in 1917 and still in use in 1934, is standing vacant. It originally contained a stage and curtain, but these were later removed. After its tenure as a theatre the structure saw a variety of uses serving at times as a creamery, machine shop, gas station and hay barn.[3]

**Langley**   ?   ?   NLS

The opera house in Langley was located above a store that burned in 1949.

**Larned**   1887   Opera House   Standing
            1889   G.A.R. Hall   NLS

Larned was the home of two performance spaces, the Opera House and the G.A.R. Hall. The Opera House building is standing, but the G.A.R. Hall is not.

Opened in March of 1887, the Larned Opera House was the joint venture by a group of the community's businessmen. An 1888 issue of *The Kansas Land Guide* published by a Larned real estate company described the opera house,

> The auditorium, located upon the second floor, is semi-circular in form and is divided into orchestral, dress circle, parquet and balcony seats. There are four private boxes on either side of the stage. The woodwork inside is finished in cherry. The scenery was painted by one of the best scenic artists in the West and is very fine. The stage, with one exception, is the largest in the state. The entire building is lighted with gas.

While many communities boasted of having the largest stage in the state, the Larned Opera House truly did have a sizable stage. It measured 28' x 80'. The seating capacity was 800. An 1889 theatrical director described the facility, "New scenery. Upholstered folding opera chairs; 5 well warmed dressing rooms; the entire house brilliantly lighted by gas." By 1907 heating and illumination were provided by stoves and electricity.

An August 1932 mention in a local paper signaled the end of the opera house era when it was reported that the seats from the theatre were sold to Mr. Crumbine at Alexander, Kansas, for the public hall there. The decline of stage shows in Larned began about 1913 with the increase in railroad fares, and high baggage and hotel rates. While this had a limiting effect on large road shows, a major factor was the advent of talking pictures.

Although large road companies were a thing of the past, Larned was the home of a very active professional theatre company with a regional reputation, the Bybee Players. A long time resident of Larned remembered that each year when the Bybees came back from touring with their tent show the neighborhood children had great fun because Mr. Bybee would let them wear the show's costumes and would help them put on plays. There was a small house in the Bybee back yard where their theatrical trunks were stored. This little house contained a small stage and that was where the amateur theatricals occurred.[4]

**Latham          1885   Opera House/Sherar's Opera House      NLS**

Built in 1885 by J. R. Harrison, the Latham Opera House, later known as Sherar's Opera House, is no longer standing.

The Opera House, located on the second floor of a stone structure, was opened on Christmas Eve of 1885, with a grand ball. A local paper reported that, "Everybody in Latham and vicinity knows J. R. Harrison, and knows that he will run a first class dance. He has placed admission at a low price; none who enjoy 'tripping the light fantastic toe' can afford to miss it." And a later report indicated that the ball was a "success in every respect. The music was the best we have listened to in a long time."

Over the years this Opera House, that seated 500, was home to high school and local talent plays, two or three traveling stock companies each year, and several seasons of vaudeville; was used by the Masonic Lodge and Modern Woodmen of America; and was an early location for the Methodist Church Sabbath School.[5]

| Lawrence | 1860 | Miller's Hall | NLS |
|---|---|---|---|
| | Mid 1860s | Frazer's Hall/ New Eldridge Hall | NLS |
| | 1869/1889 | Turnhalle | Standing/Stage |
| | 1870 | Liberty Hall | NLS |
| | 1882 | Bowersock Opera House | NLS |
| | 1908 | Lyric Theatre | NLS |
| | 1912 | Bowersock Opera House | Standing/Stage |
| | 1913 | Patee Theatre | NLS |
| | 1913 | Palace Theatre | NLS |
| | 1913 | Vaudeville Theatre | Standing |

Lawrence, rich in Kansas history, also has a significant theatre history. An early reference indicated that Miller's Hall may have pre-dated Frazer's Hall and have been the first public hall in Lawrence, but nothing else is known concerning this facility. The first performance space to be well documented was Frazer's Hall located on the third floor of the building next to the Eldridge House. This hall opened in the mid-1860s and was the site of the first opera performed in Kansas on May 29, 1869. The opera company came to Lawrence from New York City and featured the Italian tenor Pasquale Brignoli. Prior to this Ralph Waldo Emerson spoke at Frazer's Hall in March 1867. The *Lawrence Tribune*, March 11, 1867, reported that, "A large audience was present at the lecture of Mr. Emerson last evening. His subject, 'The Man of the World,' was presented in a most attractive as well as philosophical light, and was appreciatively listened to."

Among her charming reminiscences of growing up in Lawrence, Agnes Emery recounted her youthful appearance in a production in Fraser Hall.

One summer Sarah and I were members of a cast for a play which was given in this hall. Our costumes were made of white cambric. We cut gold emblems and gold letters from paper which Mother pasted and sewed onto the cambric dresses. We were really in the play, but I doubt if we had any voice in the part. Our costumes were pronounced 'proper and fitting' and our elders claimed that we gave a creditable performance. We were asked to participate in many local productions--probably because our mother was so clever in designing our costumes.

Agnes Emery also noted that in those days it was easy for men to borrow full dress clothing to use in productions because many of the local men had brought their full dress suits when they came from the East.

Emery explained that Fraser Hall was less popular than the newer Liberty Hall because "…it was not as easily reached, and it attracted a group of people with whom we were not familiar. As the years went by it was used less and less, the excuse — '…it is so inaccessible.'" Soon after Liberty Hall opened in 1870 Frazer's Hall was remodeled and renamed the New Eldridge Hall. The two halls were in competition for a while, but by 1911 Frazer's Hall was an abandoned space.

Liberty Hall, Lawrence's second theatre, was located on the northeast corner of what is now Seventh and Massachusetts. This site was first occupied by a wood-frame structure owned by the Allan and Gilmore firm. By 1858 a second story had been added, but five years later, on August 21, 1863, the building was burned to the ground during Quantrill's attack on Lawrence. In 1868 the structure was replaced by a two-story brick building that contained what was to become Liberty Hall.

Liberty Hall comprised the second floor of a building constructed by Samuel Edwin Poole. Poole's pork packing firm was located in the basement and a retail butcher shop was on the first floor. Rev. Bentley dedicated the building in 1870, and according to one account Rev. Bentley suggested that the name "Liberty Hall" was chosen because some years earlier Abraham Lincoln was reported to have called Lawrence the "cradle of liberty."

Liberty Hall seated 1,000, was 25 feet high with a 20' x 21' stage complete with three sets of scenery and footlights. The painting on the front curtain of Liberty Hall was taken from Henry Worrall's "Droughty Kansas." The drawing by Worrall, a Topeka musician and artist, depicted corn stalks with ears of corn as big as a man, pumpkins so large they had to be lifted by a team of horses, grape vines as large as trees and a fish that took four men to raise, and was used by railroads to promote Kansas.

In addition to the stage, the southeast corner of the hall was curtained off for a kitchen and various church functions such as suppers and fairs were held there. The hall was also the site of appearances by such noted speakers as Horace Greeley and Henry Ward Beecher. Renowned women abolitionists Anna Dickinson and Susan B. Anthony also appeared there.

Lawrence businessman, Justin Dewitt Bowersock bought Liberty Hall in either 1882 or 1885 and transformed it into an opera house. Over the course of the next few years Bowersock remodeled Liberty Hall twice, adding one story each time. By the time he had completed the renovations the building was the largest in town. It had a frontage of seventy-five feet and covered a half block. It was four stories in height. The name of the facility was changed to the Bowersock Opera House.

The renovated second floor opera house had a seating capacity of 1,100 with a stage 30' x 60' that contained numerous sets of scenery and a piano. On September 20, 1896, a fire broke out in the stage area of the Bowersock. Although the blaze did a great deal of damage, the theatre was repaired and re-opened in December. While the opera house survived its first fire, the fire that occurred February 18, 1911, destroyed the building. A new and very grand Bowersock Opera House was then built. This new Bowersock Opera House is standing with its original stage and is in use today.

Following the fire, Bowersock immediately began planning a new and improved opera house. An April 24, 1911, *Journal World* article explained why this opera house was going to be such a magnificent structure. "Mr. Bowersock took his time to make a thorough investigation. Wherever he heard of a particularly fine opera house he got in touch with it. The result is that he has combined in his plans all the features that make an opera house attractive and useful."

On January 22, 1912, less than a year after the devastating fire, the mayor of Lawrence dedicated the new Bowersock Opera House.

The *Lawrence Daily Journal-World* reported the occasion.

The opening night, the audience sat and marveled at the beauty of the building, and between acts of "Bright Eyes" featuring Cecil Lean and his wife Florence Holbrook, Major Bishop appeared on the stage and told just what the building meant to the owner, and expressed his thanks to the city, formally, to Mr. Bowersock, and read letters of appreciation from the council, the Merchants Association and the Commercial Club.

After the Mayor concluded his tribute, "The audience rose and gave Mr. Bowersock a standing vote of thanks."

While many Kansas towns boasted of having the most beautiful opera house in the state, the Bowersock Opera House could honestly lay claim to that distinction. The January 12, 1912, *Gazette* provided a detailed description of the wonders that awaited Lawrence theatregoers.

When the Bowersock is formally thrown open Lawrence play goers will gasp at the lavishness of its interior decoration and finish. Delicate rose tinted walls blend harmoniously with Circassian walnut furnishings. The creamy ivory proscenium arch forms a perfect background for the allegorical pastoral scene whose soft oil tones lends a greater depth of color to the richly hued draperies of the boxes just below. Encircling the proscenium are a profusion of huge sunflowers done in roman gold and oxidized bronze. The same decorations over the proscenium arch blend into forty softly shaded electric lights whose bulbs twinkling out of the floweret's centers suffuse a soft light over the parquet. On each box is a cartouche containing a gilded "B."

The Ornamentation of the theatre is exclusively Grecian. On almost every panel is a dancing girl, some of the graces of mythology, a cleverly executed scene of a Thespian masque. In no theatre of equal size in Kansas is the interior decorations so extensive, so cleverly executed, and so artistically harmonized with the entire arrangement.

The auditorium, located on the ground floor, with a seating capacity of 1,020, was larger than the previous theatre. Seating was about evenly divided between the parquet and balcony with the parquet chairs upholstered in soft brown leather. The balcony seats were folding, but not padded.

The lobby of the theatre, which retains many of the original features, was wainscoted with marble slabs. There were ticket windows on either side just inside the main entry. Also there was a ladies' retiring room on the ground floor and a ladies' retiring room and parlor and a men's smoking room on the second floor. The lobby was covered with ceramic tiling except where the floor was inclined. There rubber tile was used. The auditorium aisles were carpeted in velvet and a heavy asbestos curtain, concealed by an art drop, protected the audience should a fire occur on stage.

Over the years the Bowersock Opera House has undergone many name changes as it progressed from a primarily stage production venue to a combination of acting troupes and moving pictures to being a part of the Dickinson Motion Picture chain. In 1940, the theatre was renamed the Jayhawker Theatre. After being closed as a movie theatre in 1956, the theatre seats and screen were removed and replaced with a dance floor and stage and it became the Red Dog Inn. After the Red Dog Inn was sold in 1974 the dance floor was refurbished and the marble and stained glass windows that had been painted over were restored to their original appearance. In 1975, the name of the facility was changed to The Lawrence Opera House. Finally, in October of 1986 the venue became known as Liberty Hall, and has been returned to a theatre format with a seating capacity of 600. Liberty Hall now functions as a rental facility with a main floor and full balcony.

Over the years Lawrence has also been the location of numerous other theatres. One distinction that Lawrence can claim is that of having the first motion picture theatre in the western United States. Mrs. Mary E. "Vivian" Patee established the Nickel Theatre, located at 708 Massachusetts Street, in 1903. In 1913, the Patee's opened a new theatre at 828 Massachusetts. Other Lawrence theatres in operation between 1903 and 1917 included the Lyric Theatre (1908-1911) at 736 Massachusetts (called the Grand Theatre from 1911 to 1916), the Vaudeville Theatre (1913) at 1015 Massachusetts (known as the Varsity Theatre from 1914 on) and the People's Summer Theatre or "Air Dome" (1908-1913) located at 834 New Hampshire.

An early entertainment space was the Lawrence Turnhalle built in 1869 by the Turnverein Society at 900 Rhode Island Street. In 1889 the building was enlarged to include a stage. A beer garden was located next to the building. This structure is standing with its stage.[6]

| Leavenworth | 1857 | Turner Hall | NLS |
|---|---|---|---|
| | 1858 | Melodeon Hall | NLS |
| | 1858 | Varieties/Union Theatre | NLS |
| | 1858 | National Theatre/American Concert Hall/Varieties Theatre | NLS |
| | 1858 | Stockton Hall/Union Theatre | NLS |
| | 1864 | New Stockton Hall/Opera House/Leavenworth Theatre/Chaplin Opera House/Ummethum Opera House | NLS |
| | 1864 | Lainge's Hall | NLS |
| | 1878 | Odd Fellow's Hall | NLS |
| | 1880 | New Opera House/Grand Opera House/Crawford Grand | NLS |
| | 1889 | Soldiers' Home Opera House | NLS |
| | 1889 | Chickering Hall | NLS |
| | 1889 | Turner Halle | NLS |
| | 1904 | Crawford's Grand/New Crawford Grand | NLS |
| | 1906 | People's Theatre | NLS |
| | 1910 | Orpheum Theatre | NLS |
| | 1911 | Princess | UTD |

Leavenworth, because of its strategic location, was at the center of Western expansion. Prior to the founding of the city, General Leavenworth took advantage of the west bank of the Missouri River by establishing a fort to guard against inter-tribal Indian troubles and to protect travelers on their dangerous journeys West. The community became the main outfitting station for troops, gold seekers, and land hunters. As an example, from June 1865 to June 1866, 405 steamboats and 14,780 wagons left the levee with a total of 110,000,000 pounds of freight.

Between 1858 and 1867 the history of theatre in Kansas was the history of theatre in Leavenworth. The first reported theatrical activity in Leavenworth occurred in November of 1856 when Gabay's Theatricals played to a crowded house. The group did not perform in a theatre, but their appearance pointed out the need for a Town Hall.

Melodeon Hall, constructed in 1858, while not designated as a theatre, served in that capacity. However, the first real theatre, the Varieties or Union Theatre was opened on March 23, 1858. This was a large hall on the corner of Delaware and Third streets that was converted to a 500-seat theatre that included not only a stage, but real scenery. This theatre was in operation until April 16, 1858, when it closed for repairs and improvements. Among those was an impressive new drop curtain painted by George Burt. It was described as the national flag falling in waving folds of red, white and blue upon a marble pavement that contained the word "Union" in large gilt letters. Unfortunately, this theatre was destroyed by fire only two and one-half months after it reopened.

A short time later, the second week of November, the National Theatre opened. This structure was specifically constructed as a theatre with a stage and private boxes. The building was 40' x 100' with a 28' x 35' stage. Located at Shawnee and Fifth streets, this may have been a ground-floor theatre. In 1861 it became the American Concert Hall and in 1863 the Varieties Theatre. The theatre was partially burned in June 1870.

On March 20, 1862, a new Union Theatre was opened in the renovated Stockton's Hall. This theatre, managed by George Burt and his wife was in continuous operation until it burned January 25, 1864. A new building was erected at the site of the old Stockton Hall. This structure located on the corner of Delaware and Fourth streets was 48' x 90'. The second floor housed the new opera house with a seating capacity of 700, a stage 30' x 40', and a green room and dressing rooms below the stage. The opening of the New Union Theatre occurred September 10, 1864, with "The Hunchback" presented by the resident theatre company. During its lifetime this theatre's name underwent several changes: the Leavenworth Theatre, the Chaplin Opera House, and the Ummethum Opera House. After many years of service and numerous complaints about its deterioration, the aging opera house was replaced by a new Opera House located on Shawnee between Fifth and Sixth streets.

The new Opera House built about 1880 by the Leavenworth Lyceum Company seated 900, with a 46' x 65' stage that featured 20 sets of scenery. And, according to a theatrical guide the theatre was, "New and first class in all its appointments; heated with hot air; thoroughly ventilated and supplied with all modern appliances; patent folding chairs and elegant scenery by Noxon and Toomey of St. Louis." By 1889 L. M. Crawford of Topeka was proprietor of the theatre and it was named the Grand Opera House. In 1890 the opera house underwent another name change and was known as the Crawford Opera House. In 1904 a theatrical guide listed The New Crawford Grand Theatre, with a seating capacity of 1,100, a stage 75' x 70', and five trap doors. This was a ground-floor theatre. This theatre is no longer standing.

In 1889 there was a second opera house in Leavenworth, the Soldier's Home Opera House. This structure seated 1,500 with a stage 40' x 45' and is no longer standing.

Built in 1906, the People's Theatre was originally located at 421 Delaware and then later moved to 517-519 Delaware, had a seating capacity of 1,400 with a stage 40' x 75'. Opened in 1910, the Orpheum Theatre was located at 326-328 Delaware. This theatre had seating for 1,000 with a stage 40' x 75'. It was also a ground-floor theatre. Neither of these theatres is standing.

In addition to the previously noted theatres, Leavenworth also had several theatres that probably featured a combination of vaudeville and movies. These included the Casino Theatre/Masonic Theatre at 423 Delaware, the Fern Theatre, 302 Delaware; the Palm Theatre at 311 Delaware; the Hippodrome theatre at 524-526 Delaware and the Lyceum at 517 Delaware. None of these remains standing. The 1911 Princess Theatre located at 427 Delaware may still be standing and in use as a commercial property.

In his book, *Early History of Leavenworth: City and County*, in addition to theatres, H. Miles Moore described Leavenworth's early public halls. He reported that the first Public Hall was on the north side of Delaware between Second and Third. It was in the second story of a frame structure constructed in 1855. The next hall, larger and finer than the first was the previously mentioned Melodeon Hall. It was located on the third story of a pressed brick fronted building on the north side of Cherokee between Main and Second. Built in 1858, this structure housed the U.S. courtroom offices and the hall, both on the second floor. This Hall was totally destroyed by fire.

Leavenworth's third hall, Stockton Hall, also previously mentioned, was by far the city's most famous. Erected on the southwest corner of Fourth and Delaware in 1857, Stockton Hall was a frame building with storerooms below and a high ceilinged story above that could be used by theatrical troupes who visited the city. This hall is well remembered because it was there, on Saturday, December 3, 1859, that Abraham Lincoln spoke. Two days later he spoke outside the building because the crowed was too large for an indoor room. It was said that this speech was substantially the same as the one he gave in New York City that later won for him the presidential nomination. An Eastern reporter, Henry Villard, observed, "It was the largest mass meeting ever assembled on Kansas soil and the greatest address ever heard there." Stockton Hall was also destroyed by fire.

Another important Leavenworth hall was the Turner Hall on the northeast corner of Sixth and Delaware Streets. Erected in 1857, this hall was used for a number of years by the German community for theatricals, musicals, dancing and athletic events. After a fire partially destroyed the building, a second Turner Hall was erected on the corner of Broadway and Shawnee Streets, and finally a brick structure replaced the second hall. This third hall with its seating capacity of 800 and stage 30' x 40' was used by the Turnverein Society in the late 1800s and early 1900s, then became a public dance hall and roller rink, and finally headquarters for labor trade unions. This structure is no longer standing.

Lainge Hall was a third floor facility in the Lainge building located on the Southwest corner of Fourth and Delaware Streets. This hall was used for religious and political meetings, but never for dances because the owner was opposed to them. The hall had a seating capacity of 800 and a stage 20' x 48', but no scenery. This structure is no longer standing. Three other halls in Leavenworth were the Odd Fellows Hall, seating 800, Chickering Hall with a seating capacity of 1,200 and a stage 20' x 35', and the G.A.R. Hall. None of these is standing.[7]

| Lebanon | 1916 | Opera House | NLS |
|---|---|---|---|
| | ? | Hall | Standing |

The Opera House in Lebanon is no longer standing. A second entertainment facility is the one-story building located next to the opera house site. It was originally two stories, with the second floor used for dances and roller-skating. The second story was later removed when it became unsafe.

| Lebo | 1899 | IOOF Hall | Standing |
|---|---|---|---|

Dedicated on May 17, 1899, the new Independent Order of Odd Fellows Hall was a grand two-story stone building that served the town in many capacities. The first floor of the structure housed a bank and mercantile store. The second story was the location of a kitchen, dining room and large meeting room that originally contained a stage complete with curtains, and was the site of many community activities and stage productions. This facility is no longer used as a lodge hall and the stage has been removed, however, the first floor now houses the Lebo Senior Citizens Center.[8]

| Lehigh | 1907 | Hall | NLS |
|---|---|---|---|

The hall in Lehigh seated 300 with a stage 10' x 24' and was heated by stoves and illuminated by lamps. It is likely that this was the second floor of the Isaac Lowen drugstore. This room was reported to have served as a police court, city meeting room and band concert hall. The structure is no longer standing.[9]

| Lenora | 1904 | Lenora Opera House/ Neal's Theatre | NLS |
|---|---|---|---|

Erected in 1904, the Opera House in Lenora is no longer standing. For nearly 50 years this theatre was the focal point for much of the entertainment that occurred in Lenora.

Prior to being converted to a movie theatre, the structure was used for a combination of stage plays, operas, dances and banquets. In 1930, Henry Neal purchased the Opera House and for a number of years the theatre served as home base for the Neal Stock Company. The building was renovated and used for a combination of movies, dances and theatrical productions. The theatre contained a large stage and also a large auditorium that included a balcony.[10]

| Leon | 1885 | Hall | UTD |
|---|---|---|---|
| | 1886 | Mecham's Opera House | Standing |
| | 1889 | Sensenbaugh's Hall | UTD |
| | 1912 | Marshal Brothers and King Opera House | Standing/Stage |

Leon was the location of two halls and two opera houses. The first hall, name unknown, seated 200 and was listed in an 1885 theatrical guide. The second hall, Sensenbaugh's Hall seated 300 and was in existence in 1889. It is unlikely that either of these halls is standing.

Mecham's Opera House, a two-story brick and stone building, is standing without a stage. The theatre originally seated 300. Two stones on the front of the building identify it as MB and 1886. The MB stands for H. H. Marshall and John Butts who built the structure out of hand-cut native stone. In addition to an opera house, the building has housed a hay and grain business, a hardware store, a bank, and a restaurant.

The second and newer opera house, Marshal Brothers and King Opera House, constructed in 1912, is standing with its original stage. The theatre, located above a bank, is in use as a Masonic Hall. The Masonic Hall is located in a self-contained room built inside the auditorium of the theatre. However, the stage, located behind one of the walls, contains two sets of scenery. There are two dressing rooms on either side of the stage then stairs lead to the third floor and two more dressing rooms at the head of the stairs. In addition to the dressing rooms, the third floor contained one large room that extended over the entire stage area.[11]

| Leona | 1885 | City Hall (Odd-Fellows) | NLS |
|---|---|---|---|
| | 1889 | Leona Opera House | NLS |

Theatrical guides contained two references to performance spaces in Leona. The first reference was an 1885 listing of a City Hall or Odd Fellows Hall. The second reference was to the Leona Opera House. These two facilities might have been the same. Neither is standing.

| Leonardville | 1918 | Opera House | Standing |
|---|---|---|---|

The April 12, 1918, *Opera House Reporter* announced the new, ground-floor theatre in Leonardville with Washburn and Sikes, Managers. The theatre seated 375, had electric lights, furnace heat, piano, two dressing rooms downstairs, and new scenery. The structure is standing, without the stage, and is currently in use as part of a furniture store.[12]

| Leoti | 1918 | ? | NLS |
|---|---|---|---|

A 1918 reference indicated that an acting troupe appeared in Leoti, but not where the group performed. It is not known if Leoti had an opera house. However, the Museum of the Great Plains located in Leoti contains two roll curtains. The first is from the Grange Hall and was painted by Oliver from Paris, Texas. The second curtain is from the rural Selkirk School.[13]

| Lerado | 1886 | Opera House Block | NLS |
|---|---|---|---|

The town of Lerado was built by developers who thought two rail lines were going to intersect at that location. Unfortunately, that never happened and Lerado is now a ghost town. In 1886 the town boasted a weekly paper, a system of water works, a large steam flouring mill, three massive and substantial brick buildings with a fourth under construction. Among the town's businesses was an opera house.

In 1887 the railroads failed to materialize, and that signaled the beginning of the end for Lerado. The buildings were either moved to other locations or have fallen down. The one remaining building is part of what was known as the Opera House Block. The remaining building contained a large meeting room on the second floor. The opera house portion of the building is no longer standing.[14]

Kansas Communities | 119

| Leroy | 1886 | Opera House | Standing |

The two-story stone building that housed LeRoy's 1886 Opera House is standing. Originally the second-story Opera House had a steep sloping floor. To the right of the stage was a small area set aside for the piano player. The stage has been removed and the room is vacant. After the room was no longer used as an opera house, it was a roller skating rink and following that, the room where the mortician embalmed bodies. The first floor of the building currently houses a hardware store.

| Lewis | 1906 | Opera House | NLS |

The Opera House in Lewis was on the second floor of the Ray building which was located on the northwest corner of the intersection of Avenue A and Main Streets. The Ray Brothers constructed the building in the early 1900s. After passing through several hands, the structure burned in 1928.[15]

| Liberal | 1911 | Majestic | NLS |
|         | 1921 | Tucker | Standing |

The Majestic, a small frame building built in 1911, was located on West Second. It is no longer standing.

Built in 1921 by Henry Tucker for $60,000, the Tucker was a moving picture theatre and live theatre venue. Although the structure is standing, it contains nothing of the original theatre.

| Liberty | 1907 | Tole Hall | NLS |

The 1907 Tole Hall in Liberty is no longer standing. The structure contained seating for 300, a stage 14' x 16', was heated by stoves, illuminated by lamps, and was located one block from the Santa Fe depot.

| Lincoln Center (Lincoln) | 1886 | Bryant's Opera House | NLS |

Dr. R. F. Bryant, a leading physician, constructed the Lincoln Center opera house in 1886. It was a two-story building 50' x 85' with the Opera House located on the second floor. In addition to constructing the opera house and being a physician, Dr. Bryant was also the town's pharmacist.

The Bryant Opera House opened on October 11, 1886, with plays presented by the Madison Square Company. While this company was not well received, later that same season the Clair Pattee Dramatic Company was described as, "The best talent that has ever visited our city."

Events that took place at the Bryant Opera House ranged from amateur dramatic productions in which leading men of the business community participated, to traveling theatrical companies. Local groups such as the I.O.O.F., the Band Association, the Eastern Star and the Modern Woodmen of America staged productions at the Opera House. A particularly interesting example of a community group using the theatre occurred when the local post of the G.A.R. sponsored the first military drama presented in Lincoln, "The Spy of Atlanta." Six of the early settlers of Lincoln were Civil War veterans and at its height, the local G.A.R. post boasted 155 members. Another war play presented by the post was "The Blue and The Grey."

Visiting a neighboring town to view its home talent production was always a special treat and an event to be reported in the newspaper. In 1882 a number of people came from Beverly and Tescott on a "hand car" to see the G.A.R. production of "The Spy of Gettysburg" and were reported to have, "had a peck of fun on the trip." Then in 1887 a group from Lincoln attended the opening of the Clay Center Opera House eighty miles east. The following year fifteen people from Beverly were reported to have attended a performance of the "Mikado" staged in Lincoln.

After Dr. Bryant moved from Lincoln in the early 1900s he sold the Opera House. The new owners refurbished the scenery and installed electric lights, but over the years presentations gradually shifted from the opera house. This structure is no longer standing.

Not all of Lincoln's dramatic activity occurred in a theatre. In 1915, Lincoln's Woman's Civic Improvement Club sponsored an impressive Shakespearean production. Gilmor Brown who also directed the open air pageants in Kinsley came to Lincoln and directed and produced Shakespeare's *Midsummer Night's Dream* on the lawn of the Courthouse. This area was transformed into a wonderful setting by the addition of trees, shrubs and flowers. Lighting added a fairy-like atmosphere to the production. A second Shakespeare Festival was held in 1916, but the 1917 production was canceled due to the nation's involvement in war.[16]

| Lindsborg | 1889 | A.O.U.W. Hall | UTD |
|           | 1910 | Bethany College Auditorium/ Ling Hall | NLS |

Two performance facilities are reported to have stood in Lindsborg. In 1889 there was a reference to the A.O.U.W. Hall. This hall had a seating capacity of 300 chairs had a stage 16' x 22' and one set of scenery. It is assumed that this structure is no longer standing.

In 1895 Carl A. Swensson, the second president of Bethany College, requested permission from the college's Board of Directors to construct a large auditorium so that there could be greater attendance and participation in the "Messiah." Permission was granted and following its construction the structure was dedicated on October 4 and 5, 1895. A large space, the Bethany College Auditorium or Ling Hall, seated 2,000 and contained a stage 20' by 36'. This site housed the Messiah Festivals for a number of years. In addition, Theodore Roosevelt spoke there during his presidential campaign and Madame Schumann-Heink and Galli-Curci appeared there. In 1946, the building was destroyed by fire.[17]

| Linn | 1913 | Opera House/Aggie's Hall | NLS |
|      | 1920 | Dr. Maintz Opera House/ Edison Electric Theatre | NLS |
|      | ?    | Buck's Hall | NLS |

The first Opera House or Aggie's Hall was opened in 1913. This theatre was located on the upper floor of Aggie Schwerdtfeger's blacksmith shop. Linn had several entertainment facilities, none of which are standing.

The 1920 facility, Dr. Maintz Opera House, also known as the Edison Electric Theatre, was mainly used for motion pictures, but local talent shows and school plays were also presented there.

Linn was also the site of Buck's Hall. This hall was located in a structure that had originally been a store building. The Methodist Women and the Royal Neighbors presented plays there. Upon occasion they also presented their plays in Fact, Kansas. Plays with a mystery or family theme were the most popular.

| Little River | 1887 | The Little River Opera House | Standing |
|              | 1916 | New Majestic | UTD |

Little River is the location of one or possibly two opera houses, the Little River Opera House and the New Majestic Theatre. In 1887 the Little River Opera House was located on the second floor of a building that is currently in use as a furniture store. The opera house had a seating capacity of 600 and a stage 24' x 16'. This stage has been removed. In 1907, the theatre was illuminated with lamps. A 1916 reference also mentioned a theatre by the name of the New Majestic. No information is available on this facility. The New Majestic might have been the Opera House renamed.

The town of Little River was located where the Marion and McPherson Railroad crossed the Little Arkansas River when the line was expanded to Ellinwood. W. R. Edwards, a major developer of Little River, along with a partner, James Zent, constructed a building on Main street with a 100' front and 80' deep. This structure was two stories with a full basement. There were four rooms on the ground floor and one on the second. A stock company was formed to furnish the upper story as an opera house. On July 7, 1887, the Ruby LaFavette Company presented the first production in the newly completed opera house. In addition to performances by touring companies, weekly dances became a staple of the hall. Most citizens of Little River called the facility the Opera Hall, but contemporary newspapers referred to it as the Opera House.

For a number of years the Opera House was the largest meeting room in the community, but as fraternal and church groups constructed new and larger facilities, the opera house lost its usefulness. The final blow occurred in 1921 when a skating rink was built. This large, ground floor, space was also used as the school gymnasium and auditorium and the location of all large gatherings. As a result, the opera house space was partitioned and the rooms used for businesses and living quarters.[18]

| Logan | 1876 | Gandy Hall | NLS |
|---|---|---|---|
| | 1880 | Schultze's Hall | NLS |
| | 1891 | Opera House | NLS |
| | 1891 | G.A.R. Hall | UTD |
| | 1904 | Logan Opera House | NLS |

Logan was the site of several early performance spaces. In 1876 Gandy Hall was located on the northwest corner of Main and Washington Street. This was a two-story building with a store and post office on the ground floor and a 20' x 40' hall on the second floor. The hall was used for church services, school, dances, and social gatherings. In September 1879, a social and literary entertainment was held for the benefit of the Brass Band. This hall is no longer standing.

In 1880 Schultze's Hall was located over Schultze's Red Front Store on Main and Mill Street. This hall, which is no longer standing, was the location of Friday night dances, home talent plays and performances by traveling companies. On November 12, 1880, the Belmont Happy Minstrels appeared in Logan. This was billed as the only colored troupe traveling. The entertainment consisted of plantation scenes, farces and burlesques. Admission was 25 cents. In 1881 The G.A.R. held a reunion for all of Northwest Kansas at the hall. This became known as the Old Soldier's and Sailor's Reunion.

In 1891 a stage was built in a vacant hardware store. This theatre, known as the Opera House, was the location of such productions as "East Lynn," "Uncle Tom's Cabin," and "Ten Nights in a Barroom." This opera house was also the location of Logan's first picture show with E. A. Dye manager of both stage and picture shows. Other entertainments to occur in this theatre include an appearance by the Blind Boone Concert Company, the Princes Concert Company and the Honor Drama Company. Benefits were also held for such projects as the library and to improve the Methodist parsonage. There was also an 1891 reference to an 800-seat G.A.R. Hall. This was probably one of the existing facilities, renamed.

Constructed in 1904, the new Logan Opera House was reported to have been "a play house which would be one of the finest in the state, patterned after the famous Willis Wood Theatre in Kansas City, Missouri." The structure was financed through the Logan Opera House Company. The capital stock of $8,000 divided into 800 shares at $10 each sold quickly. This structure, once a source of great community pride, is no longer standing.

The building, 50' x 90', constructed of hard limestone quarried from a ranch northeast of Logan, was three stories high. The auditorium of the theatre consisted of the main floor, two galleries and eight private boxes. The large stage had numerous backdrops and two curtains. The dressing rooms were located under the stage and an orchestra pit was in front of the stage. The building was lighted with acetylene lights.

The Locke Dramatic and Comedy Company opened the Opera House with a full week of six performance. "Kansas Sunflower" was the audience favorite. Attendance during the first week ranged from 1,000 to 1,200 for each performance.

Sale of tickets for the first week amounted to about $1,400. In addition, the sale of tickets for the drawings that were held nightly amounted to $282. Prizes were available and each night immediately after the last act, the prizes were given away. Some of them included a Hereford Bull, an angora goat, $10 worth of dental work, a fine set of silverware, a two-year old heifer, the best suit of clothes in the store, one week's board, and $3 worth of veterinary and dental work. The grand prize, the Hereford Bull, was given away the last night of the opening week. The bull was brought on stage to the delight of the audience. He had been curried and featured a red bow on his tail. The bull was won by a man from out of town who, in turn, donated the bull to the Opera House Company to be sold with profits going to the opera house.

During its long history numerous companies performed in the opera house including Milburn Stone. In addition to traveling stage productions, the theatre was used for home talent plays, lyceum and graduation exercises, political speeches, sports and even boxing matches. Community celebrations such as Christmas and Decoration Day programs were also presented in the opera house. The last graduation ceremony to be held in the opera house occurred in 1938.

Unfortunately, after the first two years the theatre was a money-loosing proposition, and in 1916 it was declared bankrupt and sold at sheriff's sale. Finally the theatre was condemned and in 1966 replaced by the new city building.[19]

| Long Island | ? | Opera House | Standing |
|---|---|---|---|

The building that contained the Long Island Opera House is still standing, but does not contain a stage.

| Lost Springs | ? | Opera House | NLS |
|---|---|---|---|

The Lost Springs Opera House was located on the upper story of Shupe's store. This brick structure is no longer standing. The Opera House was used for lyceum courses, camp meetings and Chautauquas.[20]

| Louisburg | 1889 | Ebbert's Hall | UTD |
|---|---|---|---|
| | 1918 | ? | UTD |

There are references to one or possibly two performance spaces in Louisburg. No information is available concerning either and it can be assumed that they no longer exist. The first mention occurred in the 1889 theatrical guide. Ebbert's Hall was reported to have a seating consisting of 250 chairs. A second mention of a performance space in Louisburg appeared in a 1918 theatrical trade paper. The location or name of the theatre was not given.

| Lucas | 1913 | Rex | NLS |
|---|---|---|---|

The first theatre in Lucas was the 1913 Rex. A 1916 reference to a performance space in Lucas reported that it was a "nice ground floor house, clean, well heated." This theatre is no longer standing.

| Luray | ? | Opera House | NLS |
|---|---|---|---|

The Luray community building or opera house is no longer standing.

| Lyndon | 1889 | Bower's Opera House | UTD |
|---|---|---|---|
| | 1907 | Lyndon Opera House | Standing |

Lyndon was the location of two performance spaces, the Bower's Opera House and the Lyndon Opera House. In 1889 the Bower's Opera House, owned by Sol Bowers, seated 700 and was illuminated by gas. It is not known whether this structure is standing.

The Lyndon Opera House that seated 400 and contained an 18' x 20' stage is standing, with no stage. After the stage was removed the building was used as a roller skating rink and a plumbing shop.

| Lyons | 1882 | Butler's Opera House/ | Standing |
|---|---|---|---|
| | 1910 | Blevin's Theatre | |

T. A. Butler moved to Lyons in 1879. A few years later he opened a hardware trade and was also elected sheriff. The following year, 1882, Butler was half owner of the White and Butler block erected at a cost of $25,000. The building was 100' square and 40' high. The opera house was located over Butler's portion of the building. An 1883 theatrical guide described the opera house as seating 500 with a stage 20' x 22'. The theatre also contained ten sets of scenery and an organ. By 1910 the facility was known as the Blevins Theatre. This performance space is standing with the stage removed and in use as apartments.[21]

# M

| Macksville | 1912 | Campbell Opera House | Standing/Stage |
|---|---|---|---|

The Macksville Opera House, built in 1912 by Archie Campbell, was an attractive and active theatre. Located on the second floor of a commercial building, this theatre with its original stage is standing. The theatre portion of the building is vacant.

In the hey-day of traveling shows acting troupe managers spoke highly of the theatre. In 1917, one company manager characterized Macksville as "a real show town" and continued by praising the theatre, "…a beautiful upstairs theatre; steam heated, opera chairs and nice large stage. The best show town in western Kansas."[1]

| Madison | 1903 | Madison Opera House | Standing |
|---|---|---|---|
| | | (Opera house portion removed) | |

Completed in 1903, the Madison Opera House was a large three-story structure with the opera house located on the top two floors. Ralph Prichard, who was part of the original construction crew and years later helped remove the portion containing the opera house, reported that the theatre was financed by a group of local business men at a cost of approximately $20,000. The theatre had

Kansas Communities | 121

a large stage with dressing rooms below the stage. The door to the back stairway was located on Main Street between the drugstore and clothing store. There was a pulley at the head of the stairs and one or two horses pulled actors' trunks up the stairs. The trunks were hauled to the theatre by the drayman who also helped load the trunks into the theatre. The property boys then put the trunks in the actors' dressing rooms. Each acting company had a stage man who would give the local theatre hands lists of props needed for the shows.

The Madison Opera House had an elaborate set of 52 stage drops that were operated from a platform in the stage house above the stage. During a performance one of the stage hands stayed up there to raise the flies up and down. In addition, there were pieces of wing scenery that were ten- to 12-feet tall. These were fastened to the floor by screws and braces. The main floor of the auditorium had seating for 400 with additional seating for 200 in the balcony.

Most of the companies that appeared at the opera house played for a week at a time and presented a different show each night. Popular plays included "Uncle Tom's Cabin" and "Ten Nights in a Bar Room."

Opera Houses were at the center of many town events, and Madison was no exception. One resident, Dr. Myers, recalled taking part in the excitement of election night returns. Before there were radios or long distance telephones, on the night of a national election the results arrived by telegraph. When Dr. Myers was a boy his father would stay at the depot and take the election returns on the telegraph, then the boy would run with them to the Opera House where everybody had congregated to hear the latest results.

Time took its toll on this once grand theatre. First the balcony was condemned. Then in 1941, the building containing the opera house was sold and everything except the first floor was removed.[2]

| Mahaska | ? | Town Hall | NLS |

The Town Hall of Mahaska was the site of lyceum courses, Memorial Day programs, home talent shows, and appearances by traveling companies. In addition, city council meetings, dances, and picture shows were held there. Also, various organizations served dinners in the hall. This structure is no longer standing.

| Manchester | 1917 | Arnold's Play House | UTD |

In 1917, G. J. Arnold managed the newly remodeled Arnold's Play House in Manchester. No information is available as to whether this structure is standing. However, there is a two-story stone building that once housed a blacksmith's shop on the first floor and a dance hall on the second floor that is large enough to have been a theatre.

| Manhattan | 1872 | Peak's Hall | NLS |
| | 1883 | Coliseum Theatre/ | |
| | | Moore's Opera House/ | |
| | 1893 | Wareham's Opera House | Standing/Stage |
| | 1909 | Marshal Theatre | Standing |

Peak's Hall, Manhattan's first opera house, was located on the second floor of a stone building. The first play was presented there in 1872. The facility seated 300, with a stage 12' x 27' that contained two sets of scenery. The hall that served as a community meeting room was last listed in a theatrical guide In 1883. The building is no longer standing.

A second Manhattan theatre was listed in the 1883 theatrical guides, the Coliseum Theatre. This structure was a ground-floor theatre that seated 600. The stage was 16' x 40' and contained a fair stock of scenery. A note in an 1883 theatrical guide indicated that the theatre, also known as Moore's Opera House, "will be enlarged and refitted for seasons of 1883-84." The renovation did take place because in 1885 Moore's Opera House was listed as having seating for 1,000 and a stage 31' by 47'. There were 10 scenes and a piano.

The Coliseum Theatre or Moore's Opera House was Manhattan's first real theatre. Popular plays were "East Lynn," "Fast Mail," "Ben Hur" and "Uncle Tom's Cabin." Performers such as Blind Boone and the Spooners were favorites, and the J. C. Lewis Minstrels delighted audiences. The first three rows of downstairs seating was on comfortable opera chairs, the rest were kitchen chairs fastened to 2 x 4 boards. Balcony seating was on three rows of hard benches. Two hanging oil lamps provided lighting. Oil lamps were also used for footlights.

On August 7, 1893, Moore's Opera House was sold to Mr. Harry Wareham, a leading Manhattan businessman whose holdings, in addition to the opera house, included a telephone company, apartment buildings and a hotel. A basement-level tunnel connected all of the buildings in the Wareham block to the Court House.

In 1910, Wareham's Opera House was remodeled and the name of this ground floor facility was changed to the Wareham Theatre. The seating capacity remained the same, but the stage was expanded to 33' x 47'. Illumination was provided by electricity. This was reported to be the first theatre in Kansas to show films. In the late 1920s talking movies were added and in 1938 the theatre was again remodeled. It was during this renovation that the stage was shortened and live stage shows came to an end. The current marquee was also added at that time. In the early 1980s the theatre was remodeled in a 1910 style and its name returned to the Wareham Opera House. Today the theatre functions as a rental facility for plays and parties, and is used as a civic theatre.

Built in 1909 for stage shows, the Marshall Theatre, designed by the Boller Brothers, architects, was soon converted to show moving pictures. The theatre had a seating capacity of 1,100 with a stage 34' x 57'. This structure is used for commercial purposes and no longer contains a stage.[3]

| Mankato | 1885 | Opera House/LaMar's | |
| | | Opera House | UTD |
| | 1906 | Opera House | NLS |

Mankato was the home of two opera houses. The newer of the two is no longer standing and it is also unlikely that the first is standing. The first reference to an opera house in Mankato occurred in an 1885 theatrical guide and was simply listed as the "Opera House." By 1889 the theatre was known as LaMar's Opera House. The seating capacity was 600. Located on the upper floors of two business houses on the west side of Commercial Street, it was described as, "a good-sized audience room and dressing rooms." This opera house was the location of the Mankato High School Banquet in 1895 and was where the Christian Church met until their church building was completed. It is unlikely that this structure is standing.

Mankato's second, and much more elaborate opera house, was located on the corner of Jefferson and Center Streets. It was a two-story red brick structure designed by the Boller Brothers architects and formally opened September 28, 1906. This was a ground-floor theatre that seated 600. The auditorium contained an inclined floor, balcony, and two ornate boxes on either side of the stage. Scenery was provided by the Kansas City Scenic Company. In addition to the performance space, between 1906 and 1939 the structure also housed the public library. This structure was eventually razed and replaced by a car lot.[4]

| Mapleton | 1906 | Opera House | Standing |

Constructed in 1906, the Ball Building in Mapleton is an imposing, two-story brick structure. The building first housed the Citizens State Bank, Dr. Ball's Palace Drug Store and Office, H. R. Morris' General Merchandise, the Mapleton Press and a dentist's office. The second story of the structure housed the Opera House. This large space seated 1,000. Traveling acting companies, picture shows, graduations, and other types of entertainments occurred there. The structure is standing vacant and scheduled for demolition. The stage was removed many years ago.[5]

| Marietta | ? | Community Hall | NLS |

The Marietta Community Hall was destroyed by fire.

| Marion | 1869 | Jex Opera House | NLS |
| | 1870s | Rogers Hall | UTD |
| | 1884 | Compton Opera House | NLS |
| | 1905 | Auditorium | NLS |

Marion's first opera house was reported to have been constructed by Stephen Jex in 1869 and to have been destroyed by fire in 1920. Another early facility was Roger's Hall located in the Dr. J. N. Rogers building. During the 1870s social hops were often held in Roger's Hall. Nothing further is known concerning this space, but it is assumed that it is no longer standing.

In 1884 the Marion newspaper was extravagant in its praise for the new opera house that was under construction. The account began, "Mrs. Compton's splendid new opera building is now nearly completed." This structure, located on the north side of Main Street, in the center of the block between First and Second Streets, is no longer standing. The Compton Opera House was constructed of stone with a brick and iron front, trimmed with stone. The structure was 50' x 100' with the first floor divided into two store rooms. Between the rooms was a wide open stairway which lead to a spacious lobby from which the large double doors opened into the grand Opera Hall. On either side of this lobby were office rooms that fronted the street. There was also a stairway that led to the gallery.

The 46' x 52' auditorium with its 20-foot ceiling seated 700. The stage which was 19' x 46' with scenery painted by L. R. Close of the Kansas City Scenic Studio, contained three dressing rooms. Mr. Close who was familiar with many of the finest opera houses in the West informed the citizens of Marion that he knew of no town anywhere near the size of Marion that had as fine an Opera House. Close thought that this would be an honor to a city of 15,000 people, much less 1,500.

The whole hall was lighted with gas. Seven beautiful chandeliers, with four jets each, were suspended in the auditorium and gallery. Additional jets in other parts of the building increased the total number of jets to sixty-four. The stage was supplied with footlights and side lights. When it opened the opera house was heated with stoves, but there were pipes all the way through with a view to eventually heating it with hot air. The Compton Opera House was listed in 1883, 1885 and 1889 theatrical guides.

Around 1905 a much larger performance facility, known as the Auditorium, was constructed. Designed by Ed Runyon, a former Marion resident, the structure had turrets at each of the four corners and more closely resembled a fort than an auditorium. The facility seated 600 and contained a 24' x 55' stage. Furnaces and gas provided heat and illumination. This structure was destroyed by fire some time prior to 1920.[6]

| Marquette | 1887 | Marquette Opera House | Standing |

The Opera Block in Marquette was the idea of four businessmen. The one-half block long brick structure housed six businesses on the first floor and the Opera House on the second. Located on the East Side of Main Street, the structure is still standing. Although the opera house is no longer in existence, the 1927 ground floor movie theatre has been converted to a community theatre and has an active schedule.

The Opera Block, costing around $50,000 was completed in August 1887. The Marquette Tin Manufacturing Company produced the tin cornice work. The first event to be held in the Opera House was a festival sponsored by the women of the Lutheran Church, but the Opera House was officially inaugurated on December 23, 1887, with the Marquette Dramatic and Social Club's presentation of "Nevada or Lost Mine."

Over the years the Opera House was used for many community functions in addition to dramas presented by traveling theatre troupes and local drama clubs. From 1895 on the high school graduation exercises were held there. In 1916 when Woodrow Wilson ran for president, the election returns were brought from Western Union at the depot and posted in the opera house where everyone was gathered. In later years the Opera House was leased to the Masonic Order who converted it into a meeting hall.

Early moving pictures were shown in the second floor Opera House, but in 1920 Levi Broman moved the movies into one of the downstairs rooms of the Opera Block and in 1927 its name was changed to the Strand Theatre.[7]

| Marysville | 1873 | Waterson Hall | UTD |
| | 1881 | Turner Hall | NLS |
| | 1904 | Grand Theatre/Theatre Grand | NLS |

The first dramatic presentation in Marysville occurred in the fall of 1873 when a troupe of actors, on their way to hunt buffalo, stayed at the Tremont House and gave a week of dramatic presentations. The hall where they performed, Waterson Hall, was reported to have been crowded every night. It is unlikely that this hall is standing.

The Turner Hall of Marysville was dedicated "with considerable ceremony" on April 26 and 27, 1881. The first evening of the ceremony was concluded with a production of "Queen Ester," directed by William Becker who later became editor of the *Marysville Post* (German) and of the *Democrat* (English), and postmaster of the city. This structure, located on the corner of Eighth and Carolina Streets was 42' x 80' and cost $10,000. It was constructed from bricks made in local kilns. This ground-floor theatre had an auditorium that seated 400 and a stage 20' x 23' with a fair amount of scenery. After the erection of the Turner Hall, Marysville was the site of productions by many leading actors including John Dillon who appeared in "The Road to Selzerville" and Louie Lord in "Leah, the Forsaken." The structure was razed in 1947 following the collapse of one wall.

The Theatre Grand or Grand Theatre, a much larger facility than the Turner Hall, was located on the North side of Sixth and Broadway over the Love store. Another source reported that the Grand Theatre was located on the second floor of the Grange Hall. The Grand Theatre first appeared in theatrical guides in 1904. The theatre had a stage 36' by 20' with a proscenium opening of 20' wide and 10' high. Steam and electricity provided heating and illumination. This theatre with an auditorium that seated 525 is no longer standing.[8]

| Mayfield | 1916 | ? | NLS |

A 1916 reference in a theatrical guide indicated that an acting company appeared in Mayfield. The location of the performance is unknown, but if there was ever an opera house or performance space in Mayfield, it no longer exists.

| McCracken | 1905 | Opera House/ Art Names Opera House | NLS |

Doc Smith built the McCracken's Opera House in 1905. This cement block building that seated 500 is no longer standing. In July of 1912 Arthur Names and Leonard Ryan leased the structure and from then on it was known as the Art Names Opera House. Ryan and Names ran the opera house and produced plays for several years. After Art Names formed his own acting company, Milburn Stone, Doc Adams on "Gunsmoke," appeared throughout the Midwest with Names' traveling tent show. Stone stayed with this company for six years and appeared in a tent or in the McCracken Opera House several times.[9]

| McCune | 1889 | Sowers' Opera House | NLS |

Sowers' Opera House in McCune, a large brick structure, is no longer standing. According to an 1889 theatrical guide the theatre was managed by G. Sowers, contained 800 chairs and had a stage 22' x 40'. There was also a full set of scenery and a piano. In 1889 the theatre manager bragged that the Sowers' Opera House was the, "Finest hall in Southern Kansas, and only opera house in the city." In later years the facility was converted to a movie theatre.

| McDonald | 1916 | Electric Theatre | Standing |

The Electric Theatre in McDonald was a one-story brick building 32' x 70', with a stage 16' x 32', two dressing rooms, a piano, electric lights and furnace heat. While the outer shell of the theatre remains standing, the inside was totally gutted by fire in 1996.

| McLouth | 1894 | Opera House | NLS |
| | 1907 | Hall | Standing |

Constructed in 1894, a large two-story structure contained the Grocery and Dry Goods store on the ground floor and the Opera House on the second floor. The hall seated 300 with a stage 14' x 20'. Stoves and lamps provided heat and illumination. This structure is no longer standing.

In 1907, William Harris constructed a two-story brick building for use as a grocery store. The second floor of this structure was used for dances and for roller-skating. This building is standing and the second floor contains a floor suitable for roller skating with a platform at one end. This stage is not original.[10]

| McPherson | 1880 | Opera House/McPherson Opera House/Grand Opera House | Standing |
| | 1889 | New Opera House/Grand Opera House | Standing/Stage |

McPherson is the home of two standing opera houses. The first, referred to variously as the Opera House, the McPherson Opera House and the Grand Opera House, was constructed in 1880. While the ground floor is in use, the opera house portion of the building is vacant. The second, the New Opera House or Grand Opera House is a magnificent structure that stands with its original stage, and is in the process of being restored to its former glory.

Kansas Communities | 123

McPherson's first opera house opened in 1880 and was located above the McPherson Bank at the corner of Main and Marlin in what came to be known as the Opera House Block. The December 29, 1881, *McPherson Republican* boasted that, "the second floor has several offices and also the finest Opera House in this section of the country. It will seat 600 persons comfortably and provides a good stage, scenery, dressing rooms, etc." This second-story opera house boasted a stage 25' x 45' with eight sets of scenery. The ceiling of the auditorium featured a 12-foot decorative dome. Also, the ceiling of the theatre rose higher in the southeast corner to accommodate the stage area. This opera house was used as a courtroom, for meetings, speakers, local plays and traveling theatre companies during the 1880s. For example, in March 1887 the Edwin Clifford Dramatic Company presented "Davy Crockett"; Charles Erin Verner appeared in "Shamus O'Brien" and the very popular Louie Lord Company presented "Member of Congress" and "Fedora."

After the new opera house was completed, the older facility continued to be used primarily for speeches and local meetings. During the 1920s several renovations occurred. First the stage area was converted into a corridor and offices and finally by 1928 the entire area was turned into offices.

Organized in 1886 by E. G. Clark, the Opera House Company began with a capital stock of $35,000. But, when they fell short of this goal, the company had to borrow from the bank. The total cost of the land and building came to $42,000. The theatre's architect was George Shaffer. Located at the corner of Main and Sutherland Streets, the Opera House is 130' long, 35' wide and 40' high with a mansard roof. The entrance to the facility, located on the south side of the building is a massive two-story arch. Granite columns within the archway flank the double doors on the street entrance. The exterior walls are made of red brick and limestone. A stone cornice tops the building.

Opening on January 28, 1889, the new ground-floor theatre was magnificent. The auditorium contained seating for 900, including the ground floor, balcony and gallery. There were also two private boxes with red velvet curtains and scrollwork outlines. The blue and beige walls and ceiling were adorned with a stenciled rose and leaf pattern in red and green. The front stage curtain pictured a boy fishing on the bank of a pond, and located above the proscenium was a mural depicting a Kansas landscape. Some of this decoration is still in evidence today. The opening night production, attended by a sell-out crowd of 900, was the Topeka's Modoc Club's production of "The Chimes of Normandy."

At a time when other opera houses were still lighted by gas or kerosene, the McPherson Opera House was lit by electricity. In fact, when the Opera House was lit, the McPherson College and Industrial Institute's lights dimmed or went out. Furnaces provided heating. The stage of the New Opera House was 36' x 56'.

The opera house was the location of high school graduations, local political rallies, meetings, band concerts and other community events in addition to dramatic products by traveling companies and local talent shows. Speakers of national prominence such as Rev. Charles M. Sheldon, William Allen White, and William Jennings Bryan appeared at the McPherson Opera House.

Like many other opera houses, the McPherson Opera House saw its use as a legitimate theatre decline. Eventually movies were introduced and the facility's name was changed to the Empire. Finally the theatre closed and the building stood vacant for a number of years. But now, thanks to a dedicated group of supporters, a multi-million dollar renovation project is underway.[11]

**Meade**     1885   Opera House     UTD
          1907   Opera House     Standing/Stage

Meade or Meade Center, as it was called in 1885, was the location of two opera houses, one constructed in 1885 and a new hall built in 1908. The second building is standing with a stage, but it is not known whether this is the original stage.

The September 24, 1885, the *Meade Center Press* proudly announced that on October 1st, "will occur the grandest event that ever has occurred in the history of Mead County." The event was the opening of the Meade Center Opera House. After a day of speeches, races and games, the day concluded with a grand opening ball at the new hall and supper at midnight. It is unlikely that this building is standing.

Construction was begun on the second Meade Opera House in March 1907. The builder of the opera house was Mr. Phelps. Prior to its construction, the *Meade County News* described the opera house. It was to be a large stone building 50' x 100' feet with a 20-foot ceiling. The seating capacity was to be 1,500 and, the newspaper boasted, the stage "will be the largest west of Hutchinson and will accommodate any traveling company." On September 13, 1907, this opera house opened with what the local newspaper labeled, "the grandest ball ever held in the city." The Meade opera house is standing vacant, but is in the process of being renovated.[12]

**Medicine Lodge**   1885   Thompson's Opera House     NLS
                    1889   Mills and Sherlock's Hall     Standing

An 1889 theatrical guide listed two performance spaces in Medicine Lodge, Thompson's Opera House and Mills and Sherlock's Hall. While the opera house is no longer standing, the building that housed the hall is standing. The hall was converted to other uses and is now vacant; however, the first floor has been renovated and is in use.

In 1884 George Geppert, the cashier of the Medicine Valley Bank, began the construction of the opera house. This facility seated 600 and contained a stage 20' x 40'. Stoves and lamps provided heat and illumination. Geppert, however, did not live to see the structure completed. Following his murder, the property was sold and passed through several hands.

The Opera House, or Thompson's Opera House, was 75' wide and two-stories high. The interior of the opera house was quite elaborate with expensive mirrors and lush stage curtains. This ornate structure stood next to the hotel and the two together made a fashionable evening. The "ultimate" social activity in Medicine Lodge was to dine at the hotel and then attend a performance at the opera house. After usage of the opera house declined, the structure was used for storage and finally razed in 1937. The Medicine Lodge public library is now located where the opera house once stood.

A number of well-known Kansas stock companies played in Medicine Lodge. Some of these appeared in the opera house while others appeared in their own tent theatres. In 1917, the North Brothers Stock Company was the featured entertainment for the 4th of July festivities. Another popular Kansas company was the Art Names Players. One of their members, Milburn Stone, went on the fame on "Gun Smoke." Wallace Bruce, M. E. Bybee, and Hazel Hurd all headed companies that appeared in Medicine Lodge.[13]

**Melvern**     1894   Melvern Opera House     NLS

In 1894 a group of Melvern citizens formed a stock company and built an opera house which was also used as the town "meeting house." Events that occurred at the opera house included skating, dancing, Fourth of July celebrations, plays, and basketball games.

The Melvern Opera House, located on the southwest corner of what is now the Melvern Park, seated 500 and contained a stage 20' x 30'. The structure was heated by stoves and illuminated by lamps. The opera house was razed about 1926.[14]

**Menlo**     1890s   Hall     NLS

In the early 1890s a commodious hall was built in Menlo. This structure that was used for a variety of entertainments was razed in the 1950s.[15]

**Meriden**     1889   Town Hall     NLS
            1890   Gardner's Hall     UTD
            1890   Smith's Hall     UTD

Several halls were located in Meriden. It is unlikely that any are standing. The 1889 Town Hall was reported to have been located where the current City Hall now stands.

Two other halls, Gardner's Hall and Smith's Hall, were listed in an 1890 theatrical guide. Gardner's Hall seated 200 and had a stage 12' by 20' while Smith's Hall seated 500 and contained a 14' by 25' stage.

**Michigan Valley**   1899   ?     UTD

In 1899 the Trousdale family appeared in Michigan Valley. The location of their performance is not known.[16]

**Milan**     1893   Alton Opera House     NLS
         1900   Sappenfield Opera House     NLS

Milan was the home of two opera houses, neither of which remains. The Alton Brothers, owners of the local lumbar yard, constructed the Alton Opera House, in

1893. This theatre, located on the second floor of a commercial structure, was the site of many types of entertainment including lodge suppers.

On August 11, 1899, the Alton Opera House was destroyed by fire. At about 8:30 that evening Mr. I. S. Alton was closing up his business. The night was stormy and Mr. Alton took a hand lamp and went into the opera hall to make sure that all of the windows were secured. As he opened the door to a dressing room, the lamp exploded in his hand, severely injuring his hand and face and filling the room with burning oil. Mr. Alton succeeded in extinguishing the fire on his body then ran downstairs and sounded the alarm.

The fire spread rapidly, engulfing the Alton Brothers building and the building next door. Unfortunately, the Woodmen and G.A.R. lodges lost everything, and the fire also destroyed the city's band instruments. In addition, the telephone exchange and records were also destroyed. As soon as the alarm was sounded all of the men and boys of Milan responded, and through their efforts, the rest of the town was saved.

The loss of the opera house was felt deeply by the community and in 1900 J. T. Sappenfield built a 40' x 80' building two stories high. The upper story contained a public hall and lodge room. The hall was 42' by 64' with a 13 1/2' ceiling. The stage was 12' x 30'. The facility opened December 21, 1900, with a grand ball and banquet given by the Modern Woodmen Camp of Milan. This was the social event of the season with music furnished by the Argonia Orchestra. This structure was razed in 1946.[17]

| Miltonvale | 1887 | Kuhnle Opera House | NLS |
|---|---|---|---|
| | 1907 | Buckley's Hall | NLS |
| | 1908 | Urban Opera House | NLS |

During the early days of Miltonvale public meetings were held out of doors, but in 1887 to the community's delight, Mr. Kale Kuhnle built the Kuhnle Opera House. This Opera House was the location of many community activities including dances, Decoration Day and Fourth of July celebrations, Christmas programs, high school graduations and political rallies. The most memorable of these, a Republican Rally, occurred in 1900 when Bryan and McKinley opposed each other for the presidency. The evening's speaker and a group of followers came from Concordia. A crowd met them at the Santa Fe depot and all marched, each carrying a lighted Chinese lantern, to the Opera House. Frank McVey of Concordia, a colored man whose vocal abilities were greatly appreciated, led the singing. The favorite song of the evening was,

"I saw a ship go round the bend
Goodbye, Billy Bryan, goodbye,
'Twas loaded down with McKinley men,
Goodbye, Billy Bryan, goodbye."

Other entertainers to appear at the Opera House included Blind Boone, the pianists, and home talent plays. In 1903, the opera house was dismantled.

Another performance space in Miltonvale was Buckley's Hall. The seating capacity was 450 with a temporary stage. Heating was provided by stoves and lighting by lamps. This structure is no longer standing.

In 1908, Anton Urban built the Urban Opera House. It hosted home talent plays, traveling stock companies, Decoration Day programs and many other gatherings. Two famous men who spoke there were Charles Curtis, U.S. vice-president from 1929 to 1933, and Alfred M. Landon, the 1936 presidential candidate. This structure was also the location of silent moving pictures and later sound films. It was also used as a skating rink and as the polling place at election time. This opera house is no longer standing.[18]

| Minneapolis | 1878 | Dance Hall | NLS |
|---|---|---|---|
| | 1884 | Opera House/Minneapolis Opera House/Harbaugh Opera House | NLS |

The first location for entertainment in Minneapolis was a dance hall on the second floor of a store located at 323 W. 2nd street. This 1870's structure is no longer standing.

The second facility known as the Opera House, the Minneapolis Opera House and the Harbauagh Opera House had seating for 300 and a stage 20' x 30'. In existence in 1884, this second floor facility was torn down in the mid 1930s.[19]

| Minneola | 1916 | ? | UTD |
|---|---|---|---|

The only reference to a performance space in Minneola occurred in a 1916 theatrical guide. This information indicated that an acting company appeared in Minneola but not where the performance occurred.

| Modoc | ? | Opera House | NLS |
|---|---|---|---|

The Opera House at Modoc, the location of many community activities, is no longer standing.

| Moline | 1896 | Moline Opera House | NLS |
|---|---|---|---|

In 1896, the Moline Opera House was located on the second floor of a building midway on the west side of Main between 1st and 2nd streets. This facility was the location of dances, dramatic presentations and home talent plays produced by the Moline Dramatic Company. The facility had a seating capacity of 300 and a stage 23' x 18'. Heat and illumination were provided by gas. This structure is no longer standing.[20]

| Morantown | 1889 | Samuel's Hall | NLS |
|---|---|---|---|
| (Moran) | ? | Opera | NLS |

There are references to one or possibly two performance spaces in Moran. Neither is in existence today. The first, the 1889 Samuel's Hall, seated 300. The second reference comes from a picture in a county history book. The picture, taken at the turn of the century, shows a two-story brick structure with "OPERA" in large letters between the windows on the front of the second floor. This building had a balcony across the front and businesses on the first floor.[21]

| Morganville | 1898 | Lennard's Opera House/ Morganville Opera House | NLS |
|---|---|---|---|
| | 1915 | Elite Theatre/Opera House | NLS |

Lennard's Opera House, also called the Morganville Opera House, was constructed in 1898, and located on the second story of a building that faced the Southeast corner of Main and Allen streets. The structure was razed to make room for the Elite Movie Theatre. The Elite Theatre, also known as the Opera House, was built in 1915. This structure was razed about 1934.[22]

| Morland | 1904 | Stober Opera House | NLS |
|---|---|---|---|
| | 1920 | Clayton Hedge Opera House | UTD |

Morland's first opera house, the Stober Opera House, built in 1904, was the location of such entertainments as the Hillman Stock Company, the North Brothers Stock Company, and the Wolf Stock Company. Chautauquas and Lyceum courses were also conducted there. Unfortunately, the Opera House in Morland burned during a devastating fire on January 20, 1922.

A second facility, the Clayton Hedge Opera House, carried on the community entertainments until the 1940s. Although the current disposition of the structure is unknown, it is assumed to be no longer standing.[23]

| Morrill | 1885 | City Hall | NLS |
|---|---|---|---|
| | 1901 | Auditorium | Standing/Stage |

Morrill's 1885 City Hall is no longer standing. However, the 1901 Auditorium is not only standing, but has its original stage and roll scenery. The Auditorium is located on the second floor of the now vacant Farmer's Bank. The Auditorium has its original woodwork, stoves, piano and chairs. The scenery includes the front drop with a scene of Venice, an outdoor scene and a street scene.

| Morrowville | 1910 | Kozel Hall | NLS |
|---|---|---|---|

Completed in 1910, Kozel Hall in Morrowville was a fine two-story building 30' x 72'. This structure that served as the town's opera house was also used for a variety of cultural events, public gatherings and dances. Unfortunately, residents' objections to dances led to the structure being torn down in 1939.[24]

| Mound City | 1889 | Butcher's Hall | UTD |
|---|---|---|---|
| | 1889 | Wright's Hall | UTD |
| | ? | Livery stable | UTD |
| | 1880s | Mound City Opera House | Standing/Stage |

References can be found to several performance spaces in Mound City. Unfortunately, very little is known about Butcher's Hall that seated 200, Wright's Hall with seating for 400, or the opera house located over the Mound City livery and feed stable. This was reported to be a model institution with a frame structure and a capacity for accommodating 125 head of stock. The upstairs rooms were arranged for theatrical purposes and there was also a ballroom. The floor under the ballroom was laid with 125 car springs to give it a springy motion that was essential for ballroom dancing

Finally, the Mound City Opera House, thought to have been constructed in the 1880s and located above H. C. Mantey's store is standing with its original stage. This unique opera house features an all canvas front wall painted to resemble the front of a theatre. Even the proscenium arch is painted canvas. Two pictures are painted on the front wall, one on either side of the proscenium. There was also a scene painted on the back wall of the stage. The stage has its original footlight trough that contains gas footlights. When it was an active theatre it had its own gas well. This theatre, located on the second floor of a commercial building, is vacant.[26]

| Mound Valley | 1885 | Opera House/Hullen Opera House/ Carr's OH | NLS |
|---|---|---|---|
| | 1889 | Campbell's Hall | NLS |
| | 1889 | Riff's Hall | NLS |
| | 1941 | Township Community Center | Standing/ Stage |

There are confusing references to numerous performance spaces in Mound Valley. Several of these are likely to have been the same structure. The first reference was to an 1885 Opera House seating 300. Then, in 1889 there were references to Campbell's Hall, seating 1,500 and Riff's Hall, seating 1,000. Another reference credits Eastman with leasing the Hullen Opera House in 1911, and finally a report that the 1885 Opera House was originally a second floor theatre, but the building was gutted and a first floor theatre and auditorium created. This building is standing and still in use as a community center.

| Moundridge | 1888 | Joseph Schrag Opera Block | Standing |
|---|---|---|---|
| | 1905 | Auditorium | NLS |

Built in 1888, the second floor Joseph Schrag Opera House is standing and has been converted to apartments. Architecturally, the most outstanding feature of the building is its elaborate cornice.

In 1905, a wooden ground-floor auditorium was built. This structure is no longer standing.

| Mount Hope | 1889 | Hall/Opera House | NLS |
|---|---|---|---|
| | 1907 | Opera House/Township Hall/ Movie Theatre | NLS |

Neither the 1889 Hall/Opera House seating 300 nor the 1907 Opera House/ Township Hall remains standing. Constructed in 1907 at a cost of $7,500, the Township Hall was made of brick and stone. This structure was located on the north side of the first block on East Main. It was the scene of touring entertainments and local talent shows. Later the structure was converted to a movie theatre.[27]

| Mulberry | ? | Opera House | NLS |
|---|---|---|---|
| | ? | Thompson Opera House | NLS |
| | 1917 | Rex Theatre | NLS |

The first opera house in Mulberry, a second-story facility located above a grocery store and post office, is no longer standing. The second opera house, the Thompson Opera House was a ground-floor theatre where Chautauquas were held until the construction of the new high school. The Thompson Opera House became a motion picture theatre, but prior to that it was used by the high school as a basketball court. This theatre is no longer standing. The Rex Theatre, a combination traveling company performance space and moving picture house, was destroyed by fire.[28]

| Mullinville | 1912 | Mullinville Opera House/ Sidener Opera House | Standing |
|---|---|---|---|

The Sidener Opera House of Mullinville, built in 1912, at a cost of $12,000 is a ground floor brick structure. It is standing but without its stage. It does, however, contain its original tin ceiling.[29]

| Mulvane | 1893 | Mulvane Opera House | Standing |
|---|---|---|---|
| | 1914 | Lindel Theatre | NLS |

The first opera house in Mulvane was located on the second floor above a hardware store and a grocery store. This structure is standing, but does not contain a stage. Entrance to the opera house was by a central stairway located between the establishments. This has since been removed. The auditorium of the opera house measured 29' x 77' with a 15 1/2' ceiling. There was seating for 300 and a stage that was 17' x 29'. Stoves and lamps provided heat and illumination.

The second theatre in Mulvane, the Lindel Theatre, was unusual because it was built and managed by a woman. In 1891, Wm. H. Scheidel began a successful livery business, however, before his death, he suffered a lengthy illness. It was at this time that his wife tore down the livery stable and built the Lindel Theatre. The Lindel, constructed in 1914, was a large ground-floor theatre that is no longer standing.[30]

| Munden | 1894 | Munden Opera House | Standing |
|---|---|---|---|

The Munden Opera House was located on the second floor of a two-story frame structure. The first floor was used as a hardware and grocery store and also a post office. The building that contained the Opera House is standing, but the stage has been removed.[31]

| Muscotah | 1889 | Rink | UTD |
|---|---|---|---|
| | 1896 | Harvey Opera House | Standing |

The earliest listing of a performance space in Muscotah was the Rink with a seating capacity of 500. No further information is available concerning this structure and it is unlikely that it is standing.

The second space, the 1896 Harvey Opera House, is standing vacant without a stage. The large stone structure housed a livery stable on the ground floor and the opera house on the second floor. Doctors' offices were located across the front of the second floor with the large meeting room behind them. When the opera house occupied this space it seated 300 and contained a stage 18' x 50'.

# N

| Natoma | 1911 | Opera House | NLS |
|---|---|---|---|

While no information is available concerning the Natoma Opera House prior to 1911, an account in the July 13, 1911, *Natoma Independent* described the improvements that were being made by the new owner, Charles McFadden. These "extensive repairs" included the installation of an acetylene light plant, a complete remodeling of the stage and the addition of background and curtains, "the latter being a fine production of the painter's art." In addition to these improvements, a fire escape and enclosed stairway were added so that the building met all of the requirements of the law. These extensive additions to the opera house cost approximately $350. The article concluded, "It is very probable that many first class companies, which have been forced to pass Natoma up heretofore on account of poor facilities at the opera house, will now be glad to play here." This opera house that was located above the Farmers Union is no longer standing.[1]

| Nekoma | 1916 | Opera House/Township Hall | Standing/Stage |
|---|---|---|---|

The Nekoma Opera House or Township Hall is currently standing but in danger of collapse. The structure, a one-story brick theatre had a large auditorium and a balcony in addition to a large stage with scenery.

| Neodesha | 1872 | City Hall | Standing |
|---|---|---|---|
| | 1884 | Logsden's Hall | NLS |
| | 1910 | Blakeslee Theatre | NLS |

The City Hall constructed in 1872 at a cost of $12,000 was the location of the first performance space in Neodesha. The hall contained seating for 300 to 500 on chairs and a stage 16' x 45' with a drop curtain. This structure is standing, but the second floor hall that contained the theatre no longer has a stage and is vacant. For a number of years the space housed the public library.

An 1884 picture of downtown Neodesha contains a building with a sign that identified it as Logsden's Hall. No further information is available concerning this facility that is no longer standing.

Finally, the 1910 Blakeslee Theatre is no longer standing. The structure seated 610, and contained a 19' x 57' stage. This was a ground-floor theatre and in 1910, the only theatre in the city. At that time illumination was provided by both gas and by electricity.[2]

**Neosho Falls**     1889    Opera House                            NLS
                                1907    K.P. Opera House                  NLS

Theatrical guides list two opera houses in Neosho Falls. Neither is standing. O. S. Ward managed the 1889 Opera House. The second, the 1907 K. P. Opera House, had seating for 400 and a stage 62' x 40'. Stoves and lamps provided heat and illumination.

**Neosha Rapids**    1899    ?                                             NLS

The reference to an 1899 performance in Neosha Rapids is from a Trousdale family route list. No mention was made as to where their performance took place. There is no structure standing in Neosha Rapids that fits the description of an 1899 opera house.

**Ness City**            1885    Opera Hall/Barnd Opera House    Standing
                          1907    City Theatre                                  UTD

In 1885 Judge Barnd and the Ness City Building Association, a group of businessmen who were mostly Civil War Veterans, constructed what became known as the Opera Block. The Opera Hall was on the second floor of this structure and seated 300. Stoves and electricity provided heat and illumination. The front curtain represented a lake scene in the Alps with a castle in the distance and a bust of Shakespeare surmounted the scene. There were six drops with a full set of wings painted by Graham and Davis scenic artists in Kansas City at a cost of $225. Although not fully completed until the close of 1885, the formal opening of the hall was held in March under the auspices of the G.A.R. The opening ceremony consisted of music and speeches and a hearty old style dinner of salt pork and beans.

In 1908, Judge Barnd enlarged the facility to seat 500 on raised tiers. The stage was moved to the west side of the room and was enlarged to 20' x 40'. The main entrance was also changed. From then on the facility was known as the Barnd Opera House. Such events as high school graduations, concerts, dances and even wrestling matches occurred at the Opera House. Dramatic performances included local talent plays and presentations by traveling theatrical troops. Today the building that housed the opera house remains, as does the main stairs and the box office. The theatre portion of the structure has been removed.

Another Ness City entertainment facility mentioned in a 1907 theatrical guide was the City Theatre that seated 325 with a 12' x 21' stage. Steam and electricity provided heat and illumination. Nothing further is known about this structure.[3]

**Netawaka**          1889    Kenyon Hall                           NLS

The 1889 performance space in Netawaka, Kenyon Hall, that seated 200, is no longer standing.

**Newton**               1878    Opera House                           NLS
                            1884    Ragsdale Opera House                 NLS
                            1883    Masonic Music Hall                Standing/Stage

Built in 1878 at a cost of $20,000, Newton's Opera House Block is no longer standing. The structure was a two-story stone building 50' x 85' with the opera house located on the second floor. The Opera House seated 500 and contained a stage 18' x 20' with two sets of scenery.

The second of Newton's opera houses, the Ragsdale Opera House was a magnificent structure. Its Grand Opening was held on December 8, 1885. This massive three-story red brick and stone structure was located at the northwest corner of Main and Broadway. The first floor housed businesses and the post office. The performance space was located on the second and third stories on the west side of the structure. Finally, a winding staircase led to an observatory along the building's Mansard roof. A belfry that contained a three-faced Seth Thomas clock topped the structure. The theatre's auditorium held seating for 800. The auditorium contained a dress circle, a parquet, a balcony and a gallery. The stage was 30' x 47' and in 1885 there were sixteen sets of scenery. When the theatre opened, it was heated by steam and lighted by gas.

The Ragsdale Opera House was extremely important to the social and cultural development of Newton and for many years was the location of outstanding entertainment events. The builders of the Opera House, brothers J. M. and T. P. Ragsdale, became bankrupt in 1890 and lost possession of the opera house in 1892. In 1910, the manager of the theatre was the Murphy Mortgage Company. This imposing theatre was destroyed by fire on January 1, 1915.

The Masonic Music Hall is located on the second floor of the 1879 Masonic Temple at the corner of Main and Broadway. In 1883 the building was enlarged to provide space for a court room and opera hall which was the site of grand balls and concerts. The music hall contains a stage 22' by 48' that is still equipped with its roll scenery.[4]

**Nickerson**           1881    Opera House                           NLS

The Nickerson City Hall was constructed in either 1881 or 1888. The massive stone building housed the city library, offices, jail, fire station and post office. When opened the Opera House, located on the second floor, had seating for 400 and a stage 20' x 20'. Stoves and lamps provided heat and illumination. An ad in an 1891 *Hutchinson Clipper* described the Nickerson Opera House as having, "…elegant scenery. Stage 30 x 50 feet. Seating capacity 600. Well ventilated and lighted by electricity." The ad also gave an indication of when a company should schedule their performance in Nickerson by saying, "Railroad division. Pay roll $35,000 per month. Pay day 18th of each month." The building was destroyed by fire in the early 1920s.

**Norcatur**            1916    ?                                          UTD

A mention of Norcatur occurred in a 1916 theatrical trade paper. An acting troupe reported playing Norcatur, but did not indicate where the performance occurred. No remaining buildings in Norcatur appear to have been an opera house, but no exact information is available.

**North Topeka**    1872    Lukens Opera House                Standing
                          (Opera house portion removed)

Constructed in 1872 at a cost of $10,000, the Lukens Opera House was a three-story, native stone building. Today the third story has been removed, as has the stage on the second floor, but the remainder of the building at 807-811 North Kansas is standing. The front has been re-faced.

The building was 75' x 58 1/2'. The second floor stage was 20' x 50'. In 1883 the theatre boasted 12 changes of scenery and a Chickering grand piano. The auditorium contained seating for 800 on movable seats fastened to long boards. The floor of the auditorium was also used for dances and roller skating. There was a balcony on the third floor. Gas lights were used in the hall. Floodlights behind reflector shields provided illumination for the stage. Even though the lights would flicker when they were fanned by drafts, this was considered very up-to-date lighting for that time. The stage curtain was rolled up by hand and from the front rows the audience could view Mr. Lukens raising and lowering the heavy curtain using a windlass.

At a time when few opera houses even had a piano, Lukens Opera House boasted an elaborately carved rosewood, square grand piano. It was a Chickering purchased in the 1860s and was believed to have cost $1,000. When Blind Boone appeared at the Opera House he played on this piano and declared it was the "sweetest toned instrument that he had ever played upon." When the 1903 flood damaged many residents' pianos, this valuable opera house piano was used for practice by many children in the community. Unfortunately, when the building was remodeled in 1929 the piano was made into a table.

Lukens Opera House was opened in 1872 with a local talent show of "Ten Nights in a Barroom." Later Louie Lord, a prominent Midwestern actress, played a two-week engagement at the Opera House where one performance was scheduled as a benefit to raise money to establish a fire department. The community wanted to see Louie as Topsy in "Uncle Tom's Cabin" and while she let it be known that she would rather play in something else, she bowed to the community's wishes and performed as Topsy.

The Opera House also hosted such noted speakers as John J. Ingalls and Charles Curtis. But, one of the most memorable performances occurred outside the opera house when 12-year old Fred Stone, who later went on to national success in vaudeville, Broadway and the movies, walked back and forth across Kansas Avenue on a wire stretched from the top of Buechner's Meat Market to the top of the Lukens building.[5]

| | | | |
|---|---|---|---|
| Norton | 1885 | Norton Opera House | NLS |
| | 1907 | The Auditorium/Norton Theatre | Standing |

Prior to the construction of Norton's first opera house the courtroom, the school, and churches were used for home talent plays and by traveling theatrical companies. The Graves brothers, Albert and John Wesley, built the first opera house, a brick structure, in 1885. It was lighted by kerosene. The Opera House was opened on Thursday, December 31, 1885, by the Robert Buck Dramatic Company's production of "Fanchon, the Cricket." The opera house was used for many community functions including declamations, stage performances, dances, masquerades, lodge work, banquets, oratorios, address, and commencements. This performance space was razed in 1914.

After the old opera house was condemned, money was raised for the erection of a new Auditorium. Construction began in the spring of 1907 and the theatre was formally opened on December 17th of that year. This imposing structure, designed by the Boller Brothers, was a ground-floor theatre with a seating capacity of 400 and a stage 32' x 62'. A 110-volt Edison system provided illumination. The front curtain depicted a picture frame containing a garden view. The frame was surrounded by painted drapes. There was an orchestra pit, two boxes on either side of the stage, and beautifully painted and stenciled garlands and Greek goddesses on the plaster above the proscenium, the fronts of the balcony and gallery, and throughout the auditorium.

A most unusual event was reported to have occurred in Norton. It involved Ida Weston Rae, a popular performer in Nebraska and northern Kansas, when she appeared in Norton. She was pronounced dead by physicians at the Lathrop Hospital in Norton and later revived by the undertaker called to embalm her body.

The Auditorium is still standing. Through the efforts of community members the theatre, which had been used as a movie theatre for many years, was purchased by the town of Norton, and with public donations and a great deal of volunteer labor, was renovated into a two-screen movie theatre, the Norton Theatre.[6]

| | | | |
|---|---|---|---|
| Nortonville | 1884 | Opera House/McCarthy's Opera House | Standing |
| | 1908 | City Hall/Roxie Theatre | Standing |

C. C. McCarthy, merchant and banker, built the McCarthy's Opera House in 1884. It was located on the second floor of a brick building. Seating was for 200 with a stage 12' x 25'. Stoves and lamps provided heat and illumination. After the new opera house was constructed, this space was used as a gym and divided one side for boys, the other for girls. The stage was located between the two sides. This structure is standing and while it has been converted to apartments, a few indications of its former use as a gym can be seen. For instance, upside-down horseshoes protect the light bulbs in the ceiling.

In 1908, the new City Hall and Opera House was built. In addition to a large ground floor auditorium, the structure contained the city jail, fire department and city council room. The bell on the top of the building was the fire bell. The theatre was known as the Roxie.

The Roxie still stands, and although the auditorium portion of the building has been gutted and converted to an auto shop, the lobby remains. In fact, the lobby still contains the ticket booth, movie posters, and the stairs that used to lead to the theatre's auditorium.

| | | | |
|---|---|---|---|
| Norwich | ? | Opera House | NLS |
| | 1907 | Ashley Opera House | UTD |

Norwich's first opera house was destroyed by fire. The second opera house, the 1907 Ashley Opera House seated 300 and contained a 29' x 45' stage. Stoves and gas provided heating and illumination. It is assumed to be no longer standing.

# O

| | | | |
|---|---|---|---|
| Oakhill/ Oak Hill | ? | Dieter's Hall | NLS |
| | 1915 | Shannon Opera House | NLS |
| | 1917 | New Opera House/ Grand Opera House | UTD |

The first Oakhill opera house, Dieter's Hall, was located on the second floor above Dieter's Grocery Store on the northeast corner of Ellis and Main. This structure is no longer standing. There are references to two other performance spaces, the Shannon Opera House and the Grand Opera House. It is likely that the Grand Opera House was Dieter's Hall, renamed. A resident of Oakhill remembered that movies had been shown on the second floor of Dieter's Grocery store. This same structure may have been the Shannon Opera House. A 1915 picture identified Shannon's Opera House as being located on the second floor of a frame structure on the south side of Main Street. The building was razed.

The manager of the New Opera House/Grand Opera House, F. H. Dieter, writing in a 1917 theatrical trade paper reported that his theatre seated 350, was well equipped, and regularly lighted. Such popular companies as the Al G. Story Stock Company and the Locke Players appeared at the New Opera House during the spring of 1917 and both companies were well received.

| | | | |
|---|---|---|---|
| Oakley | 1900 | City Hall | NLS |
| | 1900 | Oakley Township Hall | NLS |

Oakley was the location to two halls, both built in 1900, the City Hall and the Oakley Township Hall. Neither is standing.

| | | | |
|---|---|---|---|
| Oberlin | 1880 | Chapman's Hall | UTD |
| | 1883 | Opera House | NLS |
| | 1891 | G.A.R. Hall | UTD |
| | 1906 | Oberlin Opera House | NLS |

The first mention of entertainment in Oberlin was the December 23, 1880, presentation of "Among the Breakers" by the Pioneer Dramatic Club at Chapman Hall. It was reported that the play was a "grand success" with about seventy reserved seats sold and standing room only. No information is available on Chapman's Hall, but it is unlikely that it is standing.

The first Opera House in Oberlin was a two-story frame building constructed in 1883. Located at 124 N. Penn, this structure is no longer standing. Minstrel shows, home talent productions, and high school graduations were held there. An 1891 reference described an event that began at the Opera House and G.A.R. Hall. This would indicate that the opera house might also have been known as the G.A.R. Hall.

A new and quite grand Oberlin Opera House, designed by the Boller Brothers, architects, was constructed in 1906. The auditorium seated 869 and contained a stage 29' x 54' with a proscenium opening 28' wide by 22' high. Scenery was by the Kansas City Scenic Company. The illumination was provided by electricity 110-volt system. In 1936, this ground-floor opera house was converted to a motion picture theatre and the name was changed to the Chief Theatre. This structure was heavily damaged by fire in 1973 and later razed.[7]

| | | | |
|---|---|---|---|
| Ogallah | 1904 | Ogallah Hall | NLS |

The 1904 Ogallah Hall is no longer standing.

| | | | |
|---|---|---|---|
| Oketo | 1905 | Oketo Opera House | Standing/Stage |

Built in 1905, the Oketo Opera House is not only standing with a stage, but is still in use as a community center. The ad curtain from the opera house hangs in the Oketo Museum. The exact date that the curtain was painted is unknown, but it was after phones came into use and prior to 1937.

The first wedding dance held in the Oketo Opera House occurred March 14, 1906, celebrating the marriage of Margaret and Hiram Herring. In addition to wedding celebrations, other community uses for the opera house included high school plays, 4-H, firemen, school reunions, family reunions, parties, showers and anniversary celebrations.

| | | | |
|---|---|---|---|
| Olathe | 1860 | Hayes Hall/Hayes Opera House | |
| | 1871 | American Hall | NLS |
| | 1880 | Hayes' Opera House/ Olathe Opera House | NLS |
| | 1904 | Grange Opera House | UTD |
| | 1910 | Eagle Opera House/ Grand Opera House | UTD |

Several early theatres are reported to have existed in Olathe. These may be the same or different structures, but none is in existence today. The first lyceum course in Olathe was organized in October 1860 and held in the Hayes Hall. A description of this hall reported that kerosene footlights lighted the stage. The audience sat in wooden chairs on the orchestra floor and upstairs was a circular balcony. Many classes of the Olathe High School graduated from this stage, and during elections people gathered at the opera house to listen to the returns.

It is likely that the Hayes Hall or Opera House was later known as the American Hall. Hayes, a prominent Civil War veteran, sold the Hayes House hotel to Colonel S. R. Burch in 1868, who changed the name to the American House. The 1874 Atlas Map of Johnson County, Kansas and an 1877 theatrical guide referred to the American Hall, located in the American Block at the corner of Park and Chestnut Streets. In 1877, the American Hall seated 400, and contained a 13' x 25' stage with a moderate amount of scenery. The last reference to this structure in any theatrical guide was 1883.

The American House became a very popular stop for traveling theatrical companies and Colonel Burch's two daughters became part of productions that required children. One daughter, Muria, had long blonde hair and was always in demand to float across the stage as one of the angels in "Uncle Tom's Cabin." The other daughter, Jessie, was used as a baby in productions. An event of great public interest occurred when Tom Thumb and his wife, who were playing in Olathe, arrived at the front of the American House in a miniature hack drawn by Shetland ponies. Colonel Burch sold the American House in 1886 after the death of his wife, but the hotel continued to be the stopping place for traveling companies.

The September 23, 1880, *Olathe Mirror* proclaimed the opening of a splendid new opera house, the Hayes' Opera House, located on north Chester Street facing west. This structure was reported to have replaced a similar auditorium of unpainted and unfinished rough lumber. To prepare for the building of the theatre, Colonel Hayes visited public buildings in several of the larger cities in order to be aware of the latest in theatrical appointments. The second floor theatre had a seating capacity of 700 with a stage 18' x 40' and a fair stock of scenery. Besides public entertainment, church groups and political parties met there.

Several other Olathe opera houses appeared in theatrical guides. A 1904 guide listed the Grange Opera House. This second floor facility with a seating capacity of 836 contained a stage 30' x 56' with scenery by The Kansas City Scenic Company. The Olathe Opera House, with the same dimensions as the Hayes Opera House, was listed in a 1907 guide. Finally, the 1910 Eagle Opera House/Grand Opera House was listed in a 1910 theatrical guide. This ground-floor theatre had a seating capacity of 475.[8]

| Olpe | ? | ? | NLS |

At one point an open-air theatre was located between the Panhandle Warehouse and Diebolt's Store in Olpe. Later a theatre, which is no longer standing, was built north of the hotel. There is no indication of whether these were theatres for traveling companies or for moving pictures.[9]

| Onaga | 1878 | Rolf Hall | Standing |
| | 1878 | Hyman Hall | NLS |
| | 1912 | Brunner Movie Theatre | Standing |

Henry Rolf erected the first stone building in Onaga in 1878. The third floor of this three-story structure was used as a public hall. This building is standing. Another hall constructed during the same period was the Hyman Hall built around 1878. The hall had a stage and was the scene of a few good vaudeville shows and where the first moving pictures were shown. This structure is no longer standing.

In 1912, J. J. Brunner constructed a two-story building on Leonard Street. The ground floor was used for stores; the second floor was the location of a theatre. This theatre was larger with a better stage and dressing room facilities than the previous theatre. The seats could be arranged around the sides of the room and the floor used for dances and for local high school basketball games. This structure is standing and in use as a factory.[10]

| Oneida | 1885 | G.A.R. Hall | UTD |
| | 1889 | Harter's Hall | UTD |
| | 1898 | Gillman Hall | Standing |

Oneida was the site of several halls. The G.A.R. Hall was first mentioned in an 1885 theatrical guide. It was managed by Noah Hardy and seated 300. It is unlikely that this structure is standing. An 1889 theatrical guide listed both the G.A.R. Hall and a second facility, Harter's Hall managed by the Harter Brothers. It is not known whether this hall is standing. The third hall, Glimmer's Hall, constructed in 1889, is standing. It is not known whether it ever contained a stage.

| Opolis | 1889 | Delong's Hall | NLS |

Delong's Hall, with seating for 200, was in operation in 1889. This facility which was used primarily as a "dancing hall" is no longer standing.

| Osage City | 1879 | Howe's Opera House/Osage City Opera House | Standing |
| | 1883 | Union Hall | UTD |
| | 1886 | Grand Opera House | NLS |

Osage City is the location of a building that once contained an opera house. Howe's Opera House, also known as the City Opera House was constructed in 1879. This was a second-story theatre with a seating capacity of 600 and a stage 20' x 50' that contained seven sets of scenery. The ceiling of the auditorium was decorated with a painted dome. Although the stage has been removed, the back stage area, papered with play posters, still exists.

An 1883 and an 1885 theatrical directory contained listings for both the City Opera House and also for Union Hall. Union Hall seated 800 with a stage 24' x 50' and 12 sets of scenery and 50 pieces on flats. It is probable that this structure was later known as the Grand Opera House.

The second opera house in Osage City was known as the Grand Opera House and also as the O'Neil Opera House. This second-story facility with a seating capacity of 500 contained a large stage 25' x 50'. The front roll curtain was raised and lowered through the use of a windlass. This structure is no longer standing.[11]

| Osage Mission/ | 1879 | Opera House | NLS |
| St. Paul | 1885 | Steadman's Hall | NLS |
| | 1885 | P.H. Moore's Hall | NLS |
| | 1889 | Koenig's Hall | NLS |
| | 1892 | Graves Hall | NLS |
| | 1912 | Graves Hall | NLS |

Osage Mission, later known as St. Paul, boasted a number of different halls, none of which remains. The first reference to a performance space was an 1879 mention of an Opera House. By 1885 two halls existed, Steadman's Hall seating 300 and P. H. Moore's Hall seating 1,000. There was also an 1889 reference to Koenig's Hall that seated 500. Several of these early halls could have been the same structure; the different names simply reflected the current owner of the building. There was also an 1889 reference to an opera house. It is not known whether this was the same structure as the 1879 opera house or to a previously mentioned hall. Finally, in 1892 W. W. Graves constructed a hall and then built a second hall in 1912. The first stage show in this building occurred on September 26, 1912.

| Osawatomie | 1885 | Agnew Opera House | NLS |
| | 1912 | Majestic Theatre | NLS |

The Agnew Opera House, constructed about 1885, is no longer standing. The facility was destroyed by fire. The Majestic Theatre constructed in 1912 is also no longer standing.[12]

| Osborne | 1879 | Town Hall | NLS |
| | 1885 | Smith and Hatch Opera House/ Osborn Opera House | Standing |
| | 1904 | Osborne Opera House /Auditorium | NLS |

The first performance space in Osborne, the Town Hall, constructed in 1879, was a one-story wooden structure that was used for all public gatherings, dances and traveling shows. Following its use as a town hall, the building served as a Presbyterian Church and later as a cabinet shop. This structure is no longer standing.

The second performance space in Osborne was the Smith and Hatch Opera House. This facility, constructed in 1883, was located on the upper floor of two buildings on Main Street. It, too, was used as a dance hall and also as a skating rink and an opera house. An 1885 theatrical guide indicated that the hall was owned by F. N. Hatch and seated 200. Companies appearing there included the Andres Opera company and the Madison Square Garden Theatre Company. The Kerkhoff and Locke Dramatic Company was organized in Osborn. They appeared extensively in that part of the state for many years. Also, the Bell Stock Company was comprised of local Osborne thespians. The building housing the Smith and Hatch Opera House is standing, but the stage has been removed and the front of the building refaced.

C. E. Cunningham built an armory for Company G of the Second Regiment of the Kansas National Guard in 1904. The armory was constructed of limestone quarried nearby. After a few years the regiment was disbanded and the building was turned into a combination theatre and opera house known as the Osborne Opera House or the Auditorium. A number of popular mid-western companies appeared there including the famous Scandinavian violin virtuoso Christian Hansen, the Hillman Stock Company, The Royal Entertainers presenting "Ten Nights in a Bar Room," and Sanford Dodge in "Julius Caesar." Following its use as an opera house the structure served as the City Hall and then as the location of various businesses. It was razed in 1959.[13]

**Oskaloosa    1884    Critchfield Opera House    NLS**

Constructed in 1884 by a prominent Oskaloosa family, the Critchfield Opera House seated 500 and contained a 28' x 22' stage. The facility was heated by stoves and illuminated by lamps. The opera house was home to masked balls at Halloween and New Years Eve in addition to appearances by magicians, hypnotists and show troupes. Blind Boone, the pianist, also appeared at the opera house. Terry Critchfield, the builder of the opera house, managed a local bank while his son, Mel, was responsible for their general store and opera house. The Critchfields always reserved the 6th row for performances. The Critchfield Opera House building, which was renovated following the devastating 1950 tornado to house the County Offices, is no longer standing.

**Oswego    1879    Oswego Hall/Opera House/**
                              **New Grand Theatre    Standing**

The 1879 structure that contained the Oswego Hall is standing. This opera house was a large second floor facility that contained a stage 20' x 30' with six sets of scenery and drop curtain. When constructed, the auditorium seated 450 but was later expanded to hold 1,000.

The Opera House opened September 5, 1879, with The Serio Comic Opera Company's performance of "H.M.S. Pinafore." The opera house was used for many community functions including dances, operas, plays, and wrestling matches. In 1915, it was renamed the Grand Theatre and became a movie theatre. The theatre later became a dance hall, then occupied by the VFW and finally as a storage space for the store below. The stage has been removed.

For many years Oswego was home to C. E. (Charles Edward) Colman who as a young man appeared as a banjoist and comedian, but later became quite well known as an accomplished scenery and sign painter and operated the Colman Scenic Shop.[14]

**Ottawa    1864    Lathrop's Hall    NLS**
                1868    Sheldon Hall/Hamblin
                           Opera House    NLS
                1880    Opera House/Ottawa Opera House    NLS
                1885    Zellner Hall/Opera House    NLS
                1889    Auditorium    NLS
                1896    Rohrbaugh Theatre    NLS
                ?         Shanner Hall    Standing
                1921    Ottawa Municipal Auditorium    Standing/Stage

In the spring of 1864, title to land held by the Ottawa Indians was secured through treaty and purchased in connection with the founding of Ottawa University. A town company was formed in September 1864. Early arrivals to this location pitched tents until the construction of permanent buildings began April 1, 1865. The old capitol building at Minneola was dismantled, moved to Ottawa, and reassembled on the northeast corner of Second and Main. The upstairs, known as Lathrop's Hall was used for town meetings, festivals, entertainments and church meetings. This historic structure was eventually destroyed by fire.

Ottawa's first real performance space was Sheldon Hall. After the Hamblin Block was constructed at Second and Main in 1867-68, H. F. Sheldon added a third story and fitted up a town hall and courtroom. This facility seated 600, contained a 25' x 60' stage, and four sets of scenery. It is likely that this structure, which is no longer standing, was later referred to as the Hamblin Opera House, and that it was destroyed in the same fire that destroyed the Ottawa Opera House.

By 1883, Col. Samuel B. Rohrbaugh had constructed a building to the south of the Hamblin Block and added a stage. This was known as the Ottawa Opera House. The Ottawa Opera House seated 900 and contained a stage 30' x 50' with 20 scenes and a piano. The Hamblin Block, including the opera house, burned in 1895, just three weeks before the Auditorium fire.

Located at Second and Main and built in 1885, the Ring-Smith-Barker Building was also known as Zellner Hall. This third floor auditorium was in general use for many years. This structure is no longer standing. Another hall, Shanner Hall, on west Second, was used for public meetings. This structure is standing, but none of the hall's original features remains.

In 1889, Col. Samuel B. Rohrbaugh, the original owner of the Ottawa Opera House and a lumberyard owner, significantly remodeled a skating rink and carriage factory into an auditorium located south of the current Ottawa Municipal Auditorium. The opera house was the site of traveling theatrical troupes, musical groups, and Ottawa University performances and speakers. This wooden structure seating 1,000 was destroyed by fire March 2, 1895.

Following the fire, Rohrbaugh offered to rebuild if the people of Ottawa would help finance the project. With $6,000 in local money and $40,000 of his own, Rohrbaugh built the Rohrbaugh Theatre. Designed by Ottawa architect George P. Washburn, the three-story brick facility seated 1,200. The auditorium contained a balcony and eight boxes, beautifully painted ceilings and walls, and huge electric chandeliers. The stage was 42' x 62'. In addition, there were 18 painted backdrops. This ground-floor theatre was illuminated with gas and electricity and contained a scene room. On opening night, January 31, 1896, the great Salvini and his company presented "The Three Guardsmen." Special trains brought dignitaries from Topeka, Kansas City and Lawrence for the theatre's grand opening. The Rohrbaugh Theatre was destroyed by fire October 2, 1915.

Built in 1919 and officially opened in 1921, the Ottawa Municipal Auditorium was a memorial to the Franklin County's soldiers who died in World War I. While smaller than the Rohrbaugh Theatre, the Municipal Auditorium seated 900 and contained a balcony. Badly damaged by the 1951 flood, the theatre was renovated in 1974, and is in use today.[15]

**Overbrook    ?    Blocker's Hall    UTD**

No information is available concerning Blocker's Hall. It is assumed to be no longer standing.[16]

**Oxford    1889    Rink Opera House    UTD**
              1907    Johnson Hall    UTD
              1909    Opera House    Standing

The first reference to a performance space in Oxford occurred in an 1889 theatrical guide. This was the Rink Opera House. The second reference to a performance space occurred in 1907 and was to Johnson Hall. This hall seated 600, had a platform for a stage, and was illuminated by lamps. Although no specific information exists, it can be assumed that neither of these structures is standing. The Oxford Opera House, a large brick structure with a ground floor auditorium, was constructed in 1909. This structure is standing vacant and without a stage.

# P

**Palco    1917    Township Hall    Standing/Stage**

The Palco Township Hall constructed in 1917 is standing with it original stage and is in use as a community center.

**Palmer    1913    Chase Opera House    NLS**

In operation between 1913 and 1925, the Chase Opera house is no longer standing. In 1905, Ed Chase moved his family from their farm into Palmer. He ran a livery stable until the first cars came to town, at which point he sold his horses and remodeled the livery stable, put in a dance floor, a stage, and bench seats around the wall. A roll curtain with painted advertisements graced the front of the stage. Chase also supplied a piano for the hall. A big stove provided heat.

When a show arrived in Palmer, the phone office would give a general ring — "Show tonight" and the residents of the community would fill the hall. Eventually the Chase family moved and the Opera House was sold and torn down for the lumber.[1]

| Paola | 1883 | Globe Hall | UTD |
|---|---|---|---|
| | 1883 | New Opera House/Paola Opera House | UTD |
| | 1889 | Grand Opera House | UTD |
| | 1897 | Mallory Opera House | NLS |
| | 1908 | Nickel Theatre | Standing |

1883 theatrical guides list two performance spaces in Paola, the New Opera House managed by L. D. White and Globe Hall, also managed by L. D. White. The New Opera House that seated 600 and contained a 24' x 40' stage with eight sets of scenery was located above White's Drug Store. Globe Hall also seated 600 but had a much smaller stage, 18' x 22'. It did, however, have a complete set of scenery. Although no specific information is available, it is assumed that neither of these structures is standing

In 1885, C. H. Mallory bought land for what was to be the Grand Opera House. This facility seated 675. The stage was 31' x 42' with seven sets of scenery and a piano.

In 1897, C. H. Mallory constructed a second opera house, The Mallory Opera House. This was a ground floor facility located in a three-story brick building. The theatre seated 950 with a stage 30' x 50'. When it opened, the facility was lighted by gas, but in 1908 electric lights were installed.

The opera house contributed significantly to the community. Such noted speakers as William Jennings Bryan, Bishop Quayle, Senators Long, Curtis and Harris, and Governors St. John, Glick, Leedy, Hoch, Bailey, Stubbs, Hodges and Capper all spoke at the opera house. Graduation exercises for the Miami County District Schools were held there as were numerous community functions. In 1904 when Richards and Pringle's Big Minstrel Show performed, the patrons were encouraged to remain and hear the election returns while being entertained by a special program. Also, because Paola had no building large enough for indoor games, in 1905 some high school girls rented the opera house and played basketball there during the winter.

Following the death of Mrs. Mallory in 1912, Charles Mallory and his daughter Lucy moved to the apartment on the third floor of the opera house. Upon Mallory's death in 1917, Lucy became the owner and manager of the opera house and received rave reviews from acting company managers. One characterized her as "one of Kansas best hustling women managers." The correspondent to the theatrical trade paper went on to say, "There is a chance at this town for some real hustler to make some money, as Miss Mallory wishes to dispose of this fine piece of property which includes many offices and an up-to-date opera house."

The opera house was never sold and Lucy continued to manage the opera house and live in her apartment in the building, as did another woman. Two businesses were located on the ground floor of the opera house building and a doctors' office was located on the second floor. In the basement and at the rear, A. Tiede and Walsh had a battery shop and station.

Late in the evening of October 27, 1921, the other woman resident of the opera house had just returned home when she discovered a fire. She rushed to Miss Mallory's room, awakened her and the two women escaped with their lives, but saved none of their belongings. Dr. Haldeman, who slept in a room adjoining his office, also escaped with nothing but the clothes he was wearing. At the time the fire began, it was confined to the battery service station in the basement and to the stage.

The firemen and volunteer workers responded to the fire bell, but for 40 minutes were not able to get any water due to low water pressure. By this time the fire had spread to the stage scenery, curtains, canvas, and the whole interior of the opera house. In just 90 minutes from the time the fire was discovered, the building was in ruins. While no lives were lost, a great deal of valuable personal property was. In addition to the contents of the other apartment and the doctors' offices, Lucy Mallory reported that her loss was about $22,000 including diamonds, silverware, heirlooms, china, furniture and an original edition of Dante's Inferno valued at $300. Because the opera house was less than a half block from the fire station, Lucy only carried $10,500 worth of insurance. It was commonly believed that with adequate water pressure, the building could have been saved.

Lucy Mallory eventually sued the city of Paola for the replacement cost of the opera house and her personal losses. Due to conflicts of interest, the case did not proceed as it should have and became quite complicated, including an arson case against the owners of the battery shop located in the basement of the opera house. They were accused of setting the fire for the insurance they carried on their shop.

A spectacular development in the case occurred when Lucy Mallory, a small woman, attacked the county attorney with a riding whip, striking him four times across the face. This followed an altercation where Miss Mallory was reported to have said, "You double-crosser! You double crossed me and defied the attorney general." The county attorney supposedly replied, "To hell with you and the attorney general's office. I'm responsible to the people of Miami County."

It was at this point that Lucy struck the county attorney with a whip she had hidden in her parasol. The court stenographer took the whip from Miss Mallory and prevented her from any further damage. Later that day, Lucy was taken before the Justice of the Peace where she was put under a bond of $1,000. The bond was given and she was released. Finally, in 1925, four years after the fire, the damage suit filed against the city of Paola by Miss Mallory was dismissed.

In 1908 a much smaller theatre, the Nickel Theatre, was housed in a building that may have been built by the Oyster brothers in 1892. In 1912, the Nickel Theatre was sold and remodeled. Opera chairs replaced the planks that were used for seating and the name changed to the O.K. Theatre. This structure is standing without a stage.[2]

| Paradise | 1916 | ? | NLS |
|---|---|---|---|

Mentioned in a 1916 theatrical trade paper, this performance space in Paradise is no longer standing.

| Parker | ? | Union Hall | NLS |
|---|---|---|---|
| | 1917 | Opera House | NLS |

There are two references to performance spaces in Parker. These may have been the same structure. The facility known as Union Hall was destroyed by fire, as was the 1917 Opera House.

| Parsons | 1878 | Hew's Hall | NLS |
|---|---|---|---|
| | 1881 | Edwards Opera House | NLS |
| | 1904 | Elks Theatre/Orpheum | NLS |
| | 1908 | Lyric Theatre | UTD |

The earliest performance space in Parsons was Hew's Hall. This facility, first mentioned in 1878, seated 300 and contained a few pieces of scenery. Then, on Washington's Birthday in 1881 the Edwards Opera House was opened. One resident observed, "It is only by comparison that anything is appreciated and the Opera House compared with Hews Hall, which had done duty for long years with its dry-goods-box stage, cramped quarters, wooden chairs and circus seats, was grandeur personified."

Located at the southeast corner of Central and Broadway, The Edwards Opera House was a second floor facility. The theatre was beautifully decorated with scenes of Switzerland. Life-sized statues of Shakespeare and Schiller were in niches in each corner fronting the stage. There were two curtains and seven scenes. The theatre seated 850 and contained a stage was 24' x 50'. Illumination was provided by gas. The Parsons Coeur de Lion Coronet band under the leadership of J. W. Smith opened the theatre. The opening night speaker was absent, but a grand march was held and dancing began and continued until 3 a.m. Neither of these first two theatres is standing.

Heralded as one of the finest theatres in the state and costing $65,000, the Elk's Theatre constructed by the Elk's Lodge of Parsons, opened December 22, 1904. The stage performance that night was "Wizard of Oz." Thirty-five years later the Technicolor movie version of the same story was shown in the theatre. All of the first night attendees were invited to attend as guests. Thirty-one persons who had been present for the original Grand Opening were present.

The Elk's Theatre, a ground floor facility, had a seating capacity of 1,209 with a stage 38' x 63'. The theatre boasted 12 dressing rooms, five on stage and seven on the second floor. In 1914, the theatre was sold to W. F. McAller, equipped for movies, and renamed the Orpheum Theatre. The structure was completely destroyed by a fire that started in the early hours of December 20, 1939.

The final theatre built during this period was the Lyric Theatre. It was located on the ground floor of a two-story brick building. The current disposition of this structure is not known.[3]

| | | | |
|---|---|---|---|
| Partridge | 1901 | Stahly Hall | NLS |

In 1901, Mose Stahly built a large brick building on the southwest corner of Main and Avenue F in Partridge. This structure contained businesses on the ground floor and the second floor housed a large room used for community activities such as dances, literaries, lecture courses, and a location for young men to play basketball. The upstairs also housed living quarters and a doctors' office. This structure is no longer standing.[4]

| | | | |
|---|---|---|---|
| Pawnee Rock | 1876 | School Hall | Standing |

An 1889 theatrical guide identified the School Hall in Pawnee Rock as a performance space. It has been suggested this was a structure built by the Santa Fe Railroad in 1876 to house newly arrived wives and children while their husbands built their homes. The building, constructed of stone blasted out of Pawnee Rock, is still standing but the second floor does not contain a stage. After its use to house settlers, the upstairs of the building served many other functions including being used as a school and as a Knights of Pithias Hall.

| | | | |
|---|---|---|---|
| Peabody | 1889 | Butler's Hall/Sawtelle Hall | NLS |
| | 1899 | Masonic Opera House | NLS |
| | 1921 | Sunflower Theatre | Standing |

The first public entertainment space in Peabody was Butler's Hall constructed in the late 1880s by W. D. Butler. Later, this structure was known as Sawtelle Hall. The facility, with a seating capacity of 600, is no longer standing. The builder of the hall, W. D. Butler willed a sum of money to be used for refreshments for children on the last day of school. This observance is called the Butler Day Picnic.

Built in 1899, the Masonic Opera House was a much more elaborate performance space. This ground-floor theatre seated 500 and contained a stage 30' x 50'. The theatre, which was heated with furnaces and illuminated with gas, was eventually destroyed by fire.

Built in 1921 and designed by the Boller Brothers architects, the Sunflower Theatre served as a combination live performance space and motion picture theatre. It is currently standing vacant without a stage.[5]

| | | | |
|---|---|---|---|
| Peck | 1887 | Roll Hall | NLS |

Peck's Roll Hall was located on the second floor of a two-story frame building constructed in 1887. The ground floor was used as a general merchandise store and post office while the upstairs was the location of many activities including community plays, dances and literaries. The second floor may also have been used as a roller rink and bowling alley. The structure is no longer standing.[6]

| | | | |
|---|---|---|---|
| Penokee | 1887 | Community Hall | NLS |

The town of Penokee was begun in 1887. Part of a frame building constructed that year was used as a community hall. This structure is no longer standing.[7]

| | | | |
|---|---|---|---|
| Perry | 1913 | Opera House | Standing |

Constructed in 1913, the two-story brick building that once housed the Perry Opera House is standing. However, nothing of the second floor theatre remains.[8]

| | | | |
|---|---|---|---|
| Peru | 1907 | M. W. of A. Hall | UTD |

In 1907, the M. W. of A. Hall was the site of performances in Peru. The hall seated 500 and contained a stage 22' x 32'. Heating and illumination were provided by gas. Although no information is available, it can be assumed that this structure is no longer standing.

| | | | |
|---|---|---|---|
| Phillipsburg | 1905 | Winship Opera House/ Majestic Theatre | Standing/Stage |

In 1905, Fred E. Winship constructed the Winship Opera House at the corner of 4th Street and State Street. Built from bricks manufactured in the city's own brick factory, the building had a 100-foot front and was a joint venture with the Masonic Lodge. The first floor of Winship's half of the building was used to house his general merchandise business with the opera house located on the second and third floors. The interior walls of the opera house were Venetian red and trimmed in gold.

Many popular entertainers performed at the Opera House including the North Brothers, Chick Boyes and Milburn Stone. An item in a 1917 theatrical trade paper recounted a pleasant Christmas Eve spent in Phillipsburg by another favorite, the No. 1 Hillman Ideal Stock Company. It was reported that the manager of the company gave a Christmas banquet for the members of his company on Christmas Eve in the dining room of the Depot Hotel at Phillipsburg. Each member of the company received a sterling silver souvenir, such as a pocketknife, card case or vanity box with engraved initials.

Other companies to appear at the opera house included the Wilkes Musical Players and the Wheldon Comedy Company. The largest traveling company to appear at the opera house was reported to have been a minstrel show of 35 people that traveled with its own band and orchestra and arrived in Phillipsburg in a chartered train.

Times changed, movies arrived and the opera house underwent a major renovation. The second and third floor opera house was changed to a ground-floor theatre with a balcony, and became a motion picture theatre. This theatre, the Majestic, is still in use and can claim the distinction of being the longest, continuous-use place of entertainment in Kansas. The secret to the theatre's success was that Ralph Winship, son of the builder of the opera house, managed it for many years. Ralph retired from this position in 1969. The town of Phillipsburg now owns the theatre.

A recent renovation changed the balcony of the Majestic into a small screen movie theatre so that an additional feature can be shown.[9]

| | | | |
|---|---|---|---|
| Pittsburg | 1882 | Hunter's New Amphitheatre/ Hunter's Opera House | NLS |
| | 1888 | New Opera House/Pittsburg Opera House | Standing |
| | 1888 | Wonderland Dime Museum and Variety Theatre | UTD |
| | 1904 | LaBelle Theatre/Orpheum | NLS |
| | 1908 | Mystic Theatre | UTD |
| | 1909 | Electric Theatre | UTD |
| | 1916 | The Klock | UTD |

Located in the heart of the Kansas coal mining district, Pittsburg has a long theatre history. Local entertainment was first presented in Hunter's Amphitheatre. Built in 1882, the structure was circular with a ring and raised seating for spectators. It was used by a circus that wintered in Pittsburg and also by traveling theatrical companies and locally produced entertainments. This was not a comfortable space. Seating was limited and in the winter it was quite cold. The facility became dilapidated and was torn down in 1908.

In 1887, the Payton Comedy Company, a repertoire show, visited Pittsburg. At that time there was no theatre, so they rented the second story of a store building, built a temporary stage, and installed seating; and for over five weeks they played to crowded houses. This company's appearance sparked the community's interest in having a theatre, so Frank Playter interested a Chicago businessman, J. Foster Rhodes, in building an opera house.

In 1888, this opera house, managed by John Ashbaugh of Topeka, opened with the comedy "Two Johns." The building was three stories and heated with steam. The Manufacturer's National Bank occupied the front of the first floor of the building with the opera house being located on the upper floors. The new opera house seated 1,000 and contained a stage 24' x 47'. With the opening of the LaBelle Opera House, the space occupied by the first opera house was converted to offices, but the building is still standing at the corner of Broadway and Fourth.

During the 1888 – 1889 season, Mary Angeline Sanders House was co-owner with her husband Isaiah Zelma House of the Wonderland Dime Museum and Variety Theatre located above the Larrimer and Donnilley's Furniture Store at 5th and Broadway. Nothing further is known concerning this structure, but it is assumed to be no longer standing.

W. W. Bell, an important person in the development of theatre in Pittsburgh, leased the Opera House in 1896 and managed it until he constructed the LaBelle theatre eight years later. Bell also managed outdoor summer theatres. Years later, Bell recalled famous performers who had appeared at the old opera house. They included Julius Brutus Booth, Eugene Mantell, Pauline Hall, Louis James, Otis Skinner, Eva Tanagway, Charles Hanford, Walker Whitesides, Amelia Bingham, Blanch Walsh, Robert Downing, Joseph Jefferson and May Irwin.

Opening on May 9, 1904, under the management of W.W. Bell and Oldendorf, the LaBelle was a plush theatre with thick Brussels carpeting, ferns and flowers decorating the stage, and the latest style opera chairs. The main floor featured box seats along the walls, two balconies and the "chicken roost," a third balcony. The seating capacity was 1,500 with a stage 38' x 63'. This ground-floor theatre was located on the corner of Fourth and Locust.

A large theatre, the LaBelle showed all of the big road shows. These included "Uncle Tom's Cabin" which would come to Pittsburgh by special railroad coach and baggage car. In addition to traveling companies, such notables as Houdini, Susan B. Anthony and Carrie Nation appeared at the LaBelle. Extremely popular for several years, the theatre suffered from the decline of interest in road companies and, in 1910, the Pittsburg Amusement Company purchased the theatre from Bell. Named the Orpheum Theatre, it reopened on September 17, 1911, with a performance by the John Phillip Sousa's band. From then on, it was a motion picture theatre. The theatre was destroyed by fire on November 24, 1915, and the space was later rebuilt as apartments.

In addition to the 1888 Opera House and the 1904 LaBelle Theatre, Pittsburg was the site of several outdoor theatres known as Air Domes. In later years, there were also several motion picture theatres that featured vaudeville. The first of these, the Mystic theatre located at 118 E. Fourth, opened in 1908. The Electric Theatre opened in 1909 and was located at 414 N. Broadway. The Electric combined pictures with vaudeville and included a full orchestra and a pipe organ. Later, this theatre was remodeled and became the Klock Theater and still later, the Fox Midland. Finally, built in 1914, The Grand, mainly a motion picture house, featured one act of vaudeville on Friday and Saturday nights in conjunction with the pictures. The current disposition of these three theatres is not known.[10]

| Plains | 1909 | Opera House | NLS |

The December 21, 1907, *Plains Journal* reported that, "It now looks as though that much talked of hall is going to be numbered among the realities. The latest developments are to build a two-story building with hall above and two storerooms below. Aside from being something that Plains is sure in need of, a building of this kind will be a good investment, as it will return at least 20 percent on the investment."

The building was constructed and for a number of years the second floor of the John W. Elder store on the southwest corner of Grand and Third street served as a city hall and Opera House. The structure was razed in 1920 following a fire.[11]

| Plainville | ? | Cronin Opera House/Plainville Opera House | NLS |
| | 1914 | City Hall | Standing |
| | 1916 | Hoff Theatre | Standing |

The original Plainville Opera House or Cronin Opera House with a seating capacity of 500 and a stage 20' x 28' was destroyed by a devastating fire in 1909. The 1914 City Hall was used as an opera house and is standing today as the Senior Citizens Center with its stage removed. Built in 1916 as a motion picture theatre, the Hoff Theatre was also used for a variety of entertainment functions. This building is also standing, but none of the original interior remains.

| Pleasanton | 1885 | Town Hall | UTD |
| | 1885 | Kincaid and Crockers Opera House | Standing |

1885 and 1889 theatrical guides listed two performance spaces in Pleasanton, the Town Hall and the Kincaid and Crocker Opera House. The disposition of the Town Hall is unknown, but the Kincaid and Crocker Opera House is standing vacant. The stage and half of the proscenium arch have been removed, but the dressing rooms and the other half of the proscenium arch remain. The last use of the opera house was as a clothing factory.

Opened with a grand ball on July 4th, 1885, the Kincaid and Crocker Opera House was a fine theatre located in a large, attractive building. The second-floor opera house consisted of an auditorium seating about 800. The stage was 20' x 30' with dressing rooms and storage space located on either side of the stage. The original lighting was oil lamps, but in 1903 the theatre was converted to gas. The stage was equipped with both a curtain that dropped and also an advertising curtain.

Over the course of its lifetime the opera house was used for a variety of entertainment and civic functions. Traveling shows, local organizations, public speeches, medicine shows and musical concerts all appeared at the opera house. Later it was used as a roller skating rink, and in 1924 as an armory with the stage used as a stock room. The auditorium was also used as a basketball court. Its final use was as a garment factory until its close in 1984.[12]

| Pomona | 1899 | White Ribbon Hall | UTD |

The only mention of a performance space in Pomona was from an 1899 reference to a Trousdale family performance in the White Ribbon Hall. No information is available on the location of the hall, but it is unlikely that it is standing.[13]

| Portis | 1916 | City Hall | NLS |

The Portis City Hall was the location of a variety of community functions. In addition, traveling acting companies appeared there. This structure is no longer standing.

| Potwin | 1885 | Whitmore Building/Rice Hall | Standing |
| | 1917 | Community House | Standing/Stage |

Built in 1885 by C. W. Potwin, the Whitmore Building was used for local talent productions, as a skating rink, and a basketball court. The structure is standing, but does not contain a stage.

The Community House of Potwin has its original stage and is still in use. This community center constructed in 1917 has been the site of home talent plays, town elections, church services, movies, various Christmas and Easter celebrations, and has served as a public library and even the city jail.[14]

| Powhattan | ? | Opera House | Standing/Stage |

The exact date of construction of the Powhattan Opera House is unknown, but it was in use by 1918. This two-story structure that contains a second-floor theatre with a stage, footlights, four dressing rooms, and the remains of some scenery is standing. Four stoves originally heated the hall. Although not currently visible from the street, the front of the building features a leaded and stained glass window that reads "Hall."

| Pratt | 1889 | Halls | UTD |
| | ? | Opera House | NLS |
| | 1911 | New Phoenix Theatre | UTD |

Theatrical guides listed several performance spaces in Pratt. An entry in an 1889 theatrical guide indicated that Pratt had "One (hall) with stage and the other conveniences. Several in which temporary stages have been erected and troupes remained a week at a time and did well." While there is no information concerning these halls, they were likely to have been located on the second floors of commercial buildings that are no longer standing.

An 1891 theatrical paper, the *Hutchinson Clipper*, indicated that Pratt had a new Opera House. This is probably the same structure mentioned in a 1907 theatrical guide. This facility seated 450 with a stage 16' x 24' and was heated with stoves and illuminated with lamps. Another reference indicated that the Pratt Opera House was a frame building located north of the post office and also served as the first municipal building. This structure is no longer standing.

The exact date of construction is not known, but the New Phoenix Theatre was a moving picture/vaudeville facility. A contemporary account indicated that, "Since this theatre opened, it has shown some of the best vaudeville and other attractions that have ever come to Pratt; and in conjunction with these shows, this theatre has always shown at least two or more long rolls of the best films it was possible to obtain." It is not known if this structure is standing.[15]

| Prescott | ? | Woodmen Hall | Standing |
| | 1920s | Victory Theatre | NLS |

Prescott was the site of several theatres. The first, the Air Dome, was located on the north side of Main Street. The Air Dome had a stage with roof, but the rest was open air. Lloyd Bortzfield painted the scenery for the Air Dome. He also painted murals on the walls of the Woodmen Hall. This hall is located on the second floor of what is now the bank. The murals, however, no longer exist.

The second performance space in Prescott, the Victory Theatre, is no longer standing. The Victory was the home of vaudeville and silent movies. The stage was at the west end and an overhead projectionist cubicle was located at the east end. Seating was on brown wooden chairs fastened together at the base. The stage curtain featured a painted outdoor scene. In addition to silent movies, occasional medicine shows took place in the theatre. It was also the location for high school plays and basketball practice.[16]

**Pretty Prairie     1936  Movie Theatre                Standing/Stage**

The Pretty Prairie Civic Theatre is located in an 1889 grocery and implement store. In 1936, the structure was converted to a motion picture theatre complete with stage, dressing room and roll curtain. This theatre, along with its original stage with footlight trough and roll curtain, is standing. While the main function of the theatre was movies, traveling shows occasionally appeared there. On the back of the curtain are messages written by traveling shows. One reads, "Good town-1939."

**Protection     1913  Pastime Theatre                Standing**

During the 1920s the second floor of the Protection Mercantile building was used as a movie theatre. The exact age of the structure is unknown, but it was standing in 1913. Although it no longer remains, there was a stage in one end of the second floor and in addition to movies, lyceum programs were presented there. By moving the seats to the sides of the auditorium, the space was also used for roller skating. An interesting architectural feature of the theatre is a center air vent. It is a four-sided tower with windows located in the ceiling of the auditorium. Originally the windows could be opened by rope, thus providing ventilation and cooling. Ventilation was especially important in buildings lighted by gas.[17]

# Q

**Quenemo     1907  Quenemo Opera House          NLS**

Although the exact date of construction is unknown, the Quenemo Opera House was listed in a 1907 theatrical guide. This second-story theatre seated 800 and contained a stage 14' x 30'. Stoves and lamps provided heating and illumination. Such traveling shows as "Uncle Tom's Cabin" and the Swiss Bell Ringers appeared in Quenemo. Local newspapers also mentioned appearances by Susan B. Anthony and Sojourner Truth. The structure is no longer standing.[18]

**Quincy          1899  ?                                     NLS**

The Trousdale Theatrical Troupe appeared in Quincy in 1899. The location of the performance is not known. No building large enough to accommodate a theatrical production remains in Quincy.[19]

**Quinter         1915  Electric Theatre                 Standing**

The building that contained the 1915 Electric Theatre is standing, but is now part of another building. Nothing remains of the theatre.

A glowing report on Quinter appeared in a theatrical trade paper. The correspondent for the Garrett Stock Company reported that they had played Quinter the week of January 1, 1916. "This is one that has been reported bad. The population is mostly Dunkards, and as a rule they do not patronize shows, but we got them coming and done a fine week's business." The Musical Reeds, a local company, also characterized Quinter as a good show town.[20]

# R

**Randal          ?       Opera House                   NLS**
                **1916  Cozy                             NLS**

There are references to two performance spaces in Randal, the Opera House and the 1916 Cozy Theatre. These might have been the same facility. Neither is standing.

**Ransom         1916  Opera House/Strand Theatre     NLS**

The Ransom Opera House, constructed in 1916, was the product of the Ransom Hall Company, an organization of Ransom businessmen. The theatre, with a stage 18' x 20', boasted $300 worth of scenery from the Kansas City Scenic Company that included six sets of scenery and a front roll curtain that featured a scene from the Arabian Knights surrounded by advertisements for the Ransom businesses. The house seated 382. The theatre, located on the second floor of a 50' x 80' brick building also contained three dressing rooms and a scenery room.

Over the course of many years the Opera House, later named the Strand Theatre, was an important feature of the community's entertainment. When the motion picture theatre was moved to the first floor of the building, the former theatre was converted to a roller skating rink with the addition of a maple floor. The Strand Theatre and Roller Rink, which carried the slogan, "Amusement Center of Northern Ness County" continued in business until 1961. The building was razed in the late 1960s.[1]

**Republic City  1885  Hall                              NLS**
**Republic        1917  Electric Theatre/Royal Theatre/**
                **1918  Opera House/City Hall       NLS**
**Republican City ?     ?**

There are several references to communities that bear similar names. Because it is not known whether they are the same or different, information will be given on all of them.

The first listing refers to a performance space in Republic City. This 1885 Hall is no longer standing. Mention of the 1917 Royal Theatre and Electric Theatre and the 1918 Opera House comes from a theatrical guide. Finally, the City Hall reference comes from residents of Republic. Local residents felt that the theatres under consideration were eventually known as City Hall. That structure contained a stage and painted scenery, and is no longer standing.

**Rexford         1903  Woodmen Hall                 NLS**
                **1922  Opera House/Legion Hall    Standing/Stage**

The exact date of construction is not available, but in 1903 Rexford had a M.W.A. Hall or Woodmen Hall. The hall, with its painted roll curtain containing advertisements for local merchants, was the site of public meetings, programs, dances, and concerts by the 20-member town band. This structure is no longer standing.

The Opera House/Legion Hall, constructed in 1922, is standing with its original stage, roll curtain, and box office. This facility, with a room that contains roller skates, is still in use.[2]

**Richland       1916  ?                                     NLS**

The only information available on Richland came from an account by a theatrical company manager who reported that the new theatre in Richland was, "one of the swellest little opera houses in that section of the country. The opera house manager has new scenery and is putting up a new piano. Shows playing this territory look him up." This theatre is no longer standing.

**Ringo           1918  Red Bird Theatre               NLS**

Ringo, a coal mining community located near Pittsburg, was the site of the Red Bird Theatre. This performance space is no longer standing. The diverse ethnic origins of the Kansas settlers were reflected in a comment by a company manager who played Ringo. He observed that many in the audience were Italian and it would be better if the plays were presented in Italian.

**Robinson      1889  Pomeroy's Hall                  NLS**
                **1920  Bird Cage Theatre               Standing/Stage**

In 1889 the performance space in Robinson was Pomeroy's Hall that seated 500. This structure is no longer standing. A second performance space in Robinson was constructed around 1920. The Bird Cage Theatre is currently used for the community theatre's annual production of a melodrama. The stage features a roll curtain from a rural school.

**Rosalia         1906  Mooso Hall                       NLS**

Built in 1906, Mooso Hall or the Town Hall was located on the second floor above the owner's hardware store. The hall served as a meeting place for various groups and was even used as a skating rink. The structure is no longer standing.

**Rosedale       1890  Union Hall                       NLS**
                **1899  Union Hall                       NLS**
                **?       McGeorge's Hall                NLS**

Rosedale is no longer listed on the state map and no information is available concerning the 1890 Union Hall, the 1899 Union Hall, or McGeorge's Hall.

**Rosemont          1887   Rosemont Hall                    NLS**

Rosemont was developed by a group of men from Kansas City. Following the completion of the railroad these men, including W. H. Frye, secured 50 acres of land and laid out a town site. Frye erected a two-story building 50' x 100'. The ground floor contained five large commercial spaces; the second floor housed 24 living rooms and a large hall. The structure was destroyed by fire in 1906.

**Rozel             1916   ?                                UTD**

Little information is available on the performance space in Rozel expect that there was a mention of Rozel in a 1916 theatrical trade paper. It is unlikely that this structure is still standing.

**Rush Center       1887   City Hall/Custer Hall            NLS**
                   **1913   Auditorium                       NLS**

Contemporary pictures of Rush Center indicate that there were two performance spaces in Rush Center. The first, City Hall or Custer Hall was standing in 1887. A 1913 picture of the flooded downtown area indicated that there was also an Auditorium. Neither of these structures is standing.[4]

**Russell           1879   Russell Opera House              NLS**
                   **1917   Isis Theatre                     NLS**

The Russell Opera House was constructed in 1879, eight years after the founding of the town. The structure was a second-floor theatre with a stage 20' x 40' and a seating capacity of 400 to 500.

An important occurrence at the Opera House was the annual high school commencement ceremony. It would begin with a welcoming address and oration given by the Salutatorian. This was followed by each member of the class giving his or her oration, as well as some musical numbers. The ceremony concluded with the address by the Valedictorian.

In addition to graduation ceremonies, banquets were also held in the opera house. These banquets were made difficult because all water had to be carried up stairs in buckets. Other functions that occurred there included home talent plays, lecture courses, and dances. This was also the site of the first movie to be presented in Russell. The Opera House was razed in the 1960s. In 1917, there was a second performance space in Russell, the Isis Theatre. This theatre was destroyed by fire.[5]

**Russell Springs   1916   Opera House/Empire Theatre       NLS**

The Russell Spring Opera House or Empire Theatre was in existence in 1916. A mention of Russell Springs in a 1916 theatrical trade paper indicated that it was a new theatre and that the company performing there played to "capacity." The structure was destroyed by fire in the 1920s.[6]

# S

**Sabetha           1883   G.A.R. Hall                      NLS**
                   **1917   Royal Theatre                    UTD**

The first performance space in Sabetha, the G.A.R. Hall, was mentioned in theatrical guides from 1883 to 1911. From 1883 to 1889 the G.A.R. Hall was listed as having a seating capacity of 1,000 and a stage 30' x 40'. From 1901 on the seating capacity was given as 500 with a stage 20' x 35'. This hall is no longer standing.

A 1917 reference in a theatrical trade paper indicated that Sabetha was the location of the Royal Theatre that contained a limited seating capacity. It is unlikely that this structure remains.

**Saint Francis     ?      Taylor's Hall                    UTD**
                   **1914   Electric Theatre                 NLS**

Because the first performance space in St. Francis, Taylor's Hall, contained neither a stage nor scenery, the 1914 Electric Theatre was a most welcome addition to the community. Established by E. W. Eggleston, an Atwood theatre owner, the Electric had a seating capacity of 350 and a stage 12' x 20' with new scenery. This theatre served as both an opera house and as a moving picture theatre. In addition, it was the location of high school commencements and community events. The theatre is no longer standing. It is also highly unlikely that Taylor's Hall is standing.

**Saint George      1916   Palace/Princess                  UTD**

The only reference to a performance space in St. George was found in a 1916 theatrical trade paper. It is doubtful that this structure remains.

**Saint John        1886   Opera House                      NLS**
                   **1889   Cornwall Opera House             UTD**
                   **1906   Convention Hall/Opera House      Standing/Stage**
                   **1916   Palace                           UTD**

St. John's first opera house, built in 1885, was a small building on the east side of the square. The structure was erected by St. John's first band leader, Charlie Harlan and by James W. Lowley. The first play presented there was "The Celebrated Case" starring Louie Lord, the most popular mid-western actress of that time. After the Convention Hall was built, the old opera house became a newspaper office; then in 1921, the structure was destroyed in the fire that consumed almost all of the businesses on the east side of the square.

No information is available concerning the 1889 theatrical guide listing of the Cornwall Opera House in St. Johns. It is likely that this is the same facility mentioned in the preceding paragraph.

In 1906, the Convention Hall, a large brick building 50' x 100', was erected. This ground-floor theatre contained a 30' x 50' stage. It was heated with furnaces and illuminated with gas. The Convention Hall opened March 5, 1906, with "Paying the Penalty" presented by the Majestic Stock Company.

Over the years the Convention Hall was used for numerous productions and community events. William Allen White and Henry J. Allen, governor and U.S. Senator, spoke there. The Redpath Lecture Course was also held there. In 1934, the building was remodeled to house the library and later the stage served as a teen recreation area while the remainder of the auditorium was used for storage. This facility now houses the town's heavy equipment.

In 1916, another performance space was the Palace Theatre. No further information is available concerning this theatre.[7]

**Saint Mary        1896   Miller Opera House               NLS**
                   **1912   Princess Theatre                 Standing**

The Miller Opera House was built as an exhibition hall at the fair grounds, but in 1896, Dr. George J. Miller moved it to the corner of Fourth and Bertrand. The opera house, located in a 32' x 80' building, had a seating capacity of 500, a stage 20' x 30' and six sets of scenery. There were also four dressing rooms. The opera house was the site of local commencements, grand balls, appearances by traveling stock companies and beginning in 1908, moving pictures and illustrated songs performed by local artists. In 1912, an article in the local paper announced that Dr. George Miller planned to tear down the opera house and use the land for other purposes.

In June of the same year, T. K. Fredorivicz of Arkansas remodeled the former Modern Woodmen of America Building at the corner of Fifth and Bertrand and opened it as the Princess Theatre. The exterior renovations included an arch with about 50 electric, colored lights, a ticket office and a recess at the entrance to the building. On the interior, the stage was located at the north end of the building. This ground-floor theatre featured vaudeville and moving pictures. In 1915, the Princess Theatre acquired a new curtain depicting a rural scene painted by a local artist, Peter Hefner. Over the years, improvements continued to be made as new projection and sound equipment was added. The Princess ceased operation as a movie theatre in the 1950s and is now used as a retail store.[8]

**Salina            1877   New Opera House/Bond Opera House/**
                          **Salina Opera House/New Theatre   NLS**
                   **1889   Coaster Park Amphitheater        UTD**
                   **1907   Convention Hall                  NLS**

In 1877, the New Opera House, financed by a joint stock company made up of local citizens, was erected on the southeast corner of Seventh and Iron at a cost of $1,500. The builders used Salina brick. This was a large second- and third-story theatre with the stage at the north end. An 1889 report gave the seating capacity as 500 with a stage 25' x 40'. Ten years later, the stage was listed as 35' x 46' and the seating capacity as 800. It is possible that these larger dimensions were the result of remodeling.

The opera house was the site of high school commencements and last-day-of-school programs by students in the lower classes. The Catholic fairs, modeled after

Kansas Communities | 135

the Mardi Gras, were also held there. Other uses of the facility included medicine shows, plays, and debates.

An unusual incident occurred at the Opera House when a young reporter for the *Saline Journal*, Henry Allen, attempted to scoop the story of a secret meeting of the Farmer's Alliance. Allen hid in the rafters in the attic of the theatre, but was discovered when he tried to straighten his cramped legs and one went through the ceiling of the auditorium. Allen was stripped of his notes and escorted to the door and told not to come back. Allen went on to become the governor of Kansas and later served as a U.S. Senator.

While important to the community, the Opera House was never a financial success and, in 1894, was sold at a sheriff's sale. W. P. Pierce bought and remodeled it. The opening featured Mattie Vickers, a well-known actress. Lionel Barrymore also appeared there in "Arizona." In 1912, the Opera House was remodeled and named the New Theater. This name was selected from suggestions submitted by the public. The structure was razed in 1928 and the United Life Building erected on the site.

An 1889 theatrical guide contained a listing for Coaster Park Amphitheatre that seated 2,000 and was "Elegantly and comfortably arranged. First-class in every particular." No further information was found concerning this venue.

The second major performance space in Salina was the Convention Hall constructed in 1907 at a cost of $48,480 by Salina United Commercial Travelers. It later passed to Putnam Investment Company and finally became a movie theatre known as the Grand Theatre. Located at the corner of Santa Fe and Walnut, this ground-floor facility had a seating capacity of 1,700 and a stage 35' x 64'. Gas and electricity provided the illumination. Convention Hall became the center for community events. Over the years many notable performers appeared there including Paderewski, Edgar Bergen and Charlie McCarthy, Blind Boone, Rin Tin Tin, Al Jolson, Houdini and Ethel Barrymore. In 1913 or 1914, a skinny freckled faced girl known as Ginger Rogers appeared with her father and mother. DeWolf Hopper, a famous singer and later husband of gossip columnist Heda Hopper, appeared at the Convention Hall in "Matinee Idol," and both William Jennings Bryan and Franklin Delano Roosevelt spoke there. This structure was razed in 1946.

Two other performance spaces, while not actually theatres, were important to entertainment in Salina. Prior to 1877 the dining room of the Pacific House was used for entertainments, concerts and balls. This was a first-class hotel located in the 400 block of West Ash and contained the largest hall in the city prior to the construction of the opera house. And much later, The Ted North Players, a well-known Kansas acting company, appeared in tent performances in Salina's Stella Park located on East Iron.[9]

**Saratoga** 1889 Town Hall NLS

In 1889 Saratoga, a town of 450 located near Pratt, was the location of a 400-seat performance space, the Town Hall. Saratoga is no longer listed on state maps.

**Savonburg** 1919 Opera House/Rhoads' Hall NLS

Rhoads' Hall or the Opera House, constructed by Dusty Rhoads in 1919, was the site of that years' annual high school commencement. By 1920, Rhoads was showing moving pictures in the facility. The structure is no longer standing.[10]

**Sawyer** 1916 Opera House NLS

Sawyer was the location of one or possibly two opera houses. None remain.

**Scammon** 1910 Scammon Theatre NLS

In 1910, Scammon was the site of a large ground-floor theatre with a seating capacity of 1,000 and a stage 30' x 53'. The theatre contained ten dressing rooms, each heated with steam, and "toilet rooms" on stage and in the house. Both gas and electricity provided illumination. The facility had its own electric system, meter and generator. In 1916, the manager advertised Scammon as, "the best Sunday town in the Southwest." The Scammon Theatre is no longer standing.[11]

**Scandia** 1889 City Hall/Opera House/
Princess Theatre NLS

Scandia's 1889 City Hall, later known as the Opera House and then Princess Theatre, is no longer standing.

**Scott City** 1890 Case's Opera House NLS
1907 Scott City Opera House Standing
? Auditorium NLS
1921 Opera House/Majestic/
Uptown/Majestic Standing/Stage

The first reference to an opera house in Scott City was an 1890 mention of a performance taking place at Case's Opera House. Mr. Case, one of the founders of the Scott City Town Company, owned the corner lot on the southeast corner of Main and DeGeer, later changed to 5th. A newspaper article announced that, "There will be a Grand Masquerade Ball at the Opera House February 12th. Oysters will be served. Music by the Valley Orchestra. Come and have a good time." The structure is no longer standing.

The Scott City Opera House was located on the second floor of the A. B. Timmerman Building. This structure, built in 1907, is standing, but no trace of the opera house remains. The facility had a seating capacity of 800 with a 30' x 12' stage.

The third performance space in Scott City was the Auditorium. Constructed at the northwest corner of Sixth and Court Streets, this eight-sided structure was used for a variety of purposes. Movable seats allowed the floor to be cleared for basketball games and roller skating. When traveling troupes such as the Wallace Bruce Players appeared, the facility could be arranged as a theatre. The Auditorium contained an elevated stage with curtain and dressing rooms. The building also contained a motion picture screen, and projection equipment was elevated behind the audience. After 1921, the structure was dismantled.

In 1921, the fourth performance space in Scott City opened. This theatre, located in the 400 block of Main Street, was first called the Opera House, but about 1930, the name was changed to the Majestic Theatre. It seated 600 with a stage and dressing rooms. The main curtain contained advertising for local merchants. There was also an orchestra pit in front of the stage and sometimes live musicians played for productions. Milburn Stone of "Gunsmoke" appeared at the Majestic, as did Smiley Burnett from the Gene Autry western films. In 1966, the name of the theatre was changed to the Uptown Theatre. The theatre is once again in use, this time as an elegant restaurant and is known as the Majestic. The stage remains and is sometimes used for performances.[12]

**Scranton** 1907 O'Brien's Opera House NLS

O'Brien's Opera House in Scranton is no longer standing. This facility seated 600 and contained a 26' x 50' stage. The opera house was heated with stoves and illuminated with lamps.

**Sedan** 1885 Opera House NLS
1896 Ackarman's Opera House NLS
1904 Sedan Opera House Standing

The Sedan Opera House, now the home of the Emmett Kelly Museum, has had a long and eventful history. The Opera House was twice destroyed by fire, and twice rebuilt at the same location.

The first structure, constructed by W. H. Bryan, was 50' x 75' and built of native stone. The lower story was divided into three rooms. The upper part was one large room that contained a stage and dressing rooms. The opera house was first used April 27, 1885, for a dinner to celebrate the anniversary of the Odd Fellows. This second-floor opera house continued to be used for dramatic productions and for community events until it was destroyed by fire April 11, 1890.

The fire, first reported fifteen minutes before midnight, originated in the two-story building next to the opera house. Despite extreme efforts to save the opera house, the timbers supporting the opera house roof were soon in flames. Next, the staging and scenery caught fire. At this point, efforts were directed to saving the contents of the opera house such as the chairs and chandeliers.

In 1895 E. C. Ackarman bought the lots of the former opera house and constructed a new native stone opera house 75' x 75'. Again, the opera house, owned by the A.O.U.W., was on the second floor of the building. The first performance held in the new opera house was an appearance by the Talbot Concert Band on March 20, 1896. As with the previous theatre, this opera house was used for community events. At various times the four churches of Sedan, Christian, Methodist, Baptist, and Presbyterian held their meetings in the opera house. Other activities to occur there, in addition to traveling theatrical troupes, included the annual Chrysanthemum Show sponsored by the Ladies Aid of the Christian Church.

History repeated itself in the early morning hours of Tuesday, December 3, 1903, when the opera house was destroyed by a fire which apparently originated in the banquet room located under the stage.

Immediately after the fire, it was decided to rebuild. The building was expanded by 25' making the structure 50' x 100'. An additional set of stairs was added, the stage was moved to the west end and a gallery added at the east end, and the seating capacity of the house was increased from 300 to 600. The Kansas City Scenic Company furnished scenery and the proprietor of the company, Mr. Bronough, personally supervised the installation of the drop curtains. The first event to be held in the new opera house was the May 26, 1904, high school commencement. The ceremony, however, was marred by the fact that the unfinished roof leaked. Audience members had to use umbrellas, and the rain pounded on the tin roof so loudly that some of the girl graduates could not be heard when they delivered their commencement addresses.

The new opera house was formally dedicated in August 1904. The Lyceum Stock Company filled every seat in the house as the audience viewed "The Woman In Red." Other performers to appear at the Sedan Opera House included a June 1904 appearance by Blind Boone. This popular black pianist was blind, but a gifted musician. His performance included imitations of musical instruments, the Marshfield tornado, and incoming trains.

By 1921, use of the opera house was waning. The new American Theatre showed the latest moving pictures and was heavily patronized while very little occurred at the opera house. One of the last events to be held in the opera house was the 1921 Chrysanthemum show. Later, the building was used as an armory for the Tank Company and the 353rd Infantry Regiment Reserves. The stage was removed and opera house portion of the building was used as a roller skating rink until the late 1950s. The first floor of the building now houses the Emmett Kelly Museum.[13]

**Sedgwick        1889   Congdon's Opera House            NLS**

Congdon's Opera House of Sedgwick is no longer standing. This facility, first mentioned in an 1889 theatrical guide, had a stage 18' x 40' and a seating capacity of 600. It was heated by stoves and illuminated by gas.

**Selden          1905   Kline Opera House                NLS**
**                1916   Grand                            NLS**
**                1916   Crystal                          NLS**

The first performance space in Selden, the Kline Opera House, built about 1905, is no longer standing. One or possibly two other theatres also existed in Selden.

A 1917 mention in a theatrical trade paper reported that "Selden has two theatres, the Grand and Crystal. The Crystal is a new house. Both houses are nice theatres and well heated but have small stages. There are two factions in town and that is the reason for the two theatres. The town is lucky to support one let alone two theatres." The Grand theatre might have been the Kline Opera House, renamed. Neither of these theatres is standing.

Not all community entertainment occurred at the opera house. Memorial Days and the Fourth of July were celebrated out of doors. These celebrations always began with a parade by the G.A.R. in uniform. Following the parade and band music, the women laid out a basket dinner on a platform and after that there were horse and foot races, ball games for the men and visiting for the women. The evening's entertainment concluded with a dance that lasted half the night. Often an organ was borrowed for the dance. One of the men in the community would bring his violin, but he only knew one tune, "Sweet Bye and Bye," which he played over and over.[14]

**Seneca          1882   Seneca Opera House               NLS**
**                1885   Opera House/Hatch Opera House    NLS**
**                ?      G.A.R. Hall                      NLS**
**                1928   Royal Theatre                    Standing/Stage**

The first opera house in Seneca was constructed prior to 1882. This theatre, the Seneca Opera House, had a seating capacity of 600 and a stage 20' x 35' with six or seven complete sets of scenery. Built by Charles G. Scrafford and J. H. H. Ford, it was known as the "leading place of amusement in the city."

The New Grand Opera House appeared in theatrical guides between 1885 and 1895. This theatre had a seating capacity of 1,000, a stage 30' x 44', with nine sets of scenery. This was a ground-floor theatre with two dressing rooms under the stage. A theatrical guide listing indicated that this was the "largest and best ventilated hall in the city; lighted by gas; 84 burners; 3 bars over stage; 25 footlights." Other names for this theatre included Martin's Opera House, Hatch Opera House and the Grand Opera House. Nothing further is known about this structure. It could have been the 1882 opera house or the G.A.R. Hall.

The exact construction date of the G.A.R. Hall is not known, but it was destroyed by a tornado in 1896.

In 1927 J. L. Lamb, a wealthy Oklahoma oil man, bought the 1882 opera house and remodeled it, retaining very little of the original structure. This theatre, named the Royal Theatre, has been remodeled several times, the last time making it into a two-screen theatre. This theatre is standing and in use today.

**Severance       1885   IOOF Hall                        NLS**

Built in 1881 by the IOOF King Lodge No. 144, the Severance IOOF Hall is no longer standing. The building was two stories, the first used as a theatre and the second for lodge functions.

A Severance resident, Hallie M. Peters, provided a detailed account of this structure that was so important to the town of Severance. Entrance to the opera house was gained through two wide, swinging doors that opened onto a small vestibule. There were ticket windows on either side. Then, double swinging doors lead into the theatre. The stage was at the far end of the building. Across the front of the stage, in the early days, was a string of oil lamps with reflectors. The wings were painted to simulate tapestry draperies and overhead was a sky blue canvas. Dressing rooms were located on either side of the stage. There were side approaches at either side of the stage and on the right hand side was a platform for the organ and later a piano. The orchestra pit was down in front.

The floor of the auditorium was level with 350 chairs arranged to have three aisles. Letters and numbers were painted on the side walls to indicate the location of the chairs. The floor was laid with hard maple suitable for dancing and skating. Two large iron stoves, one in the front and one in the rear of the auditorium, provided heat.

The second floor of the structure was used for lodge meetings and over the years a number of organizations met there including the IOOF, G.A.R., WRC, AHTA, Modern Woodmen, Masons, Knights of Columbus, VFW and Ladies Auxiliary. In the early years of the opera house, the Women's Relief Corps held a fair on the fourth Saturday in October. The money raised was used to care for the needy. In the evening, a dance was given. This was used as a coming out party for the young girls.

Another outstanding event that involved this Hall was the Decoration Day activities. The Grand Army of the Republic and the WRC gave the program early in the afternoon. Later in the day, the children, marching to the drumming of Willie Curtis or Harry Chapman, went to the cemetery on Oak Hill and decorated the graves of the soldiers and sailors.

Coming to the opera house to witness some form of entertainment was the height of excitement in the latter part of the 19th Century. People arrived by teams and wagons, buggies, surreys and, of course, men came on horseback. During the cold winter months, the women arrived with blankets tucked around them to keep out the cold. While the show was in progress, the teams were hitched to a long chain located along the side of the street south of the Opera House.

During the late 1880s and the 1890s, home talent plays were in vogue. A very popular play was "Lady Audley's Secret." This show was so well received that it was presented in towns all around Severance. Another home talent play was "Ten Nights in the Bar Room." This popular temperance play had a sad aftermath. The man who played the drunkard died from the same condition that he had depicted, not too long after playing the part. Other towns also brought their plays to the Opera House, said to be the best in the county.

Blind Boone was another performer who made an annual appearance in Severance. He played the piano wonderfully and one selection was "The Storm," a true story of a cyclone that his publicly reported having experienced when he was a small boy living in Missouri. A couple known as the Langs traveled with him. Lang delighted school children with a big green parrot named Lorita that he carried on his arm.

Other types of entertainment appeared at the Hall including traveling troupes and medicine shows, with their barkers who sold Sagwaw and Kantonka between the acts. Dances and parties were given for young folk and it was indeed a happy time. Severance was somewhat of a frontier town and folks came from miles around to attend the social events, plays, and what ever was advertised.

An important occurrence at the Hall was the yearly graduation exercise. Here, the graduates and their teachers and the school board were seated on the stage. Each graduate would step forward and deliver an oration that had taken weeks to write, prepare, and learn. The theatre would be packed, and folks came and sat on the straight, hard chairs to listen and admire their young people. Many important people crossed that stage during graduation ceremonies. James Campbell, who graduated in 1896, became Dean of Music at the University of Idaho and later Dean Emeritus of Music at the University of Los Angeles. Ed Franklin, a noted scientist at the University of Southern California, came back and brought a moving picture show to give the home folks an opportunity to view some of the interesting places and people he had seen and met while on an extended voyage with a group of British scientists.

Other activities occurring in the Hall included the first basketball games to be played in Severance. It is reported that the fun could be heard for blocks. Political campaigns were conducted from the stage. Usually a party for each side delivered an address, then the arguments would become heated and many a pitcher of water was consumed to quench the thirst of the lusty candidates. These debates could carry on for hours. The building was also used as a voting precinct. In the early years, the voters called through the small window on the outside to cast their ballots.

Hallie M. Peters closed her reminiscences by saying, "...but, nothing lasts forever, and in 1928 the IOOF lodge was dissolved and the building sold to a group of Severance residents. It was then called the Community Hall. The structure was later razed, bringing to a close a structure that stood for many years and brought pleasure to many people."[15]

**Severy**  1885  Huschart's Hall  NLS
            1889  Rink             NLS
            1907  Hall             NLS

Three performance spaces were reported in Severy. The first, listed in an 1885 theatrical guide, Huschart's Hall, seated 250. The next, reported in an 1889 theatrical guide, was the Rink. This facility was used for theatrical purposes and seated 500. Finally, a 1907 listing indicated that the performance space in Severy was the Hall, Cora Culver, manager. The Hall seated 400, contained a 20' x 10' stage, and was lighted with lamps. None of these structures is standing.

**Shady Bend**  ?  Hall  NLS

Nothing remains of Shady Bend except the foundation of a building. At one time, Shady Bend was the location of a thriving mill that produced Shady Bend flour, a bank, and a large grocery store with a hall above it. This hall was the site of everything from plays to dances.

**Sharon**  ?  Sharon Opera House  Standing/Stage

The Sharon Opera House, built by Elbert Rule, is standing with its stage. The opera house was located on the second floor of the Rule Mercantile. This facility was the site of traveling shows, lectures, high school plays, basketball games and a skating rink. Another activity that took place in the Opera House was high school graduation. In 1915, Senator Henry Allen of Wichita gave the second annual commencement address.

An interesting feature of the opera house is that signatures of acts that appeared there can be found on the back stage walls. These signatures indicate that the famous Georgia Colored Troubadours appeared there in 1920 and 1927.[16]

**Sharon Springs**  1916  Princess  Standing/Stage

The Princess Theatre mentioned in a 1916 theatrical trade paper, is probably the Strand movie theatre that is in use today. The interior of the Strand shows evidence of having been remodeled. The original stage extended further into the auditorium and there were dressing rooms in the basement.

**Sheldon**  1916  ?  NLS

Mentioned in a 1916 theatrical trade paper, this theatre is not standing. Sheldon can no longer be found on Kansas maps.

**Shoo Fly City**  1907  Ryland Hall  NLS

For many years, the 1907 Ryland Hall, located on the second floor of the Chapman building, was the center of social events in Shoo Fly City. This community no longer exists. The South Haven drive-in theatre was located where the hall once stood.[17]

**Simpson**  1916  ?  UTD

In 1916, the performance space in Simpson seated 500 and contained a stage 30' x 32' with new props, scenery, and electric lights. It is unlikely that this structure is standing.

**Smith Center**  1873  Tabernacle                NLS
                 1888  Smith Center Opera House  Standing
                 1912  Miller Opera House        Standing

In 1873, a circular wooden Tabernacle was constructed on George White's farm for use as a floral hall as part of a fair. But, due to poor crops, the fair was not a success and since the town businessmen had built the Tabernacle, the building was hauled to the city in sections. It was a large building with double entrance doors on the south side and a stage on the north. Rows of elevated seats were built around the sides like those in a circus tent. The floor of the structure could be used for skating or dancing, and when chairs were placed there, it became a performance space. This structure was razed in 1905.

In 1884, a spectacular dramatic performance, "The Spy of Shiloh," was held at the Tabernacle. Forty local people took part, in addition to several groups of children and youth appearing in different scenes. "The Spy of Shiloh" was a Civil War drama and all of the men who took part in the production were veterans, some who actually participated in the Battle of Shiloh. Years later, a 1907 newspaper article described the performance, "It was a real war drama, with soldiers carrying their muskets, marching to and fro, forming a living panorama of moving and living pictures of a great battle." The play ran ten consecutive nights.

Another important event held at the Tabernacle was the huge celebration that occurred in October 1887 on the night the Rock Island railroad laid the first rail in the east limits of the town. There were tables laden with food, bonfires and dancing far into the night.

Four businessmen erected the first real opera house in Smith Center in 1888. Each owned one of the lower floor store rooms and the opera house covered the entire second floor. The opera house was the center of community activities for many years. Finally, when movies became popular and interest in plays waned, the opera house space was divided into apartments. This large, brick building is still standing.

Ed Miller constructed the Miller Opera House in 1912. He purchased the old Odd Fellows Hall, tore it down and erected a larger one-story building on the same site. Miller purchased former Opera House furnishings such as the chairs, and called the new building the Miller Opera house. He leased the theatre for shows, movies, and high school commencements. This structure is standing and in use as a warehouse.[18]

**Solomon City**  1883  Wall's Hall                               UTD
                 1889  Opera House/Solomon Opera
                       House/Shane's Opera House                   UTD
                 1901  Solomon's Opera/Woodmen
                       Opera House                                 UTD
                 1911  Woodmen's Opera House                       NLS

Solomon City was the location of several opera houses. The first mention of a performance space occurred in an 1883 theatrical guide. Wall's Hall seated 550 and contained a 14' x 20' stage with a full set of scenery. The Wall brothers managed the hall. The next venue was a facility known variously as the Opera House, the Solomon Opera House and Shane's Opera House. It seated 300 with a stage 25' x 30'. This facility may have been the first Woodmen Opera House and Solomon's Opera House, but the stage dimensions differ. The latter was a second-floor theatre that contained a stage 12' x 15' and an auditorium that seated 250. It was heated by stoves and illuminated by lamps. While nothing is known about the current disposition of the preceding opera houses, it is unlikely that any is standing.

The final performance space, listed in a 1911 theatrical guide, was the Woodmen's Opera House located on the ground floor with a seating capacity of

400 with a stage 26' x 36'. Two large dressing rooms were located under the stage. This structure is no longer standing.

**South Haven** 1889 Hall  UTD
     (1907 Ryland Hall  NLS)

An 1889 theatrical guide listed a hall in South Haven. The seating was about 300. No information is available concerning this structure. It can be assumed that it is no longer standing.

A 1907 theatrical guide listed Ryland Hall in South Haven. The hall seated 200 with a stage 12' x 40', and was heated with stoves and illuminated by gas. It is likely that this is the same Ryland Hall that was located in Shoo Fly City. Ryland Hall is no longer standing.

**Spearville** 1909 Opera House  UTD
     1917 ?  NLS

In 1908, the Ancient Order of United Woodmen constructed a cement block structure at the corner of Avenue A and Main Street. The top floor was used for entertainment and contained a stage. The next year the group purchased chairs so that the hall could also be used as an opera house. A new schoolhouse that contained an assembly hall fitted with opera chairs was also constructed in 1909.

In 1917, T. J. Stinson, manager of the opera house, built a fireproof, tile theatre, finished in stucco with a seating capacity of 400. When this new theatre opened in July, the audience was kept comfortable by air that was circulated over ice cakes and kept moving by electric fans. The first pictures shown in the new theatre were scenes from the fighting zone in France. This structure is no longer standing.[19]

**Speed** 1916 ?  NLS

No information is available concerning the 1916 performance space in Speed. This structure is no longer standing.

**Spivey** 1889 Smalley's Hall  NLS

The only reference to a performance space in Spivey, Smalley's Hall, occurred in an 1889 theatrical guide. Nothing remains of the structure.

**Stafford** ? Peacock's Opera House  NLS
    1910 Weide Opera House  Standing
    1912 Mystic Theater  NLS

Peacock's Opera House, constructed prior to 1900, was a second floor facility that seated 400 with a stage 16' x 24'. Heat was provided by stoves and illumination by electricity. This structure is no longer standing.

The second performance space in Stafford, the Weide Opera House, was constructed in 1910. This large ground-floor theatre is standing, but the stage has been removed. At one time, the second floor was used as a movie theatre.

Stafford was the location of several movie theatres including the Electric Theater, 1904; The Gem Theater, 1910; and the Mystic Theater, 1912. A contemporary photograph indicated that the Mystic Theater contained painted scenery and was the location of local dramatic productions. None of these exists today.[20]

**Sterling** 1880 Goodson's Opera House/
       Morris Opera House  Standing
    1905 Morris Theatre  NLS

Sterling's first opera house, Goodson's Opera House, and later known as the Morris Opera House, is standing without a stage. This second floor theatre was built in 1880 with a seating capacity of 500, a stage 16' x 20', and a fair amount of scenery. The first Sterling High School commencement was held there in 1887. When Sterling's second theatre, the Morris, was built, the older theatre was taken over by the Young Men's Commercial Club, the forerunner of the Chamber of Commerce. The structure containing this opera house is standing. It is the location of the former Duckwall store.

A second, larger opera house, the Morris Theatre was constructed in 1906. This theatre contained a 30' x 44' stage with a fly loft. Four boxes were located in the auditorium. A 1906 theatrical newspaper reported that,

> The new Theatre to be built at Sterling, Kans. will cost more than $15,000, according to reports, and will be as elaborate as any of the theatres in towns many times the size of Sterling. The building will be 50' x 110', and the front will be of pressed brick. A dressing room 18' x 50' will be built on the rear. The interior will be modeled after the Orpheum in Kansas City, and there will be a room for a library and one for the Commercial Club. The lower floor will seat 500 and the gallery half as many, but in case of necessity rooms may be made so that a thousand people can witness the performances. The house will be heated by steam and lighted by electricity. Geor. A. Morris, who closed his old house about a year ago, is building the new theatre.

By the time the structure was razed in the 1990s little remained of the original theatre. The entire front and the upper story that housed the balcony were removed in 1950, and the stage and fly loft had been taken out much earlier.[21]

**Stockton** 1884 Hick's Hall/Stockton Opera House  Standing

John R. Hicks built Hicks Hall, later known as the Stockton Opera House in 1884. The first dramatic company to appear there was the Boston Theatre Company performing "East Lynn" followed by "Ten Nights in a Barroom." This was a second-floor facility. The following year, Tug Wilson painted six different scenes and a drop curtain. These were reported to be "a marvel of beauty." The next owner, M. B. Zimmer, installed maple flooring for a permanent skating rink where skating competitions were held and professionals demonstrated difficult feats.

From 1885 to 1923 when the high school was built, the Opera House was central to the life of the community. There were home talent plays, operettas, band concerts, political rallies, and memorial services in addition to commencements and appearances by professional theatrical troupes. Zimmer was generous and would donate the hall's use to groups raising money for charity. For example, a grand ball was held by the firemen to raise money for uniforms.

In later years, the stage of the opera house was removed and the space used for dances. Lawrence Welk is reported to have played in the hall several times. The VFW also used the facility. The structure that housed the Stockton Opera House is standing vacant.[22]

**Strong City** 1883 Opera House  UTD
      1901 Auditorium  Standing/Stage
      1917 Lyric Theatre  UTD

Nothing is known about the location of Strong City's first opera house except that it was mentioned in theatrical guides from 1883 to 1889. This theatre seated 400 and contained a 16' x 20' stage with a fair stock of scenery.

The second performance space in Strong City, the 1901 Auditorium, is standing with its original stage. Financed by a stock company of Strong Cityans, the structure was built of native limestone with dimensions of 50' by 80' and 40' high. The auditorium ceiling of pressed steel was painted in an artistic manner. The main floor and balcony combined for a seating capacity of 1,000. The opera chairs on the first floor were finished in oak with hat racks below. The stage was 22' x 50'.

The theatre's opening was April 19 and 20, 1901. About 1,000 patrons filled the theatre for the first performance, which was given by the Modoc Club. Following this, the opening night audience adjourned to the ballroom below the theatre for dancing where an Emporia orchestra provided music. In the early 1930s, the building was converted to a motion picture theatre, the Uptown Theatre. This building is currently vacant and suffers from extensive structural damage.

A third performance space in Strong City, the Lyric Theatre, was mentioned in a 1917 trade paper. It was described as a combination theatre for "photo plays" and live entertainment and contained a "new stage 15' x 24' with a 16' opening. Good scenery, electric lights, piano. Seats 208." Nothing further is known about this theatre.[23]

**Summerfield** 1900 Turner Hall/Opera House  NLS

The German Tournverein Society built the Turner Hall, later known as the Summerfield Opera House, located at the corner of Bethel and Front Street about 1900. The scenery was painted by Mr. Frank Powell.

A wide variety of community activities took place at the Opera House including Graduation Exercises, Baccalaureate Services, and home talent plays. Groups from neighboring communities even used the facility to stage productions for money making projects. The structure is no longer standing.[24]

**Sylvan Grove**   1895   Opera House                        Standing
                    1915   Cozy Opera House/ Theatre         NLS

The first opera house in Sylvan Grove, located above the Behrhorst Brothers Hardware Store, was constructed some time prior to 1895. Dances, parties, basketball games, and roller skating were held there. The structure, later used as the Masonic Lodge, is standing vacant.

The 1915 Cozy Opera House/Theatre was a large theatre that was used as a community building and was the site of silent movies and then "talkies," dances, basketball games, roller skating, and family reunions. A picture of the Cozy Theatre in use for roller skating showed boys in knickers and suit jackets and girls in floor length white dresses or white blouses and black skirts. A sign on the wall cautioned, "Fast Skating Not Allowed." This structure, that served the community for 40 years, was razed in the 1950s.[25]

**Sylvia**   1907   Sylvia Opera House   NLS

The Sylvia Opera House, located on the east side of Main Street, seated 350 and contained a stage 25' x 20'. Stoves provided heating, and illumination was provided by gas. This structure is no longer standing.[26]

**Syracuse**   1887   Barber Hall/City Hall/Opera House   NLS

E. P. Barber built Barber Hall, later referred to as the Opera House, in 1887 on the corner of Main Street and Avenue A. Located above Barber's general merchandise store, the hall seated 300 with an 18' x 20' stage. The building also housed the post office where Barber served as the first postmaster. His wife, Caroline, was a member of the first city council organized in 1887. This council was notable because it was made up entirely of women.

The first formal school classes were held in Barber's Hall, as were the first meetings of the Christian Church. In addition, many other community activities and dramatic productions occurred there. More recently, for a number of years Miss Thompson taught piano in the opera house. She also held piano recitals there. The structure was razed in 1982.[27]

# T

**Tasco**   ?   Opera House   NLS

The Tasco city building, also known as the Opera House, is no longer standing.

**Tescott**   1916   Odd Fellows Hall   NLS

The Odd Fellows Hall mentioned in a 1916 theatrical trade paper is no longer standing.

**Thayer**   1889   G.A.R. Hall                        UTD
              1889   K of L Hall                        UTD
              1896   Thayer Opera House/Fretwell Hall   UTD

An 1889 theatrical guide listed two performance spaces in Thayer. These were the G.A.R. Hall with a seating capacity of 150, but no stage or scenery, and the K of L Hall also with a seating capacity of 150 and no stage or scenery. Nothing is known about these structures. The guide indicated that the Presbyterian Church was sometimes opened for concerts and lectures.

Seven years later, an 1896 theatrical guide listed a Thayer Opera House located on the ground floor with a seating capacity of 200 and a 10' x 24' stage. This facility appeared in theatrical guides through 1910. Its name was also given as Fretwell Hall. The second name appeared when John Fretwell, an early 20th century mayor of Thayer, became manager of the theatre. Nothing is known about this structure, but it is unlikely that it or any of the previously mentioned performance spaces remain standing.

**Tipton**   1918   Opera House   Standing

The Tipton Opera House, mentioned in a 1918 theatrical trade paper, was a ground-floor facility. Although the original structure is standing, it has been incorporated into a larger building. The stage was removed many years ago.

**Tonganoxie**   1896   Lamming's Opera House   NLS

Lamming's Opera House, first reported in an 1896 theatrical guide, is no longer standing. It was a second-floor theatre with a seating capacity of 450 and a stage 12' x 50'.

**Topeka**   1858    Museum Hall                              NLS
              1869    Union Hall                               NLS
              1870s   Turner Hall                              NLS
              1871    Costa Opera House/Crawford Opera House   NLS
              1878    Germania Hall                            NLS
              1881    Crawford's New Opera House/ Topeka Opera House   NLS
              1882    Grand Opera House                        NLS
              1883    Globe Theatre                            NLS
              1900    Auditorium                               NLS
              1905    Novelty Theatre                          NLS
              1906    Majestic Theatre                         NLS
              1906    Star Theatre                             NLS

Located in the Ritchie Block on the southeast corner of Sixth and Kansas Avenues, the Museum Hall was the site of the first dramatic production in Topeka. On April 2, 1858, an amateur group from The Kansas Philomathic Institute presented "The Drunkard." The Museum Hall was destroyed by fire November 28, 1869.

Sol Smith Russell, a famous early-day comedian, presented the first professional production in Topeka. This occurred in 1867 when Russell appeared in the First Methodist Church building. The church wardens, however, were critical because the church was allowed to be used for such "ungodly purposes."

The first performance space, with a stage that contained a curtain and scenery, was the 1869 Union Hall with a seating capacity of 500. The design for the stage curtain was suggested by Major Tom Anderson, the local agent for the Union Pacific, and painted by Henry Worrall. Across the top of the curtain was a Union Pacific engine traveling at full speed with a cloud of smoke and a jet of steam to indicate its speed. Speed was further emphasized by the five or six train cars equipped with wings. The background of the curtain represented the streets of Topeka and showed great commercial activity. Advertisements for businesses were placed on the border of the curtain. In one corner of the curtain was a picture of Abram Burnett, the last chief of the Pottawatomie nation and in the other corner of the curtain was a picture of a popular local Indian vigorously ringing a huge dinner bell.

The first performance in this hall was by a noted Midwestern company, the Lord Dramatic Company of Chicago starring Miss Louie Lord. She was featured in an eleven day season at the Union Hall beginning January 6, 1870. The plays presented included, "The Hidden Hand," "She Stoops to Conquer," "The Sea of Ice," "Rip Van Winkle," "Uncle Tom's Cabin," and "Ten Nights in a Bar Room." This company made its second tour of eastern Kansas later that same year and played a week-long engagement at Union Hall in December 1870 and January and February 1871. For the two seasons together, 26 different plays were staged. The Union Hall is no longer standing.

Constructed in the 1870s by the Turnverein organization, the first Turner Hall was located at 507 Kansas Avenue on the second floor of the building. A later Turner Hall was erected at the corner of Crane and Harrison Streets. These halls were often the sites of band concerts. Neither hall is standing. Another 1870s hall that is no longer standing was the Germania Hall with a seating capacity of 700.

Costa's Opera House, constructed by Lorenzo Costa in 1870 and opened in 1871, had a seating capacity of 1,000 and a stage 30' x 50' with 10 scenes and a drop curtain. The first production of grand opera to occur there was the 1873 appearance of Mme. Anna Bishop. Another event of note occurred January 22, 1872, when the Grand Duke Alexis of Russia and his party were entertained there. The Grand Duke was returning from his famous buffalo hunt on the plains of western Kansas.

The first Crawford Opera House was the old Costa's Opera House remodeled. L. M. Crawford purchased the theatre in April 1880 and proceeded to spend a great deal of money on renovations. The Crawford Opera House opened in 1880 with the play "States Attorney." The renovated theatre had only been in use ninety days when it was destroyed by fire on December 2, 1880.

Crawford immediately began rebuilding and on September 5, 1881, opened his new opera house constructed at a cost of $50,000. An 1883 theatrical guide described Crawford's New Opera House as, "1st class in every particular and contains every modern appliance. Has parquet, dress circle, balcony and gallery. Heated with steam, lighted with gas and seated with latest improved opera chairs." The theatre seated 1,050 and contained a 30' x 50' stage with a full stock of scenery. The opening performance was Miss Lingard in "Our Boys." This theatre was destroyed by fire on September 24, 1906.

The Grand Opera House, a ground-floor theatre financed by a stock company, was opened in 1882 by the Emma Abbott Opera Company performing "Il Trovotore." In order to prepare for the theatre's construction Architect L. M. Wood, who also designed the Crawford, went to New York City to inspect theatres. The Grand was designed after the Booth Theatre. The seating capacity of the Grand Opera House was 1,500. The stage was 75' x 105' with 30 full sets of scenery. This theatre was constructed in the summer of 1882 at a cost of $66,000. Due to poor management and expensive upkeep, the theatre was never a financial success and had a number of managers before it was sold at auction to L. M. Crawford. Crawford continued to center his interests on his opera house, but when the New Opera House burned in 1906, he turned his major attractions to the Grand. In the summer of 1909, the Grand was remodeled and then completely rebuilt about 1915. This theatre is no longer standing.

The Globe Theatre appeared in 1883 and 1885 theatrical guides. No other information is available on this facility.

On September 25, 1900, the Auditorium was opened with a performance of "The Elijah." This featured a chorus of 300 voices and the Kansas City Orchestra. This was the city's first municipal auditorium. It was razed in 1938.

Opened in 1905, the Novelty Theater located on Kansas Avenue was managed by Roy Crawford, had a seating capacity of 870 and a stage 50' x 30'. The theatre featured traveling theatre companies, vaudeville and moving pictures. The Novelty Theater is no longer standing.

During the summer of 1906 L. M. Crawford opened what were known as Air Domes in Topeka, Emporia, Salina, Wichita, and Hutchinson. The airdome was a type of open-air theatre where high board fences were erected, the patrons were seated on planks and the sky was overhead. Only the stage, dressing rooms and box office were under roofs. If it rained, rain checks were issued. It was at an Air Dome in Topeka during the 1907 season that the Trousdale Company fired, and a few days later rehired Pearl White, an actress who later stared in the "Perils of Pauline" movie serial.

Following the destruction of Crawford's New Opera House by fire in 1906, Crawford purchased the old state printing plant at 108 E. Eighth and remodeled it into the Majestic Theatre. This theatre seated 950 and contained a 50' x 30' stage. During the 1910 season, it was managed by Roy Crawford. The Majestic presented vaudeville with the "Novel-scope," the new motion picture marvel. The North Brothers Stock Company also appeared there presenting a new play each week. The Majestic was remodeled in 1921 and is no longer standing.

A number of smaller theatres that featured vaudeville and moving pictures existed during the early part of the century. These theatres included the Best, Bijou, Elite, Lyric, Star, Metropolitan, Cozy, Novelty, Princess, Orpheum, Iris, Isis, Capital, Hip, and Olympic. None remains with the exception of the Princess located in North Topeka. That building, without stage, is standing vacant.[1]

**Toronto**         1885   Scott's Hall            UTD
                    1907   IOOF Lodge              NLS

Theatrical guides list two performance spaces in Toronto. The first, Scott's Hall, seated 300. The second, the IOOF Lodge, was located above the bank. The lodge hall seated 200 with a stage 14' x 24' and was illuminated by gas. The building is no longer standing. No information is available on Scott's Hall, but it is unlikely that it remains.

**Towanda**         1918   Opera House             UTD

The only mention of a performance space in Towanda occurred in a 1918 theatrical trade paper. The manager of an acting company reported that, "You managers will do well by booking the opera house at Towanda, Kans. This is a new oil town, and business is capacity every night." No information is available concerning this theatre.[2]

**Tribune**         1890   Court House             Standing

The upstairs courtroom in the 1890 Greeley County Courthouse was the location of all types of entertainments, dances, lodge meetings, fairs and silent picture shows.[3]

**Troy**            1868   Court House Hall        NLS
                    1885   Leland's Hall/The Leland  Standing

The first mention of a performance space in Troy was the Court House Hall. Built in 1868, this was Troy's second Court House. The hall seated 300 and contained a stage 10' x 15'. This structure is no longer standing.

Leland's Hall or The Leland was built by Cyrus Leland as the middle building in a block of three commercial buildings. This second-floor facility had a seating capacity of 500 and a 10' x 15' stage. The building is standing, but the opera house space has been converted to apartments. A long-time Troy resident remembered attending square dances with his parents and younger brothers and sisters at Leland Hall. The older children took care of the younger ones, and then, when their parents sat down to rest, the older children got to dance.[4]

**Turon**           1907   Opera House             NLS

Built in 1907, the Turon Opera House was a ground-floor theatre. It is no longer standing.

# U

**Udall**           1898   ?                       UTD

No information is available concerning where a December 1898 performance by the Trousdale family took place.

**Old Ulysis**      1887   Opera House             NLS

The Old Ulysis Opera House was built in 1887. It is not known whether any groups actually performed there, but it did function as a community center. This structure was built during the boom years, but the drought of 1889 and the hard economic times that followed hindered the town's development. In fact, the town's population decreased. In 1909, what was left of Old Ulysis was moved to a new location. At that time, the Opera House was moved to New Ulysis and became the courthouse. It is no longer standing.[5]

**Uniontown**       1885   Highbargin's Hall       NLS
                    1889   Well's Hall             NLS

Uniontown was the location of two performance spaces. An 1885 theatrical guide listed Highbargin's Hall with a seating capacity of 200, and an 1889 theatrical guide listed Well's Hall which also seated 200. These might have been the same structure. Neither is standing.

**Utica**           1917   Olympic                 UTD

In 1917, Utica was the location of a new opera house that seated 459, with a 16' x 22' stage fully equipped with scenery. This was a ground-floor theatre. No information is available concerning this theatre, but it is assumed to be no longer standing.

# V

**Valley Center**   1889   Carpenter's Hall        UTD

In 1889 Valley Center boasted one performance space, Carpenter's Hall. It is not known whether this building is standing.

**Valley Falls**    1884   Turner Opera House/
                           Valley Falls Opera House  NLS

The Turner Opera House or Valley Falls Opera House, as it was later known, was located on the second and third floors of the Turner Hall. The theatre first appeared in a theatrical guide in 1884 and was razed in the 1920s. The opera house seated 600 and contained a stage 16' x 40' with a full set of scenery. The facility was heated by stoves and illumined by lamps.[6]

**Vesper**          1916   ?                       NLS

A performance space in Vesper was mentioned in a 1916 theatrical trade paper. This venue is no longer standing.

# W

**Wabaunsee**       1901   Woodmen Hall            NLS

In 1901, Wabaunsee was the site of a two-story stone building that housed McKelvey's Store on the ground floor and the Woodmen Hall on the second floor. This structure is no longer standing.[1]

| | | | |
|---|---|---|---|
| WaKeeney | 1885 | Keeney Opera Block | NLS |
| | 1916 | Garden Theatre | UTD |

In 1880, J. K. Keeney, one of the founders of WaKeeney, began construction on a large, impressive, two-story stone structure. The walls of the building were chalk limestone while the steps, caps and sills were made from hard limestone, all taken from quarries adjacent to town. The lower story was divided into four rooms and the upper story was to be used as offices and as an opera hall. The structure was only partially completed when difficult economic times in Western Kansas halted construction. Five years later, the structure was completed. An article in the February 20, 1886, *Western Kansas World* contained this description of the newly completed opera house.

> ...the Keeney block contains an opera hall, in which every citizen of the town has a pride. It is 48 by 50 feet, 19 feet in height, has a seating capacity of 400, is well lighted, has perfect ventilation, is provided with new and beautiful scenery, and a large brass chandelier with the Rochester electric lamps. A handsome oil painting, symbolical of the various uses for which the hall is intended, adorns the center of the ceiling. The hall will be used for the district court, and for religious, social and public gatherings.

Less than ten years later, on February 4, 1895, the Keeney Block, including the opera house, was destroyed by fire.

A second theatre in WaKeeney, the Garden Theatre, was in operation in 1916. No information is available on the eventual disposition of the Garden Theatre.[2]

| | | | |
|---|---|---|---|
| Wakefield | 1896 | Dodson Opera House | NLS |

The Dodson Opera House was located on the second story of the Wakefield Bank. This structure is no longer standing.[3]

| | | | |
|---|---|---|---|
| Waldo | 1916 | ? | UTD |

No information is available on the Waldo performance space that was referred to in a 1916 theatrical trade paper.

| | | | |
|---|---|---|---|
| Wallace | 1886 | Hays Hall | NLS |

Prior to 1881, home talent plays were staged at Old Fort Wallace located two miles from the town of Wallace. This fort was abandoned in 1882. Then, in 1886 Thomas S. Hays built an opera house at Wallace. This facility, located on the second floor of a commercial building, was known as Hays Hall. The hall was the site of home talent shows, appearances by traveling troupes, political gatherings, and 4th of July and Decoration Day programs. The building is no longer standing.[4]

| | | | |
|---|---|---|---|
| Walnut | 1889 | Pierce Opera House | UTD |
| | 1907 | Walnut Opera House | NLS |
| | 1918 | Opera House/New Electric Theatre/Security Hall | Standing |

Walnut was the location of two or possibly three opera houses. The first, reported in an 1889 theatrical guide, was the Pierce Opera House. This facility seated 800. The second mention of an opera house in Walnut was in a 1907 theatrical guide. At that time, the Walnut Opera House had a reported seating capacity of 500 with a stage 20' x 30'. It is not known if these references were to the same or different theatres. The Walnut Opera House is no longer standing.

Another opera house, later known as Security Hall, is standing vacant and without its stage. This second floor facility, new in 1918, was described in most favorable terms by an acting troupe that performed there. "Played Walnut, Kans. Good town. Big business, fine new opera house and large dressing rooms with stoves in each dressing room and plenty of coal. This house is fully equipped with scenery and can handle any show, big or small."

By the summer of 1918 the name of the theatre had changed from "Opera House" to "New Electric Theatre." It seated 500 and contained an electric piano, electric lights, and two good dressing rooms with water and heat.[5]

| | | | |
|---|---|---|---|
| Walton | 1916 | ? | UTD |

A reference from a 1916 theatrical trade paper indicated that there was a performance space in Walton. It was not possible to determine if this building is standing.

| | | | |
|---|---|---|---|
| Wamego | 1882 | Leach Opera House | Standing |
| | 1895 | Rogers' Columbian Theatre | Standing/Stage |

A great deal has been written about Rogers' Columbian Theatre in Wamego, but an earlier opera house is also standing. In 1881 and 1882, Mr. Louis B. Leach constructed a building that was 50' x 100'. The ground floor contained 14 apartments, a reception room, bathrooms, heating and cooling rooms, dressing rooms and closets for giving Turkish and Russian baths. An early picture of the structure revealed its duel function. In huge letters on the front of the building was "Opera House" and under that "Turkish Bath."

Mr. Leach used information gained from visiting opera houses in other countries to design his facility. The heating and lighting apparatus for the entire building was located in the basement and sub-basement. This consisted of machinery for manufacturing gas and the most complete lighting plant of its kind in the west. The basement also contained a unique room made entirely of cement, floor, sides and ceiling. This room, completely fireproof, was where the paste for bill posting was made, and any other work that required an open flame was located there.

Entrance to the second floor Leach Opera House was from the street at the north through swinging doors, past the ticket office on the first floor. The stage was 26' x 46' with 16 sets of scenery and a piano. The scene on the drop curtain was "St. Goar On The Rhine." The auditorium seated 500. Lighting was from gas including 83 gas lights on and around the stage and 28 in the auditorium.

The Leach Opera House functioned for many years as a theatre and later, primarily as a location for banquets. The structure stands today in use as a funeral home. The chapel for the funeral home is located inside of what was once the auditorium of the theatre.

The second Wamego opera house, and the one the community is best known for, is the Rogers' Columbian Theatre. The theatre was located on the second floor above the Rogers Hardware store. Completed in 1895, the building featured ornamentation from the 1893 Columbian International Exposition held in Chicago, and purchased by J. C. Rogers in 1894 when the fair was dismantled. The fine oil paintings on the north and south walls of the opera house came from the dome of the U. S. Government building. These paintings were large, allegorical figures celebrating the country's prosperity and industry at the end of the 19th Century. The east exterior second floor windows were from the Brazil Building, and the large eagle with outstretched wings on the top of the building was also from the World's Fair.

The Rogers' Colombian Theatre had a seating capacity of 900, was heated by steam and was well lighted. The building was 50' x 180' with a stage 36' x 50'. The theatre was in continuous use from 1895 to 1950, first as a theatre and community center, then as a silent movie theatre, and finally as a modern movie theatre. Following a number of years of idleness, and thanks to tremendous community effort, the theatre and murals have been restored.[6]

| | | | |
|---|---|---|---|
| Washington | 1881 | Opera House/Knowles Opera House | NLS |
| | 1884 | G.A.R. Armory Hall | NLS |
| | 1884 | Rink | NLS |
| | 1888 | City Hall/Opera House | NLS |

Built in 1881 by a group of investors who formed a corporation, the Washington Opera House that cost $15,000 was the pride of the community. This opera house seated 700 with a stage 30' x 40' and a good stock of scenery. The theatre was opened by the Louie Lord Dramatic Company. While the Opera House was the site of numerous local productions in addition to those of traveling troupes, the opera house was not a financial success. The opera house building, seating and scenery valued at $20,000, was totally destroyed by a fire that occurred on the night of January 18, 1884.

During the period when there was no opera house in Washington, plays and other forms of entertainment were held in the G.A.R. Armory. This structure is no longer standing. Also, the skating rink that opened in February of 1884 was used for entertainment purposes. Four years later, the rink was fitted with comfortable seats and arc lights were added.

The financial well being of acting companies was often on shaky ground as the manager of a local hotel learned. The Boston Theatre Company played four nights in December of 1893 at the Armory. They presented such favorites as "East Lynne," "Lady Audley's Secret," and "Ten Nights in a Bar Room," but, the company left town without paying their board bill. The manager of the company promised to pay the bill after their first show at Wymore, Nebraska, their next stop. When the Washington hotel proprietor inquired at Wymore, he discovered that the manager of the company had left Wymore, stranding the members of the company who had not received their salaries for several weeks. The Washington hotel did not lose the entire bill, however, since some scenery had been left for collateral.

In 1888, there was civic interest in building a new opera house and the city voted in favor of bonds for a City Hall. Construction was begun and progress was made, but the first performance in the new facility featuring Miss Olive Thomson did not go as planned. First, the scenery painted by J. F. Close of Kansas City failed to arrive and the bare brick walls were draped with an awkward arrangement of flags. Next, the clammy death-like dampness peculiar to green plaster on the new walls chilled the patrons to the bone. The janitor also let the fire go out and made a great ruckus during the performance trying to get the fire started. Finally, in the middle of the first reading, the electric lights went out making it necessary for the managers to shuffle around arranging kerosene lamps. But, a week later, December 28th, the elegant new chandelier and the scenery arrived.

This new City Hall was a two-story brick structure 50' x 90'. The auditorium was 46' deep and the full width of the building. There was also a gallery projecting over the auditorium. Both the gallery and the auditorium seated 300 persons. The stage 27' x 50' contained two dressing rooms, and seven sets of scenery.

In addition to an opera house the building also was the location of a council room and an engine room. The basement contained a baggage room, a dressing room, a furnace room and a room for hook and ladder wagons and hose carts. The building was heated with a hot air furnace and the light provided by an electric arc light over the gallery and a powerful Bailey reflecting chandelier. There were also 34 stage lights. The cost of the completed building was $11,000.

The grand opening of the opera house occurred January 22, 1889, with "A Pair of Kids." Delegations from Blue Rapids, Waterville, Barnes, Greenleaf, Haddam and Morrow were present for the grand opening. The production was well received, but the next one, "Uncle Tom's Cabin," was not! The January 25, 1889, paper stated, "The 'Uncle Tom's Cabin' Company played here Tuesday night. All the actors were miserable failures except the donkey who seemed to appreciate the execrable acting of the balance and made special efforts to please."

This theatre was the site of many local productions, traveling productions, lectures and musical entertainments. But on March 3, 1908, a truly unique event took place at the opera house. Seventeen orphans from the Children's Aid Society in New York arrived by B and M Railroad. The orphans were first taken to the Nims Hotel where they had a good meal and then they were taken to the Opera House where a crowd of 700 people awaited their arrival. There were 70 applicants for the 17 orphans. The applicants had to sign contracts and show the committee that they could support the children, and had to have the endorsement of the committee before they could receive a child.

This Opera House, once so vital to the community of Washington, was destroyed by a tornado on July 4, 1932.[7]

| Waterville | 1889 | Rink | UTD |
| --- | --- | --- | --- |
| | 1889 | Opera House/Opera Hall | UTD |
| | 1903 | Waterville Opera House | Standing/Stage |

The Waterville Opera House with seating for 340 was built in 1903 by the city of Waterville at a cost of $8,000. Money for the curtain and scenery was donated. The first troupe to appear there was The Locks on September 21, 1904. Other performers to appear at the Opera House included the Hillman Stock Company and the North Players. The Opera House was also the site of revival meetings, graduation exercises, home talent plays, class plays, operettas, and many other attractions. City offices and the library were also located in the building. A large room in the basement provided space for dances and banquets. The theatre, with its original stage, has been elaborately restored and is currently used for community theatre productions.

An 1889 theatrical guide listed two earlier performance spaces in Waterville, the Opera Hall with a seating capacity of 300, and the Rink. No information is available on either of these structures. It is assumed that they are no longer standing.[8]

| Wathena | ? | City Hall | Standing |
| --- | --- | --- | --- |

The current Wathena City Hall is reported to have been the site of the local opera house. While no stage remains, there is a large room that could have served as an auditorium.

| Waverly | 1889 | Dewey's Hall | UTD |
| --- | --- | --- | --- |
| | 1913 | Bailey Theatre/Gem Theatre | NLS |

Dewey's Hall in Waverly was listed in an 1889 theatrical guide. The hall's seating capacity was 300. No further references were found to this hall and no information is available as to its current disposition. The new Gem Theatre that opened in 1913 is no longer standing.[9]

| Wayne | 1885 | Campbell's Hall | NLS |
| --- | --- | --- | --- |

The 1885 Campbell's Hall located in Wayne is no longer standing.

| Webber | 1916 | ? | NLS |
| --- | --- | --- | --- |

The Webber performance space mentioned in a 1916 theatrical trade paper is no longer standing.

| Weir City | 1889 | Bennett Opera House | UTD |
| --- | --- | --- | --- |
| | 1896 | Weir City Opera House | NLS |

The first mention of an opera house in Weir City occurred in 1887 when a license was issued for the construction of an opera house. In 1889 a theatrical guide reported that R. Bennett owned the Bennett Opera House. This frame structure seated 500. Nothing further is known concerning this facility.

The second opera house in Weir City was a ground-floor theatre located next to the Dean Hotel. The facility seated 500 with a stage 25' x 40'. In addition to numerous traveling shows, the Weir City Opera House was also the site of other community events. The Weir City Opera House is no longer standing.

Buster Keaton, the son of traveling performers, was born in Piqua, Kansas, but he also had connections to Weir. The Kentucky Hotel, operated by the Hargis family, was where many of the performers stayed when they appeared in Weir. Among these performers were the Keatons. When Buster was a small child Anna Hargis was his baby sitter.[10]

| Wellington | 1882 | Woods Opera House | NLS |
| --- | --- | --- | --- |

Constructed in 1882 at a cost of $20,000, the Woods Opera House was an elegant 50' x 85' building. Judge John G. Woods' bank and C. F. Flandro's clothing store occupied the lower floor. This second-floor theatre that seated 800, contained a stage 25' x 50' and was lighted by 70 gas jets. The theatre was opened on Tuesday, October 3rd, 1882, with "States Attorney" starring John Dillon. This structure, the site of many professional and community dramatic productions and local dances, is no longer standing.

A military pageant presented by the citizens of Wellington had an unanticipated humorous moment when, at one point, 25 Union soldiers were ambushed and lay dead upon the stage. One of the dead soldiers was a boy who owned a large Newfoundland dog. The dog managed to get up on the stage during the ambush scene. The dog began sniffing each of the soldiers and finally located his master and began to lick his face. The boy tolerated this for a while, but finally, to the amusement of the audience, got up and led the dog off stage. But, what really brought down the house was when the boy returned to the stage after disposing of the dog and resumed his place among the "dead" soldiers.[11]

| Wellsford | 1889 | Town Hall/Community Hall | NLS |
| --- | --- | --- | --- |
| | ? | Dowell Building | NLS |

Little is known about the two performance spaces in Wellsford. An 1889 theatrical guide listed a Town Hall that seated 150. A later photograph showed a large brick structure, the Dowell Building. The second floor of this building was used as a skating rink, for lodge meetings, and for community dances. Neither of these structures remains.[12]

| Wellsville | 1905 | Hill's Opera House | Standing |
| --- | --- | --- | --- |

In 1905, F. G. Hill erected a building at 516 Main in Wellsville. This structure was 32' x 85'. Barnards Clothing and Furnishing Goods was located on the ground floor and the second floor was used as an opera house. Hill's Opera House seated 550 with a stage 18' x 31'. This structure is standing and in use by the Masonic Lodge.[13]

Kansas Communities | 143

| West Mineral | ? | Opera House | NLS |

West Mineral, now well known as the home of Big Brutus, was once the location of an opera house. This structure is no longer standing.

| Westphalia | 1887 | J.C. Merrill Opera House | NLS |

Built in 1887, the J. C. Merrill Opera House is no longer standing. The beautiful stone structure, the pride of Westphalia, opened Monday evening, April 14th. Many folks came to view the hall and the scenery that included six different scenes. The front curtain contained a large picture representing the Westphalia Driving Association in the center surrounded by advertisements of the local merchants. The formal opening of the theatre occurred June 10, 1887, when a grand ball was held. The Garnett String Band furnished music for the occasion.[14]

| Wetmore | 1885 | Opera House/Morris' Hall/ Morris Opera House | UTD |
| | 1917 | Opera House | UTD |

An 1885 theatrical guide indicated that Wetmore was the location of the Morris Opera House that seated 800. Wetmore later had a second, more modern performance space because a 1917 reference indicated that the opera house in Wetmore was being remodeled with a spacious stage being added and the seating capacity increased to 450. No information is available on the disposition of these structures, but it is unlikely that they are standing.

| White City | 1889 | Monroe's Hall/ Grand Opera House | Standing |

First listed in an 1889 theatrical directory, Monroe's Hall or Opera House is standing, but in ruins. The structure no longer contains a stage. The second-story facility that seated 500 was the site of performances by both Blind Boone and Madam Schuman Heink. Wallace Bruce and the Ted North Players also appeared there. In addition to stage productions, the opera house was used by Lyceum courses and Chautauquas, and later for movies and as a lodge hall.

Traveling companies who appeared in White City used various techniques to attract an audience. When The Model Players performed "Ten Nights in a Bar Room" they would choose a local child to appear in a small part in the play. Another time the company promised that a couple would be married on stage. And once when a medicine show appeared in the opera house, they not only sold a type of "medicine," but also gave a diamond ring to one lucky woman in the audience.[15]

| White Cloud | 1862 | White Cloud Opera House/Nuzum Opera House/Kelley Opera House | Standing/Stage |

Located on the second floor of what was once a grocery store, this vacant opera house at White Cloud is the oldest standing opera house in the state. The facility still features its original stage. Before the advent of trains, White Cloud, located on the Missouri River, was a busy transportation center that saw as many as fifteen boats a day unloaded.

In 1862, the Nuzum family built the store that contained the opera house. The structure was purchased in 1893 by the Kelley family from Ireland and was in use until the 1930s. The opera house was one large room with a small stage at one end toward the front of the building. There was a small room located across the front of the building and behind the stage. This room contains the roller from an old stage curtain that had "LR Close Company" stenciled on it. This was a major scenery company located in Kansas City, Missouri. The original entrance to the opera house was exterior stairs located at the back of the building. A box office was also located at the rear of the auditorium.[16]

| Whiting | 1889 | Opera House | Standing |

The Opera House at Whiting, a 300-seat theatre, is standing vacant. If there was a stage in this second-story structure, it no longer exists.

| Wichita | 1871 | Turner Hall | NLS |
| | 1872 | North Main Street Theatre/ Variety Hall | NLS |
| | ? | Hall | NLS |
| | ? | Lewellen's Hall | NLS |
| | 1872 | Eagle Hall | NLS |
| | 1875 | Russell Hall | NLS |
| | 1879 | Turner's Hall/ Turner's Opera House/ Crawford Opera House | NLS |
| | 1887 | Wichita Museum | NLS |
| | 1887 | Garfield Opera House/ Memorial Hall/G.A.R. Hall | NLS |
| | 1888 | Crawford's Grand Opera House | NLS |
| | 1893 | Toler Auditorium | NLS |
| | 1896 | New Lyceum Theatre | NLS |
| | 1904 | Lyric Theatre | NLS |
| | 1905 | Crystal Theatre/Bijou | NLS |
| | 1905 | Lewis Summer Theatre | NLS |
| | 1906 | Wonderland Park Theatre | NLS |
| | 1908 | Orpheum Theatre | NLS |
| | 1909 | Princess Theatre | NLS |
| | 1910 | Orpheum | NLS |
| | 1910 | Pastime/Empress/Liberty | NLS |
| | 1911 | Forum | NLS |
| | 1911 | New Crawford Opera House | NLS |
| | 1918 | Arcadia Theatre | NLS |
| | 1922 | Orpheum | Standing/Stage |

Wichita was the site of numerous theatres. These ranged from simple halls to elaborate opera houses. With the exception of the relatively new Orpheum Theatre, none remains standing.

Early Wichita had several halls, second-floor rooms above commercial ventures, but reportedly the first real theatre was a one-story frame building later used as a carpenter shop. The 1872 Variety Theatre on North Main Street featured music, songs and jokes. This was not a place women would attend and it's doubtful whether any real acting took place there either. Johnnie Redding, a female impersonator, managed it. Other early places of entertainment include the 1871 Turner Hall and Russell Hall, each with a seating capacity of 300.

Lewellen's Hall, another early performance space, was nothing more than a long room above Lewellen's Grocery which was located on Main Street. Seating was on kitchen chairs and a platform with a black draw curtain was the stage. There was no scenery and kerosene lamps provided the illumination. In order to make costume changes, the actors were required to pass through the audience to a small room on the opposite end of the hall. The theatre opened with Hester's Colored Comiques, a troupe that consisted of eight Negroes who were praised for their fine voices and their ability to dance.

Another early performance space was a barn-like hall located on Douglas Avenue whose name is unknown. This hall was reported to be the first to have real opera chairs and a curtain that went up and down. The hall was used for theatrical productions for a few years, but following a shooting incident that occurred there, it fell into disrepute and disintegrated into a variety house and then into a museum which exhibited freaks and wax masks of famous men and women. The structure burned in 1882.

Eagle Hall, constructed in 1872 and seating 600, was reported to be the first venue "fit for ladies." Companies appearing at the Eagle Hall for weeklong engagements included the Kendalls Komedy Kompany and the Lord Dramatic Troupe starring Louie Lord.

The first theatre built expressly for theatrical entertainment was the 1879 Turner Hall which replaced a smaller hall erected in 1871. This two-story brick building constructed by the Turnverein Society contained a ground-floor theatre with a seating capacity of 1,000. Red and white velvet curtains draped the windows and large pictures of scenes from the Fatherland hung between the windows. Stchudy and Blomberg painted the theatre's scenery. The front curtain was pulled up and down on large wooden rollers and contained a scene of Conway Castle surrounded by mountains with a lake in the foreground. The stage was 30' x 35' with 12 full sets of scenery. Illumination was provided by gas.

An 1883 theatrical guide advertisement stated about the Turner Opera House, "all its appointments new and first class. It is not excelled by any house west of the Missouri. There were four dressing rooms." One of the first amateur productions presented in Wichita, "The Union Spy," was presented in the Turner Hall in 1880.

Because it was used for theatrical productions, the building became known as the Turner Opera House and in 1886, L. M. Crawford of Topeka, the state's most prominent theatre owner, took over management of the Turner Opera House.

L. M. Crawford constructed a lavish new opera house in Wichita that opened February 1888. This second- and third-floor facility featured an auditorium and balcony that seated 1,500 in upholstered opera chairs and a stage 35' x 60'. The stage contained 15 sets of scenery and a piano

The Crawford was the site of performances by the nation's greatest actors. In a one-year period during the winter of 1887-1888, Minnie Maddern, Marie Wainwright, Louis James, Emma Abbott, and Edwin Booth and Lawrence Barrett all appeared at the Crawford. When the New Crawford opened in 1911, this theatre's name was changed to the Lyceum. The original Crawford or the Lyceum was destroyed by fire on April 1, 1913. The Wolfe Stock Company was appearing there at the time.

Two other theatres in operation during this period were the Garfield Opera House, previously known as Memorial Hall or the G.A.R. Hall, located above the post office and the Wichita Museum which featured a museum, auditorium, and lecture hall. This facility was in operation in 1887.

A major Wichita entertainment venue was the Toler Auditorium. During the 1890s, Wichita saw the need to build a civic auditorium to attract conventions. Five thousand dollars was raised and in three months a new frame auditorium was constructed. The theatre was built in 1893, but was extensively remodeled in 1901 when H. G. Toler purchased it. The remodeled ground-floor theatre seated 1,400 with a stage 51' x 60'. In 1906, Sarah Bernhardt appeared at the Toler in "Camille." In 1907, the Wolfe Stock Company leased the Toler and changed its name to the New Auditorium. The theatre was torn down in 1918. Sidney Toler, son of the owner, went on to become famous as the second Charlie Chan.

A number of smaller theatres were built in Wichita. These included the 1896 New Lyceum Theatre, 1904 Lyric Theatre, 1905 Crystal Theatre, 1906 Wonderland Park Theatre, 1908 Orpheum, 1909 Princess, 1909 Marple, 1910 Orpheum, 1910 Pastime whose name changed to the Empress in 1912 and to the Liberty in 1918, and the 1918 Palace. Many of these became combination houses, meaning a combination of vaudeville and moving pictures was featured. None of these theatres remains standing.

In 1910 the cornerstone was laid for the Forum, a large civic auditorium that seated 5,500. The Forum featured a $1,200 Ben Hur curtain on its large stage. A year later on September 4, 1911, another major theatre, the New Crawford opened. It was located next to the Old Crawford. In 1918, the Arcadia Theatre, located in the Forum complex, opened. Neither the Forum, the Arcadia or the Crawford is standing.

The final major live performance facility constructed in Wichita was the Orpheum Theatre opened in 1922. This ground-floor theatre was designed by John Eberson with an interior that featured a Spanish motif. This was the beginning of Eberson's atmospheric theatres. There was a cloud machine that project clouds moving across the ceiling of the auditorium. The ceiling also featured lights to give the appearance of stars. The theatre was designed as a vaudeville house, but by 1929 it had switched to motion pictures although many notable stage performers continued to appear there. The Orpheum Theatre, with its original stage, is still in use and is in the process of being renovated.[17]

**Williamsburg   1889   Town Hall                            NLS**

An 1889 theatrical guide listed the Town Hall in Williamsburg as a performance space. This structure is no longer standing.

**Williamson    1917   ?                                    NLS**

The town of Williamson is no longer found on Kansas maps. A 1917 trade paper contained an add from the manager of the theatre in Williamson. He advertised, "Good show town for small companies. Playing one night or week stands."[18]

**Williamstown  1917   ?                                    NLS**

Whatever performance space that existed in Williamstown in 1917 is no longer standing.

**Wilmore       1915   Wilmore Opera House/Fisher
                       Opera House                          NLS**

The Wilmore or Fisher Opera House was an active place in 1915 with performances by the Coldwater Concert Band, the Helen Ross Comedy Company, and the Kelton and Walters Company. This facility is no longer standing.

**Wilson        1889   Leavitt Brothers' Opera House        Standing
               1901   Wilson Opera House/Turner Opera
                      House                                 Standing/Stage
               1917   ?                                     ?**

Wilson is the location of two standing opera houses, one with its original stage. The first opera house, located on the second floor above the Leavitt Mercantile Store was the Leavitt Brothers' Opera House. This 1889 facility that seated 500 with a stage 12' x 30' has been converted to apartments.

The Czech or Bohemians who settled the town of Wilson constructed the second opera house in 1901. Volunteer labor built the opera house from hand-hewn rock that came from a quarry in the north part of the town. There were very few trees in that part of Kansas, but limestone was free for the digging. The early settlers would work in the quarries during the winter when they didn't have other things to do.

The Wilson Opera House has been beautifully restored. The tin ceiling and wainscoting in the auditorium and the stage and fly gallery back stage are all original. This ground-floor theatre had a seating capacity of 500 and a stage 20' x 40'. The theatre's original front curtain still exists but is not on display.

Long an important part of the community, the Wilson Opera House was often filled with hundreds of people who crowded in to enjoy the liveliest polka music in Ellsworth County. Originally, the basement rooms housed the gym or "sokol" where the community gymnastic team practiced. One room was extremely deep to allow for the hanging apparatus.

In addition to its current use as a community center, the Wilson Opera House also contains a museum celebrating the community's Czech heritage. An interesting footnote to information on Wilson is that the hotel located across the railroad tracks from the opera house was used in the filming of the movie "Paper Moon."

Finally, Wilson may have been home to a third performance space. A 1917 theatrical trade paper contained a reference to a "New theatre in 1917." No further information is available concerning this structure.[19]

**Windom        1889   Bell's Hall                          NLS**

Windom's 1889 Bell's Hall is no longer standing.

**Winfield      1877   Mannings Opera House                 NLS
               1887   Grand Opera House                    NLS**

Winfield was the site of two opera houses. Neither is standing. E. C. Manning, president of the first town company, constructed Manning's Opera House, later known as Town Hall, in 1877. The opera house occupied the second floor of a building located 50 feet from the northwest corner of 9th Avenue and Main Street. The entrance was from Ninth Avenue with the stage at the east end of the long hall. This theatre was in use for more than 13 years. Plays, as well as entertainment of all kinds, were held there. Manning's Opera House seated 800 with a 20' x 50' stage. There were four sets of scenery and a drop curtain.

Winfield's second opera house was constructed in 1887. The formal opening of the Grand Opera House occurred on Tuesday, January 31, 1888. This lavish ground-floor theatre, costing about $60,000, was opened by the Conreid English Opera Company's presentation of the "Gypsy Baron." The Grand Opera House was described as having an enormous stage, 38' x 60'. The proscenium opening was 33' x 20'. Stage lighting was provided by 36 gas footlights and three sets of border lights above the stage that connected to 96 jets.

The auditorium, with seating for 700, featured a crystal chandelier with 64 gas burners. The theatre was leased to L. M. Crawford of Topeka. In addition to the theatre, the Winfield College of Music used the second floor. There were also apartments in the building.

When movies became popular, the opera house's name was changed to the Regent Movie Theater and in 1925 a major remodeling occurred. The last major renovations took place in 1950. At that time air conditioning was installed. The building was razed in 1962.[20]

| Winona | ? | Thouyenell Hall | NLS |
|---|---|---|---|
| | 1917 | Opera House | NLS |
| | 1917 | New Opera House | UTD |

J. N. Thouyenell constructed three performance spaces in Winona. The first, Thouvenell Hall had no stage. The second was introduced in an article that appeared in a 1917 theatrical trade paper, "Mr. Thouvenell is building and will have completed in about thirty days, a new ground floor house, with a seating capacity of about four hundred."

The next mention of this facility in a theatrical trade paper was not so upbeat. It began, "New Theatre Destroyed by Fire." J. N. Thouvenell reported, "We wish to advise you of our bad luck since you last heard of our new opera house…Saturday evening a fire originated in our garage just north of the new opera house which completely destroyed our garage, opera house and fixtures and nine cars besides all the other small items. The total loss to me is about $10,000. However, wish to say that we intend to rebuild. In fact, we have men at work already clearing the rubbish away and will begin in earnest before long."

By October of 1917 the new theatre that seated 400, with a 16' x 14' stage, was ready for business. It is doubtful that this structure is standing.[21]

| Woodruff | 1916 | Opera House | NLS |
|---|---|---|---|

The Opera House in Woodruff that was mentioned in a 1916 theatrical trade paper is no longer standing.

| Woodston | 1901 | Opera House | NLS |
|---|---|---|---|

Dedicated on Christmas night, 1901, the Woodston Opera House was located on the second floor of the Smither Brick Block. The dedication featured a masquerade ball with music provided by the Bohemian Band. T. F. Tuffley who painted many of the signs for merchants in Woodston painted scenery for the Opera House. The scenes on the curtains were of two farms in Ash Rock Township, those of E. D. Balmer and of Walter R. McNutt.

The Woodston Opera House was put to many uses. It was the site of public meetings, dramatic productions, musical programs, banquets, dancing, and beginning in 1903, roller skating. The noise caused by the skating above the bank and general store caused the 1907 newspaper editor to observe, "If one can judge from the sound, the girls can strike the floor about as hard as the boys can."

The first movie shown in the Opera House was in 1904, but it was not until 1910 that Andrew White installed a moving picture machine. A dynamo at the McNutt Machine Shop powered this machine and the electrical lines were strung on poles from the machine shop to the Opera House. The hall continued to be used for church suppers, school programs, lodge meetings and dinners, but after the high school was competed in 1921 many activities moved there. From the early 1940s until the 1960s the opera house was used as a skating rink. The building was razed in 1971.[22]

| Wyandotte | 1878 | Dunning's Hall | UTD |
|---|---|---|---|
| | 1883 | Dunning's Opera House/ Grand Opera House | UTD |

Wyandotte, now part of Kansas City, Kansas, was the site of two performance spaces. While no information is available on the status of either building, it can be assumed that they are no longer standing.

In 1878, Dunning's Hall, managed by Robert G. Dunning, seated 500. The 17' x 23' stage contained four sets of scenery. It is likely that Dunning built a second theatre because in 1883 Dunning's Opera House was listed as having an 800-person seating capacity and a stage 25' x 43' with a complete stock of scenery. No mention of this facility occurred after 1889.

# Y

| Yates Center | ? | Depew's Hall | UTD |
|---|---|---|---|
| | 1883 | Ray and Yates Opera Hall/ City Hall Opera House/Dobyn's Opera House | Standing |
| | 1896 | G.A.R. Hall | NLS |
| | 1904 | Apollo Hall/Apollo Opera House/ Temple Theatre | Standing |
| | 1907 | Auditorium | Standing |
| | 1907 | Star Theatre | NLS |

Yates Center has the distinction of being the site of three standing opera houses, although none has a stage or is used for its original purpose. The community also housed a G.A.R. Hall and later a motion picture theatre. Neither of which is standing.

The first location of public entertainment was in a hall above J. W. Depew's store on the west side of the square. This was the location of social meetings as well as political and religious meetings. The first reference to an opera house in Yates Center occurred in an 1883 theatrical directory. Ray and Yates' Opera House was managed by D. M. Ray seated 500 and the 16' x 30' stage contained a fair stock of scenery. The building, on the south side of the square in which this second-story performance space was located, is standing. It was also known as the Dobyn's Opera House and City Hall.

The 1896 G.A.R. Hall, located on east Rutledge Street, with its 250-seating capacity is no longer standing. The theatre had a 20' x 24' stage. This ground-floor theatre was last listed in a 1901 theatrical guide.

The 1904 Apollo Opera House was a second-floor facility with a seating capacity of 600 and a stage 28' x 30'. There were also two large dressing rooms. This performance space is now apartments and what was once the Temple Movie Theatre is located on the ground floor of the structure.

The fourth performance space was the Auditorium located on the second floor of the old mercantile building. The Auditorium, in existence in 1907, seated 800 with a stage 35' x 40'. The building is standing, but the stage has been removed.

Built in 1907, the Star Theatre located where the post office now stands, was designed for movies.[23]

# Z

| Zenda | 1903 | Keimig Hall | NLS |
|---|---|---|---|
| | 1916 | Opera House | Standing |

Built in 1903 by the four Keimig Brothers, this two-story frame building contained a store on the first floor and a second-floor hall where lodges met and social functions were held. Keimig Hall is no longer standing.

The Opera House was located on the second floor of the building where Henry Klein began his hardware store. The building passed through several owners and in August 1916, J. W. Evans remodeled and refurbished the building, adding a stage and converting it into the Opera House. An August 10, 1916, article in the *Zenda Citizen* described the remodeled theatre. "Just recently the Evans Meet Co. has remodeled the stage of their Opera House. The stage is being fitted up with five curtains….Upon completion of this stage the town will have one of the best on the Englewood branch and there is no reason why we should not have some good shows during the fall and winter seasons….We also understand that the contract has been let for a moving picture show one or two nights each week, and nothing but the best of pictures will be shown."

The stage of this facility has been removed and the building now houses the community's Friendship Meals. The City Council also meets in this city-owned structure.[24]

# NOTES

## Chapter I

[1] Between 1861 and 1865 only five halls were built in Kansas. These were located at White Cloud, two in Fort Scott, another in Leavenworth, and one in Ottawa.

[2] Sally Foreman Griffith, ed., *The Autobiography of William Allen White*, 13.

[3] Wolfgang Schivelbush, *The Railway Journey – The Industrialization of Time and Space in the 19th Century*, 10.

[4] Gerald M. Wagner, "Santa Fe Branch Line," 1976.

[5] Thomas D. Isner and Raymond Wilson, *Kansas Land*, 1988.

[6] The Lord's furthest destination occurred during the 1884-1885 season when they appeared in New Mexico, and it was there that James Lord passed away on January 16, 1885. James C. Malin, "James A. and Louie Lord: Theatrical Team — Their Personal Story, 1869-1889," *The Kansas Historical Quarterly*, Autumn 1956, No. 3, 249.

[7] *Wichita Eagle*, July 15, 2003.

[8] Robert W. Richmond, *Kansas: A Land of Contrasts*.

[9] Kansas historian C. Robert Haywood summarized the entertainment life of cow towns. "There was scarcely an innocent or reckless form of entertainment that did not find its way to the cattle towns to entice the free-spending, unsophisticated cowboy...There was nothing in all of Victorian Christendom quite like the bacchanalian display of young men staggering or whooping their way from one attraction to another." C. Robert Haywood, *Victorian West: Class & Culture in Kansas Cattle Towns*, 162.

[10] J. B. Edwards, *Early Days in Abilene*, 8.

[11] John F. Choitz, *A History of Ellsworth County 1854-1885*, 45.

[12] Eddie Foy and Alvin F. Harlow, "Clowning Through Life" *Collier's*, January 8, 1927, 26.

## Chapter II

[1] Union Halls were also constructed in Anthony, Rosedale and Parker.

[2] G.A.R. Halls were opened in Sabetha, Cawker City, Garnett, Washington, Fredonia, Oneida, Centralia, Colby, Beattie, Canton, Ellinwood, Ellis, Hiawatha, Hollenberg, Larned, Logan and Thayer. Later reported halls were located in Holton, Oberlin, Collyer, Yates Center and Hays.

[3] Other structures used for public entertainment were constructed by the IOOF in Severance, Lenora, Freeport, Natoma, Clearwater, Lebo, Dresden, Isabel, Toronto, Tescott, Healy and Munden.

[4] In 1885 Augusta was the location of a Good Templar's Hall.

[5] The 1907 Neosho Falls and 1916 LaCygne facilities were constructed by the Knights of Pythias; and the 1917 Columbian Theatre in Junction City was constructed by the Knights of Columbus; and the 1889 K of L Hall in Thayer.

[6] Woodmen opera houses or halls were located in Eskridge, Highland, Effingham, Solomon City, Wabaunsee, Rexford, Peru, Clifton, Elk, Cedar Bluffs and Prescott. AOUW halls were located in Hoyt and Lindsborg. There was an AOWL hall in Elk City and an AAOW hall in Bluff City.

[7] James R. Shortridge, *Peopling the Plains: Who Settled Where in Frontier Kansas*, 15.

[8] Robert W. Richmond, *Kansas: A Land of Contrasts*, 160.

[9] Thomas D. Isern and Raymond Wilson, *Kansas Land*, 95.

[10] Built in 1857, Leavenworth's Turner Hall pre-dated Kansas' entrance into the Union. Other early Turner Halls included Lawrence, 1869; Wichita, 1871; and Hanover, 1874. Turner Halls were also located in Junction City, Topeka, Marysville, Valley Falls, Belmont, Bern, Home City and Summerfield. Germania Halls were located in Topeka and Humboldt and the German Society of Ellinwood constructed a hall in 1874.

[11] James R. Shortridge, *Peopling the Plains: Who Settled Where in Frontier Kansas*, 46.

[12] Roger Carswell, *The Early Years of Osage County*, 64.

[13] Sondra Van Meter, *Marion County Kansas: Past and Present*, 157.

[14] The Augusta opera house is an example of the name changing with each change of owners, Kuster's Opera House, Hindman's Opera House and Sander's Opera House. Opera houses named for the community include the Almena Opera House built by Morgan P. Smith and the Florence Opera House commissioned by three gentlemen, Messrs. Caze, Firmin, and Aryal.

[15] Other rinks included Garden City's 1885 skating rink that was later converted into an opera house, (*Irrigator*, October 10, 1885, from Ricky W. Tyler, *Social Recreational Entertainments in Olathe, McPherson and Garden City, Kansas from the Introduction of the Railroad to the Building of the First Opera House: A Narrative History*, 199), the 1885 City Hall/Meadow's Rink in Gaylord, Muscotah's, Waterville's and Oxford's 1889 Rinks, and Noland's Rink and Opera House in Elk City that seated 600.

[16] Other community halls still in use in Kansas include the 1908 Municipal Theatre in Kincaid, the 1910 Beverly Opera House, the 1917 Township Hall in Palco, Potwin's 1917 Community House, Atlanta's 1920 City Hall, the 1922 Legion Hall in Rexford, and Gypsum City's 1925 Hall. Original painted roll scenery can be found in the halls in Atlanta, Rexford and Gypsum City.

[17] Built of native limestone, the Strong City auditorium seated 1,000 on the ground floor and balcony, both of which slanted toward the stage. The building is 500' wide and 80' long with a stage 50' wide and 22' deep. It is 22' to the rigging loft. The Waterville Opera House seated 340 in fixed seating in an auditorium 34' wide by 34' long. The stage is 34' wide by 18' deep with a proscenium arch 18' wide by 18' high.

[18] An early example of an elaborate ground floor theatre, Winfield's Grand Opera House seated 700. The stage was 60' wide by 34' deep with a proscenium arch 33' wide by 20' high. It was 18' to the grooves and 34' to the rigging loft. When the theatre opened lighting was provided by gas and included 36 gas footlights and three sets of border lights above the stage that connected to ninety-six jets. The auditorium was lit with a crystal chandelier with sixty-four gas burners. The cost of construction of this beautiful opera house was $60,000. Unfortunately this structure is no longer standing.

[19] Other theatres in this category include the 1916 Royal Theatre in Seneca and the 1917 Stella Opera House in Council Grove.

[20] Hallie M. Peters, *Old Opera Houses and Early Places of Amusement*, Woman's Kansas Day Club, 1952.

## Chapter III

[1] Hallie M. Peters, *Old Opera Houses and Early Places of Amusement*, Woman's Kansas Day Club.

[2] Woman's Kansas Day Club, *Opera Houses and Entertainment Pre-1950*.

[3] Woman's Kansas Day Club, *Opera Houses and Entertainment Pre-1950*.

[4] *Sedan Weekly Times Star*, February 12, 1904.

[5] Tyler, Ricky W., *Social Recreational Entertainments in Olathe, McPherson and Garden City, Kansas from the Introduction of the Railroad to the Building of the first Opera Houses: a Narrative History*, 1995.

[6] Leo E. Oliva. *Woodston: The Story of a Kansas Country Town 1885-1985*, 45.

[7] Woman's Kansas Day Club, *Opera Houses and Entertainment Pre-1950*.

[8] Fannie Smith Palmer and Kathryn Palmer Chilen, *Miltonvale-1982*.

[9] *Hutchinson Clipper*, July 9, 1892.

[10] "Leavenworth Centennial 1854-1954."

[11] Peters, Hallie M., *Old Opera Houses and Early Places of Amusement*, Woman's Kansas Day Club.

[12] Cynthia Mines, *The McPherson Opera House: A Prairie Landmark*, 25.

[13] *History of Latham*, Kansas, 15.

[14] Jean M. Brown, *A History of Kiowa, Old and New, On The Cowboy-Indian Frontier*, 36.

[15] Woman's Kansas Day Club, *Old Opera Houses and Early Places of Amusement*.

[16] Mary Alice Pacey, *Opera Houses and Entertainment Pre-1950*, Woman's Kansas Day Club.

[17] Cynthia Mines, *The McPherson Opera House: A Prairie Landmark*, 51.

[18] kancoll.org/articles/orphans/index.html, 5/4/04.

[19] Jean M. Brown, *A History of Kiowa, Old and New, on the Cowboy-Indian Frontier*, 348.

[20] Typed manuscript, Leroy Public Library.

## Chapter IV

[1] W.F. Pride, *The History of Fort Riley*, 164.

[2] *Topeka State Journal*, October 30, 1934.

[3] *Ellsworth Reporter*, January 8, 1880 from John F. Choitz, *A History of Ellsworth County 1854-1885*, 45.

[4] David Dary, *Lawrence Douglas County, Kansas an Informal History*, 225.
[5] *Westphalia, Kansas: The first 100 Years 1879-1979*, 14.
[6] *Blue Rapids Times*, August 1, 1895.
[7] James D. Kemmerling, *A History of the Whitley Opera House In Emporia, Kansas: 1881-1913*, 14.
[8] A list of scenery purchased in 1895 for $155 from the Kansas City Scenic Company for the Blue Rapids opera house included: 1 Handsome and attractive drop curtain; 1 Center door fancy parlor scene; 4 Parlor wings to match; 1 Rustic kitchen scene; 4 Kitchen wings to match; 1 Landscape wood scene; 4 Wood wings to match; 1 Perspective street scene; 2 Tormentor wings; 1 Grand drapery border; 2 Sky borders; 1 Drop curtain roller 4 inches diameter proper length; 4 Pairs scene frames, canvass mounted ready for use; 2 Tormentor wing frames canvassed and profiled; 4 Parlor wing frames canvassed ready for use; 4 Kitchen wings canvassed ready for use; 2 Large single and double curtain pulleys; 16 and drum with framework; 5 Nickel foot light standards; 20 Feet of nickel chain; 8 Patent foot lights; All needed rope. *Blue Rapids Times*, July 26, 1895.
[9] *The Newton Republican*, December 11, 1885.
[10] Other examples of scenery include the 1886 Stevens Opera House in Garden City with scenery by the L. P. Culberson Company of Kansas City. The 12 set of scenery included horizon, wood, landscape, garden, cut wood, parlor, chamber oak, kitchen, prison, and rocky pass could be combined to form over 100 different scenes. Larry Fowler, *History of the Stevens Opera House, Garden City, Kansas 1886-1929*, 21.
[11] The 1881 scenery for the Junction City Opera House provided by Noxon, Halley, and Toomey from St. Louis, Missouri included a landscape drop curtain, palace chamber of the Louis XV style, a plain chamber, a rustic kitchen, a Bastillion prison, a scene each of street, landscape, garden, horizon, and rocky pass, a set piece, a set house, garden statues, garden balustrades, flower vases, set rocks, set water tormentor wings, and doors, drapery borders and sky border. The scenery, 16' high and 24' wide, was flown instead of rolled. Marvin Jonason, *A History of the Junction City Opera House in Junction City Kansas: 1880-1919*, 17.
[12] Between 1885 and 1922 the Kansas City Scenic Company provided scenery for opera houses in Chanute, Garnett, Newton, Arcadia, Marion, Blue Rapids, Washington, Oberlin, Olathe, Powhattan, Mankato, Ransom, Sedan, Galena, and Gypsum City.
[13] The 1884 Newton scenery was by Sosman and Landis of Chicago; Junction City's 1881 and 1892 scenery was by Noxon, Halley and Toomey of St. Louis; and Concordia's 1907 and 1910 scenery was by the Twin City Scenic Company of Minneapolis, Minnesota.
[14] Lance Brockman, *The Twin City Scenic Collection, Popular Entertainment 1895-1929*, 98.
[15] The 1916 Edmond Opera House contained scenery by the Jessie Cox studio in Esterville, Iowa; the Omaha, Nebraska, firm of William Grabach, supplied the 1898 Junction City Opera House scenery; Jack Ballard and Son, also from Omaha, painted the scenery for the 1930 Bohemian Hall located in Cuba. This scenery includes a quite large and very beautiful drop depicting the Cathedral in Prague. Graham and Davis Scenic Artists, Kansas City, produced the scenery for the 1886 Barnd Opera House in Ness City.
[16] C. W. Sewell Scenic Company was responsible for the 1920 front curtain in the Palace Theatre in Kinsley; the Monarch Art Studio of Dodge City produced the Hosington – District 45 curtain; and J. S. Jones and Son of Wichita painted the ad curtain found in the Bohemian Hall that was originally located in the rural Jennings area.
[17] An itinerate artist painted the scenery for the Kincaid Opera House. John Techeudy from Switzerland was responsible for the 1882 scenery in Emporia's Whitley Opera House, and M. Jean Sodar who was sent to the United States by the Belgian government to decorate their building at the St. Louis exposition decorated the dome and interior walls of the 1907 Norton Auditorium and the interior of the Norton Catholic Church.
[18] Local artists who painted Kansas scenery included Fred Williams, manager of the Williams Theatre in Chanute, who painted its scenery in 1901 and 1906. Newton local, Charles Jensen supplied scenery for the town's Ragsdale Opera House. Peter Hefner & H. H. Yeager painted the 1915 scenery in St. Mary's; Ernest Hickman of Sedan who was responsible for that communities' 1913, 1914, and 1915 scenery; Lloyd Bertzfield of Prescott painted the scenery for the Air Dome and the murals in the Woodman Hall, and T. F. Tuffley painted the 1902 scenery in Woodson.
[19] *Hutchinson Clipper*, September 10, 1892.

## Chapter V

[1] Resident stock companies included ones headed by George Burt and his wife Agnes, George D. Chaplin, C. R. Thorn, and Mr. and Mrs. D. L. Scott. James C. Malin, "Theatre in Kansas, 1858-1868: Background for the Coming of the Lord Dramatic Company to Kansas, 1869," *Kansas Historical Quarterly*, Spring 1957, No. 1, 21-45.
[2] James D. Kemmerling, *A History of the Whitley Opera House in Emporia, Kansas: 1881-1913*.
[3] James C. Malin, "Traveling Theatre in Kansas: The James A. Lord Chicago Dramatic Company, 1869-1871" part 1, *Kansas Historical Quarterly*, Autumn 1957, No. 3, 298.
[4] Harry Corbet Diary, Kansas State Historical Society.
[5] Truly Trousdale Latchaw, *The Trousdale Brothers Theatrical Companies from 1896-1915*, 226.
[6] Jere C. Mickel, *Footlights on the Prairie*, 3, 8.
[7] Sarah J. Blackstone, "Alexander Byers: Play Pirate Extraordinaire," *Theatre History Studies*, 107-113.
[8] Harlowe R. Hoyt, *Town Hall Tonight*, 67.
[9] *Hutchinson Clipper*, January 1, 1902.
[10] Interview with Virginia Renfro, Lyons, Kansas, August 13, 1995.
[11] *Opera Houses and Entertainment Pre-1950*, Woman's Kansas Day Club.
[12] *Emporia Daily Republican*, September 24, 1886.
[13] D. Storms, *The Players Blue Book*, 58.
[14] *Hutchinson Clipper*, July 29, 1889.
[15] *Old Opera Houses and Early Places of Amusement*, Woman's Kansas Day Club.
[16] http://blindboone.missouri.org/history.html – February 29, 2001.
[17] February 20, 2001, NBC10 Biographies: Don Bousquet and Sissieretta Jones. Providence, RI/New Bedford, MA station home page.
[18] *Hutchinson Clipper*, January 24, 1900.
[19] Famous white minstrel acts included McIntyre and Heath, Harrigan and Hart, Montgomery and Stone, Al G. Field, George Primrose and Billy West. Black troupes to appear in the state included Callender Colored Minstrels, the Georgia Minstrels, Haverly's Minstrels, Hyer's Colored Minstrel Comedy Company, Kersand's Colored Minstrels, McCabe's Georgia Troubadours, McKanlass Company, and Richard and Prigle's Georgia Minstrels
[20] Gary D. Engle, ed. *This Grotesque Essence: Plays from the American Minstrel Stage*.
[21] *Hutchinson Clipper*, April 25, 1891; August 22, 1891.

## Chapter VI

[1] Eddie Foy and Alvin F. Harlow, "Clowning Through Life," *Collier's*, January 8, 1927, 25, 26.
[2] Jefferson De Angelis and Alvin F. Harlow, *A Vagabond Trouper*, 52-58.
[3] Luke Cosgrave, *Theater Tonight*, 29, 30, 32, 33, 34, 36, 37.
[4] Frank Montgomery, *Atchison Globe*, October 30, 1903.
[5] James C. Malin, "James A. and Louie Lord: Theatrical Team — Their Personal Story, 1869-1889," *Kansas Historical Quarterly*, 242-275.
[6] Frank Montgomery, *Atchison Globe*, October 30, 1903.
[7] Kenneth Silverman, *Houdini!!! The Career of Ehrich Weiss*, 3-18.
[8] *Kansas City Star*, 1923.
[9] *Garnett Journal*, November 26, 1897.
[10] Untitled or dated newspaper article from the Garnett library file.
[11] Information from: *Houdini: His Life-Story*, Harold Kellock from the recollections and documents of Beatrice Houdini; *Houdini: His Legend and His Magic*, Doug Henning; and *Houdini!!! The Career of Ehrich Weiss*, Kenneth Silverman.
[12] "Billboard," April 21, 1906.
[13] Buster Keaton with Charles Samuels, *My Wonderful World of Slapstick*; *Topeka Daily Capitol*, 9-6-63; *Houdini!!! The Career of Ehrich Weiss*, Kenneth Silverman.
[14] Pearl White, *Just Me*, 68, 69.

[15] *Opera House Reporter*, October 13, 1916.
[16] Peter Underwood, *Karloff: The Life of Boris Karloff*, 32-35.
[17] Letter in the Sport North materials, Kansas State Historical Society.

## Chapter VII

[1] Fred Stone, *Rolling Stone*, 1.
[2] Stone, 3.
[3] Stone, 9.
[4] Ronald L. Davis, ed. "Doc Adams of 'Gunsmoke': An Interview with Actor Milburn Stone," *Kansas History*, 250-261.
[5] W. R. Beeson, "Sidney Toler — Wichita's Own Reached Fame on Legitimate Stage and Screen Hard Way," *Wichita Eagle*, January 29, 1939.
[6] "Sidney Toler, Wichita Reared Actor, Dies," *Evening Eagle*, January 12, 1947.
[7] Ted G. Wear, "Mr. Theater — L. M. Crawford" Twentieth Anniversary Issue, *Bulletin of Shawnee County Historical Society*, 1-11.
[8] The New Crawford Circuit letterhead stationary.
[9] Neil E. Schaffner with Vance Johnson, *The Fabulous Toby and Me*, 77.
[10] Unless otherwise noted, the information is found in: Eileen Charbo, "The North Family — Clean Shows In a Cool Tent," Twentieth Anniversary Issue, *Bulletin of Shawnee County Historical Society*.
[11] Charbo, 30.
[12] Interview with Virginia Renfro, August 13, 1995.
[13] News paper clippings in the holdings of the Reno County Museum, Hutchinson, Kansas, and the Wichita Public Library, Wichita, Kansas.
[14] *Wichita Morning Eagle*, April 8, 1956.
[15] Letter from Constance Caufman to Verne Slout.
[16] Jerry L. Martin, *Henry L. Brunk and Brunk's Comedians Tent Repertoire Empire of the Southwest*.
[17] Donald W. Whisenhunt, *Tent Show: Arthur Names and His "Famous" Players*.
[18] Letter, Jaquetta Houser, September 28, 2000.
[19] *Wichita Eagle*, September 12, 1979; *Opera Houses and Entertainment Pre-1950*, Woman's Kansas Day Club.
[20] Local new paper article, October 20, 1904.

## Chapter VIII

[1] *Opera House Reporter*, 9-29-1916.
[2] *Opera House Reporter*, 1-12-1917.
[3] *Opera House Reporter*, 1-12-1917.
[4] *Jeffery's Guide*, 1889-1890.
[5] *Opera House Reporter*, 3-24-16; 9-7-1917.
[6] *Opera House Reporter*, 1-25-1918; 12-27-1918.
[7] *Opera House Reporter*, 7-16-1918.
[8] Weldon Bruce Durham, *An Invisible Armor: The United States Army's Liberty Theatres, 1917-1919*; *Opera House Reporter*, 9-6-1918.
[9] *Opera House Reporter*, 11-22-1918.
[10] *Time*, February 23, 1998.
[11] Robert W. Richmond, *Kansas: a Land of Contrasts*, 232.
[12] *Opera House Reporter*, 1-15-1918.
[13] *Opera House Reporter*, 12-27-1918.
[14] *Opera House Reporter*.

## Chapter IX

[1] *A Mound of Memories A Valley of Hope. Mound Valley Kansas 1868-1979*, 14.
[2] *Glasco Sun*, December 1, 1911.
[3] *Western Kansas World*, December 9, 1895.
[4] *Emporia Gazette*, June 19, 1913 from: James D. Kemmerling, *A History of the Whitley Opera House In Emporia, Kansas: 1881-1913*, 19.
[5] Edwin O. Sachs and Ernest A. E. Woodrow, *Modern Opera House and Theatres*, 128.
[6] Leslie Yates, *History of Milan, Kansas 1879-1979*, 58.
[7] Marvin Jonason, *A History of the Junction City Opera House in Junction City Kansas: 1880-1919*, 19.
[8] *The Newton Journal*, January 8, 1915 from Mary Jeanine Fent, *Ragsdale Opera House — Newton, Kansas, 1885-1915*, 22.
[9] *Miami Republican*, no date given.
[10] *Irrigator*, September 4, 1885 from Ricky W. Tyler, *Social Recreational Entertainments In Olathe, McPherson and Garden City, Kansas from the Introduction of the Railroad to the Building of the First Opera House: A Narrative History*, 195.
[11] *Opera House Reporter*, December 14, 1917.
[12] *Opera House Reporter*, February, 22, 1918.
[13] *Opera House Reporter*, October 26, 1917.
[14] Typed manuscript in Syracuse library.
[15] *Sedan Times Journal*, April 16, 1890 from Donna Casement, "Report on the Sedan Opera House," 1990; Sedan *Times Star*, January 8, 1904.
[16] Gwendoline and Paul Sanders, *The Harper County Story*, 127; "Condensed History of Harper."

## Chapter X

[1] A 1952 reflection by a Severance Kansas native concerning the Severance Opera House. *Old Opera Houses and Early Places of Amusement*, Woman's Kansas Day Club.
[2] Woman's Kansas Day Club. *Opera Houses and Entertainment Pre-1950*.
[3] Communities that no longer exist that had opera houses: Alanthus, Appomattox, Army City, Cooperstown, Coronado, Lerado, Richland, Rosedale, Saratoga, and Shoo Fly City.
[4] Mary Jeanine Fent, *Ragsdale Opera House — Newton, Kansas, 1885-1915*, 86.
[5] Larry Fowler, *History of the Stevens Opera House, Garden City, Kansas 1886-1929*, 42.
[6] Material located in the Reno County Museum, Hutchinson, Kansas.
[7] Motion picture theatres moved to ground floor locations: Yates Center and Marquette.
[8] Locations where the opera house portion of the structure have been removed: Chapman, Colwich, Ellis, Girard, Kensington, Madison, North Topeka, Goodland.
[9] Opera houses that later housed fraternal organizations: Cimarron, Dighton, Ellsworth, Leon, Ottawa, Wellsville.
[10] Uses: Shopping mall – Belle Plaine; army surplus store – St. Mary; auto repair shops – Canton, Nortonville; furniture stores – Little River, Osage City, Oswego.
[11] Uses: Feed store – Americus; liquor store – Holton; factory – Onaga; plumbing shops – Cherryvale, Lyndon; commercial spaces – Jetmore and Paola.
[12] Community operated movie theatres: Atwood, Norton, Phillipsburg; privately owned movie theatres – Seneca, Sharon Springs.
[13] Community Centers that contain their original stages: Oketo, Kincaid, Beverly, Palco, Potwin.
[14] Opera houses that no longer contain their original stages but are used as community centers: Ashland, Alden, Haddam, Almena, Lebo, Plainville, Zenda.
[15] Other uses for former opera houses: Chamber of Commerce meeting room – Coffeyville; Library meeting room – Baxter Springs; Library – Wathena; church owned halls – Denmark, Concordia, Hope; school bus barn – Mullinville; city's heavy equipment garage – St. John.
[16] Vacant opera houses with stages: Barnes, Brookville, Claflin, Dorrance, Hartford, the Turner Hall in Lawrence, Macksville, Morrill, Mound City, Nekoma, Powhattan, Sharon, Strong City, White Cloud.
[17] Uses: Dinner theatre – El Dorado, Scott City; movies – Robinson, Pretty Prairie; community centers – Rexford, Gypsum City; performance spaces – Orpheum in Wichita.

## A

[1] J. B. Edwards, *Early Days in Abilene*, 8.
[2] *Old Opera Houses and Early Places of Amusement*, Woman's Kansas Day Club.
[3] Deane W. Malott, *On Growing Up in Abilene, Kansas 1898-1916*, 10.
[4] *Old Opera Houses and Early Places of Amusement*, Woman's Kansas Day Club.
[5] Paul F. Long, "Old Township Hall," *Kanhistique*, 1.
[6] Daniel Fitzgerald, *Ghost Towns of Kansas*, 98.
[7] Lela J. Tidle, *Wilson County, Kansas: People of the South Wind*, 137.
[8] *Our Land-A History of Lyon County, Kansas*, 24.
[9] Ada Jaax, *A Century of Heritage, Andale, Kansas 1885-1985*, 34.
[10] Anthony, *The First Hundred Years, 1878-1978*, 23.
[11] R. R. Wilson and Ethel M. Sears, *History of Grant County, Kansas*, 207-213.

[12] *Argonia: In Retrospect...The First 100 Years*, 7.
[13] *The History of Cowley County Kansas*.
[14] *Opera House Reporter*, January 25, 1918; Unidentified, undated newspaper article.
[15] J. A. Fehr, *Arlington*, 7.
[16] *Opera House Reporter*, February 1, 1918.
[17] Daniel Fitzgerald, *Ghost Towns of Kansas: A Traveler's Guide*, 109.
[18] *Ashland Kansas: The Story of Its First 100 Years*, 24.
[19] *Opera House Reporter*, August 11, 1916.
[20] Ruth Kelley Hayden, *The Time That Was*, 155; *Opera Houses and Entertainment Pre-1950*, Woman's Kansas Day Club.
[21] Burl Allison Jr., *Augusta, Kansas 1868-1990*, 24.
[22] *Opera House Reporter*, March 24, 1916; *Opera House Reporter*, March 2, 1917.
[23] *Opera House Reporter*, January 28, 1917.

## B

[1] *Opera Houses and Entertainment Pre-1950*, Woman's Kansas Day Club.
[2] *The Baxter Springs Story Souvenir Program 1858-1958*.
[3] Mrs. N. J. Ware, *Centennial Days; Belleville, Kansas; 1869-1969*; *Opera Houses and Entertainment Pre-1950*, Woman's Kansas Day Club; *Old Opera Houses and Early Places of Amusement*, Woman's Kansas Day Club.
[4] Myrtle H. Richardson, *The Great Next Year Country: A History of Edwards County, Kansas, and the Surrounding Area for the Years from 1901 to 1925*, 344, 345.
[5] *Bennington Centennial & Fall Festival Souvenir Booklet, 1866-1966*, 2; *Opera Houses and Entertainment Pre-1950*, Woman's Kansas Day Club.
[6] Ron Koehler, *Bern, Kansas: Memories of the First 100 Years: 1887-1987*, 47; Norma Osborne, *Making Do and Doing Without: Kansas in the Great Depression*, Division of Continuing Education and KANU, 63.
[7] *Opera Houses and Entertainment Pre-1950*, Woman's Kansas Day Club.
[8] *Old Opera Houses and Early Places of Amusement*, Woman's Kansas Day Club.
[9] *Bison, Kansas: 1888-1988*, 45.
[10] *From Pioneering to the Present*, Vol. II, 375.
[11] *Marshall County, Kansas*, 147.
[12] *Blue Rapids Times*: January 21, 1892; June 21, 1894; February 28, 1895; July 11, 1895; August 1, 1895; May 6, 1897; February 11, 1897; June 14, 1897; October 10, 1985.
[13] *Century of Stars: a History of the City of Bucklin, Kansas and the Surrounding Community*, 24.
[14] *Old Opera Houses and Early Places of Amusement*, Woman's Kansas Day Club.
[15] *The History of Cowley County, Kansas*, 58; Herbert Pickens, *The City of Burden 1879-1979*, 15.
[16] *Opera Houses and Entertainment Pre-1950*, Woman's Kansas Day Club.
[17] *Burrton, Kansas 1873-1973 Centennial*.

## C

[1] *Opera House Reporter*, December 14, 1917; January 18, 1918; February 22, 1918; April 19, 1918.
[2] *Opera Houses and Entertainment Pre-1950*, Woman's Kansas Day Club.
[3] Warren Lingg, *Four Score and Ten: History of Cawker City, Kansas*, 1.
[4] *Decatur County, Kansas*, 60.
[5] *The Cedar Vale Messenger*, August 31, 1961, 37.
[6] *Handbook on the Frontier Days of Southeast Kansas, Kansas Centennial 1861-1961*, 140; *Kansas City Times*, July, 1925.
[7] Interview with Arlene Sejkora, July 10, 1997.
[8] Florence Kloxin, *Chase, America*, 20; Alpha Campbell Finkenbinder in *Chase, America*, 26.
[9] Zoe Myers Siler, *This is Our Town*, 4; Mrs. John Murphy in *This Is Our Town*, 64.
[10] *Opera House Reporter*, January 12, 1917.
[11] Interview with William Brannon, Claflin, Kansas, July 21, 1994.
[12] Scrapbook from Various Sources and from Memory – Ione Davies Russell; *Old Opera Houses and Early Places of Amusement*, Woman's Kansas Day Club; *Opera Houses and Entertainment Pre-1950*, Woman's Kansas Day Club.
[13] Athol Furman Reusser, *Clearwater, In the Valley of the Ninnescah: 1885-1985*, 219.

[14] *Opera Houses and Entertainment Pre-1950*, Woman's Kansas Day Club.
[15] *Opera House Reporter*, January 28, 1916.
[16] Interview with Leola Wood, Clyde, Kansas, February, 14, 1994; *Clyde Republican*, April 3, 1980.
[17] *Coffeyville at 100 1869-1969: History and Centennial Celebration*, 45; *Wichita Beacon*, November 2, 1963; *Coffeyville at 100 1869-1969 History and Centennial Celebration*, 4.
[18] *Old Opera Houses and Early Places of Amusement*, Woman's Kansas Day Club; Wayne C. Wingo, *A History of Thomas County, Kansas*, 37, 38, 66; *Saturday Night in the County Seat: A Walking Tour of Main Street Colby, Kansas*, 10.
[19] *Comanche County History*, 77.
[20] *Old Opera Houses and Early Places of Amusement*, Woman's Kansas Day Club; *Opera House Reporter*, August 3, 1917.
[21] Joyce Suellentrop and Dorothy Kraus, *Colwich Community Pictorial History*, 28.
[22] Janet Pease Emery, *It Takes PEOPLE to Make a Town 1871-1971 The Story of Concordia, Kansas*, 13; Peggy Doyen, *A History of Theater 1878-1925 in Concordia, Kansas*; Charles Hall, "Brown Grand Opera House," *Kansas Country Living*, June, 1976; "The Brown Grand Story," "Brown Grand Gazette," October, 1992.
[23] *Hamilton County, Kansas History*, 42; Typed manuscript in the Syracuse, Kansas library; *Hamilton County, Kansas History*, 46.
[24] Luke Cosgrave, *Theater Tonight*, 35, 36, 37.
[25] John Maloy, *History of Morris County 1820-1890*, 104; *Old Opera Houses and Early Places of Amusement*, Woman's Kansas Day Club; Lalla Maloy Brigham, *The Story of Council Grove on the Santa Fe Trail*, 93.
[26] *Opera Houses and Entertainment Pre-1950*, Woman's Kansas Day Club.
[27] Interview with Arlene Baxa, Cuba, Kansas, June 12, 1003; *History and Heritage of Gove County, Kansas*, 18.
[28] *Cullison 1886-1986 Collections & Recollections*, 2.

## D & E

[1] *Old Opera Houses and Early Places of Amusement*, Woman's Kansas Day Club; Geneva Brown, *The Story of Delphos 1876-1976*.
[2] Dorothe Tarrence Homan, *Lincoln: That County in Kansas*, 176; *Opera Houses and Entertainment Pre-1950*, Woman's Kansas Day Club.
[3] Ellen May Stanley, *Early Lane County Development*, 254.
[4] Odie B. Faulk, *Dodge City: The Most Western Town of All*, 131, 188; Samuel Carter III, *Cowboy Capitol of the World: The Saga of Dodge City*, 104; James C. Malin, "Dodge City Varieties – A Summer Interlude of Entertainment, 1878," *Kansas Historical Quarterly*, 351; Fredric R. Young, *Dodge City: Up Through a Century in Story and Pictures*, 139; *Hutchinson Clipper*, 1891; C. Robert Haywood, *Victorian West: Class & Culture in Kansas Cattle Towns*, 191; Timothy F. Wenzl, *Discovering Dodge City's Landmarks*, 36, 37; *Opera Houses and Entertainment Pre-1950*, Woman's Kansas Day Club.
[5] Esther Reilly, *The Story of Dorrance, Kansas Past...and Present*; Interview with Ken and Dorothy Mahoney, Dorrance, Kansas, July 30, 1994.
[6] Vivian Woody, *The Douglass Story 1869-1969*.
[7] *Downs The First One Hundred Years*, 48; *Old Opera Houses and Early Places of Amusement*, Woman's Kansas Day Club.
[8] *Opera Houses and Entertainment Pre-1950*, Woman's Kansas Day Club.
[9] *An Old Path: A New Direction: At 100 Edna Kans. 1876-1976*, 65.
[10] *The First Hundred Years, Effingham, Kansas, 1868-1968*.
[11] Information located in the El Dorado Oil Museum Library; William Galvani and L. M. Stallbaumer, "Main & Central: El Dorado, Kansas 1860-1985," 32, 33; *Opera House Reporter*, January 25, 1918; *Wichita Eagle*, August 26, 2001.
[12] Raydene James, *Elk City, Kansas Then and Now*, 10.
[13] *Elk County: A Narrative History of Elk County and Its People*, 57.
[14] Classic Theaters of Kansas Movie House History, http://www.reeldiaries.com/moviehouse/articles/elkhart_theater2htm, 3/31/06.
[15] Xerox page from an unnamed Ellinwood history book.
[16] *At Home in Ellis County, Kansas 1867-1992*, Volume 1, 253; Interview with Maxine Underhill Bradbury, March 1, 1993.
[17] George Jelinek, *Ellsworth Kansas 1867-1947*, 93; John F. Choitz, *A History of Ellsworth County 1854-1885*, 45.

[18] *Opera Houses and Entertainment Pre-1950*, Woman's Kansas Day Club; Ted F. McDaniel, ed., *Our Land: A History of Lyon County Kansas*, 152; James D. Kemmerling, *A History of the Whitley Opera House in Emporia, Kansas: 1881 – 1913*.

[19] Ellen Welander Peterson, *A Kansan's Enterprise: The Story of Enterprise, Kansas*, 52.

[20] Crystal Fleming, *Erie Remembrances: A Mini-biography of a Small Town in Kansas 1865-1975*.

[21] *Eudora Community Heritage of Our USA Bicentennial 1776-1976*, 96.

[22] *The History of Greenwood County, Kansas*, 31.

### F & G
[1] *History of Greenwood County*, Vol. I, 36.

[2] Sondra Van Meter, *Marion County Kansas Past and Present*, 157; *1872-1972 Century of Pride, Florence Centennial Florence, Kansas*.

[3] W. F. Pride, *The History of Fort Riley*, 163-170.

[4] T. F. Robley, *History of Bourbon County, Kansas, To the Close of 1865*, 180; James C. Malin, *Doctors, Devils and the Woman: Fort Scott, Kansas 1870-1890*, 50, 51, 52, 53; William G. Calhoun, *Fort Scott: A Pictorial History*, 122.

[5] Maynie Shearer Bush and Winifred Shearer, *The Frankfort Story: A History of Frankfort, Kansas and Surrounding Communities*, 32, 33, 89.

[6] *Fredonia Centennial: 1969*.

[7] Nathaniel Thompson Allison, *The History of Cherokee County, Kansas and Representative Citizens*, 462; Doug Henning, *Houdini His Legend and His Magic*.

[8] *The Daily Irrigator*, April 24, 1886; Larry Fowler, *History of the Stevens Opera House, Garden City, Kansas 1886-1929*.

[9] Harry Johnson, *A History of Anderson County Kansas*, 23, 69; untitled or dated news paper article from Garnett public library; *Opera Houses and Entertainment Pre-1950*, Woman's Kansas Day Club.

[10] *Opera House Reporter*, 1-19-1917.

[11] William C. Cuthbertson, *The Genesis of Girard: Stories of Early Girard, Kansas, and the Surrounding Prairie*, 95, 97.

[12] Mrs. E. F. Hollibaugh, *Biographical History of Cloud County, Kansas*, 576; *Cloud County History*.

[13] *Old Opera Houses and Early Places of Amusement*, Woman's Kansas Day Club; *The History of Glen Elder, Its People and the Surrounding Community*, 43.

[14] *Goddard 1876-1976*, 18.

[15] *Old Opera Houses and Early Places of Amusement*, Woman's Kansas Day Club; *Opera Houses and Entertainment Pre-1950*, Woman's Kansas Day Club; *They Came to Stay: Sherman County & Family History*, Volume II, 169, 260.

[16] *Opera House Reporter*, January 19, 1917.

[17] *History and Heritage of Gove County, Kansas*, 58; *Old Opera Houses and Early Places of Amusement*, Woman's Kansas Day Club.

[18] *Great Bend, Kansas: A Historical Portrait of the City, Centennial Celebration*, 44.

[19] *Opera Houses and Entertainment Pre-1950*, Woman's Kansas Day Club.

[20] *A History of Kiowa County 1880-1980: Chronicle of Kiowa County written by Kith, Kin, and Kind Friends*, 34.

[21] Margaret Fritz, ed., *Gypsum Valley History*, 9.

### H
[1] *Opera Houses and Entertainment Pre-1950*, Woman's Kansas Day Club: *Haddam's Hundred 1869-1969*, 22-25.

[2] Linda Mayfield, *Halstead: The Early Years*.

[3] Truly Trousdale Latchaw, *The Trousdale Brothers Theatrical Companies 1896-1915*, 212.

[4] *Harper Graphic*, 1884; Agnes Nye and Bob Bolitho, "A History of the 'old Opera House' Harper Kansas."

[5] *The First One Hundred Years: A History of the City of Hartford, Kansas 1857-1957*, 13, 21; *Kanhistique*, October 1991.

[6] Undated, unnamed newspaper articles from the Hays Historical Society.

[7] Karen Edson, ed., *Herington: A Century of Pride*, 7, 81.

[8] *History of Rawlins County Kansas*, 49.

[9] *Opera House Reporter*, January 28, 1916.

[10] Unnamed November 26, 1982 newspaper article; Undated, unnamed news paper article found in the Brown County Historical Society clipping file.

[11] *Old Opera Houses and Early Places of Amusement*, Woman's Kansas Day Club; Arlyn John Parish, *History of Highland Community College*, 15, 16.

[12] *Hill City Times*, October 16, 1969; *Opera House Reporter*, December 7, 1917, November 29, 1918.

[13] Raymond Wiebe, *Hillsboro, the City on the Prairie*, 64.

[14] "Barton County Historical Society Collections," 8.

[15] *Opera Houses and Entertainment Pre-1950*, Woman's Kansas Day Club.

[16] Mary Margaret Allard, *Holton, Kansas 114 Years of Growth and Development 1856-1970*, 28; *Old Opera Houses and Early Places of Amusement*, Woman's Kansas Day Club; Interview with Mildred E. Francis, Holton, Kansas, July 1, 1994; "The Perkins Theater Formal Opening," November 27, 1907.

[17] *Holyrood Centennial 100 Years 1886-1986*, 13, 14.

[18] Richard Lewis, *Early Day History of Home City, Kansas*, 11.

[19] Captions under pictures located in the Horton Public Library.

[20] *Old Opera Houses and Early Places of Amusement*, Woman's Kansas Day Club.

[21] *Old Opera Houses and Early Places of Amusement*, Woman's Kansas Day Club.

[22] *The History of Stevens County and Its People*, 432; Interview with Gladys Renfro.

[23] Genevieve L. and Harold S. Choguill, *A History of The Humboldt, Kansas, Community 1855-1988*, 42.

[24] Willard Welsh, *Hutchinson A Prairie City in Kansas*, 79; Pat Mitchell, *The Fair City Hutchinson, Kansas*; Pat Mitchell, *The Fair City, Volume Two*; *Hutchinson: The Salt City*, 33; *Opera House Reporter*, September 22, 1916, February 23, 1917.

### I, J, K
[1] Ken D. Brown, *Independence: The Way We Were*, 42, 56, 105.

[2] Mickey and Emerson Lynn, *A Pictorial History of Allen County 1855-1991*, 23, 28, 35.

[3] Lester Stites, *History of Ionia, Kansas*, 9, 19.

[4] *Barber County, Kansas*, 56; *Opera Houses and Entertainment Pre-1950*, Woman's Kansas Day Club.

[5] *Cloud County History*.

[6] *Opera House Reporter*, December 7, 1917; Interview with Bob and Neoma Tacha, Jennings, Kansas, June 13, 2003.

[7] Marvin Jonason, *A History of the Junction City Opera House in Junction City Kansas: 1880-1919*; Interview with Charles and Donna Lundeen, August 11, 2000.

[8] *Ellsworth County, Kansas*, 42; unnamed, undated newspaper article.

[9] *Centennial History of Argentine: Kansas City, Kansas 1880-1980*, 10; Margaret Landis and Larry Hancks, *Carnival Park: Circa 1907, Kansas City's White City*, 17.

[10] Interview, Al Irwin, Mound City, Kansas, July 24, 1992.

[11] *Hutchinson Clipper*, 1891; Tim Stucky, *Kingman: A Centennial View*, 15; Fred Hurd, *A History of Kingman County 1871-1969*, 123.

[12] Myron C. and Elizabeth Ann Burr, eds., *Kinsley-Edwards County Centennial: "From Prairie to People": 1873-1973*; Myrtle H. Richardson, *The Great Next Year Country: A History of Edwards County, Kansas and the Surrounding Area for the Years 1901 to 1925*; Myrtle H. Richardson, *Oft' Told Tales: A History of Edwards County, Kansas to 1900*; Woman's Kansas Day Club.

[13] Jean M. Brown, *A History of Kiowa, Old and New, on the Cowboy-Indian Frontier*, 37, 38.

[14] *Kiowa: Barber County, Kansas*, 46, 47; Jean M. Brown, *A History of Kiowa, Old and New, on the Cowboy-Indian Frontier*, 348.

[15] Ginger Anthony, ed., *The First 100 Years: A Pictorial History of Grant County*, 14; *Opera House Reporter*, December 22, 1916.

### L
[1] Margaret Hain Houser, *They Dared to Come: A Story of the Beginning of LaCrosse*, 69; "Reflections The Theatres of LaCrosse, Kansas," http://www.rushcounty.org/Reflections/index.htm, 2/19/2008.

[2] Kearny County Historical Society, *History of Kearny County Kansas*, Volume 1, 337, 375.

[3] Interview with Quenton Hobbs, Langdon, Kansas, August 8, 1997.

[4] Interview with Marcella Spreier, Larned, Kansas, March 20, 1995.

[5] Erma Ellis, *History of Latham, Kansas*, 15, 18.

[6] Agnes Emery, *Reminiscences of Early Lawrence*, 83, 84; *University Daily*

*Kansan*, August 2, August 20, 1975; David Dary, *Lawrence: Douglas County, Kansas: An Informal History*, 233, 234.

[7]*One Hundred Years of Freedom and Progress in Leavenworth, Kansas*, 29; H. Miles Moore, *Early History of Leavenworth City and County*; James C. Malin, "Theatre in Kansas, 1858-1868; Background for the Coming of the Lord Dramatic Company to Kansas, 1869, Part I," *The Kansas Historical Quarterly*, III 10,11; *Leavenworth 1854-1954*, 13; J. H. Johnson, III, *Looking Back: A Pictorial History of Leavenworth, Fort Leavenworth, and Lansing Kansas*, 16.

[8]Nancy S. Hawkins, *Simply Astounding! Lebo: The First 100 Years*, 117.

[9]Sondra Van Meter, *Marion County Kansas Past & Present*, 21.

[10]Virgil C. Dieterich, *A Story of Lenora, Kansas: 1873-1974*, 20.

[11]*Wichita Eagle*, August 15, 1994.

[12]*City of the Plains: A Story of Leonardville*, 26.

[13]Interview with Karen Walk, Leoti, Kansas, March 23, 1999.

[14]"Rural Town Origins in Southwest Reno County," *Kansas History: A Journal of the Central Plains*, Vol. 2, Number 1, Spring, 1979, 105; Alfred B. Bradshaw, *When the Prairies Were New*.

[15]*Milestones of Memories: A History of the City of Lewis and the Surrounding Community*, 294.

[16]*Opera Houses and Entertainment Pre-1950*, Woman's Kansas Day Club; Dorothe Tarrence Homan, *Lincoln-that County in Kansas*, 131, 156; *Opera Houses and Entertainment Pre-1950*, Woman's Kansas Day Club; Dorothe Tarrence Homan, *Lincoln-that County in Kansas*, 185.

[17]Selma Lind, *Living in Lindsborg and Other Possibilities*; *Opera Houses and Entertainment Pre-1950*, Woman's Kansas Day Club.

[18]*Opera Houses and Entertainment Pre-1950*, Woman's Kansas Day Club.

[19]Mrs. Summer Suhr, *Moments from History: Logan, Kansas Centennial 1871-1971*; *Opera Houses and Entertainment Pre-1950*, Woman's Kansas Day Club.

[20]Sondra Van Meter, *Marion County Kansas: Past and Present*, 230.

[21]*Opera Houses and Entertainment Pre-1950*, Woman's Kansas Day Club.

## M

[1]*Macksville, Kansas Community History 1886-1986*, 42; *Opera House Reporter*, December, 1917.

[2]*History of Greenwood County, Kansas*, Vol. II, 99, 100; *History of Greenwood County* Vol. I, 46, 47.

[3]*Old Opera Houses and Early Places of Amusement*, Woman's Kansas Day Club.

[4]*Mankato, Kansas: 100 Years Under Old Glory 1872-1972*, 44.

[5]*Footprints of Bourbon County Families*, Vol. I, 332.

[6]Sondra Van Meter, 269; undated and unnamed newspaper article in the Marion library.

[7]Allan Lindfors and Eleanor Burnison, *Pioneers on the Prairie: A History of Marquette, Kansas*, 60, 158-160.

[8]*History of Marshall County Kansas*, 123, 125.

[9]Shirley Higgins and Carolyn Thompson, eds., *McCracken, Kansas History*, Vol. II, 249, 250.

[10]*McLouth, Kansas and Jefferson County, 1882-1982*, 78, 90.

[11]Cynthia Mines, *The McPherson Opera House: A Prairie Landmark*; Charles L. Hall, "McPherson Opera House: Romanesque Architecture of the Plains," *Kansas Country Living*, July 1977, 10-A, 12-D; Interview with Jan Van Asselt, McPherson, Kansas, February 7, 1998.

[12]*Meade County News*, February 10, 1907.

[13]Nellie Snyder Yost, *Medicine Lodge: The Story of a Kansas Frontier Town*, 119, 120; Lenise Johnson, term paper found in *Opera Houses and Entertainment Pre-1950*, Woman's Kansas Day Club.

[14]Handwritten local history found in Melvern library; unnamed, undated newspaper article.

[15]*Old Opera Houses and Early Places of Amusement*, Woman's Kansas Day Club.

[16]Truly Trousdale Latchaw, *The Trousdale Brothers Theatrical Companies from 1896-1915*, 212.

[17]Leslie Yates, *History of Milan, Kansas 1879-1979*, 59.

[18]Fannie Smith Palmer and Kathryn Palmer Chilen, *Miltonvale – 1982*.

[19]*Old Opera Houses and Early Places of Amusement*, Woman's Kansas Day Club.

[20]*Elk County: A Narrative History*, 98.

[21]Mickey and Emerson Lynn, *A Pictorial History of Allen County*, 110.

[22]*Opera Houses and Entertainment Pre-1950*, Woman's Kansas Day Club; *Morganville Historical Book: 1870-1976*, 2.

[23]*Old Opera Houses and Early Places of Amusement*, Woman's Kansas Day Club; *A Centennial History of Morland and Community: February 24, 1881 to February 24, 1981*, 76.

[24]*Opera Houses and Entertainment Pre-1950*, Woman's Kansas Day Club.

[25]*From Pioneering to the Present*, Vol. III, 2, 52.

[26]Interview, Al Irwin, Mound City, Kansas, August 5, 1992.

[27]*Century of Memories: History of Mount Hope, Kansas and Greeley Township; 1870-1983*, 12, 17.

[28]Charles Irvin McCullough, *Our Yesterdays: A Story of Mulberry, Kan. 1866-1976*, 33.

[29]*Opera Houses and Entertainment Pre-1950*, Woman's Kansas Day Club.

[30]Madeline K. Farber, ed., *Mulvane: City of the Valley: Past and Present*, 77;

[31]*News and Views of Yesterday*, 27.

## N & O

[1]*Natoma History 1888-1988*, 117, 118.

[2]Joseph W. Allen, *Cho O-Nee to High Iron: The "Hidden" years of the Town Of Neodesha Wilson County, Kansas: From the Wilderness Days to the coming of the Railroads 1865-1886*, 54.

[3]Interview, Judy Delaney, Ness City, Kansas, July 22, 1994; Minnie Dubbs Millbrook, *Ness Western County Kansas*; "The Grand Opera House" handout.

[4]A. T. Andreas, *History of the State of Kansas*; Ragsdale Opera House commemorative marker; Mary Jeanine Fent, *Ragsdale Opera House — Newton, Kansas, 1885-1915*.

[5]"The History of North Topeka," *Bulletin of The Shawnee County Historical Society*, Number 24, December, 1955, 31-38.

[6]Darius N. Bowers, *Seventy Years in Norton County, Kansas, 1872-1942*, 221-223; *Kansas City Star*, March 6, 1916.

[7]*Decatur County, Kansas*, 54, 55.

[8]*History of Johnson County, Kansas*, 98; *Johnson County Democrat*, September 12, 1957; *Johnson's County Gazette*, July 17, 1990.

[9]*Our Land: A History of Lyon County Kansas*, 127.

[10]*The History of Onaga And...The Onaga Historical Society*, 6, 23, 24, 75.

[11]O. A. Copple, *History of Osage City and Osage County*.

[12]*Miami County, Kansas 1987*, 31.

[13]*Old Opera Houses and Early Places of Amusement*, Woman's Kansas Day Club; Interview with Von Rothenburg, Osborne, Kansas, October 21, 2002; *Opera Houses and Entertainment Pre-1950*, Woman's Kansas Day Club.

[14]Interview with Jerry Barnard, Oswego, Kansas, 2004.

[15]*Reflections of Franklin County and Chautauqua Days*, 39 - 41; Diane Yeamans, *My Ottawa Book: A Book on Ottawa History for Ottawa Children*; *Reflections of Franklin County and Chautauqua Days*, 34.

[16]*Old Opera Houses and Early Places of Amusement*, Woman's Kansas Day Club.

## P & Q

[1]*Opera Houses and Entertainment Pre-1950*, Woman's Kansas Day Club.

[2]*Miami County, Kansas 1987*; *Opera House Reporter*, February 18, 1918; Marjorie McLaughlin, *The Miami Republican*, undated.

[3]Mrs. Tommie J. Crispino, ed., *The Centennial Story of Parsons, Kansas*, 45; *Old Opera Houses and Early Places of Amusement*, Woman's Kansas Day Club; *Parsons, Kansas 1908, Queen City of the Great Southwest*.

[4]C. Naomi Stiggins, *Legend and Legacy Partridge, Kansas 1886-1986*, 55.

[5]Sondra Van Meter, *Marion County Kansas Past and Present*, 286.

[6]*Peck, Kansas 1887-1987*.

[7]*Old Opera Houses and Early Places of Amusement*, Woman's Kansas Day Club.

[8]John W. Frick and Carlton Ward, eds., *Directory of Historic American Theatres*, 92.

[9]January 30, 1969, unnamed newspaper article; Cecil Kingery, ed., *Phillipsburg-Phillips County Centennial 1872-1972*, B81.

[10]*Old Opera Houses and Early Places of Amusement*, Woman's Kansas Day Club.

[11]Joyce Knott, ed., *Plains, Kansas — 100 Years, 1885-1985*, 56.

[12] *Pioneering to the Present, Linn County: Its People, Evens and Ways of Life*, Vol. II, 414, 415.

[13] Truly Trousdale Latchaw, *The Trousdale Brothers Theatrical Companies From 1896 to 1915*, 212.

[14] *Wichita Eagle*, July 21, 2001.

[15] Tim Stucky, *Pratt, Kansas: A Centennial View 1884-1984*, 115; A. C. Tracy, *Chronicles of Pratt and Pratt County, Kansas: A Republication of a Book Published in 1911 by The Pratt Commercial Club*, 27.

[16] *From Pioneering to the Present: Linn County: Its People, Events and Ways of Life*, Vol. II, 321.

[17] *Comanche County History*, 111.

[18] Roger Carswell, *The Early Years of Osage County*, 79.

[19] Truly Trousdale Latchaw, *The Trousdale Brothers Theatrical Companies from 1896-1915*, 212.

[20] Interview, Wayne Mann and Waldo McBurney, Quinter, Kansas, July 7, 2000; *Opera House Reporter*, August 3, 1917.

## R & S

[1] Mark D. Horchem, *Ransom, Kansas: The First One Hundred Years 1887-1987*, 231-234.

[2] *Rexford Centennial 1888-1988*; Ronald Irvin Bruner, *Land of Windmills, Thomas County Kansas*, 23.

[3] Harold J. Borger, *A Pictorial History of Rosalia 1869-1935*.

[4] *Rush County Kansas...A Century in Story & Picture*, 234.

[5] *Old Opera Houses and Early Places of Amusement*, Woman's Kansas Day Club.

[6] *Opera House Reporter*, December 22, 1916.

[7] Typed manuscript, "St. John's Early Opera House."

[8] Joanne Hickey, "Entertainment in St. Marys."

[9] *As We Were: Pictorial History of Saline County* Vol. II; *Opera Houses and Entertainment Pre-1950*, Woman's Kansas Day Club.

[10] N. June Bennett, *Through the Years: Savonburg and Environs*, 22.

[11] *Opera House Reporter*, January 28, 1916.

[12] *History of Early Scott County*, 15, 16; *Scott County Kansas 1886-1986*, 71; *Scott County Kansas Celebrating 100 Years! 1886-1986*, 148.

[13] Sedan Opera House information compiled by Donna Casement and Osa Webb.

[14] *Opera House Reporter*, December 7, 1917.

[15] Hallie M. Peters, *Old Opera Houses and Early Places of Amusement*, Woman's Kansas Day Club.

[16] *Barber County History*, 63.

[17] Ann Jacobs Failing, *Shoo Fly City*.

[18] *Smith County Journal*, 1907; Typed manuscript, Smith Center library.

[19] Eleanor Fry, *Spearville: City of Windmills*, 87, 111; Interview with Helen Leidigh, Spearville, Kansas, August 3, 1998.

[20] *Stafford County History*.

[21] *Billboard*, May 5, 1906.

[22] *Opera Houses and Entertainment Pre-1950*, Woman's Kansas Day Club.

[23] *Chase County Centennial 1872-1972*; *Opera House Reporter*, March 2, 1917.

[24] Harriet Hughes Wright, *The History of Summerfield*, 39.

[25] Marge Lawson, *Honoring Our Heritage: A History of Sylvan Grove, Kansas*, 74.

[26] *Sylvia, Kansas 1887-1987*.

[27] Interview with Pauline Fecht, Syracuse, Kansas, March 22, 1999.

## T, U, V

[1] T. G. Wear, "Rum Play First," *Topeka State Journal*, October 30, 1935; James C. Malin, "The James A. Lord Chicago Dramatic Company, 1869-1871" part 1, *Kansas Historical Quarterly*, Autumn 1957, No. 3, 309; John W. Ripley, ed., *Town Hall Tonight: A Pictorial History of Topeka's Theatres*, 9, 10, 12, 18, 44; Euphemia Page, "Topeka Once Had Operas," *Bulletin of The Shawnee County Historical Society*, 10; "Roster of Topeka Area Theaters 1871-1941," *Bulletin of the Shawnee County Historical Society*, 93-96.

[2] *Opera House Reporter*, January 25, 1918.

[3] *History of Early Greeley County: A Story of its Tracks, Trails and Tribulations*, Vol. I. 99.

[4] Typed manuscript, Troy library.

[5] *Grant County Kansas*, 8.

[6] Interviews with Frank Shrimplin, Arthur Straion, Valley Falls, Kansas, August 6, 1992.

## W, X, Y, Z

[1] Matt Thomson, *Early History of Wabaunsee County, Kansas, with Stories of Pioneer Days and Glimpses of our Western Border*.

[2] *Western Kansas World* – 100th Anniversary Issue.

[3] *Opera Houses and Entertainment Pre-1915*, Woman's Kansas Day Club.

[4] *Old Opera Houses and Early Places of Amusement*, Woman's Kansas Day Club.

[5] *Opera House Reporter*, February 22, 1918; September 8, 1918.

[6] Inez Roberts Owens, *Welcome to Wamego, Kansas 1866-1976*, 82; "The Columbian."

[7] Mary Alice Pacey, *Opera Houses and Entertainment Pre-1950*, Woman's Kansas Day Club; Interview with Mary Alice Pacey, Washington, Kansas, August 10, 2000.

[8] *A Pictorial and Family History of Waterville, Kansas*, 92.

[9] *The Waverly History Book*, 146, 147.

[10] Ruth Turner, *Weir, Kansas 1776-1976 Bi-Centennial Salute*, 51, 74.

[11] Wellington newspaper April 11, 1946; Gwendolyn and Paul Sanders, *The Sumner County Story*, 71.

[12] *A History of Kiowa County, 1880-1980: A Kronicle of Kiowa County Written by Kith, Kin and Kind Friends*, 71.

[13] Donna Bosworth Romstedt, *Wellsville Kansas Bicentennial 1776-1976*, 41.

[14] *Westphalia, Kansas: The First 100 Years, 1879-1979*, 14.

[15] Phyllis Abernathy Taylor, *...From Time to Time*, 9, 42.

[16] Interview with Wolf River Bob, White Cloud, Kansas, June 30, 1994.

[17] Patricia Ann Mather, "The Theatrical History of Wichita Kansas 1872-1920"; R. M. "Dick" Long, *Wichita Century: A Pictorial History of Wichita, Kansas 1870-1920*; news paper articles appearing in the 1940s by Victor Murdock.

[18] *Opera House Reporter*, August 2, 1917.

[19] Interview with Jeannie Kingston, Wilson, Kansas, July 29, 1991; *Opera Houses and Entertainment Pre-1950*, Woman's Kansas Day Club.

[20] *Old Opera Houses and Early Places of Amusement*, Woman's Kansas Day Club; *Winfield: Uniquely American in the Tradition of Kansas*, 40.

[21] *Opera House Reporter*, October 26, 1917.

[22] Leo E. Oliva, *Woodston: The Story of a Kansas Country Town 1885-1985*, 45.

[23] Lottie L. Stockebrand, "Historical Development of Woodson County, Kansas, From 1855 to 1900."

[24] *Zenda, Kansas 1887-1987 Centennial: Honoring Our Heritage*, 76.

# BIBLIOGRAPHY

**Books and Theses**

Alexander, Virginia and Mary Lou Griffith. *Esbon 1887-1987*. Superior, Nebraska: Superior Publishing Company, 1987.

Allard, Mary Margaret. *Holton Kansas 114 Years of Growth and Development 1856-1970*. Holton, Kansas: Bell Graphics, 1970.

Allen, Joseph W. *Cho o-Nee to High Iron: The "Hidden" Years of the Town of Neodesha, Wilson County, Kansas: From the Wilderness Days to the Coming of the Railroads 1885-1886*. Fredonia, Kansas: Midwestern Litho and Neodesha Kansas City Federation of Women, 1962.

Allison, Burl. *Augusta, Kansas 1868-1990*. Augusta, Kansas: B. Allison, 1993.

Allison, Nathaniel Thompson. *History of Cherokee County, Kansas and Representative Citizens*. Chicago: Biographical Publishing Company, 1903.

American Association of University Women, Leavenworth Branch. *One Hundred Years of Freedom and Progress in Leavenworth, Kansas, 1861-1961*. American Printing.

Andreas, A. T. *History of the State of Kansas*. Atchison, Kansas: Atchison County Historical Society, 1976.

Anthony, *The First Hundred Years, 1878-1978*. Anthony, Kansas: Historical Museum of Anthony, 1978.

Anthony, Ginger, ed. *The First 100 Years: A Pictorial History of Grant County*. Ulysses, Kansas: Grant County Historical Society and Museum, 1990.

*Argonia: In Retrospect...The First 100 Years*. Dallas, Texas: Taylor Publishing Company, 1985.

*Ashland Kansas: The Story of Its First 100 Years*. Shawnee Mission, Kansas: Print Inc., 1984.

*Barber County History*. Medicine Lodge, Kansas: Barber County Historical Committee, 1980.

*The Baxter Springs Story Souvenir Program 1858-1958*. 1958.

Bennett, N. June. *Through the Years: Savonburg and Environs*. North Newton, Kansas: Mennonite Press, 1983.

Borger, Harold J. *A Pictorial History of Rosalia 1869-1935*. 1972.

Bowers, Darius N. *Seventy Years of Norton County, Kansas 1872-1942*. Norton, Kansas: The Norton County Champion, 1942.

Braddock, Betty. *Dodge City: Cowboy Capital...Beautiful Bibulous Babylon...Queen of Cowtowns...Wicked Little City...the Delectable Burg...*. Dodge City Kansas: Kansas Heritage Center, 1982.

Bradshow, Alfred B. *When the Prairies Were New*. Turon, Kansas: Arthur J. Allen, 1957.

Brigham, Lalla Maloy. *The Story of Council Grove on the Santa Fe Trail*. Council Grove, Kansas: Morris County Historical Society, 1989.

Brockman, C. Lance. *The Twin City Scenic Collection, Popular Entertainment 1895-1929*. Minneapolis: University Art Museum, 1987.

Brockman, C. Lance, curator. *Theatre of the Fraternity: Staging the Ritual Space of the Scottish Rite of Freemasonry, 1896-1929*: Minneapolis: Frederick R. Weisman Art Museum, University of Minnesota, distributed by University Press of Mississippi, 1996.

Brown, Geneva. *The Story of Delphos*. 1976.

Brown, Jean M. *A History of Kiowa, Old and New, on the Cowboy-Indian Frontier*. Lawrence, Kansas: House of Ushe, 1979.

Brown, Ken D. *Independence: The Way We Were*. Independence, Kansas: Brown, 1980.

Bruner, Ronald Irvin. *Land of Windmills, Thomas County Kansas*. Thomas County Historical Society, 1976.

Burr, Myron C. and Elizabeth Ann eds. *Kinsley-Edwards County Centennial "From Prairie to People," 1873-1973*. Kinsley, Kansas: Noland Publishers, 1973.

Bush, Maynie Shearer and Winifred Shearer. *The Frankfort Story: A History Of Frankfort, Kansas and Surrounding Communities*. Frankfort, Kansas: Frankfort Centennial Committee, 1967.

Calhoun, William G. *Fort Scott, A Pictorial History*. Fort Scott, Kansas: Historic Preservation Association of Bourbon County, 1981.

Carswell, Roger. *The Early Years of Osage County*. North Newton, Kansas: Mennonite Press, 1982.

Carter III, Samuel. *Cowboy Capital of the World: the Saga of Dodge City*. Garden City, New York: Doubleday and Company, 1973.

*Centennial Days; Belleville, Kansas 1868-1968*. 1968.

*Centennial History of Argentine, Kansas City, Kansas 1880-1980*. Kansas City, Kansas: Simmons Funeral Home, 1980.

*A Centennial History of Morland and Community: February 24, 1881 to February 24, 1981*. 1981.

*Century of Memories: History of Mount Hope, Kansas and Greeley Township: 1870-1983*. Mount Hope, Kansas, 1983.

*1872-1972 Century of Pride, Florence Centennial*. Florence, Kansas: Bulletin Printing, 1972.

*Century of Stars: A History of the City of Bucklin, Kansas and the Surrounding Community*. Shawnee Mission, Kansas: Kes-Print, 1986.

*Century One: History of Moundridge, Kansas 1887-1987*. Moundridge, Kansas: Centennial Committee, 1987.

*Chase County Centennial 1872-1972*. Chase County Courthouse Centennial Committee, 1972.

Choguill, Genevieve L. and Harold S. *A History of the Humboldt, Kansas, Community 1855-1988*. Newton, Kansas: Mennonite Press, 1988.

Choitz, John F. *A History of Ellsworth County 1854-1885*. Ellsworth, Kansas: Ellsworth County Historical Society, 1967.

*City of the Plains: A Story of Leonardville*.

*Cloud County History*. Concordia, Kansas: Cloud County Historical Society and Cloud County Genealogical Society, 1992.

*Coffeyville at 100, 1869-1969, History and Centennial Celebration*. Coffeyville, Kansas: Coffeyville Journal Press, 1969.

Comanche County Historical Society. *Comanche County History*. Dallas, Texas: Taylor Publishing Company, 1981.

*Condensed History of the City of Harper, Kansas and Surrounding Territory*. Harper, Kansas: DeLuxe Printing, 1977.

Connelley, William Elsey. *A Standard History of Kansas and Kansans*. Chicago: Lewis, 1918.

Cosgrave, Luke. *Theater Tonight*. Hollywood: House-Warven, Publishers, 1952.

Crispino, Mrs. Tommie J. *The Centennial Story of Parsons, Kansas*. Parsons, Kansas: Centennial Parsons, Inc., 1971.

*Cullison 1886-1986 Collections and Recollections*.

Cuthbertson, William C. *The Genesis of Girard: Stories of Early Girard, Kansas, and the surrounding Prairie*. Friends of Historic Girard, 1993.

Dary, David. *Lawrence Douglas County, Kansas an Informal History*. Lawrence, Kansas: Allen Books, 1982.

Davis, Charles Clayton. *Who's Who? A History of Kansas and Montgomery County*. Coffeyville, Kansas: Coffeyville Journal Press, 1943.

DeAngelis, Jefferson and Alvin F. Harlow. *A Vagabond Trouper*. New York: Harcourt, Brace and Company, 1931.

*Decatur County, Kansas*. Oberlin, Kansas: Decatur County Historical Book Committee, 1983.

Deterich, Virgil C. *A Story of Lenora, Kansas: 1873-1974*. Lenora Kansas, 1974.

Durham, Weldon Bruce. *An Invisible Armor: The United States Army's Liberty Theatres, 1917-1919*. Ph.D. dissertation University of Iowa, 1973.

Edna Centennial Committee. *An Old Path: A New Direction: At 100 Edna Kansas*. Edna, Kansas, 1976.

Edson, Karen, ed., Leona Lamb Nelson, Virginia Yeates Bruner. *Herington: A Century of Pride*. Herington, Kansas: Herrington Centennial, 1987.

Edwards, Floyd, ed. *Hamilton County Kansas: History*. Syracuse, Kansas: Hamilton County Historical Society, 1979.

Edwards, J. B. *Early Days in Abilene*. Abilene, Kansas: C.W. Wheeler, 1938.

*El Dorado City Directory*, 1918.

*Elk County: A Narrative History of Elk County and Its People*. Elk County Historical Society, Josten's American Yearbook Company, 1979.

Ellis, Erma. *History of Latham, Kansas, 1985*. Latham History Book Committee, 1985.

*Ellsworth County, Kansas*.

Emery, Agnes. *Reminiscences of Early Lawrence*. Lawrence, Kansas, 1954.

Emery, Janet Pease. *It Takes People to Make a Town 1871-1971, The Story of Concordia Kansas*. Salina, Kansas: Arrow Printing Company, 1971.

Engle, Gary D. ed. *This Grotesque Essence: Plays from the American Minstrel Stage*. Baton Rouge: Louisiana State University Press, 1978.

*Eudora Community Heritage of Our USA Bicentennial 1776-1976*. 1977.

Failing, Ann Jacobs. *Shoo Fly City*. Oxford, Kansas: Oxford Register, 1960.

Farber, Madeline K. ed. *Mulvane: City of the Valley: Past and Present*. Mulvane, Kansas: Mulvane Historical Society, 1977.

Faulk, Odie B. *Dodge City: The Most Western Town of All*. New York: Oxford University Press, 1977.

Fehr, J. A. *Arlington*. Wichita, Kansas: *Wichita Eagle* Press, 1937.

Fent, Mary Jeanine. *Ragsdale Opera House — Newton, Kansas, 1885-1915*, thesis, University of North Carolina, 1977.

*The First Hundred Years, Effingham, Kansas, 1868-1968*. 1968.

*The First One Hundred Years: A History of the City of Hartford Kansas 1857-1957*.

Fisher, R. H. *Biographical Sketches of El Dorado Citizens*. El Dorado, Kansas: Thompson Brothers Stationery and Printing Company, 1930.

Fitzgerald, Daniel. *Ghost Towns of Kansas*, Vol. I. 1976.

Fitzgerald, Daniel. *Ghost Towns of Kansas: A Travelers Guide*. Lawrence, Kansas: University Press of Kansas, 1988.

Fleming, Crystal. *Erie Remembrances: A Mini-biography of a Small Town in Kansas 1865-1975*. Erie, Kansas: Fleming, 1976.

Fowler, Larry. *History of the Stevens Opera House, Garden City, Kansas 1886-1929*, thesis, Kansas State Teachers College of Emporia, 1969.

*Fredonia Centennial: 1969*.

Frick, John W. and Carlton Ward, eds. *Directory of Historic American Theatres*. New York: Greenwood Press, 1987.

Friend, Madge, coordinator. *Bison, Kansas: 1888-1988*. Bison History Book Committee, 1988.

Fritz, Margaret, ed. *Gypsum Valley History*, 1993.

*From Pioneering to Present, Linn County: Its People, Events, and Ways of Life*. Vol. I-III. Pleasanton, Kansas: Linn County Historical Society, Linn County Publishing Company, 1976-1982.

Fry, Eleanor. *Spearville: City of Windmills*. Spearville, Kansas: Spearville News.

Glenn, George D. and Richard L. Poole. *The Opera Houses of Iowa*. Ames: Iowa State University Press, 1993.

*Goddard 1876-1976*.

Grant County History Commission. *Grant County Kansas*. Ulysses, Kansas: Grant County History Commission, 1982.

Griffith, Sally Foreman, ed. *The Autobiography of William Allen White* 2nd ed. Lawrence: University Press of Kansas, 1990, (1st ed. 1946).

*Haddam's Hundred 1869-1969, the Story of Haddam Kansas*. 1969.

*Handbook on the Frontier Days of Southeast Kansas, Kansas Centennial 1861-1961*.

Hawkins, Nancy S. *Simply Astounding! Lebo: The First 100 Years*. Lebo, Kansas: N. S. Hawkings, 1986.

Hayden, Ruth Kelley. *The Time That Was, The Courageous Acts and Accounts of Rawlins County, Kansas 1875-1915*. Colby, Kansas: H. F. Davis Memorial Library, Colby Community College, 1973.

Haywood, C. Robert. *Victorian West: Class and Culture in Kansas Cattle Towns*. Lawrence, Kansas: University Press of Kansas, 1991.

Heisler, E. F. *1874 Atlas Map of Johnson County, Kansas*, Olathe, Kansas: Olathe Historical Society, 1976.

Heitman, Rose Ellen, ed. *Peck, Kansas 1887-1987*. Peck, Kansas, 1987.

Henning, Doug. *Houdini: His Legend and His Magic*. New York: Times Books, 1977.

Historic Preservation Association. *Footprints of Bourbon County Families*, Vol. I. Fort Scott, Kansas: Sekan Printing, 1991.

*The History of Cowley County, Kansas*. Arkansas City, Kansas: Cowley County Heritage Book Committee, 1990.

*History of Early Greeley County A Story of its Tracks, Trails and Tribulations*, Vol. I. Tribune, Kansas: Greeley County Historical Book Committee, 1981.

*The History of Glen Elder, its People and the Surrounding Community*. Cawker City, Kansas: North Central Kansas Genealogical Society and Library, 1998.

*The History of Greenwood County, Kansas* Vol. I and II. Wichita, Kansas: Josten's Publications, 1986, 1989.

*A History of Kiowa County 1880-1930: Kronicle of Kiowa County Written by Kith, Kin, and Kind Friends*. Lubbock, Texas: Taylor Publishing Company, 1979.

*History of Marshall County Kansas*.

*The History of Onaga And...* Onaga, Kansas: The Onaga Historical Society, 1982.

*History of Rawlins County Kansas*. Atwood, Kansas: Rawlins County Genealogical Society, 1988.

*History of Early Scott County*. Scott City, Kansas: Scott County Historical Society, 1977.

Hollibaugh, Mrs. E. M. *Biographical History of Cloud County, Kansas*. 1903.

Holyrood Centennial Committee. *Holyrood Centennial 100 Years 1886-1986*. Ellsworth, Kansas: Ellsworth Printing Company, 1986.

Homan, Dorothe Tarrence. *Lincoln — That County in Kansas*. Lindsborg, Kansas: Barbos' Print, 1979.

*At Home in Ellis County, Kansas 1867-1992*. Dallas, Texas: Taylor Publishing Company, 1991.

Horchem, Mark D. *Ransom, Kansas: The First One Hundred Years 1887-1987*. 1987.

Houser, Margaret Hain. *They Dared to Come: A Story of the Beginning of La Crosse, Kansas*.

Hoyt, Harlowe R. *Town Hall Tonight*. Englewood Cliffs, NJ: Prentice-Hall, 1955.

Hurd, Fred. *A History of Kingman County 1871-1969*. North Newton, Kansas: Mennonite Press, 1970.

Isern, Thomas D. and Raymond Wilson. *Kansas Land*. Salt Lake City: Peregrine Smith Books, 1988.

James, Raydene. *Elk City, Kansas Then and Now*. Midwestern Litho. 1964.

Jameson, Henry B. *Heroes by the Dozen*. Abilene, Kansas: Shandinger-Wilson Printers, Inc., 1961.

Jaax, Ada. *A Century of Heritage, Andale, Kansas, 1885-1985*. Andale, Kansas: Centennial Committee, 1986.

Jelinek, George. *Ellsworth Kansas 1867-1947*. Salina, Kansas: Consolidated, 1947.

Johnson, Harry. *A History of Anderson County Kansas*. Garnett, Kansas: The Garnett Review Company, 1936.

Johnson III, J. H. *Looking Back: A Pictorial History of Leavenworth, Fort Leavenworth, and Lansing Kansas*. 1982.

Jonason, Marvin. *A History of the Junction City Opera House in Junction City Kansas: 1880-1919*, thesis, Kansas State Teachers College of Emporia, 1970.

Kearny County Historical Society. *History of Kearny County Kansas*, Vol. I. Jack Rollie, 1964.

Keaton, Buster and Charles Samuels. *My Wonderful World of Slapstick*. New York: Doubleday and Company, 1960.

Kemmerling, James D. *A History of the Whitley Opera House in Emporia, Kansas: 1881-1913*. The Emporia State Research Studies, XVIII, 3 (1970).

Kellock, Harold. *Houdini: His Life-Story from the Recollections and Documents of Beatrice Houdini*. New York: Harcourt, Brace and Co., 1928.

Kingery, Cecil ed. *Phillips County Centennial 1872-1972*.

*Kiowa: Barber County, Kansas*.

Kloxin, Florence. *Chase, America*. North Newton, Kansas: Mennonite Press, 1979.

Knott, Joyce, ed. *Plains, Kansas: 100 Years, 1885-1985*. Plains, Kansas: Plains Historical Committee, 1985.

Koehler, Ron. *Bern, Kansas: Memories of the First 100 Years: 1887-1987*. Seneca, Kansas: G and R Printing, 1987.

Latchaw, Truly Trousdale. *The Trousdale Brothers Theatrical Companies From 1896-1915*, M.A. thesis, University of Minnesota, 1948.

Latham History Book Committee. *History of Latham Kansas*. Shawnee Mission, Kansas: Kes-Print, 1985.

Lawson, Marge. *Honoring Our Heritage: A History of Sylvan Grove, Kansas*. Ellsworth, Kansas: Ellsworth Reporter, 2001.

Lewis Centennial Committee. *Milestones of Memories: A History of the City of Lewis and the Surrounding Community*. Lewis, Kansas: The Committee, 1986.

Lewis, Richard W. *Early Day History of Home City, Kansas*. Marysville, Kansas: Marysville Advocate, 1949.

Lind, Selma [pseud.]; Jaderborg, Elizabeth. *Living in Lindsborg and Other Possibilities*. Lindsborg, Kansas: Lindsborg News Record, 1967.

Lindfors, Allan and Eleanor Burnison. *Pioneers on the Prairie: A History of Marquette, Kansas*. 1978.

Lingg, Warren J. *Four Score and Ten: History of Cawker City, Kansas*. Cawker City, Kansas: Cawker City Ledger, 1961.

Long, R. M. *Wichita Century: A Pictorial History of Wichita, Kansas 1870-1970*. Wichita Historical Museum Association, Inc., 1969.

Lynn, Mickey and Emerson. *A Pictorial History of Allen County 1855-1991*. Iola, Kansas: The Iola Register, 1991.

*Macksville, Kansas Community History 1886-1986*. Lewis, Kansas: Lewis Press, 1986.

*Making Do and Doing Without: Kansas in the Great Depression*. Division of Continuing Education and KANU, The University of Kansas, 1990.

Malott, Deane W. *On Growing Up in Abilene, Kansas 1898-1916*. Abilene, Kansas: Dickinson County Historical Society, 1992.

Malin, James C. *Doctors Devils and the Woman: Fort Scott, Kansas 1870-1890*. Lawrence, Kansas: Coronado Press, 1975.

*Mankato, Kansas: 100 Years Under Old Glory 1872-1972*. 1972.

*Marshal County Kansas*.

Martin, Jerry L. *Henry L. Brunk and Brunk's Comedians Tent Repertoire Empire of the Southwest*. Bowling Green, Ohio: Bowling Green State University Popular Press, 1984.

Mather, Patricia Ann. *The Theatrical History of Wichita, Kansas 1872-1920*, M.A. theses, University of Kansas, 1950.

Mayfield, Linda. *Halstead: The Early Years*. Halstead, Kansas: 1987.

McCullough, Charles Irvin. *Our Yesterdays: A Story of Mulberry, Kansas 1866-1976*. Mulberry, Kansas: News-Journal, 1976.

McDaniel, Ted F. ed. *Our Land: A History of Lyon County Kansas*. Emporia, Kansas: Emporia State Press, 1976.

McLouth Centennial Committee. *McLouth, Kansas and Jefferson County, 1882-1982*, 1982.

Meltzer, George. *Social Life and Entertainment on the Frontier of Kansas, 1854-1890*, M.A. Thesis, University of Wichita. 1941.

*Miami County, Kansas*. Miami County Historical Society, 1987.

Mickel, Jere C. *Footlights on the Prairie: the Story of the Repertory Tent Players in the Midwest*. St. Cloud, Minnesota: North Star Press, 1974.

Mines, Cynthia. *The McPherson Opera House: A Prairie Landmark*. Cynthia Mines, 1992.

Millbrook, Minnie Dubbs. *Ness Western County Kansas*. Detroit, Michigan: Millbrook Printing Company, 1955.

Miller, Nyle H. and Joseph W. Snell. *Great Gunfighters of the Kansas Cowtowns, 1867-1886*. Lincoln, Nebraska: University of Nebraska Press, 1983.

Mitchell, Pat. *The Fair City: Hutchinson, Kansas*. Hutchinson, Kansas: P. Mitchell, 1983.

Mitchell, Pat. *The Fair City: Volume Two*. Hutchinson, Kansas: P. Mitchell, 1984.

Maloy, John. *History of Morris County 1820-1890*. Council Grove, Kansas: Morris County Historical Society.

Moore, H. Miles. *Early History of Leavenworth City and County*. Leavenworth, Kansas: Sam'l Dodsworth Book Co., 1906.

Morganville Chamber of Commerce. *Morganville Historical Book: 1870-1976*. Morganville Chamber of Commerce, 1976.

*A Mound of Memories, A Valley of Hope: Mound Valley Kansas 1869-1979*. Mound Valley Historical Society, 1979.

Natoma Centennial Book Committee. *Natoma History 1888-1988*. Topeka, Kansas: Jostens, 1988.

*News and Views of Yesterday*. Osborne, Kansas: *Osborne County Farmer*, 1976.

Nye, Mary E. and Lynda D. Scheele. *A Pictorial History of Dickinson County, Kansas 1855-1920*. Abilene, Kansas: Abilene Reflector-Chronicle. 1991.

*Old Opera Houses and Early Places of Amusement*. Compiled by Woman's Kansas Day Club, 1952.

Oliva, Leo E. *Woodston: The Story of a Kansas Country Town 1885-1985*. Ellsworth, Kansas: Ellsworth Printing Company, 1985.

*Opera Houses and Entertainment Pre-1950*. Compiled by Woman's Kansas Day Club, January, 1986.

*Our Land – A History of Lyon County, Kansas*. Emporia, Kansas: Emporia State Press, 1976.

Owens, Inez (Roberts). *Welcome to Wamego, Kansas 1866-1976*. Wamego, Kansas, 1975.

Palmer, Fannie Smith and Kathryn Palmer Chilen. *Miltonvale – 1982*. Miltonvale, Kansas: *Miltonvale Record*, 1982.

Parish, Arlyn John. *History of Highland Community College*. Troy, Kansas: Trojan Graphics, 1983.

Peterson, Ellen Welander. *A Kansan's Enterprise: The Story of Enterprise, Kansas*. Enterprise, Kansas: Enterprise Baptist Church, 1957.

Pickens, Herbert. *The City of Burden 1879-1979*. Burdan, Kansas, 1979.

*A Pictorial and Family History of Waterville, Kansas*. Bicentennial Committee, 1976.

Praudiere, Edelin De La, ed. *Hutchinson: The Salt City in the Heart of the Great Kansas Wheat Belt*. Hutchinson, Kansas: The Hutchinson Printing Co., 1910.

Pride, W. F. *The History of Fort Riley*. Fort Riley, Kansas: Cavalry School Book Department, 1926.

*Queen City of the Great Southwest: Parsons, Kansas*. Parsons, Kansas, 1908.

Reilly, Esther. *The Story of Dorrance, Kansas: Past and Present*. Dorrance, Kansas, 1969.

*Reflections of Franklin County and Chautauqua Days*. Ottawa, Kansas: Franklin County Historical Society, 1961.

Reusser, Athol Furman. *Clearwater: In the Valley of the Ninnescah: 1885-1985*. Clearwater, Kansas: Centennial Committee, 1985.

*Rexford Centennial 1888-1988*. The Rexford Centennial History Book Committee, 1988.

Richardson, Myrtle H. *The Great Next Year County: A History of Edwards County, Kansas, and the Surrounding Area for the Years from 1901 to 1925*. Lewis, Kansas: The Lewis Press, Inc., 1983.

Richardson, Myrtle H. *Oft' Told Tales: A History of Edwards County, Kansas to 1900*. Lewis, Kansas: Lewis Press, 1976.

Richmond, Robert W. *Kansas: A Land of Contrasts*, 3rd edition. Arlington Heights, Ill: Forum Press, Inc., 1989.

Richwine, Naomi. *Linn, Kansas, Centennial 1877-1977*.

Ripley, John W. ed., Robert W. Richmond, Mary Ritchie Jarboe, asst. eds. *Town Hall Tonight: A Pictorial History of Topeka's Theaters*. Topeka, Kansas: Shawnee County Historical Society: Art Center of Topeka, 1988.

Robley, T. F. *History of Bourbon County, Kansas to the Close of 1865*. Fort Scott, 1894.

Romstedt, Donna Bosworth. *Wellsville Kansas: The First 100 Years, 1879-1979*. Wellsville Bicentennial Heritage Committee, 1976.

*Rush County Kansas…A Century in Story and Pictures*. La Crosse, Kansas: Rush County News and Creative Printing, 2001.

Sachs, Edwin O. and Ernest A. E. Woodrow. *Modern Opera Houses and Theatres*. (orig. Pub. 1898) New York: B. Blom, 1968.

Saline County Historical Society. *As We Were: Pictorial History of Saline County*, Vol. II. Salina, Kansas: 1976-1989.

Sanders, Gwendoline and Paul Sanders. *The Harper County Story*. North Newton, Kansas: Mennonite Press, 1968.

Sanders, Gwendoline and Paul Sanders. *The Sumner County Story*. North Newton, Kansas: Mennonite Press, 1966.

*Santa Fe Railroad*. Kansas State Historical Society: Topeka, 1968.

Schaffner, Neil E. and Vance Johnson. *The Fabulous Toby and Me*. Englewood Cliffs, NJ: Prentice-Hall, 1968.

Schivelbush, Wolfgang. *The Railway Journey – The Industrialization of Time And Space in the 19th Century*. Berkley, CA: University of California Press, 1986.

Scott County Centennial Commission, *Scott County Kansas: Celebrating 100 Years, 1886-1986*. Shawnee Mission, Kansas: Kes-Print, Inc., 1986.

Shortridge, James R. *Peopling the Plains: Who Settled Where in Frontier Kansas*, Lawrence, KS: University of Kansas Press, 1995.

Siler, Zoe Myers. *This is Our Town*. Cherryvale, Kansas, 1961.

Silverman, Kenneth. *Houdini!!! The Career of Ehrich Weiss*. Harper Perennial, 1997.

Slout, William Lawrence. *Theatre in a Tent: The Development of a Provincial Entertainment*. Bowling Green, Ohio: Bowling Green University Popular Press, 1972.

Snell, Joseph W. and Don W. Wilson. *The Birth of the Atchison, Topeka and Santa Fe Railroad*. Topeka, Kansas: Kansas State Historical Society, 1968.

Stanley, Ellen May. *Early Lane County Development*. Dighton, Kansas: E. M. Stanley, 1999.

Stephenson, John C. *Downs: The First One Hundred Years*. Osborn Kansas: Osborn County Farmer, 1977.

Stevens County History Association. *The History of Stevens County and Its People*. Hugoton, Kansas: Stevens County History Association, 1979.

Stiggins, C. Naomi. *Legend and Legacy Partridge, Kansas 1886-1986*. Partridge, Kansas: C. Stiggins, 1987.

Stites, Lester. *History of Ionia, Kansas*. Ionia, Kansas: 1956.

Stockebrand, Lottie L. "Historical Development of Woodston County, Kansas, From 1855-1900." 1966.

Stone, Fred. *Rolling Stone*. New York: McGraw Hill Book Company, 1945.

Storms, A. D. *The Players Blue Book*. Worcester, Mass: Sutherland and Storms, 1901.

Stucky, Tim. *Kingman: A Centennial View*. Kingman, Kansas: Golden Valley Parks and Recreation Foundation, 1983.

Stucky, Tim. *Pratt, Kansas: A Centennial View 1884-1984*. Pretty Prairie, Kansas: Prairie Publications, 1984.

Suellentrop, Joyce and Dorothy Kraus. *Colwich Community Pictorial History*. 1972.

Suhr, Mrs., Sumner. *Moments from History: Logan, Kansas Centennial 1871-1971*. Phillips County Review, 1971.

*Sylvia, Kansas 1887-1987*. Centennial Committee. 1987.

*They Came to Stay: Sherman County and Family History*. Vol. II. Goodland, Kansas: Sherman County Historical Society, 1980.

Thomson, Matt. *Early History of Wabaunsee County, Kansas, with Stories of Pioneer Days and Glimpses of Our Western Border*. Alma, Kansas, 1901.

Tidle, Lela J. *Wilson County Kansas: People of the South Wind*. Dallas, Texas: Curtis Media Corporation, 1988.

Tracy, A. C. *Chronicles of Pratt and Pratt County, Kansas: A Republication of a Book Published in 1911 by The Pratt Club*, 1972.

Turner, Ruth. *Weir, Kansas 1776-1976 Bi-Centennial Salute*. 1976.

Tuttle, Albert B. and Mary T., ed. *History and Heritage of Gove County, Kansas*. Quinter, Kansas: Gove County Bicentennial Committee, 1982.

Tyler, Ricky W. *Social Recreational Entertainments in Olathe, McPherson and Garden City, Kansas from the Introduction of the Railroad to the Building of the First Opera House: A Narrative History*, dissertation, Michigan State University, 1995.

Underwood, Peter. *Karloff: The Life of Boris Karloff*. Drake Publishers, 1972.

VanMeter, Sondra. *Marion County Kansas: Past and Present*. Hillsboro, Kansas: M.B. Publishing House, 1972.

Vestal, Stanley. *Queen of Cowtowns: Dodge City: "the wickedest little city in America," 1872-1886*. Lincoln: University of Nebraska Press, 1998.

Waverly City Library. *The Waverly History Book*. Ottawa, Kansas: Ramsey Printing Company, 1981.

Welsh, Willard. *Hutchinson A Prairie City in Kansas*. 1946.

Wenzl, Timothy F. *Discovering Dodge City's Landmarks*. Spearville, Kansas: Spearville News, 1986.

*Westphalia, Kansas: The First 100 Years 1879-1979*. Westphalia Centennial Committee, 1979.

White, Pearl. *Just Me*. New York: George H. Doran Company, 1919.

Wiebe, Raymond. *Hillsboro, the City on the Prairie*. 1985.

Wilson, R. R. and Ethel M. Sears. *History of Grant County, Kansas*. Wichita, Kansas: Wichita Eagle Press, 1950.

*Winfield: Uniquely American in the Tradition of Kansas*.

Wingo, Wayne C. *History of Thomas County, Kansas*, MA thesis Fort Hays Kansas State College, 1964.

Wisenhunt, Donald W. *Tent Show: Arthur Names and His "Famous" Players*. College Station: Texas A and M University Press, 2000.

Woody, Vivian. *The Douglass Story 1869-1969*. 1969.

Wortman, Richard K. and Mary Ann Wortman. *History of Cowley County Kansas*. Arkansas City, Kansas: 1990.

Wright, Harriet Hughes. *History of Summerfield*. 1977.

Yates, Leslie. *History of Milan, Kansas 1879-1978*. Wellington, Kansas: 1978.

Yeamans, Diane. *My Ottawa: A Book on Ottawa History for Ottawa Children*.

Yost, Nellie Snyder. *Medicine Lodge: The Story of a Kansas Frontier Town*. Chicago, Illinois: Sage Books, 1970.

Young, Fredrick R. *Dodge City: Up Through a Century in Story and Pictures*. Dodge City, Kansas: Boot Hill Museum, 1972.

### Articles

Blackstone, Sarah J. "Alexander Byers: Play Pirate Extraordinaire." *Theatre History Studies*. (June, 1994): 107-113.

Charbo, Eileen. "The North Family — Clean Shows in a Cool Tent." *Bulletin Of Shawnee County Historical Society*, 43 (December, 1966): 28-35.

Davis, Ronald L. "Doc Adams of 'Gunsmoke': An Interview with Actor Milburn Stone." *Kansas History*, 10 (Number 4 1988): 250-261.

Foy, Eddie and Alvin F. Harlow. "Clowning Through Life." *Collier's*, January 8, 1927: 25, 26, 41: February 19, 1927, 30, 36.

Hall, Charles L. "Brown Grand Opera House," *Kansas Country Living*.

Hall, Charles L. "McPherson Opera House: Romanesque Architecture of the Plains," *Kansas County Living*, July 1977.

"History of North Topeka," *Bulletin of the Shawnee County Historical Society*, 24, (December, 1955): 31-38.

Kramme, Michael. "Opera House Illusions: Jesse Cox and Theatrical Scenery." *The Palimpsest*, 71 (Winter, 1990): 154-172.

Long, Paul F. "Old Township Hall," *Kanhistique*. 12 (April 1976): 1.

Malin, James C. "Dodge City Varieties – A Summer Interlude of Entertainment, 1878." *Kansas Historical Quarterly*, XXII Winter, vl. 4 (1956): 347-353.

Ibid., "Traveling Theatre in Kansas: The James A. Lord Chicago Dramatic Company, 1869-1871." *Kansas Historical Quarterly*, Autumn, No. 3 (1957): 298-323.

Ibid., "Traveling Theatre in Kansas: The James A. Lord Chicago Dramatic Company, 1869-1871." *Kansas Historical Quarterly*, Winter, No. 4 (1957).

Ibid., "James A. and Louie Lord: Theatrical Team - Their Personal Story, 1869-1889." *Kansas Historical Quarterly*, XXII Autumn, No. 3 (1956): 242-275.

Ibid., "Theatre in Kansas, 1858-1868: Background for the Coming of the Lord Dramatic Company to Kansas, 1869." *Kansas Historical Quarterly*, XXIII Spring, vl. 1 (1957).

Ibid., "Theatre in Kansas, 1858-1868: Background for the Coming of the Lord Dramatic Company to Kansas, 1869." *Kansas Historical Quarterly*, XXIII Summer, vl. 2 (1957): 191-203.

Ibid., "Early Theatre at Fort Scott." *Kansas Historical Quarterly*, Spring, No. 1 (1958).

Page, Euphemia. "Topeka Once Had Operas." *Bulletin of the Shawnee County Historical Society*, 18 (March, 1953): 9-10.

"Roster of Topeka Area Theaters 1871-1941," *Bulletin of the Shawnee County Historical Society*, 43 (December, 1966): 93-96.

"Rural Town Origins in Southwest Reno County." *Kansas History: A Journal of the Central Plains*, 2, No. 1 (Spring, 1979).

Russell, Don ed. "Julia Cody Goodman's Memoirs of Buffalo Bill." *The Kansas Historical Quarterly* XXVIII (4. Winter, 1962): 442-496.

"Stage, Screen and Radio Shawnee County, 1871-1941," *Bulletin of the Shawnee County Historical Society*, (December, 1966).

"The Flu Hunters," *Time* 151 (7 February 23, 1998): 54-64.

Wear, Ted G. "Mr. Theater — L. M. Crawford." *Bulletin of Shawnee County Historical Society*, 43, (December, 1966): 54-64.

### Newspapers

*Atchison Globe*, October 30, 1903.
*Barber County Indy*, December 14, 1887.
*Billboard*, April 21, 1906; May 5, 1906; April 19, 1952.
*Bill Bruno's Bulletin*, June 13, 1940.
*Blue Rapids Times*, 1892, 1894, 1895, 1897, 1985.
*Clyde Republican*, April 3, 1980.
*Emporia Daily Republican*, September 24, 1886.
*Evening Kansas Republican*, August 23, 1905.
*Garnett Journal*, November 26, 1897.

*Glasco Sun*, December 1, 1911.
*Hill City Times*, October 16, 1969.
*Hutchinson Clipper*, April 25, 1891; August 22, 1891; November 28, 1891; January 23, 1892; July 9, 1892; July 9, 1892; September 10, 1892; January 9, 1900; January 24, 1900; February 28, 1900; January 1, 1902.
*Hutchinson News-Herald*, December 18, 1955.
*Johnson County Democrat*, September 12, 1957.
*Johnson's County Gazette*, July 17, 1990.
*Kansas City Star*, March 6, 1916; 1923.
*Lakin Herald*, February 1, 1884.
*Lawrence Gazette*, January 12, 1912.
*Lawrence Journal World*, April 24, 1911.
*Lawrence Tribune*, March 11, 1867.
*Semi-Centennial Edition of The Manhattan Nationalist.*
McLaughlin, Marjorie, *The Miami Republican.*
*Meade Center Press*, September 24, 1885.
*Meade County News*, February 10, 1907; September 5, 1907; September 13, 1907.
*Medicine Lodge Cresset*, December 10, 1885.
*New York Dramatic Mirror*, November 7, 1896.
*New York Times*, November 9, 1913.
*Olathe Mirror*, September 23, 1880.
*Opera House Reporter*, 1916, 1917, 1918.
*Sedan Times Journal*, April 16, 1890.
*Sedan Times Star*, January 8, 1904; August 12, 1904.
*The Newton Republican*, December 11, 1885.
*Plains Journal*, December 21, 1907.
*The Sedan Weekly Times Star*, February 12, 1904.
*Smith County Journal*, 1907.
*Topeka Capitol Journal*, October 30, 1935.
*Topeka Daily Capitol*, September 6, 1963.
*Topeka State Journal*, October 30, 1934.
*University Daily Kansan*, August 2, 1975; August 20, 1975.
*WaKeeney World.* December 9, 1895.
Unnamed Wellington newspaper April 11, 1949.
*Western Kansas World* 100th Anniversary Edition.
*Wichita Beacon*, January 4, 1980.
*Wichita Beacon*, November 2, 1963, "Old Kansas Theatre Drew Great Stars." Alice Wade, The Coffeyville Journal.
*Wichita Eagle.* January 29, 1939; January 12, 1947; April 8, 1956; September 12, 1979; August 15, 1994; July 21, 2001; August 26, 2001; July 15, 2003.
*Zenda Citizen.* August 10, 1916.

**Manuscripts, Pamphlets, Programs**
American Sheep Breeders, "Handbook of Marion County."
"*Barton County Historical Society Collections.*"
"Bennington Centennial and Fall Festival Souvenir Booklet," 1966.
*Brown Grand Gazette*, October 1992.
"Condensed History of Harper," 1965.
"The Columbian," Columbian Theatre Foundation, Wamego, Kansas.
Galvani, William and L. M. Stallbumer. "Main and Central: El Dorado, Kansas 1860-1985."
Term paper, Hickey, Joanne, "Entertainment in St. Marys," 1977.
"The Kansas Land Guide." pamphlet published by a Larned real estate company.
Johnson, Lenise, term paper on Medicine Lodge found in *Opera Houses and Entertainment Pre-1950*.
Landis, Margaret and Larry Hancks. "Carnival Park: Circa 1907, Kansas City's White City." Kansas City, Kansas: Kansas City Kansas Community College, 1986.
"Leavenworth Centennial 1854-1954." pamphlet.
Leavenworth Historical Program. *Leavenworth 1854-1954.* Leavenworth, Kansas: The Committee, 1954.
"Melvern" Handwritten local history.
"Ness City Opera House" manuscript prepared by the city.
Nye, Agnes and Bob Bolitho. "A History of the 'old Opera House' Harper, Kansas." Harper, Kansas: *The Harper Advocate.*

Pacey, Mary Alice. Washington's Opera Houses, typed manuscript.
Patterson, Bobby. "Beloit."
"The Perkins Theater Formal Opening." November 27, 1907.
Peters, Hallie M., typed manuscript on Severance, Kansas Opera House found in *Old Opera Houses and Early Places of Amusement*, Woman's Kansas Day Club, 1952.
Report on Sedan Opera House compiled by Donna Casement, 1990.
*Saturday Night in the County Seat: A Walking Tour of Main Street Colby, Kansas.* Colby, Kansas: Leroy's Printing and Publishing, Inc.
Typed manuscript, Leroy, Kansas library.
Typed manuscript, "Saint John's Early Opera House."
Typed manuscript, Smith Center library.
Typed manuscript, Syracuse, Kansas library.
Typed manuscript, Troy, Kansas library.
Typed manuscript, Wagner, Gerald M. "Santa Fe Branch Line." May, 1976.
Wallace Bruce material, Reno County Historical Society.

**Interviews**
Bannon, William. Claflin, Kansas, July 21, 1994.
Baxa, Arlene. Cuba, Kansas, June 12, 2003.
Bradbury, Maxine Underhill. Ellis, Kansas, April 4, 1993.
Delaney, Judy. Ness City, Kansas, July 22, 1994.
Fecht, Pauline. Syracuse, Kansas, March 22, 1999.
Francis, Mildred E. Holton, Kansas, July 1, 1994.
Hobbs, Quinton. Langdon, Kansas, August 8, 1997.
Irwin, Al. Mound City, Kansas, August 5, 1992.
Kingston, Jeannie. Wilson, Kansas, July 29, 1991.
Leidigh, Helen. Spearville, Kansas, August 3, 1998.
Lundeen, Charles and Donna, Junction City, Kansas, August 11, 2000.
Mann, Wayne. Quinter, Kansas, July 7, 2000.
Mahoney, Ken and Dorothy. Dorrance, Kansas, July 30, 1994.
McBurney, Waldo. Quinter, Kansas, July 7, 2000.
McGeehee, William. Kansas City, Missouri, May, 1998.
Pacey, Mary Alice. Washington, Kansas, August 10, 2000.
Renfro, Virginia. Lyons, Kansas, August 13, 1995.
Rothenburg, Von. Osborne, Kansas, October 21, 2002.
Schaffner, Caroline. Mount Pleasant, Iowa, September 5, 1993.
Sejkora, Arlene. Chapman, Kansas, July 10, 1997.
Shrimplin, Frank, Valley Falls, Kansas, August 6, 1992.
Spreier, Marcella. Larned, Kansas, March 20, 1995.
Straion, Arthur, Valley Falls, Kansas, August 6, 1992.
Sullivan, John. Logan, Kansas, June 13, 2003.
Tacha, Bob and Neoma. Jennings, Kansas, June 13, 2003.
Van Asselt, Jan. McPherson, Kansas, February 7, 1998.
Walk, Karen. Leoti, Kansas, March 23, 1999.
Wolf River, Bob. White Cloud, Kansas, June 30, 1994.
Wood, Leola. Clyde, Kansas, February 14, 1994.

**Theatrical Guides and Directories**
Harry Miner's *American Dramatic Directory*, 1883-1884, 1884-1885.
Jno. B. Jeffery's *Guide and Directory to the Opera Houses, Theatres, Public Halls, Bill Posters, etc. of the Cities and Towns of America*, 1879-1889.
Julius Chan's *Official Theatrical Guide* 1910-1911.
Union Pacific *Theatrical Diary* 1890-1911.
*Theatres and Opera Houses on the Santa Fe*, 1907.

**Correspondence**
Letter from Constance Caufman to Verne Slout, January 29, 1948.
Letter from Jaquetta Houser to Jane Rhoads, September 28, 2000.
Letter from Marie Peters to Shawnee County Historical Society, undated.

**Internet**
http://blindboone.missouri.org/history.html, February 19, 2001.
NBC10 Biographies: Don Bousquet and Sissieretta Jones. Providence, RI/New Bedford, MA station home page.